Spiritual Exercises
of the Heart

Spiritual Exercises of the Heart

by Thomas Reade

REFORMATION HERITAGE BOOKS
Grand Rapids, Michigan

2007

Copyright © 2007

Published by
Reformation Heritage Books
2965 Leonard St., NE
Grand Rapids, MI 49525
616-977-0599 / Fax 616-285-3246
e-mail: orders@heritagebooks.org
website: www.heritagebooks.org

ISBN # 978-1-60178-006-5

Originally published in 1837.
This edition has been lightly updated and edited.

Gratitude to Grace Gems for the digital copy.
www.gracegems.org

For additional Reformed literature, both new and used, request a free book list from Reformation Heritage Books at the above address.

Contents

Preface	vii
1 Christian Retirement	1
2 Insensibility to Eternal Things	5
3 The Fall	9
4 The Prohibition in Paradise	15
5 Unbelief	18
6 The Total Depravity of the Heart	25
7 The Deceitfulness of the Heart	30
8 Keeping the Heart	35
9 The Blessedness of a New Heart	40
10 The Immensity of God	44
11 The Divine Sovereignty	52
12 The Two Covenants	58
13 The Love of God	64
14 The Gift of a Savior	71
15 The Design of the Gospel	80
16 Perverted Views of the Gospel	85
17 The Nature of Christianity	90
18 Neglecting the Gospel	94
19 Inadequate Views of Human Nature	99
20 Two Common Errors	104
21 The Cause of Skepticism	109
22 The Almost Christian	113
23 Conversion	118
24 The New Creature	124
25 Christian Unity	128
26 Following the Lord Fully	134
27 The Two Great Instruments in the Conversion of Sinners	139
28 The Two Sources	147
29 The Two Pillars	151
30 The Two Ways	158
31 Mercy Rejoicing Against Judgment	163
32 Intellectual and Spiritual Light	168
33 Knowledge and Wisdom	173
34 Passive Impressions and Active Habits	177
35 Union to Christ	182
36 The Christian Character	188
37 Christian Motives	194

38 Christian Conversation	199
39 Christian Privilege	205
40 Agreement Necessary to Communion	211
41 Separation From the World	218
42 The Importance of Self-Knowledge	224
43 The Spirit of Prayer	229
44 The Cautions and Warnings of Scripture	235
45 Self-Deception	242
46 Lukewarmness	247
47 Forgetfulness of God	253
48 Watchfulness	258
49 The Danger of Riches	266
50 The Thorns in the Parable	275
51 The Parable of the Rich Man and Lazarus	283
52 The Three Enemies	289
53 Indwelling Sin	294
54 Trials	300
55 Affliction	307
56 The Character of Martha and Mary	315
57 The Character of the Bereans	319
58 The Living Water	326
59 The Burning Bush	332
60 Adoption	339
61 Faith	345
62 Hope	352
63 Love	358
64 Joy	365
65 Peace	370
66 Humility	374
67 Meekness	379
68 Purity	383
69 Godly Fear	388
70 The Believer's Aim and Hope	392
71 True Happiness	398
72 True Religion	402
73 Election	409
74 Spiritual Vision	417
75 Heaven	421
76 The Blessedness of the Saints	427
77 Christian Obedience	433
78 The Day of Judgment	439

PREFACE

The Bible is the sacred storehouse of heavenly wisdom. Its pages are stamped with the divine seal of eternal truth and contain the charter of our hopes, our privileges, and our joys. Whatever tends to lead us from the love and study of the Holy Scriptures should be dreaded as inimical to the highest interests of mankind; while every attempt, however feeble, which has for its object the promotion of the Redeemer's glory, and the good of souls, will be received with affectionate indulgence by real Christians, who well know that success in any effort of usefulness is "from above." "Not by might, nor by power, but by my Spirit, saith the Lord of hosts" (Zech. 4:6) is a declaration at once calculated to strengthen the weak and to humble the strong. The simple design in publishing the following reflections is to induce a habit of self-examination and prayer and to excite to a more diligent perusal of the Word of God. The author, therefore, desires to come in the kindly aspect of a friendly visitor; and if privileged to enter into the sacred retirement of the Christian, would there, through the blessing of God, endeavor to lead him into a closer communion with his own heart, and with Jesus, his exalted Savior. Nothing new is here presented to the Christian. The good old way in which the patriarchs, prophets, apostles, and all true believers in every age have journeyed to the heavenly Canaan is pointed out—Jesus is the way, the only way to the Father; the living way to holiness, happiness, and heaven.

The prophet Isaiah was commanded to teach the people by line upon line, and precept upon precept; where, therefore, the same unspeakably precious truths recur again and again in these pages, their recurrence will not offend the humble believer who has tasted that the Lord is gracious. As bread and water are always pleasant to a healthy stomach, so the bread of life and the water of life are peculiarly refreshing to the soul which is hungering and thirsting after righteousness.

An original hymn is subjoined to each meditation, which, it is hoped, may assist the spirit of piety, although it can lay little claim to the charms of poetry. The Christian reader must kindly excuse the frequent lack of close connection between the hymns and the meditations to which they are attached, as they were composed before the present volume was contemplated by its author.

Should the Lord condescend to bless these humble exercises of the heart, to the guiding of some young inquirer to the Friend of sinners, to the quickening of some lukewarm professor, to the convincing of some skeptic, or the comforting of some afflicted believer—to the Triune God of our salvation be all the praise.

CHAPTER 1

Christian Retirement

How needful to the real Christian, surrounded as he is by sensible objects, which have so powerful an influence on his mind and affections, are seasons for retirement from the hurry and distracting cares of the world! The soul cannot prosper in spiritual things without much secret converse with its God and Savior.

Many duties are unavoidably of a public nature; but these, except in extraordinary cases, should not occupy those portions of time which are sacred to meditation, reading the Scriptures, and prayer.

There is something peculiarly pleasant and profitable in the interchange of activity and retirement. As activity sweetens retirement, so retirement prepares the mind for renewed activity. Those people who are most engaged in active labors for the benefit of others will find peculiar need for frequent retirement. In their closets, they must draw down from the Fountain of love, by faith and prayer, that spiritual strength, and those heavenly graces, which alone can enable them to labor perseveringly, as well as suffer patiently for Christ's sake.

The present times, which are so happily characterized by religious exertion, render this duty highly needful. It is no uncommon thing to hear excellent people complain that their whole time is nearly divided between their own jobs and the claims of multiplying religious societies, thus leaving little or no leisure for the important duty of Christian retirement. Hence, spirituality of mind is much injured from the constant bustle in which some benevolent people live. They have frequent cause to join in the lamentation of the spouse in the Song of Solomon:

"They made me the keeper of the vineyards; but mine own vineyard have I not kept" (S.S. 1:6).

The increase of valuable institutions, formed for the purpose of extending the kingdom of Christ throughout the earth, calls for perpetual gratitude to God, who thus designs to bless our favored island with the light of His truth, and to stir up His faithful servants to those interesting labors of love. But it never was the design of infinite Wisdom that one duty should extirpate another. As everything is beautiful in its season, so there is a time for everything. The art of accomplishing much consists in giving to every duty its proper place, time, and quantity. Here much wisdom is required; yet by prayer, watchfulness, and self-denial, much practical knowledge may be attained.

When we seldom retire for holy converse with God, is there not great reason to suspect some latent, though perhaps unconscious, repugnance to the more silent, unobtrusive offices of secret devotion? Some people grow almost melancholy if much alone. This surely betrays a defect either in the constitution or the heart. Absolute solitude is decidedly injurious, since He who made us has declared, "It is not good that the man should be alone" (Gen. 2:18). But occasional retirement, for the delightful purpose of holding converse with the Savior, greatly refreshes the spiritual faculties, just as rest from bodily labor recruits the wasted powers of our physical frame.

Some good men are so wedded to their studies that they can scarcely force themselves from their beloved retreat; while others are so fond of active pursuits that their minds seem averse to the sedentary employments of the closet. Like birds of passage, they live upon the wing. Both these extremes are faulty, and consequently hurtful, to each party. Every man has his circle of duty to fill up. This is larger or smaller, according to the station in which God has placed him. Let no one think that he may live for himself alone. Each individual has a sphere of usefulness to occupy, and his happiness is closely connected with the performance of his duty. Our divine Redeemer has left us an example that we should tread in His steps. May we daily study the conduct of Him whose life was one continued exercise of unwearied benevolence, "who went about doing good" (Acts 10:38).

Nothing can more beautifully exemplify the duties of holy retirement and active benevolence than the life of Jesus. In the Gospels, we read how incessant were His labors for the spiritual and temporal good of the thousands who followed Him. And there we also read, how "he went up into a mountain apart to pray"; how "when the evening was come, he was there alone" (Matt. 14:23); how "he…continued all night in prayer to God" (Luke 6:12). This He did, not occasionally, but frequently, thus setting us an illustrious example of ardent devotion, combined with unceasing exertion, for the present and future happiness of fallen man.

Come, then, oh my soul, and withdraw yourself from a thoughtless world, which is so eagerly pursuing the phantom of happiness. Look unto Jesus; place all your affections upon Him. He is the only source of spiritual felicity. While delighting yourself in the active services of a loving obedience, seek an increase of grace by daily secret converse with the Savior. We love the society of a dear friend. Can we then be strangers to communion with Jesus, if we indeed love Him? Oh, that we may feel a sweeter relish for sacred retirement, when this retirement is designed to cultivate a closer acquaintance with our own hearts, and with Him who is "the chiefest among ten thousand" (S.S. 5:10), the "altogether lovely" One (S. S. 5:16).

"Blessed Spirit of grace and truth, shed forth Thy kindly influences on my soul. Preserve me from spiritual sloth, under the specious mask of religious retirement, and from ostentatious pride, under the imposing garb of active benevolence. Oh, make me sincere in all my professions of love and obedience, simply depending on Thy grace, while laboring to promote the welfare of my fellow-creatures, that in all things I may be willing to do and suffer Thy righteous will."

―――◆◆◆―――

Jesus! my soul would now repose
Beneath the banner of Thy love:

Each rising storm dost Thou compose,
Each darkening cloud far hence remove.

Beneath Thy smile is heavenly bliss;
How sweet in solitude with Thee!
My soul, in such a world as this,
May now from anxious cares be free.

Reveal Thy mercies to my heart;
With joy my longing spirit fill;
Thy grace unceasingly impart,
To do and suffer all Thy will.

CHAPTER 2
─────────

Insensibility to Eternal Things

Come, oh my soul, call in your scattered thoughts, collect your wandering desires, and meditate with solemn awe on everlasting things. How busy is the world! How big with designs, all resting on tomorrow! But tomorrow's sun may never rise on thousands who are fondly hoping to behold a range of following years. Short-sighted mortals! He who rules over all has assigned to each a limit, beyond which the worldling cannot pass. Man has an appointed time upon earth; his days are days of an hireling. Oh, for true wisdom to learn the measure of our days and to compute with justness the extent of life!

The volume of inspiration has done this with peculiar force and beauty. There human life is compared to a sleep, to the rapidity of a flood, to a tale that is told, to a vapor that appears for a little time, to a flower which flourishes in the morning and in the evening is cut down and withered, to vanity, to a shadow that passes away.

Eternity—that solemn word soon passes from the lip, but who can grasp the mighty, the immense idea, which this word *eternity* conveys? All thought is lost in its immensity and swallowed up in its fathomless abyss. The mind may conceive, though faintly, of millions of ages heaped upon millions, until numbers lose themselves, or rather until we are lost in the vast calculation. But who can measure eternity, compared with whose everlasting lines, myriads of years are infinitely less than atoms floating in the mid-day sun?

All men are hastening to eternity. All are standing upon the brink of an interminable state of being. Yet all, except the little flock of Christ, are living as if life would never end; and they die as if beyond the grave there was nothing to awaken their solicitous concern. Awful insensibility! How fatally has sin blinded the mind of those who believe not! Men are willing to believe that which they wish to be true. They flatter themselves that all will be well at the last, though they follow the corrupt desires of their hearts, in direct opposition to the revealed will of God.

Here indeed, in this present world, the wicked, from their animal nature, have many objects to gratify their sensualistic appetites, even at the very time when their spirits are enduring the stings and lashes of an upbraiding conscience. But in eternity, where the body shall no longer be the seat of carnal desire; in eternity, where all sensual gratifications shall forever cease, the soul will experience no change from pain to pleasure or from pleasure to pain, but all will be either unmixed pain or unalloyed pleasure. Surely, no thought can be more awakening than this, and yet with what subtlety does the heart evade its force, with what shocking indifference is it treated by a world of dying sinners!

"Oh, blessed Jesus! Compassionate High Priest, awaken my drowsy sense. Deliver me from the fatal lethargy of unbelief. Captivate all my heart by the sweet constraining influence of redeeming love. Thou who art the Sun of Righteousness, dispel the mist of error; dissipate every darkening cloud which would intercept Thy cheering beam, and let all Thy brightness burst upon my ravished sight. Reveal Thyself as my Savior; let all Thy goodness pass before me; say to my trembling heart, "I am thy salvation" (Ps. 35:3); then shall I be able to contemplate eternity with joyful expectation, knowing that "to be absent from the body is to be present with the Lord" (2 Cor. 5:8).

Moses was well acquainted with the insensibility of the human heart to eternal things when he prayed: "So teach us to number our days, that we may apply our hearts unto wisdom" (Ps. 90:12). We are walking every moment on the verge of eternity! A slight accident can loosen the cords which unite soul and body, and thus bring us instantly into the world of spirits. Then why should we calculate upon length of days? Why should we act as if we had years at command? This moment only is our own. So precious is time, that infinite Bounty deals it out by seconds. And yet how prodigal we are of time, as if it were of all things the easiest to attain, or its loss the easiest to repair! Dying sinners whose consciences are awakened, and whose eyes are opened to see their danger, know the incalculable value of time. They feel every moment to be inconceivably precious, if, in this fleeting remnant of time, they can find the Savior whom they have basely slighted, and through His pardoning grace be saved from the wrath to come.

It is at dying beds that we learn something of the value of time. The keen self-reproaches of the convicted sinner show the folly of wasting days and hours, which have a value beyond the power of human calculation. The shortness of life is continually forcing itself upon us by the passing funeral-bell, the funeral procession, and the weekly voice of the obituaries. Yet its very commonness, which ought to alarm us, tends only to lull us into a strange security. This is observable in large towns, where multitudes are continually summoned into eternity; while in villages, where deaths are less frequent, a solemn awe is usually excited—at least for a time.

"Whatever others do, oh, may I think seriously on my dying hour! Lord, teach me so to number my days, that I may apply my heart unto wisdom. Enlighten my understanding to perceive what things I ought to do, and give me grace and power faithfully to fulfill the same."

We are born in sin; therefore, to be happy we must be born again. We have lived in sin—and to be happy, we must be delivered from its reigning power. As in this world there is no peace to the wicked, so, in the next, they have no rest day nor night; for the smoke of their torment ascends up forever and ever (Isa. 48:22; Rev. 14:11). Oh, that they were wise; that they understood this; that they would consider their latter end! All that sleep in the dust of the earth shall awake, some to everlasting life, and some to shame and everlasting contempt. Then those who will be wise shall shine as the brightness of the firmament, and those who turn many to righteousness, as the stars forever and ever (Dan. 12:2-3).

"Oh, blessed Lord, sit upon my heart as a refiner's fire, and as a purifier of silver, that the dross of corruption may be purged away, and my soul prepared for the hour of death and the never-ending glories of Thy heavenly kingdom."

My soul, on Pisgah's mount ascend,
Where Moses once admiring stood;
There view the promised land extend
Beyond the swelling Jordan's flood.

By faith survey the landscape over,
Where living waters gently flow;
Until earth usurp your love no more;
Until all your kindling passions glow.

In that blest region of delight,
The saints no sin nor sorrow feel;
Eternal day excludes the night,
And all possess the Spirit's seal.

The ransomed soul, in glory clad,
Shines brighter than meridian sun;
The weary pilgrim, now so sad,
There finds his toilsome journey done.

Cheer up, you saints, oppressed with grief
With joy expand your drooping wing;
Jesus affords the kind relief;
Jesus extracts the envenomed sting.

Soon will you reach the blest abode,
Where happy pilgrims ever reign;
Soon shall you see the face of God,
And all the bliss of heaven obtain.

CHAPTER 3

The Fall

He who can contemplate the introduction of moral evil into our world without feelings of deep humiliation is little prepared to receive with gratitude the stupendous mystery of redemption.

The doctrine of the fall, with all its direful consequences, shines with awful clearness in the book of God: "As by one man sin entered into the world, and death by sin; and so death passed upon all men, for that all have sinned" (Rom. 5:12).

The doctrine of the fall lies at the foundation of atonement: for "they that are whole need not a physician, but they that are sick" (Luke 5:31). Jesus came not "to call the righteous, but sinners to repentance" (Luke 5:32). He came "to seek and to save that which was lost" (Luke 19:10). "This," therefore, "is a faithful saying, and worthy of all acceptation, that Christ Jesus came into world to save sinners" (1 Tim. 1:15). His glorious work was announced to Joseph by the angel, when he said, "Thou shalt call his name JESUS: for he shall save his people from their sins" (Matt. 1:21).

While viewing the once happy pair after their awful fall, we are constrained to use the language of the weeping prophet: "How is the gold become dim! how is the most fine gold changed!" (Lam. 4:1). The sin of Adam was a compound of unbelief, pride, sensuality, ingratitude, and rebellion.

Unbelief—in giving credence to the tempter, rather than to God. Pride—in the fond desire of being wise as gods, knowing good and evil. Sensuality—in lusting after the forbidden fruit. Ingratitude—in leaguing with the fallen angels. Rebellion—in trampling the authority of Jehovah.

The apostle says: "Adam was not deceived, but the woman being deceived was in the transgression" (1 Tim. 2:14). The serpent first beguiled Eve through his subtlety and then Eve gained an easy conquest over her husband, for it is recorded: "She took of the fruit thereof, and did eat, and gave also unto her husband with her; and he did eat" (Gen. 3:6). By this act Adam acquiesced in sinful compliance with the temptation and became a full sharer in her guilt and misery. In this guilt their whole posterity was likewise involved, for it is written: "By the offence of one judgment came upon all men to condemnation" (Rom. 5:18). "In Adam all die" (1 Cor. 15:22).

The effect of the fall was shame, the never-failing companion of sin. "They knew that they were naked" (Gen. 3:7). The image of God was gone. Their native robe of innocence was gone. Their peace and purity were gone. Awful condition! They were indeed naked and exposed to all the terrors of incensed justice, without a covering from its wrath.

Another effect of the fall was the darkness of the mind. "Adam and his wife hid themselves from the presence of Lord God amongst the trees of the garden" (Gen. 3:8). Amazing blindness—to hide themselves from that Being, whose eyes are brighter than ten thousand suns, who fills heaven and earth with His presence, and from whom no secrets are hid! Slavish fear was another fruit of the fall. When God asked Adam why he hid himself, he replied: "I was afraid" (Gen. 3:10). Ah, what inward torment did sin produce in the soul of our first parents! How changed their condition! They are now afraid to look upon Him whose presence was their heaven and their joy.

Impiety and impenitence were also the baneful offspring of the fall. When God charged Adam with eating of the tree whereof He commanded that he should not eat, Adam replied: "The woman whom thou gavest to be with me, she gave me of the tree, and I did eat" (Gen. 3:12). Mark the impiety. "The woman whom thou gavest to be with me"; thus charging the guilt upon the Almighty, as if he had said, "If Thou hadst never given me this woman, I would have never sinned against Thee."

Oh, the impious insult upon divine benevolence, goodness, and love! Then mark also the impenitence of Adam: "She gave me of the tree, and I did eat," thus throwing the blame of his eating upon Eve, as if he were compelled to eat because she presented the fruit to him, and as if his own will had no part in it.

We see here no conviction of sin, no confession of guilt, no contrition on account of it. The Garden of Eden exhibited no signs of penitence, no brokenness of heart—nothing but hardness and obduracy. Eve was just as bad as her husband. She, in like manner, endeavored to exculpate herself by saying: "The serpent beguiled me, and I did eat" (Gen. 3:13).

Now observe, oh my soul; yes, observe with wonder, gratitude, and love the boundless grace and mercy of Jehovah. He, who spared not the angels that sinned, proclaimed a rich and free salvation to rebellious man. The Lord promised a deliverer, even the seed of the woman, who should bruise the serpent's head. In the fullness of time, Jesus, the Savior, was born of a pure virgin, born to save His people from their sins and to vanquish the powers of death and hell. This precious Jesus is now preached, through the everlasting gospel, to all the guilty sons and daughters of Adam, with the blessed assurance that all who believe in Him shall be saved.

From this short view of man's apostasy and recovery it is evident that man is the sole author of his destruction, and that his salvation is altogether of free, unsought-for, unmerited grace. Through the fall, man lost all spiritual power and will to love and serve God. But through the covenant of grace, he regains both, "for it is God which worketh in you both to will and to do of his good pleasure" (Phil. 2:13).

An attentive perusal of the third and fourth chapters of Genesis will convince every humble inquirer after truth, through the teaching of the divine Spirit, that every man born into this world deserves nothing but everlasting damnation, since "that which is born of the flesh is flesh" (John 3:6), and "flesh and blood cannot inherit the kingdom of God" (1 Cor. 15:50). "Marvel not that I said unto thee, Ye must be born again" (John 3:7), was the reply of the Savior to the inquiring Nicodemus.

The sinner may cavil and dispute, but his own heart will condemn him. His own life will condemn him. The law of God will condemn him. The sin of his nature, as a child of fallen Adam, will condemn him. He will find nothing but condemnation here and judgment in the world to come. But let him look outside of himself, to the second Adam, the Lord from heaven; to Jesus Christ, the promised deliverer; and there he will find everything needful to repair the ruins of the fall—yes, to raise him to a more glorious state than if Adam had never sinned.

> *And what in yonder realms above*
> *Is ransomed man ordained to be?*
> *With honor, holiness, and love,*
> *No seraph more adorned than he.*
>
> *Nearest the throne and first in song,*
> *Man shall his hallelujahs raise;*
> *While wondering angels round Him throng,*
> *And swell the chorus of His praise.*

Amazing mystery! Oh, wonderful wisdom of God, in thus educing such good out of such evil, and in making that to redound to His glory and to manifest the bright display of His perfections, which Satan intended as an awful blight on His new and fair creation!

Thus Satan is foiled, and grace reigns "through righteousness unto eternal life by Jesus Christ our Lord" (Rom. 5:21). "Sing, O ye heavens; for the LORD hath done it: shout, ye lower parts of the earth: break forth in singing, ye mountains, O forest, and every tree therein: for the LORD hath redeemed Jacob, and glorified himself in Israel" (Isa. 44:23).

Surely none but fools can make a mock at sin. Sin transformed the angels of light into powers of darkness. Sin rendered the happy pair in Eden wretched outcasts in a world of woe. Sin was the cause of the universal deluge and the fiery overthrow of the cities of the plain. Sin has ever marked its steps by misery and blood. Pride, malice, envy, murmuring, uncleanness, and every abomination hateful to a holy God, and destructive to our wretched race, spring from this poisonous root.

Every particle of sin contains an infinity of evil and deserves everlasting damnation.

But, oh my soul, if you would view sin in darkest colors and most terrible effects, go to Bethlehem, and ask, "Why did the King of heaven become an infant of days? Why was He who fills all space, wrapped in swaddling clothes and laid in a manger?" Go to Gethsemane, and ask, "Why did the incarnate God agonize, and sweat great drops of blood?" Go to the judgment hall and ask, "Why did the sovereign Judge of men and angels submit to be judged? Why did the innocent suffer such indignities? Why was the guiltless condemned to die?" Go to Calvary, and ask, "Why did the Lord of glory hang on the accursed tree? Why did the Lord of life condescend to pour out His soul unto death?"

It was to save you from your sin, to redeem you from the curse of the law by being made a curse for you, to deliver you from going down into hell, by becoming your ransom. It was to merit heaven for you by His precious atonement and obedience unto death. It was to purchase for you the eternal Spirit, by whose powerful aid you might believe and love and delight in this precious Savior, this adorable Redeemer, this almighty Deliverer, through whom your sins are pardoned and by whom you have access unto God as your reconciled Father. Oh, my soul, praise the Lord for His mercy, and never cease to speak good of His name!

Let this view of sin, and of a sin-bearing Savior, humble you in His presence and empty you of pride and vainglory. Let it, at the same time, fill you with gratitude to God for having provided such a remedy against the evils of the fall.

Sin, even your sin, nailed, pierced, and agonized the Lord of glory! Oh, then hate sin and avoid it as you would tremble to plunge a spear into your Savior's bosom, as you would shudder to trample under foot His sacred blood. "The wages of sin is death." But oh, rejoice in this gracious declaration: "The gift of God is eternal life through Jesus Christ our Lord" (Rom. 6:23).

And what is sin? "Sin is the transgression of the law" (1 John 3:4). "All unrighteousness is sin" (1 John 5:17). Sin is enmity against God, an inveterate opposition to the gospel method of salvation, a preference of our own will and the enjoyment of the creature to the will and favor of the Creator. As sin crucified the Son of God, so it hates and persecutes Him in all His faithful people. Sin is a daring rebellion against the Majesty of heaven, and would, if it were possible, pluck the Eternal from His throne. The proud sinner presumptuously asks: "Who is the Lord, that I should obey his voice?" (Exod. 5:2). And "the fool hath said in his heart, There is no God" (Ps. 14:1).

Oh, my soul, is this hideous evil the inmate of your heart? Can you cherish such a serpent in your bosom? Lord, I tremble at the thought. "Blessed Jesus, turn out Thy enemy—my sin—and make me wholly Thine; the purchase of Thy blood, the trophy of Thy grace, the monument of Thy mercy, a living temple consecrated to Thy praise."

Why is my heart so prone to leave
A God of mercy and of love?
Why dare the Holy Spirit grieve?
Why far from Christ and heaven remove?

Lord, it is the fruit of Adam's sin,
The awful taint which nature bears;
Create me all anew within;
Dissolve my flinty heart to tears.

To Thee I look, my only Lord;
On Thee, my trembling soul depends;
Blest Savior, speak the healing Word;
Thy pardoning mercy never ends.

Then will my heart overflow with joy,
My life proclaim its grateful praise,
Until safe in bliss, without alloy,
My soul shall chant celestial lays.

CHAPTER 4

The Prohibition in Paradise

Much of the beauty of Scripture is lost to us for lack of spiritual discernment. The ways of God appear dark in proportion to the thick film which rests upon our understanding.

It is awful to reflect how weak, polluted worms of earth dare to charge the infinite wisdom of Jehovah with folly. Surely we must say with the psalmist, God is strong and patient (cf. Ps. 7:11)—and God is provoked every day.

The following considerations show at once the reasonableness, holiness, and goodness of the law of Paradise.

1. As God had made man the governor of this lower world and crowned him with so many mercies, it was manifestly proper that he should require some particular instance of homage and fealty, to be a memorial to man of his dependence, and an acknowledgment on his part, that he was under the dominion of a higher Lord, to whom he owed absolute subjection and obedience.

2. What instance of homage could be more proper, circumstanced as man then was, than his being obliged, in obedience to the divine command, to abstain from one or more of the fruits of Paradise?

3. It pleased God to insist only upon his abstaining from one at the same time that He indulged him in full liberty as to the rest.

4. This easy and reasonable prohibition served both as an act of homage to the supreme Lord from whose bountiful grant he held Paradise and all its enjoyments; and it was also fitted to teach our first parents a noble and useful lesson of abstinence and self-denial. It was one of the most necessary lessons in a state of probation and of unre-

served submission to the authority and will of God, and an implicit resignation to His supreme wisdom and goodness.

5. This test of their obedience, from the nature of it, tended to habituate them to keep their sensitive appetites in subjection to the law of reason, to take them off from too close an attachment to inferior sensible good, and to engage them to place their highest happiness in God alone.

6. This injunction not to eat of the fruit of the tree of knowledge of good and evil would also tend to keep their desires after knowledge within just bounds, so as to be content with knowing what was really proper and useful for them to know, and not presume to pry with an unwarrantable curiosity into things which belong not to them and which God has not thought fit to reveal.

Now who can seriously meditate upon these valuable considerations, without being affected at the goodness of God in commanding, and at the baseness of man in transgressing, such a reasonable test of his obedience? This law was truly a law of love, and the breach of it was the highest instance of ingratitude and rebellion.

How inconceivably great is the grace of God, that at the very time when He came down to pronounce the sentence of death upon His offending creatures, He should reveal, by promise, an almighty Savior, even Himself, who should destroy the power of darkness, put an end to transgression, make an end of sin, bring in everlasting righteousness, and form a people to show forth His praise!

If we examine attentively the foregoing considerations, we shall find that nothing was imposed upon Adam that we are not now commanded to perform, with respect to the spiritual part of the injunction. We must love God supremely, acknowledge our dependence upon Him, seek our whole happiness in Him, delight in His law, be resigned to His will, keep our sensitive appetites in subjection, and check all unhallowed curiosity into the ways and wisely hidden things of God.

Every deviation from this state of heart and practice is a deviation from the holy law of God, and as a necessary consequence entails guilt and misery upon us. Thus we see that happiness is inseparable from obedience. We learn from hence that misery and wretchedness do not depend upon our station, but on the state of our souls. Adam in Paradise was happy while innocent. Adam in Paradise was miserable when guilty.

The law delivered on Mount Sinai is a standing revelation of the holiness of God; and the various precepts of the gospel are all in consonance with these pure and undefiled commandments. Both the injunctions of the moral law, and the precepts of the gospel, were virtually included in the original law given to our first parents in Paradise, thus forming a chain of holiness from the beginning to the end of time. It resembles a beautiful flower, of which the bud is seen in Eden, the expanding leaves on Mount Sinai, and its glowing beauties in Emmanuel's land.

Heaven is its native soil. There shall all the trees of righteousness be finally transplanted; and there shall the lovely flowers of Paradise expand their beauties and spread their fragrance, fed by perpetual dews of heavenly grace, and be screened forever from the blasting pestilence of this sinful world.

Oh, blessed Redeemer, Lord divine!
With beams of mercy on me shine;
Until every thought and word agree,
Until every work be done for Thee.

What is the world but grief and care?
What heaven, if Thou be absent there?
Thy glorious face illumines the sky,
And sheds ecstatic joys on high.

Thy love, with beams of heavenly grace,
Gladdens our guilty, fallen race;
In Sharon's lovely, blushing rose,
Thou deignest Thy beauties to disclose.

CHAPTER 5

Unbelief

Unbelief is a sin of much greater extent than is generally imagined. Some people confine the sin of unbelief to Jews, Mohammedans, and pagans; to atheists, deists, and skeptics. They deem it a breach of charity to charge this moral evil upon those who profess to believe the gospel to be a revelation from God and who exhibit in their outward character the amiable virtues of benevolence, kindness, and compassion.

But if we bring what the world denominates faith to the test of Scripture, and try its genuineness by the touchstone of the Word of God, we shall soon discover it to be "reprobate silver." This counterfeit coin bears some rude outlines of the King's image; but it is so badly executed that it may be easily detected by a spiritual discerner.

True faith is lively, operative, and fruitful. True faith works by love, that sacred spring which sets all the wheels of obedience in motion. True faith purifies the heart by uniting the soul to Jesus and drawing from Him through the Spirit continual supplies of grace and strength to mortify sin and walk in the ways of holy obedience. True faith overcomes the world by raising the believer above its vanities and follies and by enabling him to renounce its pomps and honors and to live as a pilgrim and stranger upon earth. True faith realizes the invisible glories of heaven and thus becomes the substance of things hoped for, the evidence of things not seen.

But how does the world's faith operate? It leads men to the house of God on the Sabbath, and then allows them to attend theaters and gayeties of every description through the week. It induces them to attend the Lord's Table on some great festival of the church, and then lulls their consciences to sleep by the assurance that they have done "some great thing" towards liquidating the contracted debt of daily transgression. It prompts them, it may be, to read their Bibles on the Sabbath, and then to close the sacred volume until the Sabbath returns again.

The faith of the nominally Christian world, bad as it is, is nevertheless valuable to civil society—inasmuch as it restrains men in some degree from the licentious and savage practices of heathen nations and preserves some portion of external decency and respect for religion among us. But it has nothing saving in it, because it has no respect to the will and favor of God. This profession of faith is consistent with worldly ambition, pride, lust, avarice, hatred of God, and enmity to the gospel. These evils abound in the lives of multitudes, with whose praises the world resounds.

Look at the great mass of our population, all of whom profess to be Christians. And what is the character of their life and conduct? Who fill the theaters? Who resort to houses of debauchery? Who tread the giddy circles of maddening pleasure? Who compose the midnight revel and waste their reason amid the fumes of intoxication? Who defraud and circumvent their neighbors? Who defile their conversation by obscenity and oaths? Who spend their time, when worldly business releases them from labor, in idle indulgences or active wickedness?

The nominal professors of Christianity—men who would be highly offended if you ranked them among the degraded idolaters of the heathen world, men who pride themselves upon their elevated scale in society, men who glory in the name of Christian. Yet these pretended admirers of Christianity abhor the spirit of the religion which they profess! They scruple not to charge the humble followers of Jesus, who "run not with them to the same excess of riot" (1 Pet. 4:4), with hypocrisy, enthusiasm, and fanaticism. They regard them with a sneer of contemptuous scorn and delight to make them the sportive subject of their bacchanalian carousals. Many of these enemies of the cross of Christ are loaded with the common bounties of an indulgent Providence.

"How terrible it will be for you who sprawl on ivory beds surrounded with luxury, eating the meat of tender lambs and choice calves.

You sing idle songs to the sound of the harp, and you fancy yourselves to be great musicians, as King David was. You drink wine by the bowlful, and you perfume yourselves with exotic fragrances, caring nothing at all that your nation is going to ruin." The poor of Christ's flock are allowed to perish around them, unheeded and despised!

But oh, what an awful change ensues when death strikes the fatal blow! Instead of beds of ivory and couches of luxurious ease, they lie down on the lake that burns with fire and brimstone. Instead of bacchanalian songs and the melody of sweet music, they hear and join in the dreadful concert, composed of weeping and wailing and gnashing of teeth! Instead of the delicious wine poured with profusion into their golden bowls, they crave in vain for a drop of water to cool their flaming tongues.

Instead of continuing their laugh of ridicule at the once despised follower of Jesus, they, repenting and groaning for anguish of spirit, are amazed at the strangeness of his salvation, so far beyond all that they looked for, and they exclaim, "This was he, whom we had once in derision and a proverb of reproach. We fools have accounted his life madness, and his end to be without honor; now is he numbered among the children of God, and his lot is among the saints! Therefore have we erred from the way of truth, and the light of righteousness has not shined unto us, and the Sun of Righteousness rose not upon us. We wearied ourselves in the way of wickedness and destruction; yes, we have gone through desert places where there lay no way, but as for the way of the Lord we have not known it. What has pride profited us? Or what good has riches with our bragging brought us? All those things are passed away like a shadow, and as a post that hastens by." Oh, that men were wise, that they understood this, that they would consider their latter end!

Unbelief manifests itself in characters of another class. Many nominal professors of Christianity are of a sweet, amiable disposition: they are temperate in their enjoyments and benevolent to their poor neighbors. They are ready to promote objects of general usefulness, and pride themselves upon their integrity of principle and strict propriety of action.

But how does their faith operate? Does it wean their affections from the world? Does it make Jesus daily more precious to their souls? Does it break them off from all self-righteous dependence? Does it produce real contrition for sin and continual application to the fountain opened for sin and for uncleanness?

Alas, they know little, and they feel less, of all this. They have never seen their absolute guilt and wretchedness as the offspring of fallen Adam; and therefore they feel not their need of a crucified Jesus to save them from the curse and dominion of sin.

They profess indeed to believe in the gospel; but they come to it as "they that are whole" (Mark 2:17). Their language is that of the young ruler, "What lack I yet?" (Matt. 19:20). Hence they deem all experimental religion, all warm affections to the Savior, all renunciation of worldly pleasures which are incompatible with the pure spirit of the gospel, as carrying matters too far, as being righteous over much. They wish to possess both worlds, to taste the joys of earth and the bliss of heaven. But eternal truth has said: "Ye cannot serve God and mammon" (Luke 16:13). Such profession of faith must therefore lead to the chambers of death; for "if any man have not the Spirit of Christ, he is none of his" (Rom. 8:9). And Christ has declared of all His true disciples: "They are not of the world, even as I am not of the world" (John 17:16).

It is also a melancholy truth that unbelief is not wholly eradicated from the hearts of believers. If it were, there would have been no need for this caution: "Take heed, brethren, lest there be in any of you an evil heart of unbelief, in departing from the living God" (Heb. 3:12). And again, speaking of the Israelites in the wilderness, Paul says: "So we see that they could not enter in because of unbelief" (Heb. 3:19). And then he adds this solemn warning: "Let us therefore fear, lest, a promise being left us of entering into his rest, any of you should seem to come short of it" (Heb. 4:1).

Those who are in the habit of observing the secret movement of their own spirit will soon perceive how this subtle evil lies at the bottom of all their languor in devotion, their inertness of duty, their dullness in spiritual perception, and their declensions from the ways of God. This acquaintance with our own heart will lead us to the continued exercise of watchfulness and prayer, through the gracious influence of the Holy Spirit.

A consciousness of inbred sin will cause us to distrust ourselves, to look continually unto Jesus, and to have no confidence in the flesh. This salutary fear, implanted in the heart through the covenant love of God, alone can keep us from falling. We shall walk over the slippery paths of this sinful world with safety when we tread with cautious step, "leaning upon our Beloved."

This knowledge of our corruption, when taught by the Spirit of truth in connection with the remedy provided to remove it, even the atoning blood of Jesus, causes the soul who receives it to sink deep in self-abasement, to rise high in heavenly affections, to renounce the vanities of the world, and to grow in a daily fitness for the inheritance of the saints in light.

How extensive, then, is the evil of unbelief. It blights the whole moral creation of God, producing sterility in every heart unrenewed by sovereign grace, while it sheds its baneful influence even over the trees of righteousness which stand in the garden of the Lord.

Just in proportion as its influence is felt in the people of God, it operates like the chilling blast in the vineyard. The blossom is injured, the fruit is checked—yes, too often withered. To this root of bitterness may be traced all the wickedness of the world, all the evils which have abounded, and do abound, in the visible church of Christ, all the declensions and falls which have unhappily stained the lives of many who, by their deep repentance, have proved themselves to be among the redeemed of the Lord.

"Blessed Savior! Thou who camest down from the throne of glory to die for poor perishing sinners, save me from the deadly sin of unbelief. Oh, give me faith in Thy precious blood. Enable me to rely upon Thee with the simplicity of a little child. On Thee may I repose my soul, for Thou didst bear my sins in Thine own body on the tree. Lord, save me from self-righteousness, from the love of the world, from pride of heart, from fleshly indulgence. Keep me near to Thyself. Wash me daily in Thy cleansing blood from every contracted defilement. Clothe me with the robe of righteousness, with the garment of salvation. Cause me to rejoice in Thee, to live in the light of Thy countenance, to taste that Thou art gracious, and to glorify Thee by a growing conformity to Thy mind and will."

In the hour of death and danger,
When the angry storms impend;
Woe to you, you wilful stranger
To the great almighty Friend.

In the days of ease and pleasure,
When your sun unclouded shone,
Every folly was your treasure,
And usurped your heart alone.

Jesus Christ was disregarded,
Love and mercy smiled in vain;
Vengeance threatened—wrath retarded;
Nothing did your lust restrain.

But behold! He now arises,
Clad with frowns and armed with woe,
He your guilty soul surprises;
Where, ah, where will you go?

Earth, with all its gilded treasures,
Cannot yield a moment's ease;
Folly, with her wanton pleasures,
Now has lost her power to please.

Swelling streams of guilt surround you,
Like an overwhelming flood;
Ah, poor sinner, haste and turn you
To a Savior's cleansing blood!

See His agonizing features;
See His pains endured for thee;
See Him bleed for rebel creatures,
Groaning on the accursed tree.

Still perhaps He may be gracious;
Still His mercy may forgive;
Like the heaven so vast and spacious,
Is the love which bids you live.

CHAPTER 6

The Total Depravity of the Heart

The corruption of the human race after the fall was radical and universal. "God saw that the wickedness of man was great in the earth, and that every imagination of the thoughts of his heart was only evil continually" (Gen. 6:5).

It would seem surprising that anyone should read this passage in the Bible and yet deny the doctrine of human depravity, did we not know the natural blindness of the understanding by reason of sin.

A painful truth is, however, plainly stated—that the heart of man is evil. And that this solemn truth may be placed in the strongest light, it is further added that not only the thoughts, but the imaginations of the thoughts of his heart are evil. By this declaration we learn how the fall has corrupted all the secret workings of the human mind, since the very outline or rude sketch of the thoughts is polluted.

If the fountain be thus poisoned, can we wonder at those deadly streams which issue from it? All who know themselves through the teaching of the divine Spirit can testify to the truth of this Scripture from their own experience. "The heart knoweth his own bitterness" (Prov. 14:10). Oh, that sovereign grace may cast down every proud and sinful imagination which is contrary to the holy law of God and bring every thought into captivity to the obedience of Christ.

Some, contending for a portion of natural goodness, may perhaps say, True, the imagination is often defiled; but must we acknowledge no remainders of virtue? What says the Scripture? "Every imagination of the thoughts of his heart was only evil continually" (Gen. 6:5). Allowing that this is true, yet may there not be some mixture of good with the evil? What says the Scripture? "Every imagination of the thoughts of his heart was only evil continually." Admitting this, yet may there not be some intervals of goodness? What says the Scripture? "Every imagination of the thoughts of his heart was only evil continually."

If this be indeed the state of man's heart, yet may not the innocent season of youth be an exemption from this awful charge? What says the Scripture? "The imagination of man's heart is evil from his youth" (Gen. 8:21). "The wicked are estranged from the womb; they go astray as soon as they be born, speaking lies" (Ps. 58:3). "Foolishness is bound in the heart of a child" (Prov. 22:15). "Childhood and youth are vanity" (Eccl. 11:10). And, as if determined to abase the pride of fallen man, and to place the doctrine of original sin beyond dispute, David, speaking under the influence of the Spirit of truth, declares: "I was shapen in iniquity; and in sin did my mother conceive me" (Ps. 51:5).

Very many pertinent and important passages might be adduced, all of which attest this solemn truth of original sin. "Who can bring a clean thing out of an unclean? not one!" (Job 14:4). "What is man, that he should be clean? and he which is born of a woman, that he should be righteous?" (Job 15:14). "How can he be clean that is born of a woman?" (Job 25:4). Hence we conclude, with divine inspiration, that we are "by nature the children of wrath" (Eph. 2:3); that "there is none righteous, no, not one" (Rom. 3:10).

Oh, my soul, cavil not with your justly offended Creator, but confess your guilt, both original and actual. Seek for grace to lie low at His feet and to accept with joyful heart those gracious offers of pardon and peace, which are so freely made to you through the great propitiatory sacrifice of His well-beloved Son.

The grace of God when viewed, as it always ought to be, in connection with the wretched state of sinful man, shines like the beauteous rainbow on the darkened cloud. Its lovely hues cheer and delight the mind in the midst of surrounding gloom.

How consoling to a soul bowed down under a sense of guilt are the following promises: "When I passed by thee, and saw thee polluted in thine own blood, I said unto thee…Live; yea, I said unto thee when thou wast in thy blood, Live" (Ezek. 16:6). Then comes the source of this mercy: "I have loved thee with an everlasting love: therefore with lovingkindness have I drawn thee" (Jer. 31:3).

But how can a polluted creature be pleasing to a pure and holy God? Behold the effects of sovereign grace: "Then will I sprinkle clean water upon you, and ye shall be clean: from all your filthiness, and from all your idols, will I cleanse you. A new heart also will I give you, and a new spirit will I put within you: and I will take away the stony heart out of your flesh, and I will give you an heart of flesh. And I will put my spirit within you, and cause you to walk in my statutes, and ye shall keep my judgments, and do them" (Ezek. 36:25-27).

The safety and perseverance of the redeemed is sweetly declared in the following delightful promise: "And I will give them one heart, and one way, that they may fear me for ever, for the good of them, and of their children after them: and I will make an everlasting covenant with them, that I will not turn away from them, to do them good; but I will put my fear in their hearts, that they shall not depart from me" (Jer. 32:39-40).

Support and final success are also promised to the believer under all the various trials and difficulties which he may be called upon to endure in the cause of his covenant God and Savior: "Fear thou not; for I am with thee: be not dismayed; for I am thy God: I will strengthen thee; yea, I will help thee; yea, I will uphold thee with the right hand of my righteousness" (Isa. 41:10). "When thou passest through the waters, I will be with thee; and through the rivers, they shall not overflow thee: when thou walkest through the fire, thou shalt not be burned; neither shall the flame kindle upon thee. For I am the Lord thy God, the Holy One of Israel, thy Saviour" (Isa. 43:2-3).

For the present and everlasting consolation of the believer, a full and free forgiveness of all sin is graciously declared: "I, even I, am he that blotteth out thy transgressions for mine own sake, and will not remember thy sins" (Isa. 43:25). "I have blotted out, as a thick cloud, thy transgressions, and, as a cloud, thy sins: return unto me; for I have redeemed thee" (Isa. 44:22). "Israel shall be saved in the Lord with an everlasting salvation: ye shall not be ashamed nor confounded world without end" (Isa. 45:17).

Well may the ransomed sinner exclaim: "O Lord, I will praise thee: though thou wast angry with me, thine anger is turned away, and thou comfortedst me. Behold, God is my salvation; I will trust, and not be afraid: for the Lord Jehovah is my strength and my song; he also is become my salvation" (Isa. 12:1-2). "I will extol thee, my God, O king; and I will bless thy name for ever and ever. Every day will I bless thee; and I will praise thy name for ever and ever" (Ps. 145:1-2). "Bless the Lord, O my soul: and all that is within me, bless his holy name. Bless the Lord, O my soul, and forget not all his benefits: who forgiveth all thine iniquities; who healeth all thy diseases; who redeemeth thy life from destruction; who crowneth thee with lovingkindness and tender mercies" (Ps. 103:1-4).

Blessed be the Lord God, the God of Israel, who only does wondrous things. And blessed be His glorious name forever. And let the whole earth be filled with His glory. Amen and amen.

———◆◆◆———

When I survey the human race,
And sin's deceitful windings trace,
Lord, what is man, amazed I cry,
That Thou for him shouldst deign to die?

How vast the love that brought Thee down,
To take affliction's thorny crown,
Midst scoffs, the gorgeous robe to wear,
Midst sneers, the sceptered reed to bear.

Yet with this crown and purple robe,
Thy kingdom far exceeds the globe;
A kingdom wide as endless space,
Prepared for man through sovereign grace.

The Total Depravity of the Heart

While others spurn this matchless love,
Thou, my warm affections move;
Drawn by Thy sacred Spirit, Lord,
May I adore the incarnate Word.

Then shall I live in heavenly rest,
And die in peace, supremely blest;
Borne on some friendly seraph's wing,
The praises of my God to sing.

CHAPTER 7

The Deceitfulness of the Heart

The Word of truth declares: "The heart is deceitful above all things, and desperately wicked: who can know it?" (Jer. 17:9). The deceitfulness of the heart is so great that no human penetration can discover its extent or detect its various windings. Fully to know this hidden evil is the prerogative of Jehovah, for when the question is asked, "Who can know it?" the important answer is given: "I the Lord search the heart, I try the reins, even to give every man according to his ways, and according to the fruit of his doings" (Jer. 17:10).

The holy, ever blessed Trinity, three persons in one Jehovah, can alone raise man from the ruins of the fall and restore him to holiness, happiness, and heaven. How vain then are all attempts to renovate the old Adam. The ancient philosopher and the modern rationalist have each found their boasted efforts ineffectual in restoring the disfigured mind of man to moral beauty.

The arts of civilization may indeed render the savage peaceable, domestic, and industrious, just as a refined education gives to the more cultivated parts of society that vigor of mind and suavity of manner which greatly add to the enjoyment of social life. But without the sanctifying grace of God, communicated through the faithful preaching of the gospel, the rude barbarian, though civilized, still retains his blindness respecting the true God and all his native propensities to evil.

If we turn our eyes from the civilized heathen to his superior in the scale of intelligence, the polished and well-educated inhabitant of a Christian country, we behold in this latter character science, taste, politeness; all that can charm the mind and imagination in the brilliancy of wit, strength of intellect, and sportive flights of fancy—yet even this polished stone, cut out of the quarry of nature, and rendered so beautiful by art, is still destitute of real worth, while devoid of those qualities which alone can render it precious in the sight of God. Such a character, the world's idol and the gospel's bane, is held up as the pinnacle of excellence, while utterly abhorrent in the eye of Him who sees not as man sees and who has declared, that while man looks at the outward appearance, He looks at the heart.

Hence we see the necessity of converting grace, whether in the crude or more polished parts of the human race. In all, the heart is deceitful above all things and desperately wicked. In all, sin reigns until divine love dethrones the tyrant and brings the humbled sinner to the feet of Jesus.

We cannot have a more convincing proof of the corruption of our nature than that proneness which we continually feel to seek rest in the creature and to find our satisfaction in earthly things.

This alienation of the heart from God may and often does exist to a most awful extent under the fair garb of amiability of temper and the creditable profession of orthodox Christianity. It is therefore possible to be highly esteemed among men, and yet be an abomination in the sight of God.

The Holy Scriptures declare that God will not accept a divided heart. We must love God supremely, or we do not love Him at all. We must rest altogether upon His grace as manifested in the gift of His beloved Son, or our partial dependence will be found a delusion. The language of the almighty Father is: "My son, give me thine heart" (Prov. 23:26). Oh, happy hour when the heart is cheerfully and without reserve given to a gracious God.

As all sin lies in the departure of the heart from God, so all holiness is concentrated in this unreserved surrender of the heart to Him. Herein lies the secret of holiness and of happiness. When the heart is once truly given to God, when the affections flow delightfully towards Him, when the will is swallowed up in the divine will, when the whole soul is devoted to the service of its Creator, Preserver, and

Redeemer—then the fruits of righteousness will appear and abound; then joy and peace will gladden the heart and hope and love will unite to prepare the believer for his eternal rest. But it is most awful to think how little the blessed God is regarded and obeyed by creatures whom He has endued with reason and reflection.

Man, although formed to show forth the praises of Jehovah, is of all His lower works the only creature who rebels against His sovereign will. "The ox knoweth his owner, and the ass his master's crib; but Israel doth not know, my people doth not consider" (Isa. 1:3). "The stork in the heaven knoweth her appointed times; and the turtle and the crane and the swallow observe the time of their coming; but my people know not the judgment of the Lord" (Jer. 8:7). "Hear now this, O foolish people, and without understanding; which have eyes, and see not; which have ears, and hear not: Fear ye not me? saith the Lord: will ye not tremble at my presence, which have placed the sand for the bound of the sea by a perpetual decree, that it cannot pass it: and though the waves thereof toss themselves, yet can they not prevail; though they roar, yet can they not pass over it? But this people hath a revolting and a rebellious heart; they are revolted and gone" (Jer. 5:21-23).

When we read the sacred pages of revealed truth, what an awful catalogue of crime meets our eye. What unbelief, what pride, what sensual lust, what covetousness, what supreme attachment to the world, what daring independence and contempt of the Almighty, what entire forgetfulness of God and abominable idolatries, what gross impurities, what envy, malice, cruelties and love of murder, what deceit and fraud, what superstition, hypocrisy and formality, what crimes of every name and character stain the history of our fallen race and prove by an incontrovertible evidence that we are born in sin and are by nature the children of wrath.

For such a world of hateful sinners, Jesus died! Oh, stupendous miracle of mercy! Well may angels desire to look into this mystery of love. But oh, amazing infatuation, man for whom this mercy was provided, man to whom this mercy is offered, man, who so greatly needs it, and who without it must perish forever, is careless and indifferent, yes, most awfully opposed to it!

We do not dislike mercy, but we dislike the channel through which it flows. We do not dislike forgiveness, but we dislike the purity of heart connected with it. We do not dislike heaven as a place of rest from toil and sorrow, but we dislike those dispositions and affections that alone can qualify us for the enjoyment of it.

While we would gladly be saved from future misery, we cannot part with present sinful attachments; therefore, we willfully renounce the infinite joys of heavenly glory and choose the pleasures of sin, which are but for a season, with all their tremendous consequences in a future world. Awful delusion! Lord save us from such a miserable choice and condition.

In the midst of this general aversion to the humbling, purifying, elevating doctrines and precepts of the gospel, there is, in every age, a "remnant according to the election of grace" (Rom. 11:5) who most gladly and thankfully embrace the rich offers of mercy made to a lost world through the atoning sacrifice of the Son of God. These happy souls receive Christ into their hearts by faith, obtain pardon and peace through His blood, and are renewed in the spirit of their minds through the power of the Holy Spirit. They walk in humble fear and holy obedience, are admitted as heirs of glory into God's everlasting kingdom, and reign with Christ their Lord and Savior forever and ever.

"Blessed Jesus! Thou who art the kind Physician of souls, heal this fatal distemper of my fallen nature—an earthly mind. Spiritualize my affections, elevate my views, enlarge my heart. Fill my soul with Thine own self. Let me not grovel here below, fond of the perishing vanities of time. Wean my heart from the transitory enjoyments of sense and fix my affections upon Thyself, the eternal, unchanging source of good. Oh, satisfy me with Thy mercy, and that soon. Hasten to help me, for Thou art my God."

Short-sighted man can only see
The outward form of piety;

But God can in a moment dart
Within the caverns of the heart.

To His all-searching, piercing eye,
Our secret evils naked lie;
Pride cannot work by Him unseen,
Nor angry passion; lust, or spleen.

Wash me in Jesus' blood divine;
May I be His, and He be mine;
From all deceitful workings, free
My heart that pants to live for Thee.

A monument of grace I stand,
Redeemed, supported by Thy hand;
Whatever I am, whatever possess,
It is all the gift of richest grace.

Then let my soul forever raise
The incense of adoring praise;
And join the heavenly choirs above,
In sweetest songs of grateful love.

CHAPTER 8

Keeping the Heart

When we are spiritually taught of God to know something of the desperate wickedness and deceitfulness of our hearts, we are prepared to feel the force of this exhortation: "Keep thy heart with all diligence; for out of it are the issues of life" (Prov. 4:23).

Our blessed Lord has told us that out of the heart proceed evil thoughts, from where we learn that the heart is the fountain of all wickedness. Evil thoughts are the springs of evil actions. Until the fountain be cleansed, all the streams which issue from it must therefore be impure.

The heart undergoes a wonderful change when renewed by the Spirit of grace. But, as man is renewed only in part, it becomes the constant duty and work of every believer to keep his heart with all diligence. Sinless perfection is the glory and blessedness of heaven. Here on earth, the most holy servant of God finds daily need of deep humiliation.

"He that is washed needeth not save to wash his feet" (John 13:10). Daily contracted defilement needs daily washing. All the children of God labor to abound yet more and more in all knowledge and in all goodness. Forgetting the things which are behind, they reach forth unto those things which are before and eagerly press toward the mark for the prize of the high calling of God in Christ Jesus. Uniting with holy David in sentiment and feeling, they can individually say: "I hate vain thoughts: but thy law do I love" (Ps. 119:113). "Let the words of my mouth, and the meditation of my heart, be acceptable in thy sight, O LORD, my strength, and my Redeemer" (Ps. 19:14).

And is this your prayer, oh my soul? Are you laboring to maintain a conscience void of offence both towards God and towards man? Is "the thought of foolishness" distressing to you? Can you with Christian sincerity join in this prayer of the psalmist: "Search me, O God, and know my heart: try me, and know my thoughts: And see if there be any wicked way in me, and lead me in the way everlasting" (Ps. 139:23-24)? The Scriptures declare: "As [a man] thinketh in his heart, so is he" (Prov. 23:7). This habitual inward state of the thoughts determines his character in the sight of God.

"Lord give me grace carefully to observe my thoughts, and to watch and pray, lest being drawn into temptation through the wiles of the devil and the deceitfulness of my heart, I should grieve Thy Holy Spirit, by whom Thy people are sealed unto the day of redemption."

Evil thoughts are not our sins, when, being injected by Satan, our will does not consent unto them but hates and opposes them, and when we earnestly entreat the Lord to save us by His grace from these fiery darts of the wicked one. But as the difficulty lies in ascertaining whether these evil suggestions spring from Satan, or the corruption of our nature, the safest way is to be humbled on account of them, to betake ourselves to Jesus for deliverance from these spiritual enemies, remembering how kindly He has said: "Come unto me, all ye that labour and are heavy laden, and I will give thee rest" (Matt. 11:28). If, through inattention, our souls lie open to the inroads of our ever watchful foe, then the evil thoughts which He stirs up within us, and which are allowed to lodge in our hearts, become our sin. All wanderings and distractions of mind in our religious exercises arising from lack of watchfulness and due keeping of the heart are sinful.

Those evil thoughts which are excited by dwelling on forbidden objects, reading immoral books, associating with carnal people, or partaking in worldly amusements calculated to inflame the passions are most awfully chargeable upon us; and they will, if not repented of and atoned for through a believing application to the blood of Jesus, sink our souls into endless perdition. If evil, ever bubbling up in the heart, so soon issues into the various actions of the life, how needful to every true believer is this exhortation of Solomon: "Keep thy heart with all diligence" (Prov. 4:23).

In order that our thoughts may please God, they must be brought into captivity to the obedience of Christ. The Word of Christ must dwell in us richly, in all wisdom and spiritual understanding, that out of the abundance of the heart our mouth may speak to His praise and glory. "Thy word," says David, "have I hid in mine heart, that I might not sin against thee" (Ps. 119:11). "Whatsoever things are true, whatsoever things are honest, whatsoever things are just, whatsoever things are pure, whatsoever things are lovely, whatsoever things are of good report; if there be any virtue, and if there be any praise, think on these things" (Phil. 4:8).

We must carefully watch against the first risings of sin, that through grace, the sprouting evil may be nipped in the bud.

We must be much in the habit of mental prayer, lifting up our heart to God on all occasions in humble, fervent ejaculations, which is what the apostle recommends when he says: "Pray without ceasing" (1 Thess. 5:17). This spirit of prayer, this holy habit of devotion, these sacred breathings of the soul, hinder no business except the evil workings of Satan on the mind. This heavenly frame, this delightful communion with the Father of Spirits, forms the purest source of enjoyment to the Christian pilgrim while journeying through a valley of tears.

To prevent the intrusion of evil thoughts, we must always take care to be usefully employed, since idleness is the soil in which Satan sows his tares with liberal hand. The best way to keep the heart is that which Jude prescribes: "Keep yourselves in the love of God" (v. 21). We must meditate often on the nature of almighty God: His majesty and glory, His truth and justice, His holiness and purity, His grace and mercy. We must also contemplate our own apostasy, vileness, and nothingness. We must think much on the love of Christ in dying for sinners, on His agony and bloody sweat, His cross and passion—and then ask, "Can I indulge a sinful thought, and cherish in my mind those dreadful evils, which nothing but the blood of God incarnate could expiate and wash away? Can I sin against such transcendent love?"

We must dwell with delight on the gracious operations of the Holy Spirit in leading the trembling sinner to Jesus; in enabling him to believe with the heart unto righteousness; and in causing him to love that precious Savior, who is the chief among ten thousand, and altogether lovely. We must be continually looking with an eye of faith to Jesus as our great example, remembering that "if any man have not have the Spirit of Christ, he is none of his" (Rom. 8:9). He left us "an example, that ye should follow his steps" (1 Pet. 2:21) and has declared, "My sheep hear my voice, and I know them, and they follow me" (John 10:27). His whole mediatorial character must be the object of our thoughts, until our souls are changed into His same image, from glory to glory, by the Spirit of the Lord.

In order to the keeping of the heart with all diligence, we must labor to set the Lord always before us. We must feel ourselves surrounded with His omnipresence, to whom the darkness and the light are both alike, who weighs the spirits, who is a discerner of the thoughts and intents of the heart.

Oh, my soul, trifle no longer with your thoughts. The irregular desire, the impure look, the angry purpose, though unseen by man, are all recorded by the omniscient God; and they will be condemned as actual transgressions of His holy law in that day when the secrets of all hearts shall be revealed.

Hasten then to Jesus for grace to save you and to keep you. Forever renounce all hope of saving yourself by any merit of your own. If "the thought of foolishness is sin" (Prov. 24:9), where is the man that lives and sins not?

"Blessed Savior, in Thee alone have I righteousness and strength. Put forth Thy mighty power. Deliver me from the assaults of Satan, and the workings of an evil heart. Enable me to watch and pray, to wrestle and fight, to labor and strive in Thy promised strength, until conflict shall end in victory; weariness in rest; and mourning in eternal songs of joy."

With guilt oppressed, bowed down with sin,
Beneath its load I groan;

Give me, dear Lord, a heart of flesh,
Remove this heart of stone.

A burdened sinner, lo! I come,
An heir of death and hell;
Oh! seal my pardon with Thy blood,
And all my fears dispel.

Nor peace, nor rest, my soul can find,
Until Thy dear cross I see;
Until there in humble faith I cry,
My Jesus died for me.

Oh, give this realizing faith,
This soul supporting view;
Until old things be forever past,
And all within be new.

CHAPTER 9

The Blessedness of a New Heart

It is delightful to contemplate the beauties that are contained in one short passage of the Holy Scriptures. In grace, as in nature, we find much beauty in what appears comparatively minute. Faith, like the microscope, discovers the hidden charms and presents to our mind those excellencies which lie undiscovered to the eye of reason. The following short promise is of this description: "I will give them one heart, and one way" (Jer. 32:39).

The whole of the Christian character is summed up in these few words. This precious promise virtually contains everything that relates to inward and outward godliness: faith working by love and love working by obedience. "I will give them one heart and one way." The two great features of the Christian character are here expressed: *singleness of heart* and *consistency of conduct*. Without a single eye, that is, without a unity of desire and a unity of design to promote the glory of God, all profession of faith and love is hypocritical and vain.

True faith is simple in its dependence and looks only unto Jesus for pardon and peace and every other spiritual blessing. It draws off the mind from all other objects and causes the believer with "one heart" to rely upon the atonement made by the Son of God for sin and to draw only out of His fullness every needful grace. This "one heart" is, therefore, a most comprehensive blessing. The more we examine into it with spiritual discernment, the more of new beauties we shall discover, unfolding themselves to our enlightened minds.

When Adam was in a state of innocence, he had only "one heart." Since the fall, the heart of man is "divided." The world, sin, and self each claim their share; and as the Almighty will have the whole or none, He has, in righteous displeasure, left His rebel creatures to the miseries of a divided and distracted heart.

But in the covenant of grace, He promises to repair the breach, to give us "one heart," that we may fear His name, seek His glory, become His portion, and thus enjoy, through the merits of the Savior, the inestimable blessings of communion with Himself, peace of conscience, and assured hope of glory. "Unite my heart to fear thy name" (Ps. 86:11) was the ardent prayer of David. Through the fall, we are dead in trespasses and sins. There is no movement for God. All is disorder and confusion, like a broken watch whose wheels lie scattered here and there and whose spring ceases to work.

But when divine grace renovates and regulates our spiritual faculties; when our heart is united; when we have "one heart" given to us; when all our soul is alive for God, and with singleness and simplicity aims at nothing but His glory and the fulfillment of His will—then we become new creatures; then we are a people formed to show forth His praise; then we possess an inward witness of our union to Jesus and our adoption into the family of God. All the family of God, possessing this "one heart," must necessarily be united to each other in brotherly love.

This loving spirit our blessed Lord made the badge of discipleship: "By this shall all men know that ye are my disciples, if ye have love one to another" (John 13:35). John makes it a mark of conversion: "We know that we have passed from death unto life, because we love the brethren" (1 John 3:14). Paul strongly exhorts to unity and fellowship and declares that all divisions mark the carnality of the mind and the unsoundness of profession. This "one heart" is then a great blessing, since it constitutes the very essence of the Christian character, as opposed to unbelief and the love of the world and sin.

"*I will give them ... one way*" (Jer. 32:39). Christ is the one only way to the Father. Faith is the one only grace whereby we become interested in the work of Jesus. Love is the one only principle that gives intrinsic excellence to our various operations. Universal holiness is the one only scriptural evidence of our possessing true faith and love and being savingly united to Jesus, the living way to the Father.

Our outward conduct must, therefore, be in consistency with our principles and professions. We must have "one way," the way of God's commandments, and walk steadily in that one way, that we may fear His name for our present and everlasting good. Thus the whole Christian character is contained in this short but beautiful promise: "I will give them one heart and one way" (Jer. 32:39). Here, we behold one of the sweet fruits of mercy hanging on the Tree of Life. All the precious promises are so many pledges of God's covenant love, which He engages to fulfill.

"Follow…holiness, without which no man shall see the Lord" (Heb. 12:14); but here holiness is promised as the work of Jehovah in the heart of poor sinners. What we cannot do, God has graciously promised to perform. He who says, "I will," is almighty and true. All His declarations of mercy are marked by solidity and stability: "The mountains shall depart, and the hills be removed; but my kindness shall not depart from thee, neither shall the covenant of my peace be removed, saith the Lord that hath mercy on thee" (Isa. 54:10). "Thy word," says David, "is very pure: therefore thy servant loveth it" (Ps. 119:140). This he could affirm from personal experience, having felt its blessed influence on his own heart. "Thy word hath quickened me" (Ps. 119:50). "Thy word is true from the beginning" (Ps. 119:160). "My soul hath kept thy testimonies; and I love them exceedingly" (Ps. 119:167). "For thy lovingkindness is before mine eyes: and I have walked in thy truth" (Ps. 26:3).

"Oh, divine Redeemer, out of whose inexhaustible fullness I would daily draw a rich supply of grace into my needy soul, be pleased to impart unto me this one heart, that to please Thee may be my greatest happiness and to promote Thy glory my highest honor. Preserve me from false motives, from a double mind, and from a divided heart. Keep me entire to Thyself, and enable me to crucify every lust which would tempt my heart from Thee. Enable me by Thy grace to walk in 'one way'—one uniform path of holy, childlike obedience. Allow me not to start aside like a broken bow. When tempted to turn aside to the right hand or to the left, may I hear a voice behind me saying, 'This is the way.' And oh, may I keep steadily therein until I reach the outer borders of the wilderness; and then, blessed Jesus, may some blessed seraph be commissioned to bear my happy and transported spirit along the shining way which leads to Thy abode, until brought before Thy throne, I see Thy face, behold Thy smile, and fall in ecstasy at Thy feet, lost in wonder, love, and praise."

Fill me, oh Lord, with holy joy,
With humble, filial fear!
My undivided heart employ
In praise to Thee and prayer.

Protect me from the power of ill;
Defend my soul from sin;
Subdue my proud rebellious will,
And make me pure within.

Create an ardent, active love,
Thy goodness to proclaim;
Oh may I sweetly feel and prove
The power of Jesus' name!

May Jesus my beloved be,
My shepherd and my friend;
Unite my soul, oh Lord, to Thee,
In bonds that never shall end!

Then will my raptured soul repeat
The wonders of Thy grace;
Until prostrate at Thy mercy-seat,
I view Thee face to face.

CHAPTER 10

The Immensity of God

It is from the Holy Scriptures alone that we can attain just views of the being, nature, and character of God. How sublime are the revelations of the divine perfections there made known to us! Who can grasp this one thought: "Thus saith the high and lofty One that inhabiteth eternity" (Isa. 57:15)? We are astonished when we read of the Egyptian pyramids and the magnificent palaces of mighty monarchs; but what sightless atoms are they, when compared with eternity, that boundless habitation of the King of kings. "From everlasting to everlasting, thou art God" (Ps. 90:2). The existence of one supreme Being, who is without beginning, is consonant with right reason; for He who made all things must necessarily be before all things. A creature cannot make itself. This would imply exertion before existence, which is an absurdity. And yet how far above our finite comprehension is the nature of the self-existent, eternal Jehovah. Our minds are lost when we plunge into infinity. "Canst thou by searching find out God? Canst thou find out the Almighty unto perfection?" (Job 11:7).

The volume of creation displays the wisdom, power, and goodness of God. What wonderful contrivance, what wise adaptation of one part to another, what power in upholding, what goodness in preserving the myriads of creatures which fill the air, the earth, the sea, is discoverable around us.

A late eminent astronomer found that in 41 minutes, not less than 258,000 stars in that part of the heaven, called the Milky Way, had passed through the field of view in his telescope! What must God be, who made, governs, and supports so many worlds, who tells the number of the stars and calls them all by their names?

It is, however, from the volume of inspiration that we derive our knowledge of the moral attributes of the Deity and obtain those awesome, yet sublimely interesting, views of Him with whom we have to do, which at once elevate and purify the soul. The Holy Bible may well be called the *book* of God; not only because it has God for its author, but because it is filled with such revelations of His glorious character, as surpass the powers of human reason fully to comprehend.

How fervently did the apostle pray for his Ephesian converts that the glory of our Lord Jesus Christ, the Father of glory, would give unto them the Spirit of wisdom and revelation in the knowledge of Him—that the eyes of their understanding being enlightened, they might know the hope of His calling and the riches of the glory of His inheritance in the saints and the exceeding greatness of His power towards those who believe; that being rooted and grounded in love, they might be able to comprehend, with all saints, what is the breadth, and length, and depth and height, and know the love of Christ which passes knowledge, and so be filled with all the fullness of God. We stand upon the seashore and survey with admiring delight the wide extended ocean, whose distant waters lose themselves in the blue horizon. But what is this great abyss of waters, compared to that ocean of almighty love, which is without a bottom and a shore?

"Oh, my God, when I contemplate Thy sovereign will, which, from eternity, in highest wisdom, consulted my welfare, I am lost in astonishment! When I reflect upon Thy omnipotence, omniscience, and omnipresence; upon Thy infinite holiness, inviolable justice, and unerring wisdom; upon Thy faithfulness and truth; upon Thy everlasting love, Thy sovereign grace, Thy patience and long-suffering—how am I filled with awe and dread! Yet faith can contemplate this bright display of uncreated excellence and rejoice in Thy infinite perfections as exhibited and harmonized in Jesus, the incarnate Word. Here I behold, as in a glass, the glory of the Lord. Oh, that while beholding, I may be transformed into the lovely image of the Savior, from glory to glory, even as by the Spirit of the Lord."

Who does not long to feel the purifying effect of these sacred views of God in Christ? "Lord, make me humble, while I meditate on Thy humility; loving, while I think upon Thy love; holy, while I dwell upon Thy purity; just, while I contemplate Thy righteousness; merciful, while I behold Thy grace; joyful, while I review Thy everlasting covenant. Oh, fill my heart with gratitude and my mouth with praise. To Thee, blessed Jesus, do I look. Remove all spiritual darkness from my mind, all spiritual deadness from my heart. Cause me to know Thee as my Savior, to follow Thee as my leader, to love Thee as my friend, to trust in Thee as my atonement, to be found in Thee as my righteousness, to feed on Thee as the living bread, to walk in Thee as the way to the Father, and to dwell with Thee in heaven forever."

What comfort may every humble believer derive from the declaration of his Lord! "Am I a God at hand, saith the LORD, and not a God afar off? Can any hide himself in secret places that I shall not see him? saith the LORD. Do not I fill heaven and earth? saith the LORD" (Jer. 23:23-24).

"Where two or three are gathered together in my name, there am I in the midst of them" (Matt. 18:20). "Lo, I am with you alway, even unto the end of the world" (Matt. 28:20). How happy must that soul be, whose refuge is always near. But to have an enemy always near us, an enemy armed with omnipotence—an enemy, made so by our willful transgressions, is a consideration most appalling.

Yet this is the case, as it respects every impenitent sinner. The thought of such a God being ever near, whose eye is ever upon us, whose power can crush us in a moment, and drive the outcast spirit into outer darkness, would, one would think, awaken every dormant sensibility, and arouse every sleeping sinner! Yet, alas, surrounded with such peril, the soul sleeps on in dreadful security, until either grace quickens it to repentance, or justice awakens it in the fire that shall never be quenched. "Lord, awaken my drowsy sense. Quicken all my powers. Draw me by the powerful, constraining influence of Thy love;

and cause me to rejoice in this sacred truth—that Thou art always near, my help in trouble and my life in death."

When we begin to measure distances with respect to natural objects, we are lost in astonishment. What thought can reach the boundary of creation? Many stars have probably been sending forth their rays in quick succession from the first moment of creation, whose light has not reached our earth. Who, then, can measure such distances? And yet, what are millions of worlds revolving round each other, compared with infinite space, and eternal duration? If we cannot, by the boldest flight of imagination, conceive the mighty stretch of creation, how shall we dare to sin against that inconceivably glorious Being who fills heaven and earth with His presence—who inhabits eternity!

How truly sublime are the questions of the enraptured prophet Isaiah! "Who hath measured the waters in the hollow of his hand, and meted out heaven with the span, and comprehended the dust of the earth in a measure, and weighed the mountains in scales, and the hills in a balance?" (Isa. 40:12).

"Behold, the nations are as a drop of a bucket, and are counted as the small dust of the balance: behold, he taketh up the isles as a very little thing" (Isa. 40:15). "All nations before him are as nothing; and they are counted to him less than nothing, and vanity" (v. 17). "It is he that sitteth upon the circle of the earth, and the inhabitants thereof are as grasshoppers; that stretcheth out the heavens as a curtain, and spreadeth them out as a tent to dwell in" (v. 22). "Hast thou not known? hast thou not heard, that the everlasting God, the LORD, the Creator of the ends of the earth, fainteth not, neither is weary? there is no searching of his understanding. He giveth power to the faint; and to them that have no might he increaseth strength. Even the youths shall faint and be weary, and the young men shall utterly fall: But they that wait upon the LORD shall renew their strength; they shall mount up with wings as eagles; they shall run, and not be weary; and they shall walk, and not faint" (vv. 28-31).

All doctrines of Scripture are designed to promote our growth in grace. They are given to us, not for speculation, but for practice. From this view of the divine immensity, we are taught humility, reverence, and circumspection. Wherever we are, whatever we are doing, the eye of God is upon us, viewing us, not as an indifferent spectator, but taking cognizance of every action, of every word, yes of every thought that rises in our minds; that, from His awesome gaze, His continued, His never to be avoided scrutiny, our eternal condition will be fixed at the judgment day.

How plain are the declarations of Scripture: "God shall bring every work into judgment, with every secret thing, whether it be good or whether it be evil" (Eccl. 12:14). "He hath appointed a day, in the which he will judge the world in righteousness" (Acts 17:31). "God shall judge the secrets of men by Jesus Christ" (Rom. 2:16). "Every one of us shall give an account of himself to God" (Rom. 14:12). "The Son of man shall come in the glory of his Father with his angels; and then he shall reward every man according to his works" (Matt. 16:27). For by actions, the sincerity of faith in Christ is best known and evidenced. And our reward, though not of debt but of grace, will be more or less glorious according to our works, those fruits of faith, done for Christ in this present world.

In like manner, the punishment of unbelievers will be proportionate to their respective degrees of wickedness and their comparative abuse of light, mercies, and privileges vouchsafed to them. "Woe unto thee, Chorazin! Woe unto thee, Bethsaida! for if the mighty works, which were done in you, had been done in Tyre and Sidon, they would have repented long ago in sackcloth and ashes. But I say unto you, It shall be more tolerable for Tyre and Sidon at the day of judgment, than for you" (Matt. 11:21-22). "Every idle word that men shall speak, they shall give account thereof in the day of judgment. For by thy words thou shalt be justified, and by thy words thou shalt be condemned" (Matt. 12:36-37). Our words will evidence the state of our hearts and therefore will prove us either in the faith or unregenerate before an assembled world.

He will "bring to light the hidden things of darkness, and will make manifest the counsels of the hearts" (1 Cor. 4:5).

How infinite is that omniscient God, who can search the deep recesses of every heart—yes, of hundreds of millions of hearts in every age, at the same moment of time, not confounding in the least degree the motives and purposes of His rational creatures; and who at the great day of account will reveal to each his secret sins, while all shall stand speechless and self-condemned before His awful tribunal!

"Lord, give me grace to judge myself now, that I may not be condemned in that day. Oh, send down Thy blessed Spirit into my heart! Sanctify every thought, every affection and desire. Purge me with the cleansing blood of Thy dear Son. Clothe me with His spotless righteousness that, being viewed by Thee in Christ my Savior, I may be saved with an everlasting salvation and never be confounded, world without end."

"Thou God seest me" (Gen. 16:13). To feel the abiding impression of this solemn truth would be a sacred preservation from sin. When an evil thought arises in my heart, should I like to divulge it to my nearest friend? Ah, no. Conscience, shame, or a regard to his good opinion checks the disclosure. What, and shall I dare to indulge in such a thought, exposed to my almighty Friend, and naked in His sight, when I would not dare to mention it to a fellow worm? Where is the fear of God? Where is the belief of His omniscience? Where is the awe of His omnipresence? Where is the dread of final judgment? Yes, where is my love to Christ, who died to save me from my sins? "Doth he not see my ways, and count all my steps?" (Job 31:4). This method of addressing conscience may, through grace, present a powerful barrier against the injections of Satan and the workings of natural corruption.

"Lord, strengthen me more and more. Give me grace never to harbor a thought which I should be ashamed to express. May I never forget that, as speaking is but thinking aloud, so thinking is speaking to Thee, who requirest not, like weak mortals, the medium of words and sounds. Thou hearest the inward voice of the soul, pouring out itself before Thee in silent yet fervent breathings of desire; and Thou knowest the subtle workings of inbred sin. May I ever consider myself as in Thy immediate presence, surrounded by Thy immensity. Thou

God seest me.' May this thought constrain me to act with purity, truth, and sincerity, when no human eye can observe my actions—or, if my actions are visible, when they cannot unveil my motives. May I do all from a principle of love to Thee, and with a simple desire in all things to promote Thy glory; for Thy eyes run to and fro throughout the whole earth, to show Thyself strong in the behalf of those whose heart is perfect towards Thee" (cf. 2 Chron. 16:9).

How consoling is this view of the divine immensity, with respect to our distant Christian friends! Wherever they are, whether crossing tempestuous oceans or dwelling in distant climates, whether traversing dreary deserts or climbing craggy steeps, God is still near them, to protect and bless them. Should He call them out of the body, separated from all they love upon earth, yet He is still near to cheer their departing spirits and to conduct them in safety to their eternal home.

"Let me then rejoice, oh Lord, in Thy presence. Let me be always happy in this sweet assurance, that Thou art a sun and shield and wilt give grace and glory to every humble follower of the Lamb. Oh, may I live daily nearer to Thee by faith and prayer! Unite my heart to fear Thy name. Bind my affections to Thy cross; and allow me not one moment to wander from Thee or lose the thought of Thy immensity and glory. It is in Thee that I live and move and have my being; it is from Thee that I derive every spiritual and temporal blessing; and it is through Thee that I humbly hope to be brought in safety, as a monument of mercy, into Thy everlasting kingdom."

Oh, holy, holy, holy Lord!
Whom angel-hosts adore;
When shall I join, in raptured strains,
The bright celestial choir?

In pity, view a sinful worm,
A prisoner here below;
A pilgrim journeying through the land
Of darkness, sin, and woe.

The Immensity of God

Ten thousand voices round Thy throne
Unite in hymns divine;
"Salvation to the Lamb!" they cry,
As high in bliss they shine.

Sincerely would I now begin the song,
To Thee, my God and friend;
Then mingle with the choirs above,
In praise which never shall end.

CHAPTER 11

The Divine Sovereignty

At the creation, amid the darkness of chaos, Jehovah said: "Let there be light: and there was light" (Gen. 1:3). When veiled in human flesh, He commanded the raging wind and waves, saying: "Peace, be still. And the wind ceased, and there was a great calm" (Mark 4:39). To His tempest-tossed people He now speaks these composing words: "Be still, and know that I am God" (Ps. 46:10)—and they find rest unto their souls. In violent public commotions, God can still the madness of the people; and in inward mental agonies, He can calm the agitated spirit. "When he giveth quietness, who then can make trouble? and when he hideth his face, who then can behold him? whether it be done against a nation, or against a man only" (Job 34:29).

When we read the history of past ages and consider the ever-changing scene before us; when we study man and perceive though but a small portion of the passions and contending interests which shake the fabric of society—how delightful, how composing to the mind, is this all-gracious declaration: "Be still, and know that I am God"!

The political world, like the air and sea that surround us, is ever in motion; but the happy believer finds his rest in God. In the present day, the human mind seems to be acted upon in a most remarkable manner. Knowledge is diffusing its light in every direction, and the intellectual powers are acquiring an expansion, which their ancient boundaries can neither limit nor control. The Christian world is all awake to the spiritual and moral degradation of mankind and is laboring to disseminate the sacred truths of revelation, which alone can raise our fallen race.

The enemies of the gospel and of social order are alike awake to their deeds of darkness. There is, therefore, at the present eventful period, an evident struggle between light and darkness. The struggle may be violent, but the believer hears the cheering voice from heaven, which dissipates every rising fear: "Be still, and know that I am God."

Oh, my soul, rejoice that the Lord reigns! He can calm the rough surges of the mind. He can bid the inward tempest cease. He can pour an enlivening ray upon the drooping heart and cause a sweet serenity and peace to reign within. Trust in the Lord at all times. Be still, and know that He is God.

There is something peculiarly soothing to the heart of a pious Christian to know that He who rules over all worlds, in whose hands are the destinies of nations, and who guides the minutest concerns of families and individuals, is his Father and his friend. The more we know of God, of His power, wisdom, love, faithfulness, and truth, the more we shall bow before His throne in humble adoration and filial confidence and love.

To know God in Christ, to know Him as a covenant God, to know Him as our God, is to possess all the sources and secrets of true peace in the midst of surrounding storms and tempests. This knowledge will raise us above the agitated elements of the world and place us in that pure region where the soul can breathe more freely and expand her powers more fully. Faith views with admiration the perfections of Jehovah. Hope rests the fulfillment of her expectations on these perfections. Love delights in them and gradually assimilates the soul to them, while patience calmly waits, under every changing dispensation, for that abundant harvest of rich blessings, which the God of truth has promised and which His faithfulness will perform.

Come, then, oh my soul, and learn, from this view of your privileges, the blessedness of trusting in God, "with whom is no variableness, neither shadow of turning" (James 1:17). All His promises are yea and amen. All His ways are righteous and true. Cast your care upon Him who cares for you; and, under every trying event, be still, and know that He is God.

It is truly animating to reflect that, while every thing seems given to change, the Almighty has declared: "My counsel shall stand, and I will do all my pleasure" (Isa. 46:10). "I change not" (Mal. 3:6). The purposes of God are moving steadily and directly towards their fulfillment. Many things, according to our shortsightedness, appear to thwart His designs. Persecutors arise and cut off His most zealous servants. Death seizes eminent laborers in His vineyard. Unforeseen circumstances spring up and appear to check the progress of the gospel. Hence we are ready to exclaim with David: "Let me not fall into the hand of man" (2 Sam. 24:14). But is not this the language of despondency, the language of a soul looking through a dark and gloomy medium? Man never had, and never shall have, the upper hand. David was in a right frame when he sang: "The Lord reigneth" (Ps. 96:10). This is the triumphant song of the redeemed above. "Alleluia: for the Lord God omnipotent reigneth" (Rev. 19:6).

Nothing can happen without the divine will and permission. The Almighty sees the end from the beginning. Unto Him are known all His works and all events from eternal ages. He has firmly laid His eternal plans of goodness, justice, and mercy. All things serve Him. "The Lord hath made all things for himself: yeah, even the wicked for the day of evil" (Prov. 16:4).

Can anything, then, unforeseen, strike across His purposes or derange His plans? Can any man who is crushed before the moth, the creature of a day, turn aside the grand machine of providence, whose constant wheels revolve their everlasting rounds? Ah, no! As every thing respecting the eternal purposes of Jehovah springs from His own will, so every thing shall terminate in His own glory. Higher and farther than this, we cannot go. "I am Alpha and Omega, the beginning and the end, the first and the last" (Rev. 22:13). Clouds and darkness may surround the throne of the Eternal and veil His bright designs, but faith can pierce the veil and view, beyond this darkening scene, the rising glories of Emmanuel's kingdom.

How great, then, is the blessedness of true religion! How highly privileged is the child of God! As nothing can happen without the divine permission, so everything shall work together for good to those who love God, to those who are the called according to His purpose.

Satan may rage, the world may frown, the flesh may rebel, and providence may seem to cross the humble believer; but yet, notwithstanding all this tempest, his soul is safe, being hid with Christ in God. He may groan, being burdened; yet still he can rejoice. He looks through the curtain of time, which hangs over the glories of eternity; and, in joyful expectation of soon entering within the veil, he endures, with much patience, the trials of this transitory state.

Not so the worldling. He knows no joys but those of sense, or those perhaps of a more refined nature, flowing from intellectual pursuits. But in respect of heavenly pleasures, arising from communion with his Savior and a delightful foretaste of future bliss, he is an utter stranger. To him, "the future is a dark unknown." His views are indistinct and dim when he reads or hears of joys forever flowing from those sources that are now the objects of his unvarying dislike.

What happiness can arise from the contemplation of being eternally with Jesus, when prayer and meditation are now irksome and insipid to him? What happiness from the idea of being made like Jesus, when holiness is offensive to him, or from the consideration of beholding His glory, when the splendors of this world have far more powerful attractions to him?

It is true, he prefers heaven to hell, as a choice of two evils; but he secretly disbelieves the Word of revelation and therefore hopes that hell has no existence and that death is an eternal sleep. If he is not thus far advanced in infidelity, yet he flatters himself that God will be more lenient and merciful than His own Word declares Him to be. Thus he ventures upon the dreadful step of putting the truth of God to its most awful test, and passes through death to learn by tremendous experience the madness of his unbelief!

Happy, thrice happy, is the man who receives with childlike simplicity the Word of God and acts upon it. He sees God in everything and can feed upon the hidden manna. He finds the promises to be full of truth and comfort. On them, as on a rock, he rests in safety. With wonder he beholds the raging tempest, which, sweeping over the nations of the earth, clears away deep-rooted prejudices and prepares a smoother path for the chariot of the everlasting gospel.

He knows that glorious days are hastening on and therefore is not discouraged, though they be preceded by a stormy night. He hears the voice of his almighty Father speaking in gracious accents to allay his fears, "Be still, and know that I am God" (Ps. 46:10), and he is kept in perfect peace.

Come, then, oh my soul, and take courage. Fear not the face, nor the frown, of man. The Lord reigns, be the earth ever so unquiet. Sing with David, unite with Luther, and say: "God is our refuge and strength, a very present help in trouble" (Ps. 46:1). Do not be dismayed at the troubles of the earth. Tremble not at the convulsions of empires. Only fear God; only believe in His promises; only love and serve Him; and all things shall work together for your good, as they assuredly will for His glory.

Life is hastening quickly away. Eternity is at the door. Live, then, for eternity, and leave with God the concerns of time. Leave in His hands the safety of His church and the security of His cause. Cleave to Him with childlike simplicity. Seek His glory. Aim at perfection. Look high, and look forward; and soon you shall be removed out of the reach of evil and be placed securely in the paradise above!

In times which are gloomy and sad,
When nations are trembling with fears,
The Christian, in confidence clad,
Serene amid dangers appears.

He knows that the black lowering sky,
Whose bosom destruction contains;
In a moment will vanish and fly,
When God His dread vengeance restrains.

The Divine Sovereignty

In Him, whom archangels adore,
In Him, whom the cherubs obey,
While thunders tremendously roar,
He trusts without fear and dismay.

It is Jesus who reigns in his heart,
While Satan is raging around;
It is faith quenches every dart,
As pointless they fall to the ground.

The peace he enjoys in his breast,
Descends from a reconciled God:
While sinners, those strangers to rest,
Groan under the stroke of His rod.

When troubles invade and oppress,
When death rips his comforts away,
He still, in the midst of distress,
Has God for his comfort and stay.

Thrice blessed, you saint of the Lord;
In Jesus your refuge is found;
Oh, trust to His promise and Word,
And joys shall increase and abound.

Yes, joy shall increase like a stream;
Your peace, like the waves of the sea;
Your grace into glory shall beam;
And Jesus your portion shall be.

CHAPTER 12

The Two Covenants

The covenant of *works*, in the order of time, was proclaimed to Adam before the covenant of *grace*. But the covenant of grace, called in Scripture the everlasting covenant, was entered into by the divine persons in the Godhead before the world was made. While contemplating this dispensation of mercy, our views must stretch themselves into eternity. We must pass beyond the origin of earth and enter into those revelations which record the purposes of God before time began. And how wonderful are the counsels of infinite love, wisdom, and power!

Jesus, in the volume of inspired truth, is declared to be the Lamb of God, "who verily was foreordained before the foundation of the world" (1 Peter 1:20). He was "slain from the foundation of the world" (Rev. 13:8). His redeemed ones were "chosen…in him before the foundation of the world" (Eph. 1:4). They were "from the beginning chosen…to salvation" (2 Thess. 2:13) "according to his own purpose and grace, which was given us in Christ Jesus before the world began" (2 Tim. 1:9), "elect according to the foreknowledge of God the Father" (1 Pet. 1:2), and "predestinated according to the purpose of him who worketh all things after the counsel of his own will" (Eph. 1:11).

From these glorious passages, and many others of similar import, it is evident that the whole economy of human redemption was devised and planned in the eternal counsels of Jehovah before the earth or man was formed. Hence we are taught that the covenant of grace originated in the everlasting love of God. But with respect to us finite creatures, who can know nothing of the purposes of God, but as He is pleased to reveal them, it may aptly be called a *new* covenant.

When Adam was created in the image of God, the Lord placed him in a garden of delights, surrounded with everything that could gratify his pure and innocent desires. In the midst, however, of this garden was placed the tree of knowledge of good and evil as a reasonable test of his obedience; for God created man in righteousness and true holiness, with powers and faculties to know and serve Him. In the garden was also placed the Tree of Life as a pledge of immortality. Of this tree he might freely eat while he continued obedient to the divine command. But man, alas, ate of the forbidden fruit through the subtle temptations of the serpent, and thus the covenant of works was broken, and death entered into the world by sin. His whole posterity are involved in the dreadful consequences of the fall; for the Scriptures declare: "In Adam all die" (1 Cor. 15:22). All die spiritually; for we are "shapen in iniquity" (Ps. 51:5). We are "by nature the children of wrath" (Eph. 2:3).

All die naturally. The sentence "Dust thou art, and unto dust shalt thou return" (Gen. 3:19) extends to all the children of Adam. "It is appointed unto men once to die" (Heb. 9:27). "By man came death" (1 Cor. 15:21). "Death passed upon all men, for that all have sinned" (Rom. 5:12).

All die eternally if left in righteous judgment to the awful consequences of transgression: "The wicked shall be turned into hell, and all the nations that forget God" (Ps. 9:17). "The soul that sinneth, it shall die" (Ezek. 18:20). "He that believeth not shall be damned" (Mark 16:16).

In this wretched, lost, and sinful condition, when he was without strength and without hope, Adam heard the voice of mercy. The "seed of the woman" was proclaimed and promised. Jehovah spoke the word of life at the very moment when justice was lifting up the sword of vengeance, as if determined to magnify His mercy. Oh, what encouragement is this to trust in Him, whose love outstripped His justice, or rather provided a satisfaction to it, that mercy might have free course and be glorified in the salvation of a ruined world!

The new covenant was then made known to Adam and (may we not hope?) was more delightful to his guilty, trembling soul than all the sweet harmony of birds that had regaled his ear in the lovely groves of Eden. At the voice of pardoning grace, hope revives, love rekindles, and joyful admiration holds the mind in wondering meditation on the goodness of our justly offended Creator!

The covenant of works made with Adam being broken, all hope of happiness from that covenant is done away forever. But the covenant of grace made with Christ, the second Adam, is immutable and everlasting. Jesus, in our nature, fulfilled all the conditions, performed all the requirements, and answered all the demands of the broken covenant of works. By His unsinning obedience and meritorious death, He brought in everlasting righteousness and thus became the author of eternal salvation to all those who obey Him. So that now, all the blessings of the covenant of grace are made over to every fallen son and daughter of Adam who truly believes in Jesus.

Here, then, is the spring of the believer's hope and peace and joy. Here he finds security and stability. Here he reposes his soul and smiles at every storm. Oh, how rich, how full, how sovereign is the covenant of grace! This covenant, as we have seen from the pages of eternal truth, was made before the world began—made from eternity. What a wide expanse for the mind to range in! But we need a guide, or else our minds will soon be lost in wandering mazes and dangerous speculations.

This guide is the Bible, read with prayer in a spirit of humility and faith, under the teaching of the Holy Spirit. Where the line of revelation stops, there we must stop; or rather, where it enters into the unfathomable depths of eternal wisdom, there we must pause, and wonder, and adore. We must not dare to tread within the veil or curiously to pry into those hidden mysteries which God has wisely concealed from mortal eyes. "Thou knowest not now; but thou shalt know hereafter" (John 13:7) will quiet and satisfy every humble, loving, obedient, grateful follower of the Lamb.

What personally concerns every believer is this: have I the spirit and character of those who are interested in the covenant of grace? If not, what will all its glories and blessings avail me? I shall only resemble a person looking over the title deeds of a vast estate in which he has no interest.

How plain and express is the Word of God in describing the character of the redeemed! Here is no ambiguity, no darkness, no mystery. It is a faithful mirror, held up to all mankind. Happy indeed are they, who beholding, as in a glass, the glory of the Lord, are changed into the same image, from glory to glory, even as by the Spirit of the Lord!

The character of God's peculiar people is thus portrayed by the pen of unerring truth: They are "chosen…in him…that we should be holy and without blame before him in love" (Eph. 1:4). "God hath…chosen you to salvation through sanctification of the Spirit and belief of the truth" (2 Thess. 2:13). God "hath saved us, and called us with an holy calling, not according to our works, but according to his own purpose and grace" (2 Tim. 1:9). They are "elect according to the foreknowledge of God the Father, through sanctification of the Spirit, unto obedience and sprinkling of the blood of Jesus Christ" (1 Pet. 1:2). They are "predestinated…unto the adoption of children" (Eph. 1:5). They are predestinated "to be conformed to the image of his Son" (Rom. 8:29). They are "created in Christ Jesus unto good works, which God hath before ordained that we should walk in them" (Eph. 2:10). "Ye are a chosen generation, a royal priesthood, an holy nation, a peculiar people; that ye should shew forth the praises of him who hath called you out of darkness into his marvellous light" (1 Pet. 2:9). He "gave himself for us, that he might redeem us from all iniquity, and purify unto himself a peculiar people, zealous of good works" (Titus. 2:14).

Such is the spirit and character of those happy souls who have fled for refuge to lay hold upon the hope set before them in the gospel—the character of all who truly believe in Jesus. To them all the promises of God in Christ Jesus are yea and amen, sure and abiding. To them the most affectionate exhortations are addressed. "Put on therefore, as the elect of God, holy and beloved, bowels of mercies, kindness, humbleness of mind, meekness, longsuffering; Forbearing one another, and forgiving one another, if any man have a quarrel against any: even as Christ forgave you, so also do ye" (Col. 3:12-13). "Be ye kind one to another, tenderhearted, forgiving one another, even as God for Christ's sake hath forgiven you" (Eph. 4:32). "Be ye therefore followers of God, as dear children; and walk in love, as Christ also hath loved us, and hath given himself for us an offering and a sacrifice to God for a sweet-smelling savour" (Eph. 5:1-2). "Let the peace of God rule in your hearts" (Col. 3:15). "Put on charity" (Col. 3:14) and "the ornament of a meek and quiet spirit" (1 Pet. 3:4). "Be clothed with humility" (1 Pet. 5:5). "Love not the world, neither the things that are in the world" (1 John 2:15). "Seek those things which are above" (Col. 3:1). "Set your affection on things above" (v. 2). "Let your speech be alway with grace" (Col. 4:6). "Rejoice evermore. Pray without ceasing" (1 Thess. 5:16-17). "Abstain from all appearance of evil" (1 Thess. 5:22). "Fight the good fight of faith" (1 Tim. 6:12). "Be thou faithful unto death" (Rev. 2:10). These beautiful exhortations contain a lively portrait of the true believer. How different from the worldling, the nominal Christian, the cold-hearted adherer to the gospel, the double-minded professor! With the true believer, all is life and energy. Here, all is spirit, unction, and power. Here, we see the workmanship of God, the new creation in Christ Jesus (Eph. 2:10). Where these lineaments are found, there grace is begun; where they are lacking, all pretensions to religion, all hope of final salvation, all self-appropriation of the promises, is delusion—a device of Satan, to lull the soul to sleep on the lap of carnal security, until it drop into the flames of hell. "Lord, open my eyes, that I may see wondrous things out of Thy law. Change my heart by the powerful influence of Thy Holy Spirit. Fill my soul with humility, love, and purity. May Christ be formed in me the hope of glory. May Christ dwell in my heart by faith. May love and every grace abound within me, until I am brought by sovereign mercy to the general assembly of the church of the firstborn, whose names are written in heaven."

How free the love, how rich the grace,
A pardoning God bestows;
To Adam's vile apostate race
In boundless streams it flows.

*What joy arises in the heart
When Jesus' cross appears—
Salvation to my soul impart,
Subdue my guilty fears.*

*Blessed Savior, speak the healing word,
Bid all my sorrows cease;
Be Thou my great atoning Lord,
My righteousness and peace.*

*Oh, let Thy precious blood divine
Wash all my sins away!
Then will my soul resplendent shine,
Through heaven's eternal day.*

CHAPTER 13

The Love of God

"God is love" (1 John 4:8)! Sweet truth! Oh, my soul, rejoice daily in this blessed revelation, "God is love." Before all worlds, before any being was formed, "God is love"—love eternal and unchangeable. He is the same yesterday, today, and forever. He is love. How inconceivably great is the love of God! All worlds rolling in the infinite expanse, all beings inhabiting those innumerable spheres, which extend far beyond the boundaries of the most excursive imagination, all the myriads of angelic spirits which dwell forever in the bright effulgence of uncreated light, are only the overflowings of that love, which is inexhaustible. The immense fountain loses not one drop, though countless millions are filled by its streams. It is ever flowing, ever full. "Lord, Thou art love. Oh, fill my soul with Thy love! Thou canst not be diminished, and I shall be made everlastingly blessed."

When the Almighty created the angels in heaven, and man in Paradise, He endued both with powers suited to their distinctive degrees of excellence. Both were formed holy, and consequently happy. All nature proclaims the benevolence of the deity, the unbounded goodness of Jehovah. The moral law emanated from the love of God. This law was stamped upon the heart of Adam when he was in a state of innocence. It is a transcript of the divine mind as holy, just, and good.

When man sinned, he broke the law of God. He fell under its curse. To redeem him from this wretched state, Jesus, the Son of God, assumed our mortal nature, expiated our guilt, and brought in an everlasting righteousness. He burst the bars of death. He ascended up on high and reigns as the sovereign Lord of angels and of men.

When the royal law of love was broken in Paradise, how soon did Adam's first-born imbrue his hand in a brother's blood! Violence overspread the earth with awful rapidity until God, in righteous judgment, swept the guilty rebels from the earth by a tremendous flood of waters. Every succeeding age has been marked by miseries of every name, all flowing from one common source—an evil heart of unbelief. Sin is the cause of all misery, and sin originates with man.

If it be asked, what is the true cause of man's inability to love and serve God, may we not answer, a criminal indisposition of heart so to do? It is not that man cannot love God, from a natural incapacity, arising from a total destitution of understanding, will, and affections; but rather that he will not, owing to a deep-rooted enmity against the holy character and commands of God.

This aversion of the heart from God constitutes the chief guilt of man. Man is a responsible being and must render an account to God, from whom he receives all his powers, for the abuse of those talents committed to his trust. He has a heart that can love the world: he can love sensual delights, he can love riches and honors— yes, he can love everything which tends to gratify his passions and to exalt him in his own eyes or in the estimation of others. He has a will to choose what is pleasing to his animal appetites and to refuse what is painful or distasteful to him. He has an understanding to judge upon worldly matters and a quick eye to discover the path to temporal advancement. He finds his hopes and fears, his joys and griefs, his loves and hatreds, brought into continual exercise with the ever-varying events of life.

Hence man does not labor under a natural incapacity. His inability is altogether of a moral kind. Sin has darkened and corrupted all the higher faculties of the soul, so that "the world by wisdom knew not God" (1 Cor. 1:21). "Men loved darkness rather than light, because their deeds were evil" (John 3:19), for "the carnal mind is enmity against God" (Rom. 8:7).

This wrong state of the heart, this evil bias of the soul, this radical corruption of our nature, is universal. It spreads itself through the whole human race, without exception—for all are born in sin, all are by nature the children of wrath and the heirs of hell. So powerful is this innate evil, this natural indisposition of the heart towards God, that neither reason, conscience, nor philosophy can remove it. God alone can turn the heart of the sinner to Himself. The language of divine revelation is: "Thou hast destroyed thyself; but in me is thine help" (Hos. 13:9).

While, therefore, in deepest self-abasement we bear the burden of our guilt and acknowledge that we have destroyed ourselves, we must ascribe all the glory of our salvation to omnipotent love, in whom our help is found, and say, with the grateful psalmist: "Not unto us, O Lord, not unto us, but unto thy name give glory, for thy mercy, and for thy truth's sake" (Ps. 115:1).

The whole human race must soon stand before the judgment seat of Christ. No plea will then be accepted in arrest of judgment. In that awful day, every mouth shall be stopped, and all the world will become guilty before God, "for whatsoever a man soweth, that shall he also reap" (Gal. 6:7). From this view of our fallen state, we may scripturally conclude that sinners, if left to themselves, would never turn to God. And hence we see the blessedness and necessity of that grace which turns us from darkness unto light and from the power of Satan unto God.

It is a true saying of Augustine, that without free will there could be no condemnation, and without free grace there could be no salvation. But the voice of sovereign love declares to the great Melchizedek: "Thy people shall be willing in the day of thy power" (Ps. 110:3). Here is set forth the power of God, the people on whom that power is exerted, and the blessed effects of it upon their souls. This power is the power of God unto salvation. When He works, who can resist it? It is convincing power, converting power, sustaining power. Oh, that this divine power, this *energy* of *love*, may be felt in every soul! Lord, may I feel it in mine!

But on whom is this power exerted? When we view the whole human race sunk in sin and misery, in a state of open rebellion against the majesty of heaven, where shall we find His people? The very words, they "shall be willing," imply that they were not always so. Prior to this great change, they were enemies in their minds by wicked works (Col. 1:21). They are His people in purpose and grace, "chosen…in him before the foundation of the world, that we [they] should be holy and without blame before him in love" (Eph. 1:4), "predestinated to be conformed to the image of his Son" (Rom. 8:29).

When Paul was at Corinth, the Lord appeared to His persecuted servant and said: "Be not afraid, but speak, and hold not thy peace: For I am with thee, and no man shall set on thee to hurt thee: for I have much people in this city" (Acts 18:9-10). Oh, that my proud heart could submit to receive salvation as the free gift of unmerited mercy! Lord, make me willing in the day of Thy power to yield myself unto Thee as a living sacrifice, as my most reasonable service.

We see what is the effect produced by this power on the minds of His people. They "shall be willing"—willing to receive Christ, willing to suffer for Christ, willing to give up all for Christ. This change in their will is not effected by any natural effort of their own or by the moral persuasion of others, but solely by the power of God, through the instrumentality of the gospel.

"I am not ashamed of the gospel of Christ," wrote the apostle to the Romans, "for it is the power of God unto salvation to every one that believeth" (Rom. 1:16). Those favored souls who are thus made willing in the day of God's power are not compelled by an unwelcome force to embrace salvation, but are sweetly and lovingly inclined, through the soft influences of heavenly grace, to choose, delight in, and appreciate the work and service of Emmanuel. They are made willing. Their whole heart goes forth towards the Savior, as when Jesus said to Levi at the receipt of custom: "Follow me" (Luke 5:27). They love the Lord Jesus Christ in sincerity. They embrace Him as their only Savior and His precepts as their only rule, His promises as their only support, His cross as their only glory, His righteousness as their only boast, His people as their only friends, His heaven as their only home. Oh, what a change! "Lord, may I long, and pant, and labor after this blessedness. Stir up my soul to seek it more and more."

I have here an evidence to judge of my own character. "Thy people shall be willing." If, then, I belong to this happy number, I must be willing to be saved on God's terms, to delight in His salvation, to choose His ways. Do I feel my will subdued and cheerfully inclined to embrace in humble faith the whole revelation of mercy, as made known to me through a crucified Jesus? "Lord, put forth Thy mighty grace. Let this very day be the day of Thy power. Tomorrow may find me in the eternal world. Oh, may I now be willing to be wholly Thine, that every succeeding hour may only increase my willingness to do and suffer Thy whole righteous will."

How different is earth to heaven! Here on earth, an awful disinclination of heart to love God is discoverable in all the fallen children of Adam. Even the regenerate feel with grief this hated deadness of soul to God. "My soul cleaveth unto the dust" was the lamentation, and "quicken thou me according to thy word" (Ps. 119:25) was the fervent prayer of David.

In heaven, all is governed by the sweet constraining principle of pure, undivided love. Were a soul to leave this earth under the influence of alienated affections, how could such a soul be either fit for, or happy in, that blessed place where every note is harmony and every heart is love? Reason, even in its present beclouded state, must see the unfitness of such a soul for glory when that glory consists in loving God with a supreme affection and being made like Him in all His communicable perfections.

How great, then, is the happiness of loving and serving God while journeying through this valley of tears! This is the sweet peculiarity of the religion of Jesus. It diffuses joy and gladness wherever it is received in the simplicity of faith. "God is love" (1 John 4:8), and "every one that loveth is born of God, and knoweth God" (v. 7). Loving God and being the object of His love constitute the bliss of angels. The opposite of this is hell.

What poor miserable creatures we are while in a state of nature and under the power of sin and Satan! We smile when we should sigh. We laugh when we should mourn. We appear gay and sprightly when we should be of a sorrowful spirit. But oh, the change which takes place when the gospel comes to the heart, not in word only, but in power! Then we receive beauty for ashes, the oil of joy for mourning, and the garment of praise for the spirit of heaviness. Then we are privileged to rejoice always and to delight ourselves in the abundance of peace. Oh happy, blissful state, to be the genuine disciples of the blessed Jesus, who has assured His faithful people that He will manifest Himself to them, as He does not unto the world; yes, He will even come unto them, and make His abode with them. Who can contemplate these wonders of grace and not feel the holy influence of this precious revelation: "God is love!" Surely none but they who know not God; for thus says the apostle: "He that loveth not knoweth not God; for God is love" (1 John 4:8).

You trembling saint, cast off your fear,
Your mourning garments lay aside;
It is Jesus speaks: "Be of good cheer,
My love, my sister, and my bride."

Oh listen to the voice of love!
Its gentle accents whisper peace;
The Savior, from His throne above,
Delights to view your joys increase.

Blessed Jesus, cheer each drooping heart;
Uplift, revive, each fainting soul;
Thy presence, gracious Lord, impart;
Oh, make each wounded sinner whole!

Then shall Thy church more beauteous grow,
"As lilies" in Judea's vale;
Like widening streams "her peace shall flow,"
Whose "springs in Thee" can never fail.

You trembling saints, no longer fear,
Your mourning garments lay aside;
Since Jesus is forever near,
The church's husband and her guide.

CHAPTER 14

The Gift of a Savior

Before the earth was formed or man was created upon it, the Almighty foreknew that His moral creatures would apostatize from Him. The angels had already sinned and were cast into the place prepared for them. They were doomed, in righteous judgment, to be the eternal monuments of divine indignation.

A just, yet infinitely gracious Sovereign, did not determine to leave man under the same hopeless condemnation. The revelation is truly wonderful. Jesus Christ, the eternal Son of God, "who is over all, God blessed for ever" (Rom. 9:5), was foreordained in the councils of heaven to be a sacrifice, a propitiation, an atonement, for the sins of apostate man. As "all things were made by him" (John 1:3), so all things were made for Him. Earth was to be the theater on which should be displayed the mercy and justice of Jehovah.

The glorious plan was gradually unfolded through succeeding ages. The bleeding lamb was instituted as the appointed emblem of the Savior of the world. When offered up in faith, in humble reliance on the divine mercy, and with a contrite heart, the believing suppliant, thus approaching the mercy-seat through the bleeding victim, found pardon and peace.

In this way, the ancient believers obtained rest unto their souls. They trusted in God and were not confounded.

The prophets depicted in glowing colors the glories of Emmanuel, while they blended the deepened shades of His amazing humiliation with the resplendent luster of His divine nature. When the "fulness of the time was come" (Gal. 4:4), how grand to the eye of saints and angels was the entrance of the Messiah into our world!

The angel Gabriel was commissioned to convey the glad tidings to Zacharias, that he should be the father of him whom Isaiah and Malachi had predicted as "the voice," "the messenger," who should prepare the way of the Lord. He was then sent with joyful news to the humble virgin at Nazareth, announcing to her that she should be the highly favored mother of the Messiah, of whose kingdom there should be no end. The tender fears of Joseph were next dispelled by a dream in which he was assured that He who should be born of Mary, his espoused wife, was no less than the Son of God, who should save His people from their sins.

The emperor Augustus was made the instrument, though unconsciously, of bringing the virgin mother to Bethlehem, thus fulfilling the prophetic declaration of Micah and establishing the truth of the descent of Jesus in the line of David by a public enrollment.

When born in the city of David, the infant Savior was announced by the angel of the Lord to the humble shepherds of Judea, who were keeping watch over their flocks by night, while the angelic host sang in exulting strains: "Glory to God in the highest, and on earth peace, good will toward men" (Luke 2:14). In the temple, during the ceremony of Mary's purification and the dedication of her Son to the Lord, Simeon took the blessed child in his arms and declared Him to be a light to lighten the Gentiles, and the glory of His people Israel (Luke 2:32); while Anna, the prophetess, spoke of Him to all those who looked for redemption in Jerusalem.

After Jesus was returned to Bethlehem, the divinely directed Magi of the East came to pay their homage to the infant King, presenting to Him gifts of gold, frankincense, and myrrh. Herod and all Jerusalem were troubled, while saints and angels were rejoicing at the birth of the long-expected Deliverer. When John entered upon his prophetic office, he bore witness to the dignity of the Messiah and pointed to Jesus as the Lamb of God who takes away the sin of the world. The Father Himself testified of His Son: "Jesus, when he was baptized, went up straightway out of the water: and, lo, the heavens were opened unto Him, and he saw the Spirit of God descending like a dove, and lighting upon Him: and lo a voice from heaven, saying, This is my beloved Son, in whom I am well pleased" (Matt. 3:16-17). The blessed Jesus, when He made himself public to the world, astonished the thronging crowds by His stupendous yet beneficent miracles, by His heavenly wisdom, by His holy example, by His unwearied labors to do good.

The worldly, the proud, and the self-righteous could not endure the light of His doctrine and the keenness of His reproof. Hence they conspired against Him, however discordant were their peculiar views and practices. Herod and the high priest, Pilate and the Scribes, Sadducees and Pharisees, heathens and the professed worshipers of Jehovah—all allowed their national antipathies and religious differences to merge into one common cause against the Lord and against His anointed. Herod, from jealousy; the chief priests and scribes, from envy; Pilate, from slavish fear; and the common people, from popular feeling excited by their rulers, conspired the death of Jesus, whose meekness and innocence, contrasted with the rage of His bloody enemies, shone like the arch of heaven on the angry cloud.

He died praying for His murderers. He died a sacrifice for their sins. He died a sacrifice for the sins of a lost world. Amazing love! Oh, my soul, look to this precious, bleeding Savior; trust in Him for your whole salvation; rejoice in His grace, and adore that wisdom that could overrule so much wickedness to produce so much good!

How awful the period! The sun was darkened, the rocks were split apart, the veil of the temple was torn in two, the graves were opened, and many bodies of the saints who had died arose and appeared in the holy city after His resurrection.

On the third day, the conquering Savior rose triumphant from the dead, appeared to His weeping followers, ascended into heaven in their sight, and soon after His session at the right hand of power, poured out upon His infant church that great promise of the Father— the Holy Spirit.

How wonderful was the effect of this heavenly gift! The apostles, once illiterate, now spoke with new tongues; their former fears were lost in an undaunted courage; timidity gave place to zeal. In the emphatic language of the sacred historian: "They were all filled with the Holy Ghost, and they spake the Word of God with boldness" (Acts 4:31). They preached Christ in the face of danger and of death. Thousands, through their labors, were turned from Satan unto God. Churches were planted in all the known countries of the world, and at length they sealed their truth with their blood, counting it all joy to suffer for the sake of their beloved Lord.

Great is the mystery of godliness—God manifest in the flesh. That the Almighty should become the Savior of His rebellious creatures by taking upon Him their nature; that He, who rules over all worlds, should stoop, not to be a mighty monarch, but a humble carpenter; that He, who cared for and provided the foxes and the birds with holes and nests, should voluntarily leave Himself destitute of a place where to lay His head; that He, who is the great proprietor of all things, should condescend to be supported by pious females, who ministered to Him of their substance; that the Fountain of felicity should become a man of sorrows and acquainted with grief; that the Lord of glory should be despised and rejected of men; that the Judge of the living and the dead should stand, like a criminal, at an earthly tribunal, charged with crimes which He never committed, and condemned for transgressions of which He was declared innocent; that the Majesty of heaven should be spit upon, scourged, and crucified; that the Lord of life should pour out His soul unto death; this, this is the wonder of wonders—the unsearchable riches of Christ,

> *Not to be thought of; but with tides of joy;*
> *Not to be mentioned, but with shouts of praise.*

Well may Christ be styled by the enraptured prophet as "Wonderful!" (Isa. 9:6).

Men are naturally fond of great things, and yet they feel an aversion to the greatest thing in the world, the redemption of the soul. This would be inexplicable, had we not the volume of inspiration to unfold to us the hidden reason. This aversion to so glorious a work arises from the state of the human heart and the nature of redemption. The heart is in love with sin; yes, it is itself desperately wicked. Sin is its food, its element, its very constitution.

Salvation by Christ is a deliverance from sin, a renovation of the heart to holiness, a surrender of the soul to God. Hence arises the enmity. Darkness is opposed to light; and Satan, reigning in the sinner, is opposed to Christ the Savior claiming His usurped possession.

This enmity is universal and proves the universality of the fall. Wherever redemption by Christ is faithfully preached and honestly exhibited in the life, there it is powerfully resisted by both the worldly laity and mercenary priests. As the bitterest enemies of our blessed Lord were those who wore the priestly vestments, so multitudes of the faithful have, in all ages, been devoured by wolves in sheep's clothing. Lord, clothe Thy ministers with righteousness, that Thy people may sing with joyfulness!

None can receive the gospel in the love and power of it but those who are enabled by sovereign grace to do so. All others lie under the just condemnation of willfully rejecting it and shall be punished for such rejection. Men may cavil at such a statement as this and call it inconsistent; but God will, before long, vindicate His own cause. If it be true that "by grace are ye saved" (Eph. 2:8), it is equally true, that "this is the condemnation, that light is come into the world, and men loved darkness rather than light, because their deeds were evil" (John 3:19).

This great redemption is by price. And oh, what a price! The precious blood of Jesus, the Lamb of God. This blood cleanses from all sin, satisfies offended justice, clears away the obstacles in the sinner's path to glory, and procures pardon and peace and the gift of the Holy Spirit. He "made peace through the blood of his cross" (Col. 1:20). "We have redemption through his blood, even the forgiveness of sins" (Col. 1:14). This redemption is by power. God, the Holy Spirit, descends into the sinner's heart, applies the healing balm to the previously smitten conscience, and, by His almighty influence, produces the new birth, the new creation. He leads the trembling sinner to the bleeding sacrifice, points to the cross, gives saving faith, causes joy to spring up in the heart, and thus enables the soul, delivered from the penalty and pollution of sin, to "sing in the ways of the LORD" (Ps. 138:5) and to glorify the rock of his salvation.

None can love this work of grace but the subjects of grace. This sadly wounds the pride of man; but so it is. We must forever stand indebted to unmerited love for this great salvation. All boasting is here excluded. He that glories must glory in the Lord. The language of the redeemed is, "In the LORD have I righteousness and strength" (Isa. 45:24).

Oh, that I may now put the crown upon the head of Jesus! May all my affections center in Him. To Him may I devote every power and be altogether consecrated to His praise.

Oh, my soul, forever bless your beloved Lord for thus becoming your Redeemer! He is always near His people to support and comfort them. He dwells in their hearts by faith. He abides in them by His Spirit to enlighten their minds, to purify their hearts, to regulate their wills, to direct their walks, and to lead them in the paths of righteousness for His name's sake.

Thus they are safe and happy under the Shepherd's care. Their union with their divine Lord is sweet and constant. They lean upon their beloved and are supported through the wilderness. They are made strong by His strength, wise by His wisdom, righteous in His righteousness, holy by His grace. They daily receive out of His fullness, who of God is made unto them "wisdom, and righteousness, and sanctification, and redemption" (1 Cor. 1:30).

Jesus is the head over all things to His church. All power is given unto Him in heaven and in earth. As He rules over all, so He overrules all for the good of His people. Hence the apostle could confidently declare: "All things work together for good to them that love God, to them who are the called according to his purpose" (Rom. 8:28). All this is cheering to the humble followers of the Lamb. Are they in trouble? Jesus appoints it for their good. Are they joyful? The joy of the Lord is their strength. Well may the believer triumphantly exclaim: "Who shall separate us from the love of Christ?" (Rom. 8:35). "We are more than conquerors through him that loved us" (v. 37).

Jesus is the universal Lord: to Him every knee shall bow, of things in heaven, and things in earth, and things under the earth. Jesus will be the almighty judge: all nations shall be assembled before His throne, and He will render unto every man according to his works.

When, through faith, the sinner is admitted into the family of God and changes both his state and nature through the blood and spirit of Jesus, then his desire is to maintain the peace which he has happily obtained through believing. This he learns to do from the prophet Isaiah: "Thou wilt keep him in perfect peace, whose mind is stayed on thee: because he trusteth in thee" (Isa. 26:3). A wandering, backsliding, double heart can never enjoy peace. To possess the blessing of peace, the mind must be stayed upon God. This is the same as abiding in Christ and being steadfast in the faith, "rooted and grounded in love" (Eph. 3:17).

It implies stability, constancy, perseverance. The mind must be stayed upon the covenant of grace as an unchangeable, everlasting covenant, ordered in all things and sure. In this covenant, every thing is treasured up which can furnish the believer with grace here and glory hereafter. Staying his mind, therefore, upon this covenant of life and peace, he finds rest unto his soul.

The mind must bow with humble reverence to the authority of God. Pride and rebellion destroy peace. Humility and submission promote it. The believer must wait the Lord's time for deliverance: "Oh! tarry you the Lord's leisure; be strong, and he shall comfort your heart," is the affectionate advice of David, the sweet psalmist of Israel. This childlike reliance on the divine goodness tranquilizes the mind in seasons of darkness, perplexity, trial, and temptation. That soul is the most happy which can the most cheerfully acquiesce in the appointments of infinite wisdom. Murmuring and repining grieve the Holy Spirit. Resignation and contentment produce serenity and sweetness of mind.

While cultivating these important duties, which are brought into daily exercise by the very nature of Christian experience, the mind is kept in peace, holiness is promoted, and God, the author of all good, is equally glorified. Who, then, dare say that the doctrine of grace, abounding to the chief of sinners through a crucified Redeemer, is a doctrine which tends to licentiousness? As a sick stomach may corrupt the most wholesome food, so a wicked heart can turn the grace of God into lasciviousness, and, under a most dreadful delusion of Satan, sin that grace may abound. But let not this evil be charged upon the holy gospel of Jesus, any more than the disordered frame upon the wholesome food. The natural and spiritual consequences in both cases are similar. The one arises from a bad stomach; the other, from a bad heart.

"Blessed Jesus! bestow upon me, Thy unworthy servant, that realizing faith, that tranquilizing hope, that operative love, which will enable me to know and serve Thee more and more, until my soul shall be made fit for that happy world, where all sin and sorrow shall flee away and where perpetual peace and purity shall gladden the redeemed forever and ever!"

What soul can reach the lofty height,
From where the Savior came to die?
What soul can trace the Lord of might
In His profound humility?

Angels, who stand before the throne,
Here feel the weakness of their powers;
In wonder, they, adoring, own
The Lord of life, both theirs and ours.

Oh, for a heart of faith and love,
To taste the Savior's richest grace,
To emulate the choirs above,
Who ever see His blissful face.

Blest Spirit! Beautify my soul
With humble joy and holy fear;

Thy power can make the wounded whole
And bring each gospel blessing near.

Descend and dwell within my heart;
The Savior's image let me bear;
Then bid me hence with joy depart,
And angels' bliss forever share.

CHAPTER 15

The Design of the Gospel

What a dreadful change sin has made in man! His heart, once the abode of peace and every heavenly disposition, is now the cage of every unclean and hateful bird, a den of wild beasts, a nest of vipers, a loathsome sepulcher.

How is the gold become dim—how is the fine gold changed! In this deplorable condition grace finds us, and from this state of wretchedness grace redeems us!

The glorious design of the gospel is to throw a luster around the Godhead by affording a display to all intelligent beings of those infinite perfections which harmonize at the cross of Christ, and by this sacred union of mercy, truth, righteousness, and peace, to restore fallen man to the favor and image of his Creator.

Holiness is the glory and happiness of man. When he lost his holiness, he lost his happiness. Through the atoning blood of Jesus, we obtain the removal of our guilt; and by the power of the divine Spirit, the renewal of our nature. Being thus made holy, we become once more happy. A great spiritual change is effected—no less than a new creation, for if any man be in Christ Jesus, he is a new creature.

This, then, is the will of God, even our sanctification. Hence we find that the gospel is designed to reveal to us, yes, to put us in possession of, the richest blessings: pardon of sin; justification of our person, by faith in Jesus; the renovation of our souls; adoption into the family of God; peace with God; access to God; union with Christ; communion with the Father and the Holy Spirit, through Him; victory over sin, Satan, and the world; consolation in trouble; light in darkness; life in death; assurance of future glory; and fruition of bliss in the world to come.

How little is the genuine nature and design of Christianity considered by the generality of professing Christians! How inadequately is its power felt and its sweetness enjoyed, even by those who sustain the character of believers in Jesus! We live lamentably below our privileges. Oh, that a spirit of revival may be felt among us! "Lord, revive Thy work in the midst of our days. Revive it in my heart!"

Christ is the salvation of all His dear, believing people. They look to no other, they love no other—or, if they love others, it is Christ in them who is the chief object of their affection.

It is, therefore, evident that the great design of God in the gospel is to form a people unto Himself who shall show forth His praise—a peculiar people, zealous of good works.

Here I behold a way of access opened to poor perishing sinners, through faith in the atonement of Jesus. "Lord, give me faith in Thy dear Son. Enable me to cast my soul without reserve upon Thy covenanted mercies in Christ Jesus. In Him alone is eternal life. In Him alone are treasured up grace, mercy, and peace. He that has the Son has life, for this is eternal life: to know Thee, the only true God, and Jesus Christ, whom Thou hast sent. Oh, for a heart to believe unto righteousness! Blessed Lord, this heart Thou only canst bestow. Thou knowest my wickedness and wretchedness, my frailties and follies, my helplessness and total alienation of heart from Thee. Thou knowest from what height of happiness I am fallen through original sin, and into what depth of misery I am plunged through willful transgression. But oh, sovereign love! Oh, matchless grace! Thou hast pitied me—Thou hast sent Thy Son, Thine only Son, to save me. Thou hast assured me that all who believe in Him shall not perish, but have everlasting life. Yet, in the midst of all this profusion of mercy, examine yourself, oh, my soul, whether you are in the faith."

Have I ever yet believed unto life? Have I that faith which is given to all the children of God, called by the apostle "the faith of God's elect" (Titus 1:1), a faith "according to godliness" (1 Tim. 6:3), a "faith which worketh by love" (Gal. 5:6), which " purifies the heart" (1 John 3:3), which "overcometh the world" (1 John 5:4), which is the "substance of things hoped for, the evidence of things not seen" (Heb. 11:1)? Jesus has said: "By their fruits ye shall know them" (Matt. 7:20). "The tree is known by his fruit" (Matt. 12:33). Here, then, is an unerring standard, a sure criterion of judging; for men do not gather grapes from thorn bushes, nor figs of thistles.

What, then, are the fruits that I am daily bringing forth? What is the general tenor of my thoughts? If sinful thoughts arise, do I cherish them? Am I fond of retaining them? Or have I obtained the mastery over my imaginations, so as to be able almost instantly to suppress them when they are contrary to purity and holiness? Do I find delight in secret retirement, meditation, reading the Scriptures, and prayer? Am I careful with my words? Do I love to discourse about the things of God in such a manner as to render my conversation profitable? Is Jesus, that endearing name, often upon my tongue—not from mere profession or religious parade, but from a heart-felt love to Him? What is the nature of my actions? Do they spring from a lively faith, that by them my faith may be known, as a tree by its fruits? Am I careful "to maintain good works" (Titus 3:14), knowing that if I am a child of God, I am created in Christ Jesus unto good works, which God has before ordained that I should walk in them?

By some people, this train of self-examination may be termed legal; but where these evidences of grace in the soul are lacking, all pretension to gospel liberty is a device, a delusion of Satan. John has declared, "If we ask any thing according to his will, he heareth us" (1 John 5:14); therefore, it follows as a consequence that if we are not sanctified, it is because we do not in sincerity ask this blessing from our heavenly Father. We are not only to ask, as it respects the subject matter of our prayers, what is agreeable to the will of God; but, to obtain the blessing, we must also ask in that spirit which He requires and which He alone can impart. We must ask in faith first, and then comes the blessing: "Whatsoever ye shall ask in prayer, believing, ye shall receive" (Matt. 21:22).

We have here the reason why so few are saved. Either they do not pray at all—or, if they pray, they do not ask in faith. Hence, the whole guilt lies upon the unbeliever. He has no desire to be sanctified, being destitute of true faith, and so his prayers are formal, heartless, and unanswered. But, oh, when we duly contemplate the grand design of the gospel, what an encouragement is held out to the awakened sinner who is crying out: "What must I do to be saved?" (Acts 16:30). What an encouragement to know that God wills his salvation, and that if he ask according to the will of God, he shall assuredly obtain his request! He listens to this declaration of love, "Believe on the Lord Jesus Christ, and thou shalt be saved" (v. 31); and relying, through grace, on the merits of his Savior, and making mention of His righteousness only, he supplicates at the mercy-seat for pardon and purity, for peace and perseverance, and obtains all the riches of the everlasting covenant, to the praise and glory of God.

However disputants may marshal one part of divine truth against another, the glorious doctrines of the gospel, like stones in a well-built edifice, are firmly united together. No created power can separate them. Men may disagree in sentiment, but they cannot destroy the unity of truth. The Word of the Lord endures forever.

The gospel of Christ, like the rivers in Eden, branches itself out into many fertilizing streams. Each truth makes glad the city of God, the church of the Most High. This sacred river shall continue to flow, with progressive increase of blessedness, until the whole earth shall be filled with spiritual beauty and gladness through the knowledge of the glory of the Lord.

When the rosy streaks of morning
Flit across the darkened cloud:
When the growing splendors brighten
O'er the midnight's sable shroud;

Then we know the sun, advancing,
Will diffuse the genial ray,

Until its beam, profusely pouring,
Form the bright, the perfect day.

Thus the waiting saints, beholding,
Midst the shades of mental night,
Streaks of light, divinely shining,
Flail with joy the rapturous sight.

Now they know their Lord is coming;
Jesus' praise they sweetly sing;
Hail! they cry, oh Son of glory,
Rise with healing on Thy wing.

Nations wrapped in awful darkness,
See the glorious light appear;
Deserts wild and barren places
All the charms of Eden wear.

Truth, and love, and hope concord,
Bless the desolated earth;
Sighs, and tears, and bitter anguish
Yield to joy and sacred mirth.

Hasten on this happy period,
Shine, blessed Savior, from above,
Until each nation be Thy portion,
Fruit of Thy redeeming love!

CHAPTER 16

Perverted Views of the Gospel

Men, in general, have awfully low conceptions of true religion. They neither understand its nature nor desire to understand it. When we look into the nominally Christian world, it would almost seem as if the great bulk of professing Christians thought nothing about the holy design of the Christian dispensation or of their own responsibility respecting it. Their views are alarmingly erroneous on a subject of all others the most important. Taking their own wisdom for their guide, they go on stumbling in the dark, until either sovereign grace makes them wise unto salvation, or infinite justice allows them to reap the fruit of their own folly in "the blackness of darkness for ever" (Jude 1:13).

Some consider the gospel as a mitigated law, whereby the standard of holiness is lowered and a door is opened for the commission of venial offenses. Others imagine that mercy, by being ultimately extended to all, will triumph in the final judgment; though all may not reach that standard, which some over-righteous enthusiasts deem essential to salvation. Some view the plan of salvation as happily accommodated to the needs of sinners. Jesus they acknowledge as the only Savior, whose merits are apportioned to the deficiencies of each applicant for mercy, so that very moral people need less of the Savior's merits than the profligate, as their own excellencies help to fill up the scale of righteousness. Thus Jesus becomes a mere additional weight in the balance of their good works. Oh, the pride and blindness of the human heart!

Others blasphemously make Christ the minister of sin, declaring that nothing can hurt the privileged believer—no, not even the cherished evils of his own deluded heart. They assert that Christ has done all and left him nothing to do but to rejoice, although unsubdued corruptions are continually breaking out in his life and conversation. They maintain that divine grace is the more glorified by thus rising superior, in its gifts of mercy, to the infirmities and allowed sins of believers. Thus, the moral law is set aside, and holiness is considered as a burden from which they are happily freed.

How Satan can transform himself into an angel of light, the more effectually to allure and destroy! Awful delusions indeed! Such self-deceivers love darkness rather than light, because their deeds are evil. Of divine truth, they "willingly are ignorant" (2 Pet. 3:5). How great is the change when God, who commanded the light to shine out of darkness, shines into our hearts to give the light of the knowledge of His glory in the face of Jesus Christ! By this divine process, we become new creatures, bear the image of the Savior, shine forth in the beauty of holiness, and live to His glory, who works all things after the counsel of His will.

The redeemed sinner is a child of God. He is born from above and resembles his heavenly Father in His imitable perfections. "God is love" (1 John 4:8). Hence, every one that loves is born of God and knows God. God is "glorious in holiness" (Exod. 15:11). His people are, therefore, a holy people, being called with a "holy calling" (2 Tim. 1:9). God is just. And His children are all righteous. They walk before Him in uprightness, simplicity, and godly sincerity. God is eternal truth. His redeemed ones speak the truth from the heart. They abhor deceit and lies. God is almighty. His people are "strengthened with might by his Spirit in the inner man" (Eph. 3:16) and come off "more than conquerors through him that loved them" (Rom. 8:37). God is "rich in mercy" (Eph. 2:4). His children are commanded to be merciful, even as their Father who is in heaven is merciful. God is wisdom. All His faithful servants are enlightened by His Spirit, guided into all truth, and made wise unto salvation. Thus, every communicable perfection which resides in the Deity is reflected by the new creature to the praise of His glory, from whom comes every good and perfect gift.

From this view, we perceive that the mere externals of religion will avail nothing unto salvation. There must be the accompanying power of godliness and an inward experience of the truth upon the heart. Head knowledge, without heart work, is but a shadow, good for nothing. The gracious promise of our all-merciful God is sweetly proclaimed by the prophet Jeremiah: "I will give them an heart to know me, that I am the Lord" (Jer. 24:7); and Paul declares: "With the heart man believeth unto righteousness" (Rom. 10:10). "My son, give me thine heart" (Prov. 23:26) is the paternal command of the Almighty, at once reasonable, loving, and delightful.

Now, let me ask myself seriously, as in the sight of the all-searching God: am I reflecting the bright beams of His grace on my own soul? Do I love God, His people, and His ways? If I am a child, I must, of necessity, be filled with love, for God is love. Do I hate all sin and walk in all the commandments of God, knowing that, without holiness, no man shall see the Lord? Am I just and equitable in all my dealings, remembering that God has declared His abhorrence of all unrighteousness of men? Are deceitful lies hateful to my soul? Do I love the truth and practice it in all my intentions, words, and conduct? Am I ready to forgive, knowing how mercy shines forth in the covenant of grace and how much I stand in need of divine mercy every moment of my life? Oh, that I could feel more of the sweet influence of those graces in my heart!

"Lord, pity a poor sinful worm of the earth. Let me not be destitute of this sure and certain evidence of belonging to Thee, even that of bearing Thy holy image. Fill me with love; make me holy in all my life; just and true in all my ways; powerful in resisting evil; merciful to my offending brethren; and wise in all heavenly wisdom. Thus may my light shine before men to Thy glory, until, by Thy sovereign grace, I am admitted through the gates into the city, clothed with the righteousness of Jesus, and having the inward seal and witness by the Spirit, enabling me to exclaim, 'Abba, Father!' in the courts above."

Almighty God, to Thee belong
The heart-felt praise, the grateful song;
From Thee all joy and peace proceed,
And grace to help Thy people's need.

Who can recount Thy mercies o'er,
Or fathom that unbounded store
Of love divine, which freely gave
Thy Son, rebellious man to save?

Here language fails, nor can express,
The riches of redeeming grace.
Its depth exceeds an angel's ken;
Its height, the feeble eye of men.

Behold its length, its breadth survey,
Co-equal with eternity;
For everlasting love alone,
Could place a rebel on the throne.

And is this love held forth to me?
Amazing thought! Ah! can it be?
Angelic tongue can never express
The vastness of redeeming grace!

For me, a rebel worm, He died!
For me "my Lord was crucified!"
Away you sins—you lusts, be gone;
I will be His, and His alone.

Almighty Jesus, make me Thine;
Oh, wash me in Thy blood divine;
Preserve my soul from every sin,
And reign the sovereign Lord within.

Oh, clothe me in that beauteous dress;
The garment of Thy righteousness;
Then may I look towards Thy throne,
And claim each promise as my own.

With joy shall I appear among
The blood-bought flock, the ransomed throng;
And when Thou bidst time be no more,
Thy grace in endless worlds adore!

CHAPTER 17

The Nature of Christianity

Christianity is a religion of love. It flowed from the eternal love of God the Father, was published in lines of blood on the cross of God the Son, and is graciously revealed to every contrite soul through the power of God the Holy Spirit.

Christianity breathes nothing but love to the penitent sinner. It woos, it entreats, it invites all, without exception, to partake of its blessings and to live. It holds forth the free mercy of God through Christ and offers pardon and acceptance even to the vilest who come, weary and heavy laden, unto Jesus as the Savior and friend of sinners.

Can you, oh my soul, refuse such an offer as this? Can you reject so loving a Savior, so rich an offer of grace and mercy? "Blessed Jesus! Behold a wretched sinner at the foot of Thy cross. Enable me to look unto Thee alone for salvation. Draw me, and I will run after Thee. Oh, may I daily live upon Thee, the true bread from heaven, by faith! Unite me to Thyself as the branch to the vine, the member to the head, and bring me in joyful triumph to Thy celestial kingdom. But what am I now asking? Blessings rich as heaven and extensive as eternity. I am imploring blessings bought with blood—the blood of God incarnate! Amazing price, yet freely paid, to purchase heaven for me!"

Christianity spreads happiness around her path. True happiness can be found only in a covenant God in Christ, who has declared Himself to be a just God, and yet a Savior; just, and yet the justifier of all who believe in Jesus; yes, faithful and just to forgive us our sins and to cleanse us from all unrighteousness.

Outside of Christ, when we contemplate the great Jehovah in His essential character, we behold every perfection in array against us, demanding our everlasting punishment as rebel creatures. Infinite holiness and justice, truth and goodness, require that sin should be punished. Hence the Scriptures declare that "our God is a consuming fire" (Heb. 12:29) "that will by no means clear the guilty" (Exod. 34:7).

But when we view God in Christ reconciling the world unto Himself, not imputing their trespasses unto them; when we behold the eternal Word becoming flesh, and dwelling among us; when we see the babe of Bethlehem, Emmanuel, God with us; then hope revives and leans with sweet, delightful confidence on the Rock of ages; love kindles into a bright and ardent flame; faith contemplates with rapture the stupendous plan of mercy; all our enraptured powers unite their efforts to adore the great Redeemer's name.

Lord, "what is man, that thou art mindful of him? and the son of man, that thou visitest him?" (Ps. 8:4). Oh, how wonderful is the love of God towards lost, rebellious sinners!

"Who is a God like unto thee, that pardoneth iniquity, and passeth by the transgression of the remnant of his heritage? he retaineth not his anger for ever, because he delighteth in mercy. He will turn again, he will have compassion upon us; he will subdue our iniquities; and thou wilt cast all their sins into the depths of the sea" (Micah 7:18-19).

The religion of Jesus is a religion of peace. The angels sang "Glory to God in the highest, and on earth peace, good will toward men" (Luke 2:14) when they announced to the wondering shepherds the glad tidings of the Savior's birth. Wherever the power of the gospel is felt, there joy and peace reign. "The wilderness and the solitary place shall be glad for them; and the desert shall rejoice, and blossom as the rose. It shall blossom abundantly, and rejoice even with joy and singing" (Isa. 35:1-2).

Christianity displays the wisdom of God. "Happy is the man that findeth wisdom, and the man that getteth understanding. For the merchandise of it is better than the merchandise of silver, and the gain thereof than fine gold. She is more precious than rubies: and all the things thou canst desire are not to be compared unto her. Length of days is in her right hand; and in her left hand riches and honour. Her ways are ways of pleasantness, and all her paths are peace. She is a tree of life to them that lay hold upon her: and happy is every one that retaineth her" (Prov. 3:13-18).

"Take, then, to Thyself, oh mighty Savior, Thy great power, and reign over all the earth! Fulfill Thy promise to Thy ancient Israel, and to the benighted millions of the heathen world. Let Satan no longer maintain his empire in the human heart. Hurl him from his seat. Dislodge him from his citadel. Command him into the deep; for Thou hast said, 'All Israel shall be saved' (Rom. 11:26), and 'the Lord shall be the King of the whole earth' (cf. 1 Cor. 15). Adorable Emmanuel, Prince of Peace, Sovereign of souls! Take away the veil from the hearts of the poor Jews, who have so long been 'scattered and peeled' (Isa. 18:2), 'without a king, and without a prince, and without a sacrifice' (Hos. 3:4). Hear the prayers of Gentile Christians on their behalf, that they may look upon Thee whom they have pierced, and mourn until their sorrow, through Thy forgiving grace, shall be turned into joy. Open the eyes of the perishing heathens, that they may see the misery of their condition, the hard bondage under which they labor, the cruel tyrant whom they serve, and the awful doom which awaits them in another world. Oh, do reveal to them, through the preaching of the gospel, Thy agony and bloody sweat, Thy cross and passion—all the mysteries of Gethsemane and Calvary. Show them the crown of glory which Thou hast purchased, the kingdom which Thou hast prepared, the inheritance incorruptible and undefiled, which is reserved for all who live a life of faith in Thee. Endue them with strength to renounce their sins and to burst the chains which bind their captive spirits. Shed abroad Thy love in their hearts and transform them into Thine own most holy image. And oh, loving Savior, have mercy upon those thousands of nominal professors of the gospel, who are by Thee esteemed the worst of sinners! These, oh Lord, do unto Thee the greatest dishonor. They hear of Thee without emotion. They talk of Thee without affection. They know Thy gospel, speculatively, but experience nothing of its power. They call Thee Lord, but do not obey Thee. They have the light shining around them, yet love darkness rather than light. They hear the sweet sound of grace, yet find no chord of unison within. They see the waters of life flowing on every side, yet never taste of their refreshing stream. They have a name that they live, and yet are dead. They profess that they know God, yet in works deny Him. They have the form of godliness, yet deny the power thereof. They express a self-complaisant pity for the poor Jew and Gentile, while they themselves are in a far more wretched state than these objects of their commiseration. Oh, that the Spirit may be poured out from on high, that the wilderness may become a fruitful field, that every heart may experience the transforming power of Thy sovereign grace and the whole earth be filled with Thy glory! Thou hast said, 'Surely I come quickly.' Amen. Even so, come, Lord Jesus" (Rev. 22:20)!

Eternal God, Thy power display;
Chase all the shades of night away;
Let every foe before Thee fly,
And bring each gospel blessing nigh.

Thy dying love, oh Lord, reveal,
That love which melts the heart of steel;
Each stubborn will in mercy bow,
And lay the rebel sinner low.

Arise, oh Sun of Righteousness,
And all Thy waiting people bless;
Arise upon our hearts, and shine
Until every heart be wholly Thine.

Inflame our cold affections, Lord;
Renew them by Thy quickening Word;
Bind every thought in willing chains,
Until not a rebel thought remains.

CHAPTER 18

Neglecting the Gospel

This declaration of the apostle, "How shall we escape, if we neglect so great salvation?" (Heb. 2:3) is both a solemn question and an awful conclusion. Those who hold infidel principles, who live in a total disregard of religious ordinances, and who persecute the followers of Jesus despise the salvation of God. But there are other marks equally legible to the discerning eye, though often unseen by the people who bear them, on account of the blinding nature of sin, which point out the neglecters of salvation.

The three following should excite alarm, and call forth the important exercise of strict self-examination:

1. If we are living in the allowed indulgence of one known sin, whether that sin be internal or external, whether it be cherished in the secret recesses of the heart, or whether it ripen into overt acts, we are neglecting the salvation of the gospel. We may have knowledge and zeal and gifts of various kinds; we may do much in active exertion to promote the general cause of religion; we may associate with pious characters, and be ourselves esteemed pious; we may be regular at church, maintain family worship, and, like Herod, do many things; yet if, after all, we are living in the allowed indulgence of one known sin, we are neglecting this great salvation and, dying in this state, must inevitably perish. Should we knock and say, "Lord, open unto us," Jesus would profess unto us, "I never knew you: depart from me, ye that work iniquity" (Matt. 7:23). How awful is this consideration, and yet how just! We may destroy all of the Amalekites; yet, if we preserve Agag and the rest of the flock alive—if we retain some beloved lust in the

heart—we manifest a spirit in direct opposition to the will and command of God.

2. If we are building upon any other foundation, in whole or in part, than Jesus Christ and Him crucified, we are neglecting His great salvation. To be saved from the dreadful consequences of sin, we must build simply and entirely on that foundation which God has laid in Zion, without daring to bring any of the materials of corrupt nature to mix with it. On this foundation we must pray for grace to build gold, silver, and precious stones. This must be done by adding to faith virtue, and to virtue knowledge, and to knowledge temperance, and to temperance patience, and to patience godliness, and to godliness brotherly kindness, and to brotherly kindness charity. If these things be in us, and abound, they make us that we shall neither be barren nor unfruitful in the knowledge of our Lord and Savior Jesus Christ, while an entrance shall be ministered to us abundantly into His heavenly kingdom.

3. If we are preferring any earthly object, of whatever kind, to Jesus Christ; if our affections are placed on any other being in opposition to Him; or if we are seeking our delight in any created thing, as distinct from Him and independent of Him, we are neglecting His great salvation; yes, we are setting up idols in our hearts. We must love the adorable Savior with a supreme affection, and we must love other objects only for His sake. Our temporal blessings must be enjoyed as flowing from Him; our friends and domestic comforts must be received as gifts coming to us through His redeeming grace. All we possess must be held at His disposal, and with a view to that account which we must one day give. Thus, Christ must be the Alpha and Omega, the beginning and ending of all our desires and affections.

Oh, how strait is the gate, and narrow is the way, that leads unto life; and few there be that find it. May I never forget this unchangeable truth, that Jesus is the only way of escape from hell and the only way of access to heaven. Lord, let Thy Holy Spirit guide me into this consecrated way. Hold me up, and I shall be safe.

It is truly awakening to reflect how far a person may go in the circumstantials and externals of religion, and yet be entirely destitute of the life of God in the soul. The Holy Scriptures abound with declarations to this effect, which prove the deceitfulness of the human heart and the danger of resting in mere outward forms and orthodox opinions. Thus, Job describes the character of the hypocrite: "What is the hope of the hypocrite, though he hath gained, when God taketh away his soul? Will he delight himself in the Almighty? will he always call upon God?" (Job 27:8, 10), evidently implying that, not having the root of the matter in him, though he had gained the applause of men for his seeming piety, he would soon grow weary of the service of God.

David also shows, in awful colors, the wickedness of false teachers: "Unto the wicked God saith, What hast thou to do to declare my statutes, or that thou shouldest take my covenant in thy mouth? Seeing thou hatest instruction, and castest my words behind thee" (Ps. 50:16-17). Thus, wicked men may enter into the priestly office, preach the gospel, and talk about that covenant, in the blessings of which they have no personal interest whatever.

The prophet Isaiah, by the Spirit of God, sets forth the extreme hypocrisy of the Jews: "Cry aloud, spare not, lift up thy voice like a trumpet, and shew my people their transgression, and the house of Jacob their sins. Yet they seek me daily, and delight to know my ways, as a nation that did righteousness, and forsook not the ordinance of their God: they ask of me the ordinances of justice; they take delight in approaching to God" (Isa. 58:1-2). Thus, their conduct was a strange mixture of apparent devotion and decided rebellion.

The prophet Ezekiel was shown the true character of those who waited upon him: "They come unto thee as the people cometh, and they sit before thee as my people, and they hear thy words, but they will not do them: for with their mouth they shew much love, but their heart goeth after their covetousness" (Ezek. 33:31). Our divine Redeemer has painted the hypocrite in his true colors: "Woe unto you, scribes and Pharisees, hypocrites! for ye pay tithe of mint and anise and cummin, and have omitted the weightier matters of the law, judgment, mercy, and faith" (Matt. 23:23). "Woe unto you, scribes and Pharisees, hypocrites! for ye make clean the outside of the cup and of the platter, but within they are full of extortion and excess" (v. 25). "Woe unto you, scribes and Pharisees, hypocrites! for ye are like unto whited sepulchres, which indeed appear beautiful outward, but are within full of dead men's bones, and of all uncleanness" (v. 27). "Ye serpents, ye generation of vipers, how can ye escape the damnation of hell?" (v. 33).

When we consider that these men were held in the highest esteem and veneration among the Jews for their outward sanctity and devotion, we see how far people may go in the externals of religion, and yet be in the very gall of bitterness and in the bond of iniquity. It was on this account that the apostle Paul so constantly warned the churches to whom he wrote against false profession and receiving the grace of God in vain. He speaks of those who hold the truth, but who hold it in unrighteousness. The epistles of Peter, John, and Jude are full of warnings against false teachers, antichrists, and deceivers. The charges to the seven churches in the book of Revelation most awfully show the danger of declension, of leaving our first love, of becoming lukewarm, and, consequently, loathsome to an infinitely holy God.

Many, it is to be feared, have the reputation of being spiritually alive, whose souls, in the sight of God, are dead to all the vital influences of the Holy Spirit.

Oh, my soul, let not these solemn portions of God's sacred Word be lost upon you. Pray without ceasing for that grace which can alone preserve you from falling and, through the merits of Jesus, present you faultless before the presence of His glory with exceeding joy.

"Almighty Savior, awaken my drowsy senses, and make me alive to my real condition. Allow me not to neglect Thy blessed gospel, but draw me to Thyself continually, for Thy grace is sufficient for me. Wash me in the cleansing fountain of Thy blood. Place me upon that foundation which can never be moved. Arm me for the spiritual combat, and at last make me more than conqueror, through the power of Thy might and the riches of Thy grace."

Why should I linger here below,
When Jesus calls my heart above?

Why, oh, my soul, the bliss forego,
The joy of everlasting love?

I feel the weight of nature's guilt,
Beneath its ponderous load I groan;
Oh, may the blood on Calvary spilt
For all my crimson sins atone!

Blest Jesus, speak the pardoning word;
Salvation to my spirit bring!
Then will Thy grace those joys afford,
Which from Thy cross to sinners spring.

Redeemed from guilt and slavish fear,
My soul shall wing its way to Thee!
While faith beholds her tide clear
To blissful immortality.

CHAPTER 19

Inadequate Views of Human Nature

The world is full of mourning, lamentation, and woe. We see many dancing along in thoughtless gaiety and sporting on the brink of perdition. But this lightness of spirit is transient; sorrow soon darkens the glare of human happiness and leaves the soul in sad dejection and despair. This picture may be gloomy, yet it is true. Sin has defaced the moral excellence of man—yes, more, has converted him into whatever is base, polluted, and depraved. All his faculties and powers are now employed as weapons against his Maker, and the very plan of mercy, whereby alone he can be restored to holiness, happiness, and heaven, is opposed, neglected, or despised.

And yet we talk of moral excellence in a fallen creature, of goodness in a heart which is desperately wicked, of righteousness in a condemned criminal, of amiable qualities in a mind at enmity against God, of strength in a helpless worm, of wisdom in a soul beclouded in all its powers.

Strange inconsistency! "What communion hath light with darkness?" (2 Cor. 6:14). The Word of God condemns such a motley character and pronounces a woe on that which the world so much admires.

It is no uncommon thing to hear people talk about their good hearts and good intentions, when love to God, and a desire to please Him, are utter strangers to their souls.

These self-admiring people consider as libelous every attempt to tear away the mask and to expose the native vileness of the inner man. Thus, pride, vanity, self-love, and unbelief, the deadly roots that all sin springs from, conspire to keep us in a state of bondage and enveloped in the mist of error.

It is quite compatible with the vanity of our fallen nature to extol, as the highest excellence, those benevolent and patriotic feelings which often exist in a heart totally alienated from God. The Bible acknowledges no real excellence but what arises from the regenerating work of grace upon the soul. An attentive reader of that holy Book must be struck with the faithful delineations which it gives of the human heart. Man is there represented as he appears in the sight of God, when divested of all his meretricious ornaments.

What we call virtues will be found, when analyzed, to be mere selfish principles, and human approbation to be the secret spring of many a splendid action. This disclosure is revolting to our pride. But proud man must be humbled. The Scripture has concluded all under sin. In this state, grace at first finds the sinner. There is naturally no movement of the soul towards God, no affection for Him, no trust in Him, no obedience to Him.

The first inclination of the heart to God is the sole operation of God's own secret power by such instruments or means as He, in His wisdom and sovereignty, is pleased to employ. The work, once begun, gradually, and sometimes rapidly, increases. The blade, the ear, and the full corn in the ear are of a longer or shorter period in their growth, as the principle is weaker or stronger; for there are mysteries in grace, as well as in nature.

But in both kingdoms, the work is of God. He begins, carries on, and completes the vast design. All originates in His will, and all shall terminate in His glory. His language is, "I am the LORD thy God,...for there is no savior beside me" (Hos. 13:4). "In the LORD shall all the seed of Israel be justified, and shall glory" (Isa. 45:25).

Yet man is a responsible creature, a moral agent. In this work of grace, God does not force, but inclines the heart to seek Him. He does not compel the sinner, with reluctant steps, to enter in at the strait gate; but, by enlightening his mind, and touching his heart, he sweetly constrains him to enter in, that he may be saved.

His refusing to submit to the yoke of Jesus, and to accept of mercy on gospel terms, is altogether the fruit and effect of his own depraved heart and will justly be punished, if persisted in, with everlasting destruction. Thus, all the praise of our salvation is due to God alone, while all the guilt and final misery, flowing from our transgressions, are chargeable solely upon ourselves.

Men may now argue, and dispute, and cavil, about the truths of revelation; but a day is fast approaching when "every mouth that is now opened against him, God will condemn" (cf. Rom. 3:19). In that tremendous day of just judgment, the guilty conscience will speak in loudest thunder to the self-convicted soul, while notes of praise will forever ascend from hearts renewed by sovereign grace to the fountain of eternal love.

We sin, and forget the sin. But God remembers all our wickedness. Awful, dreadful thought! Every impure imagination, every unhallowed affection, every sinful purpose, though unripened into action, every secret and unknown iniquity, is remembered by that omniscient God, who will judge the secrets of men's hearts by Jesus Christ, and strictly render to every man according to his works. Oh, what a day will that be, which plucks away the mask of hypocrisy from the face of sin, which rolls away the whitened stone from off the loathsome sepulcher, which discloses the impure chambers of imagery, and discovers all the hidden evils of a heart once admired, but now abhorred by an assembled world of saints and angels!

In that day, the wicked will bewail, in bitter reproaches, their forgetfulness of God, and their love of sin; but this bitterness of soul, being utterly destitute of every gracious feeling, will only increase the sharpness of their torment, and give additional strength to the sting of that worm which never dies! Thus, their self-reproaches, and hatred of God, will be commensurate with eternity. Hating God, hating themselves, and hating the dreadful fiends who torment them, they will be wretched beyond all conception, forever and ever!

Happy are they who receive the truth as little children. Lord, give me right views of the truth, as it is in Jesus; and right feelings and affections towards Thee, who art the God of my life and of my salvation. Put Thy fear into my heart, that I may not depart from Thee. Fill me with a reverential awe of Thy holy name. Let me never pry into the wisely concealed purposes of Thy grace, but ever remember, and practically regard, this important declaration of Moses: "The secret things belong unto the Lord our God: but those things which are revealed belong unto us and to our children for ever, that we may do all the words of this law" (Deut. 29:29).

When I hear a sinner boasting
Of the goodness of his heart,
And how easy it is for mortals
With their dearest sins to part;

Then, methinks, this man's a stranger
To the work of grace and faith.
All he speaks betrays his blindness,
All is darkness that he says.

Did he once but feel the workings
Of the Spirit's mighty power,
He would feel the flesh rebelling,
From that highly favored hour.

Satan would not let him conquer,
Without many battles fought;
This the Lord permits, that sinners
Their own vileness may be taught.

*It is the traitor lodged within us
Seeks to admit the foe without;
When, by grace divinely potent,
Satan has been once cast out.*

*Inbred evils, dread corruptions,
Natives of the human heart,
League with Satan against the Savior,
And determine not to part.*

CHAPTER 20

Two Common Errors

There are two fatal errors, which, it is to be feared, abound among professing Christians. The one considers divine grace as disrobed of its glory by insisting upon the necessity of human endeavors in the great work of salvation. The other declares as injurious to morality the emphasis that is laid upon the absolute necessity of divine grace to the production of every thing that is spiritually good in any man.

The truth embraces both these propositions: that is, the absolute need of divine grace, without which "nothing is holy," and the absolute necessity of human endeavors, since God works in us both to will and to do of His good pleasure. Though salvation be all of grace, yet God is pleased to work by means. A Paul must plant, and an Apollos water, while God gives the increase. The husbandman deposits his seed in the ground, yet God alone can crown his labors with an abundant harvest. To depend upon the divine blessing, without using the means which infinite wisdom has appointed, is enthusiasm. To use the means appointed, without an entire dependence upon the promised blessing, is impiety.

If a father, for instance, should pray for the conversion of his children, and yet allow them to run wild, without presenting any checks to their evils, under the impression that the Almighty in His good time will save them if they are to be saved, and that if they are not among the elect, no blame can attach to him should they finally perish—would he not, by such erroneous views of the plan of salvation, be actually aiding the cause of Satan and the destruction of his unhappy offspring under the false notion of glorifying the sovereignty of God and the freeness of divine grace?

So, on the other hand, if a father should endeavor to train up his children in virtuous habits and be anxious to guard them against the seductions of the world, and yet draw all his hopes of success from his own exertions and paternal instructions, without once feeling the force of that all-important declaration of the Savior, "Without me ye can do nothing" (John 15:5), would he not, by such conduct, manifest great impiety? And might not the Almighty withhold His spiritual blessing to show how easily He can blight the most powerful human endeavors?

To trust God with all our hearts in the diligent use of the appointed means is the path which infinite wisdom has marked out for man as a moral agent. To be enabled to do this in a right spirit is the work of divine grace and is the way to obtain the divine blessing.

The Bible, while it reveals the utter inability of man to do anything that is good by any natural power of his own, addresses him as a creature endued with rational powers and of high responsibilities. Hence, the sacred volume abounds with exhortations to diligence, motives to obedience, and promises of grace and strength both to do and suffer the holy will.

Spiritual pride and spiritual sloth are alike condemned. He who says "I will not," and he who says "I cannot," may be equally under the influence of a bad spirit. The latter, which has a show of humility, may spring from spiritual sloth, as the former does from spiritual pride. When grace really enlightens the mind and affects the heart, the sinner, though deeply conscious of his utter inability to save himself, dares not make this an excuse for continuing in sin. Under the influence of the Holy Spirit, he cries mightily to God, through Christ, for deliverance from the guilt and power of sin, and is graciously helped by Him who never said to the seed of Jacob, "Seek ye me in vain" (Isa. 45:19).

The antinomian, and the self-righteous error, are both reprobated in the Scriptures of truth. While we would carefully avoid those metaphysical niceties which darken the simplicity of the gospel, we should pray to discover those subtle webs which Satan weaves to catch the feet of the unwary. Divine truth is beautiful in its own simplicity—and grand in its own sublimity. Every human addition, like paint on the diamond, obscures its luster. An honest heart, and a sincere intention to please God in all things, will clear the path of duty from many a stumbling-block, which the pride of human reason has cast up; for "if any man will do his will, he shall know of the doctrine, whether it be of God" (John 7:17).

People, in general, are more ready to argue a point in theology than to crucify a beloved lust. Those who are much acquainted with the religious world will find many theological disputants for one self-denying follower of Jesus.

The apostle was compelled to say in his day: "There are many unruly and vain talkers" (Titus 1:10). And such characters have been found in every age of the church, to the annoyance of the humble Christian.

The Bible is not given to us for disputation, but for edification; and its doctrines are designed to have a practical tendency on the mind and heart. If real Christians, who differ from each other on some abstruse points of theology, were to meet on the ground of our common Christianity, they would be surprised to find how nearly they approximate each other in genuine experience and practice. They would, with delightful feeling of joy, recognize a brother, where they expected to meet a foe. The weapons of controversy being thus laid aside, and agreeing to differ on points confessedly abstruse and beyond the power of finite reason to solve, they would cheerfully hold out the right hand of fellowship and exhibit to the world that charity which is the bond of perfectness and the beauty of the church of Christ.

This is a state of feeling devoutly to be wished. May this spirit of mutual love and affection abound more and more among the true followers of the Lamb. Then will each member of the church, by his holy walk and conversation, prove his election of God; and all the members of the mystical body, deriving daily nourishment and strength from their glorified head, be growing in a fitness for the "general assembly of the first-born," however they may differ in their views or some of those "deep things of God" which can only be unraveled in the world of light and glory. It is no small craftiness of Satan to engage the mind about non-essentials and to beget among Christians a spirit of strife and contention. This crafty enemy has succeeded too well in all ages, to the grief of good men, to the weakening of the good cause, and to the joy of the enemies of the gospel of Christ. All this only tends to confirm the Scripture doctrine of human corruption and satanic agency. It calls for great watchfulness, circumspection, and prayer, as well as humility and dependence on the Spirit of truth.

The grand design of God, in His revelation of mercy, is the display of His own perfections in the salvation of His fallen creatures. Hence, the command to perishing sinners is: "Look unto me, and be ye saved, all the ends of the earth: for I am God, and there is none else" (Isa. 45:22), "and besides me there is no saviour" (Isa. 43:11). While the exhortation to believers is: "Work out your own salvation with fear and trembling. For it is God which worketh in you both to will and to do of his good pleasure" (Phil. 2:12-13).

"Blessed Lord, give me that wisdom which is from above. Preserve me from falling into those errors, which would excuse spiritual sloth, or feed spiritual pride. Bestow upon me the spirit of prayer and give me grace to live in the spirit of my prayers. Cause me to walk before Thee with a humble, loving, obedient heart, that, living a life of faith in Thy beloved Son, I may work by Thee and for Thee while it is called today, before 'the night cometh, when no man can work'" (John 9:4).

Wherever I turn my eyes within,
What loads of guilt, what depths of sin,
Like oceans deep, like mountains high,
Call for the vengeance of the sky!

Deceit, ambition, lust, and pride,
Within the human heart reside;
There Satan, seated on his throne,
Claims the whole empire as his own.

But Jesus comes! The mighty Lord!
He wields the bright celestial sword;
The strong man armed is forced to fly,
While angels chant the victory.

Glory to God in heaven above,
On earth sweet peace and sacred love;
Good-will to men—the foe is foiled,
And God and sinners reconciled.

Come, mighty Conqueror of the heart,
Subdue my soul in every part;
Ascend Thy long-usurped throne:
Oh, be my King, and reign alone.

CHAPTER 21

The Cause of Skepticism

What a multitude of opinions we find in the religious world—how many different sects and parties, each walling itself round with its own peculiar tenets and maintaining its own view of doctrine as the only standard of truth! But, in the midst of all this diversity of sentiment, how busy is the great enemy of souls in sowing the tares of uncharitableness, angry zeal, violent passions, and every unchristian temper in the gospel field. The visible church has too long been the arena for combats which have ended in deluges of blood. Witness those many persecutions which have been carried on by Christians against Christians in almost every age.

"Oh, almighty God, look down upon Thy church, the vine which Thine own right hand hast planted, that the boar out of the woods may not waste it, nor the wild beast of the field devour it. Return, we beseech Thee, oh God of hosts; look down from heaven, behold, and visit this vine."

It may be useful to inquire, From where arises all this angry disputation in the professing Christian world? It arises, chiefly, from the pride of our hearts. To contend earnestly for the faith once delivered to the saints is a duty; to give place, "no, not for an hour" (Gal. 2:5), to those who seek to destroy the foundation of our faith is a duty. There is, however, an existing evil of great magnitude, and which springs from that pride of intellect, which seeks to be wise above what is written.

Man is not willing to act upon the plain, revealed command of heaven. He must search and pry into the secret counsels of Jehovah. He wishes to ascertain why the Almighty issues such-and-such commands. He endeavors to bring every revelation from God to the rule and standard of his own peculiar mode of reasoning; and when two declarations present themselves before him, apparently opposed to each other, though practically leading to the same point—that is, the glory of God and the salvation of the soul—instead of humbly receiving both, as stated in the Word of truth, and seeking to draw from each the practical improvement intended by them, he cannot rest until he has filled up the seeming chasm with his own confused ideas, thinking thereby to vindicate the ways of God to man!

Now, as each inquirer claims an equal right to fill up this chasm in his own way, and as very few will entirely submit to the system of another, so on this account it is that the Christian world is filled with such heterodox opinions. Thus, leaving the sure path of revealed truth, men plunge into an ocean of inexplicable difficulties, and, by laboring to be wise above what is written, become very fools in divine things.

"Lord, grant that I may never exercise myself in matters which are too high for me, which Thou didst never intend should be fully known in this present state—no, which I cannot comprehend, until the natural blindness of my understanding be wholly removed. In heaven, all darkness will be excluded. Here, I know but in part; there, if admitted by Thy grace, I shall know, even as also I am known. Make my soul then, oh Lord, as a weaned child. Give me that simplicity of faith which cheerfully receives, as truth, all that Thou hast revealed, though mystery surrounds me on every side."

I find many plain and clear declarations, which nothing but a willful hatred of the truth can misrepresent and pervert. On these I would continually dwell; from them I would draw all the sweetness and comfort, wisdom and strength, which they were mercifully designed to convey. As a newborn babe, may I desire the sincere milk of the Word, that I may grow thereby (1 Pet. 2:2).

I find other declarations high and sublime, far surpassing man's understanding. From these, I would learn humility. To these, I would submit my reason with humble reverence. By these, I would exercise my faith and place implicit confidence in the Word of truth, although many things therein be difficult to comprehend and many past finding out.

While Peter acknowledges that, in the epistles of his beloved brother Paul, are some things hard to be understood, he also declares that the unlearned and unstable twist them, as they do also the other Scriptures, unto their own destruction. From these considerations, I perceive how wonderfully the Holy Scriptures are calculated to instruct the humble believer, while they bewilder the proud skeptic. Like the cloud in the wilderness, they afford light to the Israel of God, while "the disputer of this world" (1 Cor. 1:20) is left in darkness. "Who is wise, and he shall understand these things? prudent, and he shall know them? for the ways of the LORD are right, and the just shall walk in them: but the transgressors shall fall therein" (Hosea 14:9).

All theological and practical errors originate in the unbelief and pride of our hearts. We are continually pained with instances illustrative of this truth. Many who, to all outward appearance, set out well, holding the grand essentials of Christianity, and exhibiting the humble walk of the Christian, have, by degrees, got so high in doctrines as to pass over the limits of the precepts, considering every enforcement of the moral law as derogatory to the freeness and liberty of the gospel. The promises are to them like the manna for sweetness, while the precepts resemble the bitter waters of Marah. By this perverted view of the gospel of grace, which makes provision for the holiness, as well as the acceptance, of the believer, they endeavor to disunite what God has inseparably joined together.

Advancing in their career of bold inquiry and daring investigation, leaving the precincts of the written Word, and soaring into the interminable region of wild conjecture, they fall at length, giddy with their flight, into the fatal revelries of fanatical delusion, skeptical indifference, Socinian heresy, or deistical profaneness. Such wandering stars, leaving their proper orbit, afford an awful warning to the church of Christ; and happy is he who learns wisdom from their end, and thereby resists the first risings of pride and unhallowed speculation.

Some, indeed, are restored by that sovereign grace which they have abused, while others are left to the misery of their own delusions, according to Jude, who denominates them "wandering stars, to whom is reserved the blackness of darkness forever" (Jude 1:13). In the midst of surrounding darkness and abounding iniquity, in the midst of distracting opinions and guilty fears:

Where must we look for saving help?
To whom for refuge fly?
Who dare presume to plead our cause
Before the throne on high?

It is Jesus pleads His people's cause,
Before the eternal throne;
Presents the merit of His blood,
And claims them for His own.

Oh, for a lively, vigorous faith,
To feel this blessing mine;
Make me, oh Lord, of saving grace
A monument divine.

On Thee, a helpless worm I fall,
On Thee alone depend;
I'll trust Thy grace—'tis infinite,
And knows nor bound nor end.

Father, behold me in Thy Son;
Oh, send Thy Spirit down,
To fit me for eternal joys,
And seal me for Thine own.

CHAPTER 22

The Almost Christian

In this day of outward profession, it is most needful frequently to reflect how far a person may go in the way of religion and yet prove nothing at the last but an "almost Christian." This will prove to us the importance of self-examination, since nothing is genuine that will not stand the test of Scripture, that only touchstone of real godliness. A person may have a clear knowledge of the gospel way of salvation, be able to declare the truths of Christianity with interest and edification, have much fluency in prayer, be punctual in his attendance on the means of grace, engage actively in religious and benevolent institutions, maintain family worship, join the society of pious characters, abstain from worldly amusements and all outward immoralities—and yet, with all these shining appendages, be only an almost Christian.

This, to many, may appear uncharitable, and lead them to exclaim with the disciples, "Who then can be saved?" (Luke 18:26). The fact is, all these important gifts and talents may be possessed, and these active exertions may be made, upon the principles of our fallen nature. A man may have a taste for scriptural studies and a fondness for biblical criticism; he may have a natural fluency of discourse; his connections may be such as imperceptibly lead him to join the friends of religion in their activities, and, by degrees, influence him to establish family worship, to separate himself from worldly amusements and worldly associates; and yet there may be a total destitution of evangelical principles. "Faith which worketh by love" (Gal. 5:6) may be a stranger to his heart.

The gospel declares that "if any man have not the Spirit of Christ, he is none of his" (Rom. 8:9); that "if any man be in Christ, he is a new creature" (2 Cor. 5:17); that "except a man be born again, he cannot see the kingdom of God" (John 3:3).

The work of grace being altogether spiritual and internal, its operations must be felt and experienced in the heart. This work consists in a deep humiliation on account of sin, both original and actual, whether of omission or commission; in a deep sense and feeling of spiritual helplessness and wretchedness; in a hearty reception of Jesus Christ, as revealed and offered in the gospel to perishing sinners; in a supreme love of Him who died to save the vilest who come unto Him in a childlike obedience to His will and commands, however self-denying.

If these things be lacking, all else is nothing but dross in the sight of God. All short of this divine work in the soul is only "almost Christianity." It is painful to the friends of Jesus to behold many droop and wither who have given promising hopes of future excellence and almost confirmed the expectations of pious friends concerning their religious sincerity.

These hopeful professors walk well for a season, but at length they begin to draw back, by slow degrees, it may be, at the first; but, increasing in their speed as they advance in the path of declension, they finally plunge into the world, and thus verify the true proverb: "The dog is turned to his own vomit again; and the sow that was washed to her wallowing in the mire" (2 Pet. 2:22). With uneasy consciences, they endeavor to justify their return by slandering the lives of professors and speaking evil of those things with which they were never savingly acquainted. Such people, if they die in their apostasy, give every reason to believe that they never knew the grace of God in truth, that they never received the truth in the love of it. Hence the apostle John, speaking of such characters, plainly says: "They went out from us, but they were not of us; for if they had been of us, they would no doubt have continued with us: but they went out, that they might be manifest that they were not all of us" (1 John 2:19).

We may equally presume that they never tasted the inward blessedness of true religion—peace with God and joy in the Holy Spirit, arising from a believing, self-appropriating view of the atonement of Jesus.

When, therefore, their new mode of thinking and acting subsided, when prosperity gilded their path or persecution covered it with thorns, not having root in themselves and being destitute of saving faith, they became weary of a service in which their entire souls were never engaged. They cast off a yoke, to them galling and grievous, and ran back again with delight into the secretly beloved pastures of the world. "Demas hath forsaken me," said the sorrowing apostle, "having loved this present world" (2 Tim. 4:10).

Where is the congregation of professing Christians which does not from time to time afford melancholy proofs of this hollowness of character, this emptiness of profession, this influence of the world, to the grief of its faithful pastor and the pious part of his flock? Such awful characters may be considered as spies, who "feign themselves just men" (Luke 20:20), whom Satan sends into the camp of the true Israel of God, in order to discover the failings and infirmities of real Christians. These they traitorously expose to the derision of an ungodly world, hoping thereby to bring discredit upon the gospel of Christ and keep men more quietly in their sins. God can indeed overrule all for good, but woe unto them by whom these offenses come.

It is, then, both awakening and alarming to reflect how far a person may go in outward profession and yet be a hypocrite with God, an almost Christian, a "castaway" (1 Cor. 9:27). If the new creature in Christ Jesus can be so counterfeited as to deceive for a time the children of God, whose judgment is always guided by that charity which hopes all things, how ought I to examine into the principles, motives, and springs of my own actions, lest, after having made a profession before men, I should be rejected as "reprobate silver" (Jer. 6:30) in that day when "the fire shall try every man's work of what sort it is" (1 Cor. 3:13)! Oh, what need there is for sifting ourselves!

"Blessed Lord, make me a humble, sincere disciple. Let me not covet after gifts so much as graces and divine gifts, only that I may be useful to others and glorify Thee. I may live in the bustle of religious institutions while devoid of religious affections. I may be able to advocate the cause of Christ while destitute of a saving interest in His blood. I may mingle in the companies of the pious and yet be an utter stranger to their spirit and experience."

Nothing will stand the test of the great day but faith which works by love. My soul must be united to Christ by a living faith before my works can be acceptable to a holy God. Out of Christ, I am a dead branch. In Christ, I become fruitful through the skill of the heavenly husbandman, who prunes the living branches that they may bring forth more fruit to the glory of His grace. This blessed receiving of Jesus, through the power of the Holy Spirit, will be accompanied by a gradual renewal of the soul into His image; and this divine transformation will be productive of works of faith, labors of love, and patience of hope. My heart will become the abode of peace and purity. High and holy principles will be implanted in richer abundance. I shall live for Christ. His glory will be my chief aim, His law my soul's delight. Holy love will guide my movements and become the unceasing spring of holy actions. All my desires will be to Him who loved me and gave Himself for me. This is true Christianity. Oh, that I may feel the power of this sacred truth! "Lord, save me from insincerity and hypocrisy, from declension and apostasy. Let me not be satisfied with barren knowledge and outward profession, but let Thy love rule in my heart and shine forth in my daily words and actions until I am translated, through grace, to those pure regions of unsullied happiness, where all Thy redeemed people shall shine forth as the sun in the kingdom of their Father, forever and ever."

Dear Jesus, fill my soul
With holiness and peace;
Arise with healing in Thy wings,
Thou Sun of Righteousness.

May all beneath the sky
Usurp my heart no more;

May Thou be my first, my chief delight,
My soul's unbounded store.

In Thee all treasures lie,
From Thee all blessings flow;
Thou art the bliss of saints above,
The joy of saints below.

Oh come and make me Thine,
A sinner saved by grace;
Then shall I sing with loudest strains
In heaven, Thy dwelling-place.

When standing round the throne,
Amid the ransomed throng,
Thy praise shall be my sweet employ,
While love inspires my song.

CHAPTER 23

Conversion

Wherever we look, we behold some part of God's works; some remembrancer of His power and goodness. Then, why are our thoughts so seldom led through nature, up to nature's God? Here we discover the influence of sin, which so fills our hearts with the love of the creature as to leave no room for the love of the Creator.

When the Savior was born into the world, there was no room for Him in the inn. Just so it is with our depraved hearts. Yet, wonderful condescension! Jesus stands at the door and knocks, saying: "If any man hear my voice, and open the door, I will come in to him, and will sup with him, and he with me" (Rev. 3:20).

And does not every heart fly open to receive the heavenly visitant? Alas, no! Satan puts on the threefold bar of unbelief, pride, and prejudice, while inbred sin, afraid of losing its darling gratifications, opposes every effort to admit so kind a friend. The flesh pleads hard for self-indulgence; the world spreads its painted baubles, its deceitful riches, its empty honors, its intoxicating pleasures; and thus the sinner is held in vassalage to the powers of darkness.

Is, then, the heart forever barred against the Prince of Peace? Forever barred it would be, did not sovereign grace, by its almighty power, drive out the strong man armed, crucify each rebellious lust, and bring every thought into captivity to the obedience of Christ. When grace opens the sinner's heart, all the powers of the soul are made willing to admit the conquering Savior and to acknowledge Him to be the Lord. Old favorite sins now become hateful; darling lusts appear like inbred vipers. Satan is beheld in all his horrors, and vice in its true deformity.

The world loses its charms. Heaven opens on the enraptured eye of faith. Holiness captivates the heart by its celestial beauties. Jesus is beheld with rising admiration and becomes each day more precious to the soul. Such is the wonderful change wrought in the conversion of a sinner, through the power of the Holy Spirit.

Unbelief gives way to faith, pride to humility, anger to meekness, impatience to resignation, hatred to love, and sin to universal holiness. The idol, self, falls prostrate before Jesus Christ, and nothing is extolled, or trusted in, or pleaded before the throne of God, but the precious blood and righteousness of Emmanuel. All glory is now given to the Father, Son, and Holy Spirit; and the Triune God is *all in all*.

It is to be feared that thousands who call themselves Christians will never be acknowledged as such in that great day when the secrets of all hearts shall be revealed and the real character of every professor of godliness distinctly known. Too many, it is to be feared, substitute a general acknowledgment of the truths of the Bible for that faith in those truths which purify the heart and assimilate the soul to the image of Jesus.

It is no difficult thing to say, "I believe in God the Father Almighty, maker of heaven and earth; and in Jesus Christ, his only Son our Lord"; but to feel all the love, reverence, and obedience, which, as creatures and redeemed sinners, we owe to our God and Savior, is not so easy to fallen nature. It is no way contrary to our carnal heart to profess, and even strenuously to contend for, those truths which we have been taught from our infancy to consider as sacred, or to extol that church in whose bosom we have grown up from earliest years.

But to exhibit the fruit of those doctrines and to act agreeably to the spiritual formularies of our venerable establishment is not so congenial to the natural state of our depraved hearts. So long as thousands who bear the Christian name live in all the gayeties and follies of the world, neglecting the gospel and manifesting a spirit in direct opposition to it, we cannot wonder that such multitudes, carried away by the potent stream of public example, rest satisfied with a faith which passes current in the world, which attaches no transformation to the character, which requires no self-denial, no painful sacrifices on the part of its possessors.

Many, no doubt, rejoice that they are preserved from such delusions as they suppose the people of God labor under, who debar themselves from what they term the innocent gayeties of life and the delights of fashionable extravagance. These people pride themselves on their superior wisdom in being able to grasp both worlds at once: to acknowledge the importance of Christianity, and yet to enjoy those carnal gratifications which give such a zest to their existence. Thus they go on like the rich man in the parable, faring sumptuously every day, and never find out their dreadful mistake, until, like him, they open their eyes in hell, being in torments!

How awfully blinded is the soul of man, until illuminated by the Holy Spirit of truth! Until His glorious light irradiate our minds, we can form no accurate ideas either of God or of ourselves. All is chaos and confusion. We do not even "see men as trees, walking" (Mark 8:24). We are in a state of complete blindness, and all our conceptions are erroneous. We grope in the dark. We stumble even at noonday.

How different from that cold assent of the understanding to the general truths of the gospel, which satisfies an unbelieving world, is the faith which the Spirit of God works in the hearts of His people. The believer in Jesus is the new creation of God. His mind is enlightened from above. His heart is made to feel its guilt and misery. He reads the Word of God with an interest unfelt before. He reads it as a revelation of love from the God of mercy, proclaiming pardon to the guilty, peace to the miserable, and purity to the polluted. Every declaration bears, to his mind, the stamp of truth. He requires no other sanction than "thus saith the Lord"; and, finding this, he reads with reverence, and seeks for grace to receive with all meekness the engrafted Word which is able to save his soul. He finds his own character exactly portrayed in its sacred pages. He looks within and is able to trace sin through the dark recesses and secret windings of his heart. He discovers those latent seeds of evil, those bitter springs of misery, unbelief, pride, lust, and covetousness, which are continually pouring forth their deadly streams into his outward life. He traces all this evil to the fall of man and finds that the deadly poison has contaminated the whole posterity of Adam. He owns himself a sinner, both by nature and practice. He justifies the righteous judgment of God, whose law he has broken, and whose tremendous curse he has so awfully incurred. He no longer tries to palliate his offenses or invent soft names whereby to varnish over the deformity of sin. He frankly and fully confesses himself a rebel, guilty of death, and deserving of nothing less than eternal damnation.

Into this humble, broken, contrite state of heart he is brought by the deep convictions of that Holy Spirit, whose office it is to "reprove the world of sin" (John 16:8). But does this divine agent leave him in this awakened state of agony and despair? Ah, no! How good, how gracious, how merciful is God! He wounds in order to heal; He kills in order to make alive!

When a person labors under a violent fever, every expedient is tried to reduce the wasting malady. The means used seem, for a time, to increase the weakness and debility of the patient; but he is thus weakened only that he may eventually become strong. No sooner is the consuming fever abated than cordials and restoratives are freely administered, which, given before, would have augmented the dangerous symptoms and thus have hastened on the fatal consequences of the disease. Thus, our heavenly Physician humbles and subdues the proud heart of the sinner and destroys the feverish thirst and burning desire after sinful gratifications before He imparts the reviving cordials of pardon and peace to restore the sin-sick soul to spiritual strength and vigor.

Then the bloom of health begins to appear in the sweet tints of peace and joy, of love and humility, of meekness and heavenly mindedness, which beautify the soul and cause the believer to shine in the image of his divine Redeemer.

The happy believer now knows his malady and his remedy. He takes with gratitude those medicines which infinite wisdom prescribes. He daily feeds upon Christ by faith and daily derives strength from this gracious source of blessedness. He feels his own weakness and experiences the power of Jesus. He loathes himself and truly loves his Savior, in whose righteousness he appears all lovely in the eyes of his heavenly Father. As a pilgrim, he journeys onwards under the guidance of that Holy Spirit who dwells in him as in a temple and who has promised to keep him by His mighty power through faith unto salvation. The world fascinates no longer. The mask falls from its face, and he beholds the idol in its natural deformity. He sees the emptiness of human applause, the madness of ambition, the deceitfulness of riches, the folly of extravagance. Everything beneath the sun assumes its true character while he views it through the medium of God's holy Word.

He learns to form a proper estimate of temporal things. He prays for grace to use the world as not abusing it and to be moderate in the enjoyment of all created good, knowing that the fashion of this world passes away. Has the believer no enjoyment of life? Is he destitute of all rational delights because he makes the Lord his portion? It would be an impeachment of the goodness of God to suppose His service a mere Egyptian bondage.

The true believer in Jesus has the sweetest enjoyment of life. He can eat his food with singleness of heart, praising God. He can taste the sweets of Christian friendship and domestic life; he can enjoy all the endearing charities of husband, father, brother; he can feel his heart expanding towards the poor and find his joy in pouring the balm of consolation into the troubled breast; he can delight in all the beauties of natural scenery and relish all the charms of sound philosophy; he can rejoice in every opening prospect for the extension of the Redeemer's kingdom through institutions devised by Christian wisdom and conducted in Christian simplicity; he can weep in his best moments over the ruins of the fall, not only as felt in his own heart, but as beheld in the abject condition of the millions of mankind; he can rejoice with those who rejoice and weep with those who weep. Say, then, can such a man be miserable? Can such a man be destitute of sources of real enjoyment? He lives by faith; he longs for heaven; he desires to be daily conformed to Jesus and to glorify Him more, whether it be by life or death. To him, to live is Christ and to die is gain. Such is the character of the converted sinner. Oh, how precious, how divine, how rare a character!

"Lord, impart this grace unto me, who am less than the least of all Thy mercies, until faith shall end in the glorious fruition of Thyself in Thy everlasting kingdom of light and glory."

⎯⎯◆◆⎯⎯

*Blest Savior, condescend
To dwell within my heart;
Oh, be my advocate and friend;
Bid every sin depart.*

*Incline my soul to love
The path of life divine;
In concord let my passions move,
Let all my heart be Thine.*

*Preserve me by Thy care;
Protect me, lest I stray;
Keep me from Satan's deadly snare,
From every devious way.*

*Let angel-guards surround,
And shield my soul from ill;
While traveling over temptation's ground,
To Zion's holy hill.*

*When death the message brings
To call me hence away,
Oh, may I stretch my joyful wings
To heaven's eternal day!*

CHAPTER 24

The New Creature

The heart cannot be too deeply impressed with the absolute necessity of regenerating grace, nor seek too earnestly for the promised blessing. If the value of one immortal soul exceeds in amount all the wealth of the globe, yes, of millions of material worlds, how strange that men should barter their souls for trifles light as air and empty as vanity itself! Awful infatuation! By many people, faith is considered as the cheapest commodity and of the most easy attainment, forgetting that the eternal Son of God paid the price of His own most precious blood, that we might receive this heavenly grace and be made partakers of everlasting glory.

Faith is the gift of God, and, if any man be in Christ—or, in other words, if any man possess this gift of faith—he is a new creature; with him, old things have passed away, and behold, all things have become new. Ah, how little is this delightful yet solemn truth considered by the great bulk of professing Christians! Solemn indeed, when viewed in reference to Christians in general; delightful, when contemplated in connection with the present holiness and future happiness of the new creation of God. To be made new creatures, two important changes must pass upon us. We must be renewed in the spirit of our mind, and we must walk before God in newness of life.

He who commanded the light to shine out of darkness must shine into our hearts to give us the light of the knowledge of His glory in the face of Jesus Christ, before we can walk in the light, as He is in the light. When thus enlightened, we shall walk circumspectly, watch ourselves closely, feel our own helplessness, lament our depravity, cast ourselves on Jesus unreservedly, plead His merits, implore His mediation, pray without ceasing, delight in the Scriptures, love the people of God, shun carnal pleasures, delight in labor for Christ and souls, stem the torrent of general impiety, and seek to abound in every good word and work. If this be a faithful miniature of the new creature, we must, while looking at unconverted man, exclaim, "What hath God wrought!"

The true believer has been justly compared to a little flame miraculously burning in the midst of mighty waters. There is everything around him and within him that is calculated to extinguish the holy fire. Satan, the prince of the powers of the air, is constantly agitating these troubled waters. The world is dashing its surges against it; and the flesh, with its mire and dirt, is laboring to smother the sacred flame. But all is vain. He who kindled it, is almighty; He who has promised that it shall never go out, is almighty.

Oh, then, let not the afflicted, tempest-tossed believer be dismayed, but rather rejoice, inasmuch as the power and grace of Jesus are glorified by those very trials, which tend to increase the graces of His redeemed people. John has declared that "he that believeth on the Son of God hath the witness in himself" (1 John 5:10). If, then, we are new creatures in Christ Jesus, we shall have the following indubitable evidence of regeneration in our souls:

Our perceptions will be new. A divine light will break in upon our minds. The darkness of error, which obscured the truth from our view, will be dissipated. We shall see with unveiled face, as in a glass, the glory of the Lord, and shall be changed into the same image, from glory to glory, even as by the Spirit of the Lord. In His light, we shall see light; and, following Jesus, who is the light of the world, we shall become the children of the light and of the day.

Our principles will be new. We shall act from pure, holy, unselfish motives. Faith working by love will be the grand moving principle. Self will no longer be the pivot on which we turn, but Jesus will be our all in all.

Our practice will be new. We shall live no longer according to the sinful customs of the world, or the powerful solicitations of the flesh, but according to the holy precepts of the everlasting gospel. We shall delight in the law of God after the inward man. It will be our food and drink to do the will of our Father which is in heaven.

Our plans will be new. We shall dedicate ourselves, and all we have and are, to the service of that divine Savior who loved us and gave Himself for us. We shall not be daily occupied in forming plans for worldly pleasure or projecting schemes for the acquisition of worldly profit, but in devising means for carrying on the cause of truth and for spreading the knowledge of a crucified Redeemer throughout the earth.

Our prospects will be new. The darkness being past, and the true light now shining, we shall see the distant radiance of the heavenly Zion and behold, with the telescopic eye of faith, the land which is very far off.

Our privileges will be new. God will be now our reconciled Father; Jesus, our elder brother, Savior, and friend; the Holy Spirit, our sanctifier and comforter; angels, our ministering spirits; and heaven, our eternal home.

Our portion will be new. All those exceeding great and precious promises, which in Christ are yea, and in Him amen, to the praise and glory of God, will be ours. We shall be heirs of God and joint heirs with Christ. We shall be the citizens of the New Jerusalem and shall inherit that kingdom which is incorruptible and undefiled, prepared for all the new creatures in Christ Jesus before the foundation of the world.

To sum up all this blessedness, we shall experience in this world a progression in holiness, and in the world to come a perpetuity of bliss.

"Blessed Lord, my soul longs for this rich grace, this unspeakably glorious state. Oh, allow me not to lie a moment longer in nature's darkness; but speak the word, and light shall start into existence. Then shall the lineaments of the new creature, formed to Thy glory, be daily unfolding themselves in greater likeness to Thyself, until the happy hour shall arrive, when every remnant of corruption shall be forever destroyed, and my soul be made perfect in Thine everlasting kingdom."

The New Creature

Lord, what I want, and still implore,
Is grace to love Thee more and more;
A heart renewed—set free from sin,
And filled with heavenly light within.

Oh could I reach this blissful state!
For this, my longing soul shall wait,
Until sovereign love, with mighty power,
Shall on my soul the blessing shower.

Then, when the sacred drops descend
From Jesus, my almighty friend,
The fruits of joy and peace shall grow,
And all the garden spices flow.

With holy love and humble joy
Shall grace my every power employ,
Until, far removed from sin and shame,
My soul shall ever bless Thy name.

CHAPTER 25

Christian Unity

We read much in the New Testament about Christian unity. The strength and beauty of the church consists in the oneness between Christ and His people. How powerful were the pleadings of our great Advocate for the unity of His redeemed people: "Holy Father, keep through thine own name those whom thou hast given me, that they may be one, as we are" (John 17:11), "that they all may be one; as thou, Father, art in me, and I in thee, that they also may be one in us: that the world may believe that thou hast sent me. And the glory which thou gavest me I have given them; that they may be one, even as we are one: I in them, and thou in me, that they may be made perfect in one; and that the world may know that thou hast sent me, and hast loved them, as thou hast loved me" (John 17:21-23).

Paul also dwells much on this important subject: "By one Spirit are we all baptized into one body…; and have been all made to drink into one Spirit" (1 Cor. 12:13). "Be perfect, be of good comfort, be of one mind" (2 Cor. 13:11). "I beseech you, brethren, by the name of our Lord Jesus Christ, that ye all speak the same thing, and that there be no divisions among you; but that ye be perfectly joined together in the same mind and in the same judgment" (1 Cor. 1:10). "Now the God of patience and consolation grant you to be likeminded one toward another according to Christ Jesus: that ye may with one mind and one mouth glorify God, even the Father of our Lord Jesus Christ" (Rom. 15:5-6).

From our Lord's intercessory prayer, we learn that all who are the subjects of grace are the gift of the Father to the Son; that to such the Son gives eternal life; that the beginning of this eternal life is to know the only true God and Jesus Christ whom He has sent; that this knowledge is imparted by Jesus Christ through the teaching of the Spirit of truth, the Comforter; that this knowledge is of a sanctifying nature; that it leads to a separation from the world and a union to each other; that these happy souls are kept from the evil that is in the world and are preserved unto eternal glory.

Hence, all strife, divisions, and contentions disfigure the beauty and tarnish the glory of the church of God. Paul sharply reproves the Corinthian church for its lack of unity: "Ye are yet carnal: for whereas there is among you envying, and strife, and divisions, are ye not carnal, and walk as men?" (1 Cor. 3:3). Meanwhile, to the Ephesian converts he gives this beautiful exhortation: "I therefore, the prisoner of the Lord, beseech you that ye walk worthy of the vocation wherewith ye are called, with all lowliness and meekness, with longsuffering, forbearing one another in love; endeavouring to keep the unity of the Spirit in the bond of peace. There is one body, and one Spirit, even as ye are called in one hope of your calling; one Lord, one faith, one baptism, one God and Father of all, who is above all, and through all, and in you all" (Eph. 4:1-6).

It may be asked, "Is it possible that all who profess to believe in the truths of the Bible will ever be brought to see everything in the same light and to follow, in every minute particular, the same track of thinking and acting?" This unity may be, and ought to be, maintained in the grand essentials of the gospel. And a beautiful union of faith and practice, of sentiment and feeling, does exist among real Christians of all denominations, however they may differ about the terms and explications of some abstruse doctrines, or respecting the outward forms and modes of church government: "For the kingdom of God is not in word, but in power" (1 Cor. 4:20). It "is not meat and drink; but righteousness, and peace, and joy in the Holy Ghost" (Rom. 14:17). When these holy characters freely unbosom their hearts to each other, and discourse together on experimental and practical subjects, they find themselves standing on one common ground, connected by one common tie, united in one common cause, and drinking into one and the self-same spirit.

They all mourn over, and are deeply humbled on account of, the corruption of their nature and the sin of their lives. They all feel the plague of their own hearts, and so groan, being burdened. They all are conscious of their utter inability to save themselves. They all know that they are naturally without strength. They are all enabled, through grace, to look unto Jesus, the eternal Son of God, as their only Savior, whose blood cleanses them from all sin; whose merits, received and applied by faith, form their only justifying righteousness; whose intercession for them prevails with God; whose promised gift, the Spirit of truth, dwells in their hearts, causing them to cry with filial love and confidence, "Abba, Father." They all know and feel that they thus become the children of God by faith in Christ Jesus; and, enjoying the presence and grace of their heavenly Father through the Son of His love, they are all enabled to resist the devil, to crucify the flesh, to renounce the world, and gradually to perfect holiness in the fear of God.

They all confess how low their highest efforts fall beneath the elevated standard of gospel holiness; yet, forgetting the things which are behind, they press forward towards those things which are before, and long for that happy period when, having laid down their bodies of sin and death, they shall shine in spotless purity in the courts above.

With these feelings and impressions, they all confess themselves to be pilgrims and strangers upon earth. Their hearts are set upon things above. They sympathize with each other's sorrows and gladden with each other's joy. They love to bear each other's burdens, and so fulfill the law of Christ.

As they all believe in the glorious doctrine of the Trinity in unity and in the divine and human nature of Jesus Christ, so they unitedly confess themselves to be sinners saved by grace through faith in a crucified Redeemer, and ascribe all their salvation, from first to last, to the free, unmerited mercy of God in Christ. Thus, while they acknowledge the justice of that sentence which condemns them, as sinners, to everlasting misery, they extol the vastness of that love which so freely saves them from the wrath to come. With these holy views of the truth, they can each say from the heart:

> *My power is lost—the fault is wholly mine;*
> *Yet bid me live—the glory shall be Thine.*

Now, if every faithful follower of Jesus can subscribe to these common points of Christian doctrine and experience, what is it that divides and separates the true family of Christ? Is it not the remaining corruption of our nature, the remaining darkness of our minds, and the subtle enemy of our souls? These are the foes which disturb the peace of the church and destroy much of her purity and spiritual prosperity.

Oh, that the Holy Spirit may purge away this old leaven of malice and wickedness and fill us with sincerity and truth, that we may become a new lump, be all new creatures in Christ Jesus, shine as lights in the world, and so advance that kingdom of holiness upon earth, which is criminally impeded in its progress and marred in its beauty by the disfiguring contentions, strifes, and divisions of those who call themselves the followers of the Lamb!

In the "revelation of mercy," as in the visible works of creation, there are mysteries which our finite minds cannot fathom; for what is man that he should be wise as his Maker? And yet how many dare to reject the oracles of God because they cannot comprehend their elevated truths or square their seemingly discordant statements with their preconceived systematic opinions!

The Word of God is "as a city which is at unity with itself." All is plain and clear to the divine Mind, who sees the end from the beginning, and who knows the infinitely varied movements of His own vast design. We see but a small part of His ways. Many a wheel, which we cannot trace, enters into those darknesses of His impenetrable counsel. But still it is moving onward in direct progression towards that glorious period, when the whole stupendous work of mercy shall be displayed to the church triumphant in heaven and shall call forth her eternal songs of praise. There, in that bright world, those saints of God who differed here below respecting some mysterious points of deep concealment will see with one vision.

The darkness being gone, the veil being withdrawn, and the truth standing fully revealed to their enraptured souls in all its beauty, symmetry, and perfection, they will then utter no jarring sentiment, feel no uncharitable emotion, experience no shyness of approach; but, wrapped in holy admiration and humble reverence before the throne of God, every feeling will be love, and every view of the truth will be in perfect accordance with the mind and will of their Creator. There, with one heart and mouth, they will glorify God and the Lamb, join in the same song, delight in the same work, being, in every sense, one in the presence of Him who, when upon earth, interceded for His people: "The glory which thou gavest me I have given them; that they may be one, even as we are one: I in them, and thou in me, that they may be made perfect in one" (John 17:22-23). Well, then, might the apostle say to the Corinthians, when lamenting their unhappy dissensions, "Are ye not carnal, and walk as men" (1 Cor. 3:3), as people unconverted, as men destitute of the Spirit of Christ?

While we remain in the body, differences of opinion on points confessedly mysterious must be expected; but may not this be designed by infinite Wisdom, for the exercise of charity and patience towards each other, provided the great essentials of genuine Christianity are maintained and practically believed?

This incapacity of our minds to grasp the mighty design of everlasting love towards creatures helpless in themselves and unable to come to God (John 6:44), and yet chargeable with the guilt of not coming to Him (John 5:39-40), should teach us humility and entire dependence on the Spirit of truth, to direct us aright in the way of life and salvation.

The more we know ourselves, the more we shall learn to renounce our own reasonings and to follow simply the direction of that blessed Word which is given us to be a light unto our feet and a lamp unto our path. Jesus said, "I am the light of the world: he that followeth me shall not walk in darkness, but shall have the light of life" (John 8:12). "Walk while ye have the light, lest darkness come upon you: for he that walketh in darkness knoweth not whither he goeth. While ye have light, believe in the light, that ye may be the children of light" (John 12:35-36).

"Merciful Lord, be pleased to cast Thy bright beams of light upon Thy church, that all Thy people, being enlightened by the doctrines of Thy Word, may so walk in the light of Thy truth, that at length they may attain to everlasting life. Preserve me, Thine unworthy servant, from that unhallowed curiosity which would presumptuously pry into those deep things around which Thou hast thrown an impenetrable veil. Give me a mind enlightened to discover the truth as it is in Jesus and a heart to love and practice the truth, as it is revealed to my soul in the fullness of Christian charity, enabling me to say, 'Grace be with all those who love our Lord Jesus Christ in sincerity,' and enabling me to call every one a brother who bears Thy holy image, takes up his cross, and follows Thee."

Sweet is the joy of those possessed,
Who know and love the Lord;
No guilty fears disturb their rest,
While leaning on His Word.

Amid the ruffling scenes of life,
They trust a covenant God;
While all the angry sons of strife
Despise His chastening rod.

Jesus to them His peace imparts,
To them His presence gives;
He dwells by faith in all their hearts,
And all their needs relieves.

Thus, holy Lord, may I be blessed
With graces from above;
Until peace and joy reign in my breast,
The fruit of dying love.

CHAPTER 26

Following the Lord Fully

True humility is a sweet and blessed grace. It is the product of almighty power. How calm is the humble soul! While storms and tempests rage with unrelenting fury among the proud and haughty of mankind, a serene and lovely sky smiles over those who are clothed with humility. To promote this desirable state of heart, it is very useful to study those characters on which infinite truth has stamped a worth which revolving ages cannot diminish nor impair. Such are Enoch, Noah, Abraham, Job, David, Daniel, and many others, who shine like stars in the book of God.

We cannot but be struck, while taking this survey, with the blessed testimony which God gave to Caleb. He is there said to be a man of "another spirit" from the unbelieving Israelites around him and to have followed the Lord fully, at a time when the most awful defection took place among the professed people of God (Num. 14:24).

To follow the Lord fully is, indeed, a great work; and yet, nothing less than this will bring us to heaven. The work is the Lord's. "By grace are ye saved through faith; and that not of yourselves: it is the gift of God" (Eph. 2:8). The unbelief of the Israelites was their sin, for which they suffered, not being permitted to enter into the promised land.

The faith of Caleb was the gift of God; and his privilege of being favored with a fruitful possession in the land of Canaan, in consequence of it, was of grace and not of debt.

This strictly applies to me in a spiritual sense. Oh, for more self-condemnation and self-abasement, when I see and feel the awful unbelief which dwells in my evil heart! And yet, if I have any reason to hope that the Lord has given me another spirit from the carnal world around me, or from what I once had, and if this new spirit evidences itself by an obedience to His holy command, and a delight in His will, to Him be all the undivided praise!

To follow the Lord fully, I must have a lively faith in the promises of God made to me in Jesus Christ; I must experience the love of God shed abroad in my heart through the Holy Spirit given unto me; I must have a good hope through grace, a hope full of immortality; I must feel the sweet drawings of the Spirit, uniting me closer to Jesus in heart and affection; I must renounce all self-dependence and all creature dependence; I must renounce both my sins and my own supposed righteousness; I must abandon the flattering vanities of the world, and labor to subdue the lusts of the flesh; I must be willing to bear the cross, to deny myself, and to do anything for Christ; I must submit to the righteousness of God—yes, esteem it so inestimably precious, as to count all things else in comparison of it but dung and dross; I must have my will swallowed up in the holy, sovereign will of God; I must lie passive in His hand, while actively engaged in His service, being ever desirous, with childlike simplicity, to do and suffer, at all times and in all places, the will of my heavenly Father. If this be to follow the Lord fully, then, oh my soul, lie prostrate at His feet in shame and confusion of face.

God will not accept of a divided heart. To follow Him fully, I must follow Him only. The language of the church is: "Other lords beside thee have had dominion over us: but by thee only will we make mention of thy name" (Isa. 26:13). "Whom have I in heaven but thee? and there is none upon earth that I desire beside thee" (Ps. 73:25). "The Lord is my portion, saith my soul" (Lam. 3:24). Oh that this may be the language of my heart! I can never know true peace, until Jesus reign the unrivaled sovereign of my affections. "Blessed Savior, be my only Savior! Let me not trust in any thing but Thee. Let me love nothing but Thee, or for Thy sake. May I love Thee supremely, and love all Thy people, because they belong to Thee."

To follow the Lord fully, I must follow Him at all times—not only when the sun shines, but when the tempest comes. This often puts faith and love to the severest trial, when the line of duty runs through rugged paths and hostile foes. Yet, if I draw back in the day of trouble, I cannot follow the Lord fully. I must not choose my path, but "run with patience the race" which is set before me (Heb. 12:1). I must still keep in the narrow way, however few there be who walk in it, or however unfashionable this path may be among the rich and learned of the earth; I must ever remember that the promise of eternal life is made to those only who are found in the King's highway of holiness. If through fear of man, or love of ease, I deviate into bye-paths and crooked ways to avoid the difficulties of the road, I shall assuredly find them multiply upon me, without one sustaining promise, for, thus says the Lord: "If any man draw back, my soul shall have no pleasure in him" (Heb. 10:38).

To follow the Lord fully, I must confess Him with courage and constancy before an unbelieving world. A cowardly believer dishonors his heavenly King and betrays the cause of truth. I say a cowardly believer, for such was Peter when left to himself. Caleb was valiant for the truth. He believed in God and dared to confess his faith and allegiance in the face of the whole congregation, when they would stone him with stones like another Stephen. Thus he experienced the blessedness of this divine declaration: "Them that honor me I will honor" (1 Sam. 2:30).

But, through the deceitfulness of sin, I am in danger of falling into two extremes: vainglory, and the fear of man. Our beloved Redeemer, however, has given me an exact direction how to avoid both these evils: "Take heed that ye do not your alms before men, to be seen of them: otherwise ye have no reward of your Father which is in heaven" (Matt. 6:1). "Let your light so shine before men, that they may see your good works, and glorify your Father which is in heaven" (Matt. 5:16). By observing the first precept, I shall avoid vainglory, which is the evil forbidden; by observing the second, I shall maintain a holy courage in exhibiting the power of godliness to the glory of God, which is the duty enjoined.

To follow the Lord fully, I must cleave to Him in seasons of general defection. Here Caleb proved that he was a man of another spirit from those around him by cleaving steadfastly to God. Thus did the apostles, when, on many forsaking Jesus, He said to them, "Will ye also go away?" Peter replied, "Lord, to whom shall we go? thou hast the words of eternal life" (John 6:67-68).

This entire surrender of the heart to God is the work of the Spirit, for "a man can receive nothing, except it be given him from heaven" (John 3:27). Nothing short of this will bring us to glory. Nothing short of this can give true assurance, peace, and joy. I can never taste the real comforts of religion until I follow the Lord fully. It is the lack of this undivided state of heart which causes so much unsteadiness in the walk and so much discomfort in the experience of many professors who, separating what God has joined together, maintain with warmth the high doctrines of grace, while they esteem of small importance the social and relative duties of the gospel. Such people seem to forget that to be really holy, is to be relatively holy, and that no truth can do us any personal good, but as it influences and purifies our hearts and lives. What can we think of those professors who, while they appear saints abroad, are fiends at home? Can it be a matter of surprise that they should feel no real satisfaction either in religion or in the world? They profess so much religion, as to render them the objects of the world's derision; and yet, they possess too little of its power to enable them to taste the sweets of genuine piety. Hence, they grow morose in their temper and uncharitable in their spirit. They are quick-sighted in discovering the mote in a brother's eye, while utter strangers to the beam in their own. They are spots and blemishes in the visible church and verify the declaration of the prophet: "There is no peace, saith my God, to the wicked" (Isa. 57:21).

But how great is the happiness of the true follower of Jesus! His sins are blotted out. His soul is beautified with salvation. He has no double aims. All his intentions are simple and single: his one desire is to promote the glory of his God and Savior. His heart is the abode of peace. His house is the dwelling-place of joy and gladness. He has his conflicts, and he has his comforts. He has his sorrow, and he has his support. God is his Father. Angels minister to him, and all things work together for his good. He may be hated of men, but he is beloved of God. He may have to pass through deep waters, but underneath are the everlasting arms. He may often groan, being burdened; but in heaven all his tears shall be wiped away. He shall there follow the Lamb wherever He goes. He shall there experience the eternal blessedness of that glorious promise: "He that overcometh shall inherit all things; and I will be his God, and he shall be my son" (Rev. 21:7).

Oh blessed Redeemer, fill my soul
With love and grace divine;
Subdue the power of every sin,
And make me wholly Thine.

In Thee, oh Christ, may I be found
From every blemish free;
Though vile and worthless in myself,
Yet all complete in Thee.

Oh, send Thy Holy Spirit, Lord,
In larger portions down,
To witness with my waiting heart,
And seal me for Thine own.

May holiness my life adorn;
May all my soul be love;
May every wish be formed by Thee,
And placed on things above.

Thus will a holy evidence
Confirm that I am Thine;
And faith, by works made manifest,
Shall prove the work divine.

CHAPTER 27

The Two Great Instruments in the Conversion of Sinners

The written Word of God is one of the sacred instruments in the hands of the eternal Spirit for the regeneration of sinners. "The law of the LORD is perfect, converting the soul" (Ps. 19:7).

The preaching of the gospel is another instituted means for awakening dead souls and leading them to Jesus Christ, through the accompanying power of the Holy Spirit; for "faith cometh by hearing, and hearing by the word of God" (Rom. 10:17).

All men, without exception, are by nature dead in trespasses and sins. Multitudes, however, are quickened to a life of faith and holiness.

But, how are they quickened? How are they born again? As God is pleased to work by means, what instruments does He employ in this great work of bringing dead souls to spiritual life and vigor? Our blessed Lord Himself has told us, when He said, "The hour is coming, and now is, when the dead shall hear the voice of the Son of God: and they that hear shall live" (John 5:25). This voice is heard when the gospel is preached, and wonderful is the effect produced by it. That our Lord meant dead souls is evident from His mentioning another hour, when all who are in the graves shall hear His voice and come forth to judgment. Those preachers of the gospel must therefore be very defective in their views, who will not exhort sinners, under the idea of its being useless to speak to the dead, making no difference between those who are naturally and those who are spiritually dead. The hour is indeed coming when the former shall be aroused from their slumber by the voice of the archangel and the trump of God; but the hour now is, when the latter are awakened, through grace, by the sweet sound of the trumpet of the gospel of peace.

When Ezekiel was commanded to prophesy in the valley of dry bones and was asked, "Son of man, can these bones live?" he modestly replied, "Oh Lord God, thou knowest" (Ezek. 37:3). Without reasoning upon the subject or objecting to the work of prophesying to dry bones, he implicitly obeyed the divine command; and immediately there was a shaking, and the bones came together, and the sinews and flesh came upon them. Then he was again commanded to prophesy unto the wind, and the breath came into them, and they lived. So also when the apostles went forth at the command of Jesus, to preach the Word of life to thousands "dead in trespasses and sins" (Eph. 2:1), an agitation was felt wherever they came, and multitudes were turned unto the Lord through the power of the Holy Spirit.

Paul writes thus to the Ephesian church: "In whom ye also trusted, after that ye heard the word of truth, the gospel of your salvation" (Eph. 1:13), and also to the Thessalonians: "Our gospel came not unto you in word only," (like Ezekiel's first prophesying,) "but also in power, and in the Holy Ghost, and in much assurance" (1 Thess. 1:5). A quickening influence accompanied the Word; and souls, before dead in sins, were quickened and saved by almighty grace. "For this cause," says the apostle, "thank we God without ceasing, because, when ye received the word of God which ye heard of us, ye received it not as the word of men, but as it is in truth, the word of God, which effectually worketh also in you that believe" (1 Thess. 2:13).

James, in like manner, plainly declares, "Of his own will begat he us with the word of truth" (James 1:18). Peter, again, fully confirms this doctrine: "Being born again, not of corruptible seed, but of incorruptible, by the word of God, which liveth and abideth for ever" (1 Pet. 1:23). "The word of the Lord endureth for ever. And this is the word which by the gospel is preached unto you" (1 Pet. 1:25). Surely, then, may the messenger of peace say to a ruined world, "Awake thou that sleepest, and arise from the dead, and Christ shall give thee light" (Eph.

5:14). His duty is to preach the Word. The promise of God is, "it shall not return unto me void" (Isa. 55:11).

Our blessed Lord, in His beautiful parable of the sower, compares the Word of God to seed sown on various grounds. There is the hard-beaten pathway, which cannot receive the seed: it lies on the surface, and is devoured by the fowls of the air. There is the rocky ground, lightly covered with earth, which admits indeed the seed; but, affording from its shallowness no moisture, in seasons of heat and drought the plant withers away. There is the thorny ground, so covered with weeds and brambles that the seed, if it spring up at all, can bring no fruit to perfection. There is the good ground, which being ploughed and broken up, is brought into a proper state to admit the scattered grain from the sower's hand and plentifully rewards his toil.

Wherever the gospel is faithfully preached, there the good seed of the Word is sown. The soil is the human heart. Careless hearers receive no good whatever from the most faithful preaching of the gospel. Mere carnal excitements are of short duration, while the stony heart remains unchanged. Worldly riches, cares, and pleasures check the growth of the gospel in the soul.

One soil, and only one, is good: a heart prepared by divine grace; a heart deeply impressed with the command of God, "Break up your fallow ground, and sow not among thorns…lest my fury come forth like fire, and burn that none can quench it" (Jer. 4:3-4); a heart groaning under the burden of conscious guilt, and crying out, "What must I do to be saved?" (Acts. 16:30). Such a heart, like soil that has been ploughed and broken up, is prepared to receive the precious seed of gospel grace, those glad tidings of great joy which proclaim pardon and peace through a crucified Redeemer.

According to the strength of faith is the produce which this blessed soul yields, in some thirty, in some sixty, in some a hundred fold. Fruit is invariably produced by such a soil in a greater or lesser degree; it is "the ground which the Lord has blessed." Happy is he who abounds in the fruits of righteousness, for Jesus has declared: "Herein is my Father glorified, that ye bear much fruit; so shall ye be my disciples" (John 15:8).

Now, if the Word of God, or the great truths drawn from that Word, be the instrument of our regeneration, if a spiritual change be thus effected by spiritual means, how invaluable are the two great blessings which a God of mercy has bestowed upon mankind, "the scriptures of the prophets" and "the preaching of Jesus Christ." Paul knew their value when he wrote, "Now to him that is of power to stablish you according to my gospel, and the preaching of Jesus Christ, according to the revelation of the mystery, which was kept secret since the world began, but now is made manifest, and by the scriptures of the prophets, according to the commandment of the everlasting God, made known to all nations for the obedience of faith: To God only wise, be glory through Jesus Christ for ever. Amen" (Rom. 16:25-27).

Thus the wisdom, as well as the grace, of God is manifested in appointing the Holy Scriptures and a preached gospel as the two grand instruments in the hands of the eternal Spirit for the bringing of all nations to the obedience of faith. If such be the great authority, and such the sure foundation, on which Bible and missionary societies are established, what must we think of those who, professing to be guardians of the truth, labor to paralyze the exertions or suppress the endeavors of the zealous servants of Christ, whose only aim is to extend the knowledge of salvation among the perishing millions of mankind by those very means which infinite love has ordained for our present and future happiness?

From lack of due consideration, some people confound the regeneration of the soul with the rite of baptism and suppose that every person baptized is invariably born again during the celebration of that sacred ordinance. A man cannot be born twice in a spiritual, any more than in a natural, sense. If an infant be truly regenerated in baptism, (and who dare limit the holy One of Israel?) he will, no doubt, manifest the change by corresponding fruits, at least in childhood, before the influence of bad example has unhappily corrupted his renewed nature. But does not the painful experience of almost every family testify that infants in general unfold the sinful powers of their souls, without manifesting one genuine fruit of the Holy Spirit? Lies, dissimulation, and perverseness in childhood; frivolity and licentiousness in youth; ambition and love of the world in manhood; covetousness and peevishness in old age; all awfully prove the soul to be dead in sin and an heir of hell.

Should the Almighty transform a child after the holy image of its Savior when presented to Him in baptism, this would only evidence the sovereign mercy and grace of a compassionate God, but it does not disprove the former statement of facts. Man, under the Christian economy, as under the Jewish economy, is not necessarily and invariably changed by the outward rite of either baptism or circumcision, for Paul expressly declares: "He is not a Jew, which is one outwardly; neither is that circumcision, which is outward in the flesh: but he is a Jew, which is one inwardly; and circumcision is that of the heart, in the spirit, and not in the letter; whose praise is not of men, but of God" (Rom. 2:28-29).

Thousands, however, are turned from darkness unto light through the grace of God accompanying the faithful preaching of the gospel. Those who have been baptized, and who have grown up in the visible church in the commission of every crime, have been converted from the error of their way and made the humble, holy followers of Jesus through the Word of His grace. The change produced by the Spirit, when thus bringing the truth to the heart, is radical and universal. They become, in every sense, new creatures. They are quite different from what they were before. Surely, then, all must confess that the "word of God is quick, and powerful, and sharper than any twoedged sword" (Heb. 4:12), when wielded by the almighty Spirit through the instrumentality of men appointed to preach to a world of sinners the unsearchable riches of Christ.

So invaluable to fallen man is the gospel of salvation, that the apostle exhorted the Thessalonians to pray for himself and his fellow-laborers, "that the word of the Lord may have free course, and be glorified" (2 Thess. 3:1). There is something peculiarly impressive in the object of the petition, "have free course." When the gospel was first preached, it met with continual opposition. Yet, like some mighty river, checked in its progress by opposing rocks, it forced its way and fertilized all the regions through which it bent its course. The gospel still flows onwards, and shall continue to flow, until the earth be filled with the knowledge of the glory of the Lord, as the waters cover the sea. This prayer is always needful, because the enmity of the human heart is in every age the same.

In the first family, we find a Cain opposing the work of faith and love. The same spirit continues to manifest itself wherever the worship of the true God is established. The Israelites misused their prophets who spoke to them the Word of the Lord, stoning some and killing some (cf. Matt. 21:35). The pagan powers, as well as the Jewish rulers, set themselves against the Lord and against His anointed. The holy apostles of our Lord were called to perpetual sufferings while they spread abroad, through a preached gospel, a Savior's dying love. Papal Rome has long carried on the work of slaughter among the sheep of Christ, checking by fire, tortures, and anathemas the progress of genuine Christianity, lest the pure, unadulterated Word of God should have free course and be glorified. No wonder, then, that the thunders of the Vatican are heard to roar against the most blessed of all human institutions, the British and Foreign Bible Society.

But the gospel has other enemies who labor to check its progress. Infidelity directs the shafts of ridicule against its holy mysteries. Socinianism, under the specious name of rational Christianity, seeks to rob the gospel of its brightest jewel: "God…manifest in the flesh" (1 Tim. 3:16). Indifference, worldly mindedness, formality, and hypocrisy, while they render the mere nominal professors of Christianity barren as the sand, tend more to check the spread of the truth than do all the united attacks of its most hostile foes.

There is, however, a goodly company of faithful Christians who delight in the gospel of Christ and whose lives are devoted to advance its progress throughout the earth. These are the happy servants of the Lord, who pray in secret and are willing to spend and be spent, that in all things God may be glorified through Jesus Christ. They meet with a double hindrance: the one outward, from the enmity of the world; the other inward, from the sin which dwells in them. Yet they are enabled, through grace, to press forward and to help forward the work of the Lord. Oh, that my station may ever be among this blessed flock! Lord, make me one of the humble laborers in Thy vineyard. Give me a heart to receive the truth in the love of it and to feel its power. Teach me to pray with holy fervor, "Thy kingdom come," and to rejoice in every opening prospect of that blessed period when the earth shall be filled with Thy glory. Even now, the morning streaks begin to appear on the distant mountains; even now, the Sun of Righteousness is arising with healing in his beams (Mal. 4:2).

Oh, what glorious times are dawning
On a dark and ruined world!
It is the long-expected morning;
Satan from his seat is hurled.
Hallelujah—Amen.

Hark! The jubilee horn is sounding,
Gladsome notes are echoed round;
Every heart, with joy resounding,
Hails the gospel's welcome sound.
Hallelujah—Amen.

As the light is still advancing,
Backward shrinks the hellish foe;
Faith, through future ages glancing,
Views another Eden glow.
Hallelujah—Amen.

Idols now—the spell discovered—
Dashed as potters' vessels, fall;
Slaves, from pagan chains recovered,
Own Messiah Lord of all.
Hallelujah—Amen.

Hasten, Lord, the joyful season;
Claim the heathen as Thine own;
Break the pride of human reason;
Reign as sovereign Lord alone.
Hallelujah—Amen.

CHAPTER 28

The Two Sources

While men of philosophic minds are busily employed in tracing effects to their causes, and others, of a more adventurous spirit, in traversing unknown regions to trace some mighty river to its source, how few, considering the magnitude of the object, are employed in discovering the two most important of all sources—the source of misery, and the source of mercy. This discovery—so essential to our happiness, and, without an experimental knowledge of which, we must forever remain in a state of spiritual death—is but little regarded by the great bulk of mankind.

Human wisdom and philosophy have been laboring for ages to find out the origin of moral evil and a remedy against it; but they have failed in the attempt. The world, by wisdom, knows not God, for darkness has covered the earth, and gross darkness the people.

We need only to pursue the fabled absurdities of heathen mythology, to witness the self-inflicted tortures of the Hindu devotee, to behold the superstitious penances imposed by the Church of Rome—yes, all the errors and evils which have abounded among Christians, Jews, Mohammedans, and Pagans, in every age—to be convinced that man can never, by any effort of his unassisted reason, discover the true source either of misery or of mercy.

The Bible alone reveals them both. There I learn that the sin of Adam is the source of human misery. "By one man sin entered into the world, and death by sin" (Rom. 5:12). "In Adam all die" (1 Cor. 15:22). From this fountain issue ten thousand poisonous streams, which embitter life, fill the world with wretchedness, and carry unnumbered millions on their boisterous waves until they are plunged into endless perdition.

There I learn, that God in Christ is the only source of mercy. "God was in Christ, reconciling the world unto himself" (2 Cor. 5:19). "Beside me," says Jehovah, "there is no saviour" (Isa. 43:11). "There is none other name under heaven given among men, whereby we must be saved" (Acts 4:12). "Other foundation can no man lay than that is laid, which is Jesus Christ" (1 Cor. 3:11). All good, in time and in eternity, flows from Him who is goodness itself. When man had destroyed himself, and was justly reaping the fruit of his doings, it pleased almighty God, of His own free mercy and grace, to reveal the wondrous plan of salvation by declaring that the seed of the woman should bruise the serpent's head (Gen. 3:15).

This declaration of grace was unasked for and unexpected, and therefore proves to us fallen creatures that God is the only source of mercy, that God is love; for He "so loved the world, that he gave his only begotten Son, that whosoever believeth in him should not perish, but have everlasting life" (John 3:16).

As God is the source of mercy, so the channel through which this grace descends is all of mercy. Jesus Christ, the eternal Son of God, gave Himself for us, an offering and a sacrifice to God for a sweet smelling savor.

By this stupendous sacrifice, divine justice is satisfied, the holy law is magnified, the holiness of Jehovah is unsullied, and eternal truth remains inviolate; yes, by this amazing sacrifice all the divine perfections receive additional luster in the eyes of saints and angels. The whole volume of inspiration is occupied with tracing the various streams which flow from these sources of misery and of mercy, in opening the nature and effects of sin, and in revealing the nature and operations of infinite love. To understand these aright through the teaching of the Spirit is to understand the Scriptures. To have an inward practical knowledge of them in the heart is to be made wise unto salvation.

The excellent Archbishop Leighton thus beautifully describes this stream of mercy, flowing from the fountain of eternal love: "The spring of these waters of salvation, hid in the councils of God before time began, was opened immediately after the fall, and began to flow in a small but reviving brook. Increasing by degrees, and, from the very beginning, making every place it passed through fertile and pleasant, it soon became a large stream. At length the main current of the gospel flowed in, and now it rolls on full of water, greatly enriching the earth, a pure river of water of life, clear as crystal; the streams whereof make glad the city of God, and shall do so, until this river empties itself into the ocean of eternity." It is truly interesting to trace the windings of this sacred stream, sometimes blessing one country and sometimes another, according to the purpose and grace of Him who directs its course with wise and unerring skill.

What cause for gratitude, that this river of the water of life flows in every direction through this highly favored island. But oh, how delightful to taste its sweetness, and to feel, through faith, its purifying and refreshing virtues! "Blessed Lord, be pleased to open my understanding, that I may understand the Scriptures. Give me the Spirit of wisdom and revelation, that I may know myself as a helpless sinner and Thee as my only Savior. Let me never cavil at the deep mysteries of Thy holy Word; but make me as a little child, humble, teachable, and submissive to Thy righteous will. May the knowledge of my ruined state, through original and actual transgression, fill me with shame and self-abhorrence. May the knowledge of Thy sovereign grace and purposes of mercy, through a crucified Redeemer, fill me with gratitude and adoring praise. Make me more and more acquainted with the deceitfulness of sin, that I may watch against its subtle workings; and make me more and more acquainted with Thee, my almighty Savior, that I may daily rejoice in Thy salvation, be exalted in Thy righteousness, and live to Thy glory."

Oh, that I felt my soul upborne
On pure devotion's wings;
Far above earth's deceitful joys
And sublunary things!

Where Thou, blessed Savior, art enthroned
In everlasting light;
The glory of the angelic host,
The source of its delight.

There, in Thy blissful presence, reigns
Immortal joy serene;
No wintry storms are heard to roar,
Nor desolation seen.

Around Thee flow unmixed delights,
Like rivers deep and wide;
While, from the ocean of Thy love,
Proceeds an endless tide.

Can such a sinful creature, Lord,
Partake this wondrous grace,
To dwell with Thee in heavenly bliss,
And view Thy glorious face?

Ah, then, let sin and earth usurp
My wayward heart no more;
Oh be, through life, my all in all,
My soul's unbounded store.

CHAPTER 29

The Two Pillars

"The religion of a sinner," as good Mr. Newton used to say, "stands upon two pillars: what Christ has done for us in the flesh; and what he does in us by his Spirit." Christ dying for us; and Christ living in us, is the very ground and pillar of the truth. Come, oh my soul, retire from a busy, thoughtless world; collect your scattered powers; explore the sacred volume, and examine with delight these glorious pillars, which support the fabric of your hopes, and point to realms on high. Consider what Jesus Christ, the Lord of glory, has done for you, when He became incarnate. And may the review of this stupendous mercy kindle such a flame of love, as never, never will expire!

The mighty God graciously "made himself of no reputation, and took upon him the form of a servant, and was made in the likeness of men: and, being found in fashion as a man, he humbled himself, and became obedient unto death, even the death of the cross" (Phil. 2:7-8). And why did the ever-blessed Jesus thus humble Himself? Oh, mystery of love! It was to "save his people from their sins" (Matt. 1:21). It was that He, who knew no sin, might be made sin for us, that we might be made the righteousness of God in Him (2 Cor. 5:21). It was "to finish the transgression, and to make an end of sins, and to make reconciliation for iniquity, and to bring in everlasting righteousness (Dan. 9:24).

"Christ died for our sins according to the scriptures" (1 Cor. 15). He has "once suffered for sins, the just for the unjust, that He might bring us to God" (1 Pet. 3:18). He bore "our sins in his own body on the tree, that we, being dead to sins, should live unto righteousness: by whose stripes we were healed" (1 Pet. 2:24). He "was once offered to bear the sins of many" (Heb. 9:28). He is the Lamb of God, that takes away the sin of the world (John 1:29). Jesus, the beloved of the Father, "was manifested, that he might destroy the works of the devil" (1 John 3:8), "that we might live through him" (1 John 4:9), that He might "be the propitiation for our sins" (1 John 4:10), and that He might "be the Saviour of the world" (1 John 4:14). He "gave himself for our sins, that he might deliver us from this present evil world" (Gal. 1:4) and from the wrath to come, and "that through death he might destroy him that had the power of death, that is, the devil" (Heb. 2:14).

These are some of the glorious things which Jesus has done for us in the flesh. That none may despair of salvation on account of their multiplied transgressions, it is further declared in the everlasting gospel that "Christ Jesus came into the world to save sinners" (1 Tim. 1:15), that He "came to seek and to save that which was lost" (Luke 19:10), that He "died for the ungodly" (Rom. 5:6), "that, while we were yet sinners, Christ died for us" (Rom. 5:8), and that "the blood of Jesus Christ…cleanseth us from all sin" (1 John 1:7)—by which precious blood we are redeemed (1 Pet. 1:19) and justified (Rom. 5:9) and by which we, who were sometimes far off, are made near (Eph. 2:13) and obtain the forgiveness of sins (Eph. 1:7).

Jesus is further declared in Scripture to be our peace (Eph. 2:14;), our "wisdom, righteousness, sanctification, and redemption" (1 Cor. 1:30), the "one mediator between God and men" (1 Tim. 2:5), our "advocate with the Father" (1 John 2:1), our compassionate high priest (Heb. 4:15), our all-prevailing intercessor (Heb. 7:25) "who gave himself a ransom for all" (1 Tim. 2:6) and who tasted death for every man (Heb. 2:9). Therefore, says the apostle, "Christ our passover is sacrificed for us" (1 Cor. 5:7). "Christ hath redeemed us from the curse of the law, being made a curse for us" (Gal. 3:13). And the Lord himself declared that He came not to destroy the law, but to fulfill it (Matt. 5:17).

Oh, the depth of the riches both of the wisdom and knowledge of God! (Rom. 11:33). How unsearchable is His wisdom, who can "be just, and [yet] the justifier of him which believeth in Jesus" (Rom. 3:26). A door of hope is now opened to perishing sinners, for, through

Jesus, "we have access by one Spirit unto the Father" (Eph. 2:18). He is the only Savior (Acts 4:12), the only foundation (1 Cor. 3:11), the only way—for no man cometh unto the Father but by Him (John 14:6).

"This is the record, that God hath given to us eternal life, and this life is in his Son" (1 John 5:11). "To him give all the prophets witness, that through his name whosoever believeth in him shall receive remission of sins" (Acts 10:43). "Him hath God exalted with his right hand to be a Prince and a Saviour, for to give repentance to Israel, and forgiveness of sins" (Acts 5:31). "Through this man is preached unto you the forgiveness of sins: And by him all that believe are justified from all things, from which ye could not be justified by the law of Moses" (Acts 13:38-39).

Much, very much more is revealed in the Scriptures of truth concerning the freeness, fullness, and all-sufficiency of this great salvation wrought out for us by the blood of Jesus when He took upon Himself our nature and stood in the place of sinners. But ah, my soul, enough is here written to raise your warmest notes of grateful adoration! May every succeeding meditation on the love of your Redeemer, drawn from the sacred fountain of revealed truth, add fresh fervor to your praise and constrain you to live more to His glory, who loved you and gave Himself for you. "Blessed Savior, increase my faith, while I consider what Thou art now doing in the hearts of Thy people through the influence and agency of the Holy Spirit."

Man, through the fall, was not only excluded from the kingdom of heaven, but was very far gone, gone as far as possible, from original righteousness. The image of God was gone from him, and the image of the evil one was stamped upon him. He became a guilty and polluted creature, unable either to satisfy offended justice or to perform one single act of acceptable obedience. By the fall, he lost all title to the heavenly inheritance and all fitness for the mansions of celestial glory, and thus he became an outcast, an heir of misery and death. To deliver fallen man from this state of condemnation, God sent His only begotten Son into the world, "made of a woman, made under the law, to redeem them that were under the law, that we might receive the adoption of sons" (Gal. 4:4-5).

And in order to prepare and make us fit for the inheritance of the saints in light, God sends the Spirit of His Son into our hearts, enabling us to cry "Abba, Father" (Gal. 4:6). At the creation, God said, "Let there be light: and there was light" (Gen. 1:3). So in the new creation, He shines into our hearts to give us the light of the knowledge of His glory in the face of Jesus Christ.

The first work of the Holy Spirit is to enlighten the eyes of our understanding (Eph. 1:18), to convince us of sin (John 16:8), to show us the spirituality of the law (Rom. 7:9) and the purity of the divine nature (1 Pet. 2:16), to bring us into an intimate acquaintance of our own hearts, that by this knowledge of our own corruption (Jer. 17:9) and helplessness (2 Cor. 3:5) we may be deeply humbled (Job 42:6) and led to seek for deliverance from these evils by the aid of some power greater than our own (Isa. 41:10). Being thus emptied of all self-righteous notions and proud conceptions of our own strength, and groaning under the guilt of sin through a spiritual application of the divine law to our consciences, we are prepared for the joyful reception of the gospel where pardon is freely offered to every coming sinner, and grace, mercy, and peace are extended to the weary and heavy-laden soul.

Thus the Holy Spirit guides us into all truth (John 16:13). He testifies of Christ (John 16:14). He gives us an inward witness of His power and mercy in the conversion of our souls (Rom. 8:16). He makes us the trophies of His victory over sin and death, and, finally, makes us the precious jewels in the Redeemer's crown.

The Spirit carries on the great work of salvation which Jesus began in the days of His flesh when he gave Himself for us that He might redeem us from all iniquity and purify unto Himself a peculiar people zealous of good works. He renewed us in the spirit of our minds (Eph. 4:23) by making us new creatures (2 Cor. 5:17), by sanctifying us wholly in body, soul, and spirit (1 Thess. 5:23), by consecrating us as temples of the Lord Almighty (2 Cor. 6:16), and by filling us with those fruits of righteousness which are by Jesus Christ to the praise and glory of God (Phil. 1:11).

Being, through the operation of the Spirit, united by faith to Jesus Christ, as branches to the vine (John 15:5) and members to the head (Eph. 4:16), we receive out of His fullness grace for grace (John 1:16). We can do all things through Christ who strengthens us (Phil. 4:13), and we are made more than conquerors through Him that has loved us and has given Himself for us (Rom. 8: 37). We are enabled to crucify the flesh (Gal. 5:34), to resist the devil (James 4:7), to renounce the world, to mortify the corrupt affections (Col. 3:5), to walk in newness of life (Rom. 6:4), and to glorify God with our bodies and our spirits, which are His, knowing that we are not our own, being bought with a price (1 Cor. 6:20), even with the precious blood of Christ, as of a lamb without blemish and without spot (1 Pet. 1:19). Thus the love of Christ constrains us to obedience (2 Cor. 5:14). The patience of God leads us to repentance (2 Pet. 3:15). And by all the tender mercies of God, we are sweetly influenced through the Spirit of grace to present our bodies a "living sacrifice, holy, acceptable unto God," which is our reasonable service (Rom. 12:1).

This part of that glorious work of redemption, which Christ performs in us by His Spirit, is so essential that, without it, all our views of gospel truths, however orthodox, and all our trust in His atonement, however consoling, are mere delusions; for "whom he justified, them he also glorified" (Rom. 8:30). Sanctification is as essential to our enjoyment of heaven as justification is to our admittance into it. Without faith, it is impossible to please God (Heb. 11:6). Without holiness, no man shall see the Lord (Heb. 12:14). Happy, then, is the man whose hopes of heaven rest upon these two adamantine pillars, without either of which the fabric cannot stand.

"Blessed Jesus, may my hope be fixed wholly upon Thee. Be my rock, my only confidence, my soul's unbounded trust. While simply resting on Thy great atonement, may I daily feel this inward work of grace, that so Thy living care may perfect what Thy dying love began."

Great God of mercy, hail!
To Thee I lift my voice;
Thy comforts never fail
The faithful to rejoice.

What matchless wonders shine
In rich, redeeming love;
Where attributes divine
In sweetest concord move.

Stern Justice smiles content,
And lays His thunders by,
Since Jesus underwent
The death of Calvary.

The trembling sinner now
Can boldly plead with God:
And mercy can bestow
The pardon bought with blood.

Thy truth, which never fails,
A blessed assurance gives;
For Christ the Lord prevails,
And high in glory lives.

He lives, to intercede;
To send the Spirit down
To help His people's need,
And all His mercies crown.

What depth of sovereign love,
What breadth, before me lies!
Its height is heaven above,
Its length exceeds the skies.

The Two Pillars

An ocean deep and wide,
Where angel minds are lost;
An ever-swelling tide
Refreshing every coast.

How rich the prospect glows
Beyond this vale of tears;
Where crystal water flows,
And verdure crowns the years.

Oh, blessed Spirit, come,
Conduct me, by Thy grace,
To that eternal home
Where I shall see Thy face!

You happy saints, rejoice,
Who feel the Spirit's power;
Lift up your grateful voice,
And wait the joyful hour.

'Twill soon arrive, with smile;
With healing on its wing;
To bear us far from toils,
To Christ our heavenly King.

CHAPTER 30

The Two Ways

"And unto this people thou shalt say, Thus saith the Lord; Behold, I set before you the way of life, and the way of death" (Jer. 21:8). These important words were spoken to the Jews when the king of Babylon was drawing near to besiege the city of Jerusalem. Those who went to the Chaldeans should find the way of life, while those who remained in the city should be in the way of death. But these expressive words may be addressed to all in every age, and more especially to those who live in gospel times.

The commission given by our Lord to His apostles just before His ascension into heaven speaks the same language: "Go ye into all the world, and preach the gospel to every creature. He that believeth and is baptized shall be saved; but he that believeth not shall be damned" (Mark 16:15-16). Thus, faith in Jesus is the way of life; rejection of Him is the way of death. The gospel, therefore, sets before us life and death. Hence, John says: "He that hath the Son hath life; and he that hath not the Son of God hath not life" (1 John 5:12).

In conformity with which truth, John the Baptist declared, when bearing witness to the divinity and messiahship of Jesus: "He that believeth on the Son hath everlasting life: and he that believeth not the Son shall not see life; but the wrath of God abideth on him" (John 3:36). Our Lord declares also respecting Himself, in terms too plain to be misunderstood, "I am the way, the truth, and the life: no man cometh unto the Father, but by me" (John 14:6).

All, then, who receive the Lord Jesus Christ by a true and living faith are in the way of life. They draw near to God by that new and living way which He has consecrated for us; and, persevering in this way, shall reach the heavenly Zion and have right to enter by the gates into the city. This way of life our blessed Lord represents as difficult to fallen nature: "Strait is the gate, and narrow is the way, which leadeth unto life, and few there be that find it" (Matt. 7:14). This difficulty arises not from the road itself, but from the nature of those who walk in it.

The first entrance is truly difficult to the awakened sinner, owing to the abounding evils of his heart, all rising up against the strait, self-denying, flesh-crucifying gate by which he must enter. Grace, however, enables him to overcome these workings of corruption and to pass, by deep repentance and humble faith, through the strait gate. This is a blessed step towards eternal felicity.

But when in the way of life, he finds it narrow, for his desires, being sadly mixed with evil, too often wander after those gratifications which lie beyond the limits of the way in which he is to walk. This grieves the Holy Spirit, wounds his conscience, and occasions that warfare with his corrupt inclinations which constitutes no small part of the fight of faith. He labors to keep his heart within the boundary of the narrow way and to bring every thought into captivity to the obedience of Christ. But still, when he would do good, evil is present with him. The law in his members wars against the law of his mind and compels him to cry out: "O wretched man that I am! who shall deliver me?" (Rom. 7:24). Yet, this painful consciousness of evil is mercifully overruled for good by driving him continually to the strong for salvation—to the Savior. By experience, he learns that his sufficiency is of God; that under all exigencies, the grace of Jesus is sufficient for him; that when he is weak, then he is strong.

The Christian has to journey to the heavenly Canaan through the wilderness of this world; therefore, like the Israelites of old, his soul is sometimes discouraged because of the difficulty of the way. The world frowns, Satan assaults, providences darken, corruptions harass. All these things produce, for a season, much discouragement. Like Peter, he looks at the raging waves instead of at the omnipotent Savior; and then he begins to sink into despondency and would be overwhelmed in the depths of mental affliction, did not the compassionate Jesus stretch out the hand of mercy and uphold him by His mighty power.

He now learns the evil of unbelief and mistrust of a Savior's love. He is much in prayer for the guidance and help of the Holy Spirit, by whose sacred influence and direction he is enabled to look unto Jesus under every trial and to walk before Him in love and childlike obedience. Thus, to every humble pilgrim, strength is imparted; realizing views of the faithfulness of Emmanuel are granted; and he is made to rise superior to every discouragement and to walk, with increasing alacrity and joy, along the narrow way which leads unto life eternal.

How awful is the condition of those who, entering by the wide gate into the broad way, enlarge their desires as hell (Hab. 2:5) until, having filled up the measure of their iniquity, they come, as "vessels of wrath fitted to destruction" (Rom. 9:22), by their own willful transgressions, into the place of everlasting torment.

What a painful consideration that, respecting the narrow way, "few there be that find it" (Matt. 7:14), while of the wide gate our Lord has said: "Many there be which go in thereat" (Matt. 7:13). I am a dying creature walking on the verge of an awful eternity. Heaven and hell lie before me; to one of these places I am, at the close of every day, advanced a day's journey. This day may bring me to my eternal abode of happiness or misery. The sleep which I take this night may be the sleep of death—and should it be so, where would my spirit, dislodged from earth, find itself? Oh, my soul, ask yourself, with all the solemnity which becomes so awful a question, Where am I going? Soon I must be called into the presence of my Judge, but what reception shall I meet with there? What award does conscience now make? Have I believed with the heart unto righteousness? Is the life which I now live a life of faith in the Son of God? I find from the Word of God that two roads lie through the wilderness of this world. The one, at its beginning, is pleasant to carnal nature, being strewed with forbidden pleasures, sensual delights, and materialistic gratifications; but, growing darker, and more crooked and thorny as it advances, it ends abruptly in eternal misery. The other, difficult at the entrance, requires many sacrifices and much self-denial; but, gradually increasing in light and beauty, it terminates in the blissful regions of immortal glory. In which of these roads am I now walking?

"Oh, my beloved Savior! Thou knowest my heart; Thou art acquainted with every thought, affection, and desire that rises within me. Thou knowest that I would follow Thee along the narrow way. Lead me in the paths of righteousness—draw me, and I will run after Thee (S.S. 1:4). Thou art Thyself the way to heavenly glory. When I find a cross laid before me, help me not to turn aside, but give me strength to take it up and follow after Thee. When the travelers in the broad road, with specious arguments and smiling faces, though with aching hearts, would labor to entice me from the path of life, let me not be deceived by their sophistry or ensnared by their wiles. When the clouds of adversity darken my prospects and the night of sorrow obscures my way, then, oh blessed Jesus, support my fainting steps, cheer my drooping soul with Thy celestial promises, and give me strength and courage equal to my day. When Satan tempts and harasses my soul, when inbred evils rise within me and rebel; then, gracious Savior, put forth Thy mighty arm in my defense, lest I fall through manifold temptations from the heavenly road. Thou alone art my strength. In Thee I am strong. Increase my faith that I may be daily united more closely to Thyself. Wean me from the vanities of the world. Screen me from the enticements of sin. Guard me from the fiery darts of Satan. Thus may I walk, oh blessed Emmanuel, in close communion with Thee, in the consolations of Thy Spirit, in the enjoyment of Thy love, in peace of conscience and serenity of mind, until I arrive at the gates of death, where some appointed herald of glory may be stationed to conduct my disembodied spirit into Thy blissful presence, there to dwell with Thee and gaze on Thy glories with rapture and delight forever!"

Oh, could I feel the sweet transforming power,
The holy influence of my heavenly Friend;
Then should I hail the last dissolving hour,
When sin and sorrow would forever end.

A pilgrim journeying through a land of woe,
I daily need the Shepherd's guardian care;
It is He alone my every grief can know,
It is He alone can break the fatal snare.

Blessed Savior, look in pity on my soul,
Enfold me in Thine arms of boundless love;
Permit a traveler on Thy strength to roll
That burden, which Thou only canst remove.

Oh give me faith, to reach the blissful place
Where joyful hope shall to fruition grow;
Where Zion's pilgrims shall behold Thy face,
And ever dwell where living waters flow!

CHAPTER 31

Mercy Rejoicing Against Judgment

The promises of God, which in Christ are yea, and in Him amen, shine with resplendent luster in the pages of eternal truth. Nothing but unbelief can prevent the soul from enjoying the sweetness, or experiencing the purifying efficacy, of those exceeding great and precious promises of grace and mercy. The manner in which many of them are introduced by the prophets must have filled the ancient believers with astonishment. When the prophet, in the name of Jehovah, had been declaring to his rebellious people their multiplied transgressions, we might naturally expect to find the catalogue of their crimes dosed by a denunciation of deserved vengeance and final abandonment. But how great is our surprise to behold mercy rejoicing against judgment, to find that where sin abounded, grace did much more abound.

The following striking passages will fully verify this assertion. In the first chapter of Isaiah, the Jews are called a "sinful nation, a people laden with iniquity, a seed of evil-doers, children that are corrupters" (Isa. 1:4). The Almighty declares His aversion to their "solemn meeting" (Isa. 1:13); that when they spread forth their hands, He would hide His face from them; when they made many prayers, He would not hear. And then, instead of threatened destruction, the prophet adds, "Wash you, make you clean; put away the evil of your doings from before mine eyes; cease to do evil; Learn to do well; seek judgment, relieve the oppressed, judge the fatherless, plead for the widow. Come now, and let us reason together, saith the LORD: though your sins be as scarlet, they shall be as white as snow; though they be red like crimson, they shall be as wool" (Isa. 1:16-18).

In the thirtieth chapter, the sinfulness of the Jews is proclaimed in forsaking the Lord and trusting in the shadows of Egypt. The awful consequences of this departure are declared: "One thousand shall flee at the rebuke of one; at the rebuke of five shall ye flee: till ye be left as a beacon upon the top of a mountain, and as an ensign on an hill. And therefore"—mark the surprising termination—"will the Lord wait, that he may be gracious unto you, and therefore will he be exalted, that he may have mercy upon you: for the Lord is a God of judgment: blessed are all they that wait for him" (Isa. 30:17-18).

Thus we behold the lovely character of our God. Vengeance is His strange work, while mercy is His delight. "As I live, saith the Lord, I have no pleasure in the death of the wicked; but that the wicked turn from his way and live" (Ezek. 33:11). Again, in the thirty-second chapter, the prophet declares: "Many days and years shall ye be troubled, ye careless women.... Upon the land of my people shall come up thorns and briers;... the palaces shall be forsaken; the multitude of the city shall be left; the forts and towers shall be for dens for ever, a joy of wild asses, a pasture of flocks" (Isa. 32:10, 13-14). How long shall this desolation continue? Is the prospect of misery boundless? Ah, no! For thus only shall it be, "until the spirit be poured upon us from on high, and the wilderness be a fruitful field, and the fruitful field be counted for a forest. Then judgment shall dwell in the wilderness, and righteousness remain in the fruitful field. And the work of righteousness shall be peace; and the effect of righteousness quietness and assurance for ever" (vv. 15-17).

Mercy promised forbids despair. Patience leads to repentance. How touchingly beautiful is the following display of judgment and mercy! "Who gave Jacob for a spoil, and Israel to the robbers? did not the Lord, he against whom we have sinned? for they would not walk in his ways, neither were they obedient unto his law. Therefore he hath poured upon him the fury of his anger, and the strength of battle: and it hath set him on fire round about, yet he knew not; and it burned him, yet he laid it not to heart. But now thus saith the Lord that created thee, O Jacob, and he that formed thee, O Israel, Fear not: for I have redeemed thee, I have called thee by thy name; thou art mine. When thou passest through the waters, I will be with thee; and through the rivers, they shall not overflow thee: when thou walkest through the fire, thou shalt not be burned; neither shall the flame kindle upon thee" (Isa. 42:24-25 and 43:1-2).

The almighty Creator, taking, as it were, a survey of His moral creatures, says of His chosen people: "This people have I formed for myself; they shall shew forth my praise. But thou hast not called upon me, O Jacob; but thou hast been weary of me, O Israel. Thou hast not brought me the small cattle of thy burnt offerings; neither hast thou honoured me with thy sacrifices. I have not caused thee to serve with an offering, nor wearied thee with incense. Thou hast bought me no sweet cane with money, neither hast thou filled me with the fat of thy sacrifices: but thou hast made me to serve with thy sins, thou hast wearied me with thine iniquities" (Isa. 43:21-24). Surely now the deserved vengeance will be pronounced. Oh, my soul, read with holy admiration these accents of mercy! "I, even I, am he that blotteth out thy transgressions for mine own sake, and will not remember thy sins" (Isa. 43:25).

Must we not exclaim with David, "There is forgiveness with thee, that thou mayest be feared" (Ps. 130:4)? Must we not acknowledge the force of John's declaration: "We love him, because he first loved us" (1 John 4:19)? Must we not confess with Paul: "Not by works of righteousness which we have done, but according to his mercy he saved us" (Titus 3:5)? How precious are the Scriptures of truth! They are full of the loving-kindness of the Lord, of the goodness of our God.

The few specimens here given will serve to show the extraordinary manner in which the promises are often introduced. The prophet first declares the guilt of God's professing people in order to humble their hearts and convince them of sin. He then proclaims the divine mercy on their true faith and repentance, as is strikingly shown in the first chapter of Isaiah. Well may we join the holy prophet and say: "Sing, O ye heavens; for the LORD hath done it: shout, ye lower parts of the earth: break forth into singing, ye mountains, O forest, and every tree therein: for the Lord hath redeemed Jacob, and glorified himself in Israel" (Isa. 44:23).

Surely mercy rejoices against judgment while it exclaims, in accents of redeeming love: "Deliver him from going down to the pit: I have found a ransom" (Job 33:24). "If any man sin, we have an advocate with the Father, Jesus Christ the righteous" (1 John 2:1). "If we confess our sins, he is faithful and just to forgive us our sins, and to cleanse us from all unrighteousness" (1 John 1:9). "Come, and let us return unto the Lord: for he hath torn, and he will heal us; he hath smitten, and he will bind us up" (Hos. 6:1). "Truly in vain is salvation hoped for from the hills, and from the multitude of mountains: truly in the Lord our God is the salvation of Israel" (Jer. 3:23). "Behold, we come unto thee; for thou art the Lord our God" (Jer. 3:22).

"Bless the Lord, O my soul: and all that is within me, bless his holy name" (Ps. 103:1), for he is a "just God and a Saviour" (Isa. 45:21)—just, and yet the justifier of him that believes in Jesus (Rom. 3:26). "God is love" (1 John 4:8). "Blessed is the man that trusteth in the Lord" (Jer. 17:7).

My soul, in grateful strains record
The love of Thy redeeming Lord;
To all around His praises tell,
Who snatched you from the verge of hell.

Why should Jehovah condescend
To call Himself the sinner's friend?
Or why in terms so sweet proclaim
His mercy in a Father's name?

Blessed Savior, in Thy work I see
Why God is merciful to me;
How He a rebel can receive;
How He can all my sins forgive.

'Tis faith in Thy atoning blood
Averts of wrath the angry flood;
'Tis faith in righteousness divine
Makes all Thy saving merits mine.

Descend, blessed Spirit, from above,
In all the energy of love;
To me Thy heavenly gifts impart,
And seal salvation to my heart.

Then, in those sweet abodes of peace,
Where grateful accents never cease,
A living monument of grace,
I'll strive to sing Thy loudest praise.

CHAPTER 32

Intellectual and Spiritual Light

The whole world lies in wickedness, in a state of spiritual darkness. Out of this darkness, sinners are called by the gospel; and when, through grace, they arise and depart out of this valley of the shadow of death, they are admitted into the marvelous light of the everlasting covenant and become the children of light and of the day. Thus they who once were not a people become the people of God; and they are called beloved, who were once not beloved (Rom. 9:25). Those who were afar off are made near by the blood of Christ, and those who were strangers and foreigners are made fellow-citizens with the saints and of the household of God. Thus grace reigns through righteousness unto eternal life by Jesus Christ our Lord.

Hence a most important and vital distinction must be made between mere intellectual light and the divine illumination of the Holy Spirit—a distinction which, like a powerful scythe, will cut down many a fair herb, many a beautiful flower, in the garden of nature. Natural light, improved by human instruction and study, is confined altogether to the head.

Spiritual light, derived from above, enlightens the understanding, while it renews and purifies the heart. History furnishes us with many instances of men endowed with all the riches of science whose hearts were full of enmity against God, though some happy exceptions have, through grace, blessed and benefited the world.

Intellectual light may soften the character and improve the morals, but experience testifies that nothing but the power of the Holy Spirit can newly create the soul. God works by His Word. Hence the Scriptural exhortation to sinners is: "Awake thou that sleepest, and arise from the dead, and Christ shall give thee light" (Eph. 5:14). When divine power accompanies the command, the dead soul arises to spiritual life and action.

To believers, the command is: "Arise, shine; for thy light is come, and the glory of the Lord is risen upon thee" (Isa. 60:1); and then new vigor and energy is felt in these seasons of refreshing, when Jesus arises on His people with healing in His wings. Spiritual light, thus descending from "the Sun of righteousness" (Mal. 4:2), is received through the medium of the Holy Scriptures, read with prayer, and, through the instrumentality of the gospel, faithfully preached and heard in a spirit of faith. But through whatever channel it is received, it is always communicated by the Holy Spirit and is known by its sanctifying effects on the mind, conscience, and heart.

All who do not possess this spiritual light are in a state of darkness, however bright and luminous their intellectual light may be. How frequently do we find men of science and deep research completely blinded with respect to the divine science of living to God!

And, what is still more painful, how often do we meet with people, in this day of gospel light, who have very clear views of the truth, who are able not only to speak fluently upon the mysteries of grace, but also to delight and edify those who hear them—and yet, who are themselves destitute of true humility, genuine love to the Savior, and that spiritual-mindedness which is life and peace. Thus, however illuminated their understandings may be, they are, in the eye of a heart-searching God, in a state of spiritual blindness.

Surely, then, the above distinction is most important. How many bright professors does it involve in darkness! How many shining candles does it put out! "The natural man receiveth not the things of the Spirit of God: for they are foolishness unto him: neither can he know them, because they are spiritually discerned" (1 Cor. 2:14). "Though I …understand all mysteries, and all knowledge;… and have not charity, I am nothing" (1 Cor. 13:2). "The world by wisdom knew not God" (1 Cor. 1:21). "O that there were such an heart in them, that they would fear me, and keep all my commandments always" (Deut. 5:29). "Not every one that saith unto me, Lord, Lord, shall enter into the kingdom of heaven; but he that doeth the will of my Father which is in heaven" (Matt. 7:21). "If ye know these things, happy are ye if ye do them" (John 13:17). These, and many other passages which might be adduced, prove the immense difference between head knowledge and heart religion. The former is the pride of the hypocrite; the latter is the portion of the humble penitent.

Oh my soul, examine well into your real state and condition before God. Do not be satisfied with how much you know, but see what effect the knowledge which you have attained has upon the heart and life! Are you acquainted with your fallen state by nature and your added wretchedness through actual transgression? If this awful truth has been admitted into your understanding, so far it is well. But rest not here. This is merely intellectual light if its rays extend no further. Search and see whether its piercing beams have reached your conscience and, like forked lightning in the midst of Sinai's thunder, struck you with conviction and dismay. Like Saul of Tarsus, has it struck you to the ground and laid you low in the dust of deep humiliation?

Without this self-abasing experience of the total corruption of your nature, and this heart-humbling sense of your own extreme depravity, all your knowledge is merely human, "taught by the precept of men" (Isa. 29:13), and leaves you in a state of spiritual insensibility—the more dangerous because the more liable to make you contented with the barren knowledge of your condition and to substitute the shadow for the substance.

With respect to all the other great and glorious doctrines of grace, the same important questions must be put to the heart; for faith without works is dead. The Christians to whom Peter wrote were called "out of darkness into his marvelous light" (1 Pet. 2:9). Have I been thus called by sovereign grace, by almighty love, into a light which may be denominated "marvelous"? The mere reception of divine truth into the mind does not deserve this appellation. But, when the light of truth discovers to myself the hidden evils of my heart, when it shows me the deformity of sin, the vileness of my nature, and thus fills me with shame and self-abhorrence, it is, indeed, a "marvelous light."

When the light of truth reveals to my soul the blessed Jesus in the essential dignity of His person; the suitableness of His glorious offices in the covenant of redemption; the greatness, freeness, and extent of His love in becoming man and expiring on the cross that He might save rebellious sinners—when this view of a loving Savior fills my soul with love, admiration, delight, and joy, it may well be called a "marvelous light."

When the light of truth takes away the false glare of the world and shows me its real worth, that all is vanity and vexation of spirit; when everything is placed in its true light and seen through a clear medium; and when this view sobers my expectations and weans my affections from the world—then it is truly a "marvelous light."

When the light of truth unveils the world of spirits and opens to my wondering sight the unutterable glories of eternity; when I behold the blissful seats, the happy mansions, and the peaceful abodes of the redeemed; when I contemplate the fulness of their joy in being forever with their Lord and like their Lord; when this prospect of the saints' felicity makes holiness more lovely and my breathings for the Spirit of grace more ardent; when it makes me long and labor after an admittance, through faith in Jesus, into those bright abodes—then it is a "marvelous light."

"Oh, glorious Sun of Righteousness, light of the world, shine into my heart, that I may be light in the Lord and walk as a child of light, shining, by reflection, to Thy praise and glory! Preserve me from resting in outward forms or barren speculations. Let nothing satisfy my soul but the possession of Thyself, dwelling in my heart by faith and filling me with peace and joy, blended with holy fear. Grant that I may ever prefer Thee to everything in earth or heaven; for Thou, blessed Jesus, with the Father and the Holy Spirit, three Persons in one Jehovah, art alone worthy of all love, adoration, and praise. Everlasting praises shall be given unto Thee by men and angels. Oh my soul, begin now the eternal anthem. However feeble the string, yet let it vibrate to the praise of your God. However weak your notes, yet let them ascend, in grateful adorations, to Him who has loved you and washed you from your sins in His own blood. To Him be all honor, glory, and power, ascribed by every tongue, henceforth and forever. Amen and amen."

Oh Thou, from whom all blessings spring,
Accept the offering which I bring:
A grateful tribute—heartfelt praise,
For all the riches of Thy grace.

Shall I enjoy Thy bounty, Lord,
And not Thy boundless love record?
Oh, let me tell to all around
What joys in Jesus' name abound.

Jesus! Thy saving name contains
Eternal glories—endless gains;
The sinner, pardoned by Thy grace,
Is made Thy chosen dwelling-place.

Bless the Lord, my soul, and sing
Unceasing praises to Thy King,
Whose love through all His counsels shine,
Transcendent, matchless, and divine.

CHAPTER 33

Knowledge and Wisdom

What can be more agreeable to the dictates of true wisdom than that a creature should love and obey its Creator, when that creature is endued with faculties capable of loving and obeying the author of its existence? The reverse of this constitutes the grossest impiety. No man of reflection, however carried away by his passions or perverted in his views of divine revelation, can help allowing that to love the supreme good is the truest wisdom; and to obey the supreme governor, the highest duty.

Yet men, who pass for philosophers, who can unfold the beauties of nature and even expatiate on the charms of virtue, not infrequently are the slaves of sensual pleasure and enemies to the gospel of Christ, thus proving that human knowledge, however refined, can never reduce the rebel state of the affections to the love and fear of God or convert the wild, tumultuous passions to spiritual order and peace.

Men may talk wisely about worldly matters, for our blessed Lord has declared that "the children of this world are in their generation wiser than the children of light" (Luke 16:8); but the wisest worldly character can never, by any natural effort of the understanding, think and act wisely about spiritual and eternal things.

Orthodox notions of the truth may indeed be imbibed while the heart continues under the influence of evil, for we read of people who "hold the truth in unrighteousness" (Rom. 1:18). But true wisdom consists not in the bare knowledge of what is good, but in reducing that knowledge to practice. Thus, I may know that it is my duty to love and obey God; but I am only wise when I really do love and obey Him.

If I had to cross a river in winter, which was frozen over, and were told that, owing to a current in the middle of the stream, the ice would be too weak to bear my weight, this knowledge would only prove beneficial in case I had wisdom enough to desist from the hazardous attempt. Should I, after this knowledge of the state of the ice, still persist in crossing the river, my conduct would be termed recklessness; and, if drowned, men would condemn my folly. This distinction runs through all the transactions of political, civil, and commercial life. The truth is too obvious to need further illustration; it must therefore be apparent, that

> *Knowledge and wisdom, far from being one,*
> *Have oftentimes no connection.*

Job, with beautiful clearness, points out to us the nature of true wisdom. It is not the knowledge of natural objects; neither can created things impart it. "The depth saith, It is not in me: and the sea saith, It is not with me" (Job 28:14). "God understandeth the way thereof, and he knoweth the place thereof" (Job 28:23). "Unto man he said, Behold, the fear of the Lord, that is wisdom; and to depart from evil is understanding" (Job 28:28).

There is in all men a natural desire after happiness. All are anxiously in quest of it. The inquiry is: "Who will shew us any good?" (Ps. 4:6).

Man, having lost his way through the Fall, is now stumbling upon the dark mountains of vanity in search of that treasure which he never can find in earthly things. He needs to be happy. To obtain this blessing, he is willing to forego many present enjoyments.

Some brave the billows of the ocean; others dare the cannon's mouth; multitudes rise early, and late take rest, and eat the bread of carefulness, in order to accumulate those golden stores, which they fondly hope will purchase happiness. Riches perchance increase, but cares and vexatious anxieties grow up together with them. Happiness, like a flying phantom, still eludes their eager grasp, until, compelled at length to give up the chase, they exclaim with Solomon: "All is vanity and vexation of spirit" (Eccl. 1:14).

Here we may ask, Why is man thus restless after an imaginary good? Why does every possession lose its value, and every enjoyment its zest, while that certain something, still desired, yet unpossessed, fastens on the mind and renders all other earthly pleasures comparatively insipid?

Is it not that man was originally created for nobler ends than those which he is now pursuing? He resembles a noble temple in ruins. We see the fragments of ancient grandeur; but they are so mutilated and destroyed that no feeling is excited but that of pain while viewing the desolation.

The gospel, like a guardian angel, points out to man the way to happiness. Here he may know how to obtain felicity; and here, through grace, he may be made wise unto salvation.

Is he anxious to be rich? The gospel unfolds to his view the unsearchable riches while the Spirit is freely offered to enable him, like the wise merchantman in the parable, to sell all and buy this treasure.

Is he thirsting after glory? The gospel reveals to him that honor which comes from God only, and that glory which is prepared for the righteous in a future world.

Is he desirous to obtain a name? The gospel assures him that, if a believer, his name is written in heaven, for the righteous shall be had in everlasting remembrance.

Is he panting after pleasure? The gospel tells him of joy unspeakable, of a peace which passes understanding, of rivers of pleasure which flow at God's right hand for evermore.

Thus the gospel of grace discovers to fallen man not only the nature of true happiness, but the way to obtain it. It shows him the source of all misery, the fall of our first parents, and conducts him to the fountain of all blessedness, God manifest in the flesh.

Through faith in this gracious Deliverer, the soul is saved from the guilt and power of sin. The world and all its vanities, like the retiring tide, recede from the heart, while the joys of God's salvation flow in and fill the soul with substantial and satisfying delights. The sinner made thus wise unto salvation by the eternal Spirit finds the way of peace and becomes at length what worldlings can never be, truly happy.

"Oh, blessed Jesus! Thou in whom are hid all the treasures of wisdom and knowledge, make me wise unto salvation. Preserve me from being satisfied with the false glare of human knowledge, which possesses only the name, but nothing of the qualities, of wisdom.

"Come, divine Redeemer, with all Thy full salvation, into my longing heart. Without Thee, I cannot be happy; with Thee, I cannot be miserable. The world may smile; but if Thou dost frown, I must be wretched. The world may frown; but if Thou dost smile, I am blessed. Let me no longer seek my comforts from creatures, however fair and excellent. 'All my springs are in thee' (Ps. 87:7). Oh, be my all in all, in adverse days and in pleasant seasons. Let Thy grace be in me as a well of water, springing up into everlasting life. Then I shall be holy and happy. All will be serene within, the sweet presage of eternal rest!"

Touched by the power of love divine,
To Thee, my gracious Lord, I come;
Thy Spirit speaks—I hear the call:
Dear Savior, make my heart Thy home.

Too long, alas, a wandering sheep,
Far from Thy blessed fold I strayed;
But now my hopes on Thee are fixed;
On Thee my grateful soul is staid.

Thou art my refuge and my rest,
Sweet peace in Thee I now may find;
The richest streams of heavenly grace,
To soothe and calm my troubled mind.

Oh, may I never from Thee roam;
Or feel a single wish to stray;
Since Thou hast led my wandering feet
To Christ, the true, the living way.

CHAPTER 34

Passive Impressions and Active Habits

It is very important to distinguish rightly between passive impressions and active habits. We are continually liable to receive impressions of one kind or another: impressions of love and aversion, joy and grief, hope and fear. A pleasing representation of a person produces a favorable impression upon the mind, bordering upon love. How common to hear it said, "Your description makes me quite love him"; and yet this is often but a mere impression. The description and the feeling are soon lost in the succeeding objects which crowd upon the mind. Thus, many people are deeply impressed by awful representations of the day of judgment and the horrors of hell, who yet never break off from their sins or turn truly to God.

We often hear of an impressive sermon, a sermon calculated deeply to affect the mind and heart of the congregation. And yet, how seldom do we hear of conversions, which are the consequences of abiding impressions producing active habits. It is a truth that impressions, if only passive, and forming no active habits in the soul, lose their power by repetition.

Hence many people, who were much affected when first they heard the gospel and, in consequence, made some considerable profession, yet, owing to this impression being simply passive, and not leading to the formation of gracious habits in the soul, have become by degrees so gospel-hardened that the sharpest rebuke, as well as the most affectionate entreaty, has lost its edge and influence on their minds; they hear as though they heard not. This view of the subject may lead us to distinguish between what is the operation of natural causes and what is the operation of the Spirit of God.

Impressions, however strong at the time, if merely the result of lively description upon the imagination, will soon wear away, as the imagination loses the vivid coloring which fascinated it—just as the beautiful tints of an evening sky gradually disappear as the sun retires beneath the horizon.

But the impressions made on the soul by the Spirit of God, being of a nature peculiar to themselves, produce an immediate change (though apparently small at first) on the views and feelings of the person affected, which, deepening by repetition, form those active habits that give a new character to the whole man.

Hatred of sin, a holy fear of God, love to the Savior, joy in the Holy Spirit, delight in holiness, patience under suffering, and deadness to the world are the result of those saving, quickening impressions which are made on the heart by the almighty energy of the divine Spirit.

When this is the case, the same subjects which at first impressed, continue to impress. The habits of the soul become more active and holy. Faith waxes stronger, love abounds yet more and more, hope becomes livelier, and obedience in heart and life grows more regular and delightful.

But the same subjects are heard with complete indifference after a time, when the impressions are passive and occasioned by the simple effect of natural eloquence on the mind.

This proves that no oratory, however fascinating, can truly reach the heart or produce gracious habits in the soul if unaccompanied by a divine power. The understanding may be convinced, the conscience may tremble; but the affections can never be firmly fixed upon God through the power of human eloquence or the arts of moral persuasion.

"A new heart also will I give you, and a new spirit will I put within you" (Ezek. 36:26) is both the promise and work of almighty love. Popular ministers of the gospel, who gather crowds of admiring auditors around them, may learn from this subject both humility and dependence.

No eloquence of language, no force of expression, no pathetic appeals to the emotions, can produce one saving impression upon that adamant rock which lies within the human breast. He who commanded Moses to strike the rock must graciously accompany the stroke with His supernatural power, or the waters of true contrition will never flow.

The humble and comparatively weak instrument may from hence take encouragement, knowing that it is not by might, nor by power, but by the Spirit of the Lord, that Satan is dislodged from his stronghold and the sinner saved.

The weakest instrument becomes effective in proportion to the skill and power of him who wields it. Hence, infinite Wisdom is pleased, in general, to employ the weak things of the world to confound the things that are mighty, that no flesh may glory in His presence.

Instances not infrequently occur in the experience of faithful ministers, of sermons, which they had rejected for their supposed lack of good style and arrangement, but which they afterwards preached, for lack of time to write better, being made the blessed instruments of fastening conviction on the conscience and leading the sinner to the cross of Christ; while many an elaborate discourse, on which they had bestowed hours of thought, and from which they expected great results, produced no other effect than that of drawing forth flattering commendation or critical remarks.

We are taught in the Word of God not to despise the day of small things, nor to lean unto our own understanding, nor trust to an arm of flesh. Those holy precepts operated powerfully on the mind and practice of the great apostle to the gentiles. "I…came not," said he to the Corinthians, "with excellency of speech or of wisdom, declaring unto you the testimony of God. For I determined not to know any thing among you, save Jesus Christ, and him crucified.… My speech and my preaching was not with enticing words of man's wisdom, but in demonstration of the Spirit and of power: that your faith should not stand in the wisdom of men, but in the power of God" (1 Cor. 2:1-2, 4-5).

And again, to the Thessalonians he wrote: "As we were allowed of God to be put in trust with the gospel, even so we speak; not as pleasing men, but God, which trieth our hearts. For neither at any time used we flattering words, as ye know, nor a cloke of covetousness; God is witness" (1 Thess. 2:4-5).

And while declaring that the gospel came not unto them in word only, but also in power and in the Holy Spirit, and in much assurance, he rejoiced that they received the Word, which they heard of him, not as the word of men, but as it is in truth, the Word of God, which effectually works in those who believe.

Thus I am taught, that while the ambassadors of Christ are willing to spend and be spent in the blessed work of proclaiming the gospel of peace, it is God alone who can give efficacy to the Word of His grace, according to the purpose of His own will; for His counsel shall stand, and He will do all His pleasure.

Let me then learn to cease from depending on man. May all my expectations be from God, whose power changes the heart and who can form a people unto Himself who shall show forth His praise. "Lord, preserve me from transient feelings and momentary impressions. Give me a deep and an abiding conviction of the evil of sin, a growing love for the blessed Savior, and an increasing relish for holy duties. May I be rooted and grounded in love, established and built up in Christ, and thus enabled to hold the beginning of my confidence steadfast unto the end. The habitual frame of my heart and the daily tenor of my life will then prove the genuineness of my faith and keep me, through the power of the indwelling Spirit, from those awful falls which bring such misery on false professors and cause so many to stumble and forsake the right way of the Lord."

Give me, oh Lord, that holy fear,
That constant dread of sin;
The brightest evidence of grace,
Of light and love within.

Guide me along the narrow way,
Conduct me by Thy grace

To Jesus, my almighty friend,
The sinner's hiding-place.

Oh, for a seraph's tongue to speak
The praises of my God;
Lord, fit my heart to sing Thy praise
In heaven, Thy blest abode.

Until then, I would in lisping notes
Chant forth Thy matchless love;
Adore Thee in the church below,
Then join the church above.

CHAPTER 35

Union to Christ

How beautiful is our Savior's parable of the vine! It illustrates in the most convincing manner this great truth, that "he that hath the Son hath life; and he that hath not the Son of God hath not life" (1 John 5:12). We have in this parable a striking view of the true church of Christ, which grows out of Jesus the true vine, hangs upon Him, and derives all its nourishment and fruitfulness from Him, just as the branches do from the parent stem.

Until the soul be united to Christ by faith, it cannot produce one fruit of the Spirit any more than a branch can bear fruit of itself when severed from the vine. A soul out of Christ, and a branch cut off from the parent stem, must be alike barren and withered.

Hence it is evident that before the great act of justification by faith, that spiritual ingrafting of the soul into Christ, there can be no holy fruits in the heart or life. By this gracious operation of the Holy Spirit, the sinner becomes a living branch in the true vine—a part of Christ's mystical body—and immediately receives spiritual nourishment and strength, for "without me," says Christ, "ye can do nothing" (John 15:5).

But we read of barren branches in Him which are taken away. These are nominal professors of the gospel, which abound in the visible church. They become members of the outward church by the ordinance of baptism; but being destitute of true faith, they yield none of the fruits of righteousness to the glory of God. These characters form the great bulk of the people in nations denominated Christian.

They may be called branches in Christ, considering the church in its present condition as represented by fruitful and barren branches, by wheat and tares, by good and bad fishes, by wise and foolish virgins, in the several parables of our blessed Lord. These barren branches easily fall off in time of temptation. Being attached to Christ only by the slender thread of an outward profession, they are soon blown away by the stormy winds of persecution. Like Demas, they forsake Christ either through the fear of man or the love of this present evil world. But what says our blessed Lord? "Every branch in me that beareth not fruit he taketh away" (John 15:2). The almighty Husbandman at length cuts them off in His providence by the hand of death. But where are they cast? Into the fire of hell, to be burned!

Oh, how should this awaken all my fears and apprehensions, lest I should be found at the last to have been only a barren branch, full indeed of the leaves of profession and the worthless fruit of head-knowledge and party zeal, but destitute of those heavenly graces of humility, love, and purity, which prove the reality of a union to Jesus!

"Every branch in me," said our divine Savior, "that beareth fruit, he purgeth it, that it may bring forth more fruit" (John 15:2). Thus, the pruning-knife of affliction is applied to the true branches to cut off all their exuberances and to render them more abundant in the fruits of holiness.

Hence it is worthy of remark that the very trials which take away the unfruitful branches do, by a skillful operation of spiritual husbandry, promote the fertility of those branches which derive their nourishment by a vital union to the parent stem.

This blessedness is closely connected with perseverance. "Abide in me, and I in you" (John 15:4). There must be a constant abiding in Christ until the hour of death; otherwise there can be no perpetuity of fruitfulness. Let a branch be in a vine for a hundred years and every year be loaded with fruit, yet if it be severed at the last, it must wither and die.

So our union to Christ must be perpetual. Being once in Him, we must abide in Him, or all our fruitfulness will be at an end. "He that abideth in me, and I in him, the same bringeth forth much fruit: for without me, [or severed from me,] ye can do nothing" (John 15:5).

How careful, then, I ought to be, lest I am deceiving myself with mere temporary feelings and impressions. Nothing will abide but true faith. Nothing but true grace can endure unto the end. What sweet privileges are connected with this union and this fruitfulness.

"Herein is my father glorified, that ye bear much fruit" (John 15:8). Thus the more fruit we bear, the more God is glorified. What wonderful condescension!

"So shall ye be my disciples" (John 15:8). This fruitfulness proves us to be the genuine disciples of the Lord Jesus.

"Ye shall ask what ye will, and it shall be done unto you" (John 15:7). Our prayers will then be graciously heard and answered.

"As the father hath loved me, so have I loved you" (John 15:9). Thus, if fruitful believers, we shall through eternity enjoy the Savior's constant love.

These beautiful sayings of Jesus are closed by an exhortation to perseverance: "Continue ye in my love" (John 15:9).

Thus Christ is all and in all to His believing people. He is the true vine from which proceeds all the grace, which, flowing through the branches, produces fertility and beauty. He is also the Sun of Righteousness, whose bright and nourishing beams cause the trees of righteousness to abound in fruitfulness.

Every image is thus used by the divine Spirit, when guiding the pen of inspiration, to set forth the all-sufficiency of both the power and grace of Jesus.

As there is no spiritual life separate from Him, so without Him there is no blessedness in time or eternity. In Him "are hid all the treasures of wisdom and knowledge" (Col. 2:3). In Him "dwelleth all the fulness of the Godhead bodily" (Col. 2:9). Are any chosen unto salvation? They are "chosen…in him before the foundation of the world," that they "should be holy and without blame before him in love" (Eph. 1:4). Are any adopted into the family of God? It is "by Jesus Christ …, according to the good pleasure of his will" (Eph. 1:5). Do any receive pardon? It is "through his blood,... according to the riches of his grace" (Eph. 1:7).

How great, then, is the love of God, in thus giving His well-beloved Son to die for us, that through His precious death upon the cross, He might save us from sin and hell.

But, oh my soul, how great soever the love of God to perishing sinners may be, how rich soever the promises of mercy, how glorious soever the inheritance of the saints—what will all this avail if you are destitute of that faith, without which it is impossible to please God, and of that holiness, without which no man shall see the Lord? I would ask myself with all seriousness, as in the presence of God, who searches the heart and tries the thoughts, Have I received the Lord Jesus into my heart by a humble loving faith?

His name is as ointment poured forth, healing the wounded conscience and shedding a rich fragrance through the soul. But have I felt the deadly wound which sin has made? Have I with joy received the atonement and thus obtained peace through believing? I may have a knowledge of the way of salvation, but have I been brought into this way by the Spirit of truth, and am I walking therein by faith? Do I now experience the power of the cross in the crucifixion of my lusts and the mortification of every sinful desire? Do I know Christ in the power of His resurrection, being raised from a death in sin to a life of righteousness?

"As many as are led by the Spirit of God, they are the sons of God" (Rom. 8:14). Am I daily led by the Spirit through the light of the revealed Word into a saving acquaintance with Jesus Christ as my wisdom, righteousness, sanctification, and redemption?

"If any man be in Christ, he is a new creature" (2 Cor. 5:17). Have I experienced a spiritual change in my understanding, will, and affections? Are my views, purposes, motives, desires, inclinations, and pursuits quite different from what they once were? Can it be said, in the strong language of Scripture, that "I am born again"? Is the change visible to others? Is it felt by myself?

Am I devoted to the service of God, ardent in my love to the Savior, and anxious for the happiness of all around me? Are my religious views and feelings thus influential, pervading—like the hidden sap—all the branches of personal and relative duties?

The doctrines of the gospel are practical in their tendency. They at once humble and elevate. Like rays emanating from the sun, they enlighten, warm, cheer, and fructify. "Shine, then, blessed Savior, with Thy bright beams of grace into my heart. Preserve me from everything that is false and insincere. Let Thy work be deep and abiding. Nothing can uphold me but Thy sustaining grace. Without Thee, I am like the chaff before the wind, like a withered branch ready to be carried away by every blast. Abide in me, blessed Lord, that I may abide in Thee. Unite me to Thyself, and never leave me nor forsake me; then shall I praise Thee with unceasing hallelujahs, when my happy spirit shall be transplanted to the paradise above."

Jesus, true and living vine,
Unite my soul to Thee;
Oh, let my barren, withered heart,
A fruitful scion be.

Too long, alas, my guilty soul
A fruitless branch has been;
Fit fuel for the eternal fire,
The slave of lust and sin.

Oh, may I now, through sovereign grace,
This blessed union know,
From where all peace and pardon too,
And endless glories grow.

Grafted by faith, my joyful heart
Shall be forever Thine;

While clustering fruits of heavenly growth
Will prove the work divine.

Come, Holy Spirit, Thou Lord of life,
Make all these blessings mine;
Make me a fruitful living branch
In Christ, the living vine.

CHAPTER 36

The Christian Character

The beatitudes with which our Lord begins His Sermon on the Mount most strikingly show what is the inward state and outward conduct of true believers, as well as the general reception which such characters meet with from the world.

Their inward state is described by poverty of spirit, mourning for sin, and hungering and thirsting after righteousness and purity of heart; their outward conduct by meekness, mercifulness, and peaceableness. Their general reception from an unbelieving world is declared to be persecution, reviling, and slander. The promises made to the various branches of the Christian character are most encouraging.

The poor in spirit, who are humble on account of sin, who are emptied of all self-righteousness, and who feel their constant need of Jesus, are made the happy partakers of every gospel blessing. Receiving Christ into their hearts by faith, they daily grow in grace and in a fitness for the heavenly inheritance.

The Savior comforts these mourners in Zion, binds up their broken hearts, and gives them beauty for ashes, the oil of joy for mourning, and the garment of praise for the spirit of heaviness. While they are hungering and thirsting after righteousness, the good Shepherd leads them into green pastures and nourishes their souls unto eternal life. They receive the desire of their hearts, even the presence and image of God in their souls.

Being justified by faith, they are accepted in the Beloved; and, being made the temples of the Holy Spirit, they become vessels unto honor, sanctified for the Master's use.

Sincerity and uprightness mark their character. Purity of intention, a hatred of sin, and a love of holiness, flowing from that faith which purifies the heart, prepare them for present manifestations of God in Christ, as revealed in the gospel, and for brighter visions of His glory in the world to come.

With these internal principles and affections, they show forth, by their daily walk and conversation, the praises of Him who has called them out of darkness into marvelous light. They are meek in their words and actions. The law of kindness dwells upon their tongues. They are patient, bearing with one another in love. Thus they avoid many troubles which those endure whose spirits are violent and whose actions are unkind.

They glide along the stream of life upon the still waters of meekness and gentleness, while the contentious and petulant are ever struggling with the rough surges of their own creating. Being firm in purpose, as well as mild in spirit, they cannot always escape the storm; but while they "earnestly contend for the faith which was once delivered unto the saints" (Jude 1:3), when duty calls them so to do, they labor to possess their souls in patience (Luke 21:19) and strive "in meekness instructing those that oppose themselves" (2 Tim. 2:25). When they are reviled, they revile not again; when they suffer, they threaten not; but, committing themselves unto Him who judges righteously and who will one day vindicate the cause of His people, they are kept "in perfect peace" (Isa. 26:3) and, in the truest sense of the promise, "inherit the earth" (Matt. 5:5).

They are merciful when opportunities offer for the exercise of mercy, whether it be in acts of forgiveness or benevolence. Like their heavenly Father, they delight in mercy. Having been much forgiven, they are ready to forgive much, considering that the greatest possible injury done to themselves, when compared with their offenses against God, is but like the hundred pence to the ten thousand talents. They pray for grace to resemble their beneficent Creator, who makes His sun to arise on the evil and on the good and who causes His rain to descend on the just and on the unjust.

They love to do good unto all men, especially to those who are of the household of faith, remembering that gospel precept, "Be not overcome of evil, but overcome evil with good" (Rom. 12:21). They love peace, and they study, as far as is consistent with the truth of the gospel and a good conscience, to live peaceably with all men. They delight in pouring the balm of consolation into the troubled breast and in smoothing the rigors of angry feeling wherever their influence extends.

These are the lineaments of that beautiful character, which is formed by the Holy Spirit; our blessed Savior calls it "the salt of the earth" and "the light of the world" (Matt. 5:13-14) and preserves it from universal corruption and total darkness.

This character is the great preparative for the enjoyment of heavenly glory—and yet, though beloved of God, this is the character which is despised, persecuted, reviled, and slandered by an unbelieving world. No real Christian, bearing this exalted character, need droop or despond, for he is assured by eternal truth itself that great shall be his reward in heaven.

But is this the character of all of the Lord's people, without exception? It is. All do not, indeed, attain to the same degree of holy conformity to Jesus, but all must and do bear this divine image, since it is expressly said: "If any man have not the Spirit of Christ, he is none of his" (Rom. 8:9). All true believers possess these inward principles of holiness, all have these outward marks of true discipleship, all have to encounter the world's derision—though, like the good seed in the parable, there may be in some thirty, in some sixty, and in some a hundred-fold.

Let none of the children of God, then, startle at the sight of the cross, for "all that will live godly in Christ Jesus shall suffer persecution" (2 Tim. 3:12). Rather let them rejoice, since it is recorded by the pen of inspiration: "If we be dead with him, we shall also live with him: if we suffer, we shall also reign with him" (2 Tim. 2:11-12).

Happy, indeed, are they who most resemble the Savior and suffer the most cheerfully for His sake. I learn from these beatitudes that all the graces which our divine Redeemer pronounces blessed meet, like the radii of a circle, in one common center—the heart of the true believer. These graces do not form so many distinct characters, but unitedly they form one character, the child of God. Some of God's children have shone brighter in one grace, and some in another; but each possesses the whole.

Abraham is exhibited to us as a pattern for faith; Job, for patience; Joseph, for purity; Moses, for meekness; Samuel, for integrity; David, for contrition and spiritual-mindedness; Daniel, for devotion; Peter, for zeal; John, for tenderness; Paul, for contempt of the world and delight in the cross—yet all were filled with love, all were clothed with humility, for humility and love are the characteristic features of genuine excellence.

The angels are humble as, standing before the throne of God, they veil their faces with their wings. The glorified saints are humble when, high in bliss, they cast their crowns at the feet of Jesus, exclaiming, "Worthy is the Lamb" (Rev. 5:12).

But oh, amazing thought! Even the great Jehovah, who humbles Himself to behold the things that are in heaven and earth, condescended to empty Himself of all but love and, in infinite compassion, to take upon Him the nature of man and to bleed upon the accursed tree! And for whom did He die? For His rebellious creatures, whom He could in a moment have annihilated and whose place He could have supplied by myriads of holy beings.

This almighty Savior, who inhabits eternity, even now condescends to dwell in the humble and contrite heart, to revive the spirit of the humble, and to revive the heart of the contrite ones. Oh, for faith to contemplate this great sight! Oh, for a heart to feel the power of this grace and to taste the sweetness of this redeeming love! "Lord, come with all Thy full salvation to my soul, that all my powers may be wholly consecrated unto Thee."

Here I behold humility exhibited in its divinest form. Shall we, then, boast of our humility and extol the lowly bendings of a sinful worm? Ah, how little do our most abased feelings deserve the name of humility when contrasted with the inconceivable abasement of the eternal Word, when He was made flesh and dwelt among us!

Look and gaze, oh my soul, on your condescending Savior, until you are laid prostrate in the dust of humiliation at the foot of the cross; and there drink deep into that spirit which will assimilate you to the Friend of sinners and prepare you for the bliss of heaven. Oh, how should I loathe myself! He, so humble, and I, so proud; He, so pure, and I, so polluted!

The thirsty traveler sees a cistern at a distance and labors hard to reach it; but when he comes with longing desire to quench his thirst, he finds it broken. Thus earth disappoints all who trust in its supplies. It is a broken cistern. I look for its refreshing streams but find none. Where, then, must I turn? To the Fountain of living waters. Jesus is this fountain of life and glory. To Him I would now hasten. In Him I shall ever find a never-failing stream of grace and comfort. He can delight and refresh my soul; and, coming unto Him by faith, I shall never be disappointed.

From these considerations I learn that to seek first the kingdom of God and His righteousness is the highest wisdom of man; for, while so doing, all other needful things shall be added unto me. I also learn that Jesus has made an inseparable connection between the precepts and promises of the gospel, between the character and the privileges of His people.

If I am renewed in the spirit of my mind, and thus made humble, contrite, meek, spiritually minded, pure, and peaceable, I shall enjoy His presence and love while journeying through this valley of tears and His everlasting glory in the world above.

Then why should the souls of the faithful be discouraged because of the hardness of the way (Num. 21:4), seeing that the way of the cross is the way to the crown? The world may light up its fires; friends may betray us to death; Satan may roar like a lion; the flesh may cry out for indulgence and tempt us to yield to our foes—yet, if Jesus be the God of our hearts, He will raise us above every temptation; He will strengthen us for every assault; and, at length, He will make us more than conquerors, to the praise and glory of His grace.

> Oh, love without compare,
> Oh, love beyond degree;
> That He, whom cherubim adore,
> Should bleed and die for me!
>
> For me, a wretch so vile,
> For me, a rebel worm,
> His love its sacred power displayed,
> In its divinest form.
>
> It is Jesus died to save,
> It is Jesus lives to bless;
> On high He dwells—the sinner's friend,
> The Lord, our righteousness.
>
> Then, oh my soul, rejoice,
> Extol your Savior's name;
> Make mention of His dying love,
> And celebrate His fame.
>
> He claims your heart, your love;
> He claims you for His own;
> Oh cast yourself in willing bonds
> Before His heavenly throne.

CHAPTER 37

Christian Motives

Christianity has justly been called a religion of motives—and yet, alas, how little are those sublime motives to action, which the gospel inspires, considered by the great mass of professing Christians!

Men carry out their worldly concerns under the powerful influence of some constraining motive which impels them forward with unabating ardor. But in the affairs of eternity, they commonly act at random, without any fixed purpose whatever. Education, or custom, gives the coloring to their religion; and if they are asked to give a reason of the hope that is in them, a total absence of motive or purpose will soon be discovered.

They think as the world thinks, and they act as the world acts. Treading in the steps of their forefathers, they retain the impression of early habits. And finding little leisure, amid the accumulating engagements of life, to investigate the claims of eternity, they are satisfied with the observance of outward ordinances and a few crude notions of the Christian religion.

They pity those who are so weak as to prefer future to present enjoyments, and they can scarcely conceive any rational motive sufficiently powerful to induce men to pass by the flattering prospects of the world for the unseen possessions of futurity. Hence they condemn such people as visionary and enthusiastic, while they applaud the wisdom of those who endeavor to make sure of present profit and advantage. To secure the main prospect is their standard of wisdom, their highest object of pursuit.

This, we may fear, is but too faithful a picture of thousands who call themselves Christians but who possess nothing beyond the name. Esteeming themselves wise, they become fools—and will, except they repent, eternally bewail their folly.

It is of immense importance to examine well into the motives of our actions, for "whatsoever is not of faith is sin" (Rom. 14:23).

Saul of Tarsus in his blind zeal conceived that he ought to do many things contrary to the name of Jesus of Nazareth; but when his understanding was enlightened, he saw himself to have been a persecutor, a blasphemer, and an injurer.

When Abraham went to offer up his beloved Isaac, it was an eminent instance of faith. He acted on this trying occasion from a good motive, in simple compliance with a divine command, though it was an apparent frustration of a divine promise. Yet he believed God and cheerfully obeyed His will.

This childlike reliance on the truth and faithfulness of Jehovah was honored by a rich promise of abundant blessings. But when the Israelites, on the contrary, caused their children to pass through the fire to Moloch, it was an awful instance of human depravity. Their conduct sprang from a bad motive, being in direct violation of a divine prohibition, and was therefore quickly followed by heavy judgments upon the nation.

The command to Abraham was designed by the Almighty to be a trial of his faith, a test of his obedience, a proof of his love. But more especially to Abraham was a signal representation of His own unspeakable love, in not withholding His own—His well-beloved Son—from us, when He gave Him to be a sacrifice for sin on one of those very mountains of Moriah.

Now, can anyone for a moment suppose that these two actions—sacrifice of Isaac to God and sacrifice of children to Moloch—shall receive the same recompense of reward? We shudder while we contemplate the unnatural infatuation of the idolatrous Israelites. We feel humbled while we meditate on the astonishing exercise of faith, obedience, and self-denial which was exhibited in the case of Abraham.

Their motives were as widely distant as the east is from the west, as distant as holy faith is from rebellious unbelief.

Some actions are criminal in their very nature, while others may be good or bad according to the motives from where they spring. The hypocrites, whom Jesus condemns in His Sermon on the Mount, gave alms, and prayed, and fasted. But when they distributed their charities, they sounded a trumpet before them; when they prayed, they stood in the synagogues and in the corners of the streets; when they fasted, they disfigured their faces—thus making their religious performance as public as possible. And why did they take such pains to be seen? Our Lord tells us: "That they may have glory of men" (Matt. 6:2). They obtained that which was the governing motive of their actions, and consequently they had their reward.

Our blessed Savior exhorts His people to the performance of the same duties, but from a far different motive. Secrecy in giving, retirement in devotion, and unostentatiousness in fasting are opposed to pharisaical display. Duties, thus performed from a principle of faith and love, and directed simply to the glory of God, will be approved of by Him who sees in secret and who will graciously reward them openly.

We hear of a man extolled for his charity and benevolence to the poor. His name appears in the list of benefactors to almost every laudable institution; but if to be extolled is the secret motive of his actions, this man has his reward.

Another is very regular in his attendance on public ordinances. His seat is never vacant. He talks much about doctrines and seeks the society of religious people. Hence he obtains the appellation of pious. If to be so esteemed is the moving spring of his conduct, truly he has his reward.

All this is equitable. Those who act from no higher motive than human approbation, on receiving such commendation, have their coveted reward.

They may speak with the tongues of men and of angels; they may understand all mysteries and all knowledge; they may bestow all their goods to feed the poor; yes, in a season of fiery persecution they may even give their bodies to be burned—and yet, if faith working by love is not their principle of action, all these splendid gifts and costly sacrifices will profit them nothing. In the day of judgment, they will be found no better than sounding brass or a tinkling cymbal (1 Cor. 13), while the widow's mite (Mark 12:42-44), and the cup of cold water given to the least of the brethren of Jesus (Matt. 10:42), out of love to His name, shall in no way lose its reward.

How important then is self-examination! How necessary to ascertain the motives of our actions, lest self-seeking, vainglory, and the desire of human applause should render them odious in the sight of God.

Oh, that I may never forget this gospel truth, that no work is accounted good in the judgment of heaven, but what springs from faith in Jesus Christ. Therefore, until I am united to Christ by faith and justified through His righteousness, all my boasted moral virtues are nothing but "splendid sins." Brought to this touchstone, how many actions, highly esteemed and far-famed among men, will be rejected as "reprobate silver" by that holy Being who searches the heart and tries the reins. For lack of due consideration in time, many thousands, it is to be feared, will reap the fruit of their criminal indifference through an awful eternity.

From this view of the subject, I learn that where there is a desire to serve God, it is accepted according to that a man has, and not according to that he has not. The holy purpose will be recognized, even when circumstances prevent the performance. Nathan, when informed of David's purpose to build a house for the God of Israel, said: "Go, do all that is in thine heart; for the LORD is with thee" (2 Sam. 7:3).

David, though not permitted to erect the temple, received the most gracious assurance of the divine approbation, which Solomon took special notice of in his beautiful prayer at its dedication: "The LORD said unto David my father, Whereas it was in thine heart to build an house unto my name, thou didst well that it was in thine heart. Nevertheless thou shalt not build the house; but thy son that shall come forth out of thy loins, he shall build the house unto my name" (1 Kings 8:18-19).

Let no one then despise the day of small things, since the inward ardent desire to promote the cause of Christ in the earth may be accomplished through the good hand of our God upon us (Ezra 7:9), by our children, and our children's children.

"Blessed Lord, be pleased to give me the precious grace of simplicity and godly sincerity. May all my desires be to Thee, and to the glory of Thy name. Reign in my heart the Lord of every motion there. Purify my motives. Elevate my purposes. Preserve me from seeking the applause of men. Guard me from the poisonous influence of flattery and self-love. Clothe me with humility; and whatever I do in word or deed, may I do all in the name of the Lord Jesus."

Assist Thy servant, Lord, to pray;
Illuminate my mind;
Oh, guide me in that heavenly way,
Where sinners comfort find.

In mercy, Lord, Thine ear incline
To every fervent prayer;
Let rays of love, and grace divine,
My soul for heaven prepare.

Reveal Thy great salvation, Lord,
Dispel each rising doubt;
Oh, speak that soul-enlivening word,
"Your sins are blotted out."

Then shall I raise the cheerful song.
To my redeeming God;
And join the raptured choral throng,
In Zion's blest abode.

CHAPTER 38

Christian Conversation

The spirit in which Christian speech should be conducted is delineated with peculiar accuracy in the Word of God. How delightful would be the society of professing Christians if the humble, loving, gracious, improving spirit, so much enforced in the Holy Scriptures, filled every circle. How needful, then, at all times is the prayer of David: "Set a watch, O Lord, before my mouth; keep the door of my lips" (Ps. 141:3).

The true believer is a new creature. He is surrounded by a holy atmosphere in which the trifler cannot live. As his motives are elevated, so his conversation is pure. The giddy and the vain avoid his society, not because he is repulsive in manner, but because his views and feelings are so spiritual and heavenly. He is ridiculed as "the saint" and taxed with pride and self-conceit. But his heart is known unto God, with whom he holds sweet converse in the midst of an ungodly world. Such is the Christian. His character is little understood by the thoughtless multitude, whose time is occupied and whose affections are absorbed in the trifles of the day. But before long he shall shine as the sun in the kingdom of his Father.

The following suggestions may tend to improve our fellowship with each other.

We ought never to speak unfavorably, not even by insinuation, of absent people, except when duty positively requires it; and even then, there should be a marked and sincere regret that the occasion calls for such an exposure of character.

We must guard against attributing wrong motives to the actions of others, even when appearances might favor such a conclusion, remembering that God alone knows the heart—and who are we, that we should judge our brother?

We should avoid every thing that borders upon flattering adulation, especially towards those who are present, knowing how pernicious praise is to a fallen creature and how few are able to withstand its influence.

This does not exclude a proper commendation, or a suitable encouragement, when dictated by Christian simplicity and prudence.

We must not indulge in those exaggerations, those strong hyperboles, those embellished representations, which seem to give force to conversation, but which actually destroy its delicacy and beauty. This mode of speaking, by stretching out too far, touches upon the confines of falsehood. Truth appears most beautiful in its own native simplicity.

Christian conversation is marked by love, humility, and purity. These are the peculiar features by which it is known. Although so attractive from its nature and excellence, yet how few know how to appreciate or relish its charms.

Love leads us to converse with delight on all subjects connected with the glory of God and the good of man. Humility draws a veil over her own graces and delicately discovers the excellencies of others. It frankly confesses our own faults and carefully conceals the failings of our brethren. Purity, like the refreshing rose, sheds a fragrance peculiarly its own over our whole conversation; and, like that lovely flower, leaves its reviving scent when we are gone.

How different from the conversation of the wicked, whose throat is compared in Scripture to an open sepulcher, loathsome and offensive, disgusting and pestilential.

We naturally love to discourse on subjects which lie nearest our hearts. No wonder, then, if real Christians, who feel the love of Christ constraining them, delight to talk together on the most glorious of all subjects, the love of God in the gift of His Son. May not believers now say with the disciples of old: "Did not our heart burn within us, while he talked with us by the way?" (Luke 24:32).

But, alas, how little is there of this spiritual discourse among us! The men of the world, when they meet together, can enter with enthusiastic ardor on their various objects of pursuit, whether political, commercial, or philosophical. The warrior recounts his battles, the sportsman his pleasures, the merchant his adventures, the politician his schemes, the philosopher his discovery, the worldling his excesses, with a feeling and animation which demonstrate at once that his soul is engaged in the subject. And shall Christians be less alive when they meet together for the avowed purpose of strengthening each other's hearts and kindling each other's devotion? If our faith and love were stronger, our communion would be more profitable and delightful.

In this our day of outward prosperity and religious liberty, there is a great danger of imbibing a worldly spirit and of allowing our fellowship to degenerate into religious trifling and religious gossiping. The conversation of too many, although it may be technically called religious, resembles the cloud and the well without water, so strongly reprobated by Peter (2 Pet. 2:17). When such people separate from each other, they feel no real good derived to their souls. And why? Because their conversation was destitute of that "unction from the Holy One" (1 John 2:20), which is life and peace.

Jesus and His salvation—heart experience and genuine godliness, as felt and exhibited in the soul and conduct of the believer—were not the subject matter of discourse. The head, and not the heart, was called into exercise. Some religious publication, some popular preacher, some recent occurrence, some commonplace remarks filled up the hour; and no wonder if the mind, at parting, retained its usual flatness and leanness after such an insubstantial meal.

If it be asked, Must our conversation be altogether confined to evangelical subjects? we answer that our conversation must always be in the spirit of the gospel. If our hearts be right, we shall always have one end in view: the glory of God and the edification of our neighbor.

With this aim constantly before us, we shall not wander far from true Christian discourse. The danger arises from entering on religious conversation without religious motives and religious affections, and from having a desire to talk merely for the sake of talking. The apostolic injunction, "Whatsoever ye do in word or deed, do all in the name of the Lord Jesus" (Col. 3:17), if duly obeyed, would cut off every idle and unprofitable word.

How pertinent is Malachi on this point: "Then they that feared the Lord spake often one to another: and the Lord hearkened, and heard it, and a book of remembrance was written before him for those who feared the Lord, and that thought upon his name. And they shall be mine, saith the Lord of hosts, in that day when I make up my jewels; and I will spare them, as a man spareth his own son that serveth him" (Mal. 3:16-17). From the whole tenor of this beautiful passage, we may be assured that what these believers spoke about so often one to another was highly pleasing to the Lord of hosts. He was their theme. Their delight was in Him. They feared the Lord and thought upon His name.

The following portions of Scripture may serve to show the nature and spirit of godly conversation:

"Hear, O Israel: The Lord our God is one Lord: And thou shalt love the Lord thy God with all thine heart, and with all thy soul, and with all thy might. And these words, which I command thee this day, shall be in thine heart: And thou shalt teach them diligently unto thy children, and shalt talk of them when thou sittest in thine house, and when thou walkest by the way, and when thou liest down, and when thou risest up" (Deut. 6:4-7). "My tongue shall speak of thy righteousness and of thy praise all the day long" (Ps. 35:28). "I will meditate also of all thy work, and talk of thy doings" (Ps. 77:12). "My tongue shall speak of thy word: for all thy commandments are righteousness" (Ps. 119:172). "The mouth of a righteous man is a well of life" (Prov. 10:11). "In the lips of him that hath understanding wisdom is found" (v. 13). "The tongue of the just is as choice silver" (v. 20). "The lips of the righteous feed many" (v. 21). "The mouth of the just bringeth forth wisdom" (v. 31). "The lips of the righteous know what is acceptable" (v. 32). "The lips of the wise disperse knowledge" (Prov. 15:7). "The lips of knowledge are a precious jewel" (Prov. 20:15). "A good man out of the good treasure of the heart bringeth forth good things" (Matt. 12:35). "Let no corrupt communication proceed out of your mouth, but that which is good to the use of edifying, that it may minister grace unto the hearers" (Eph. 4:29). "Let the word of Christ dwell in you richly in all wisdom; teaching and admonishing one another in psalms and hymns and spiritual songs, singing with grace in your hearts to the Lord" (Col. 3:16). "Let your speech be always with grace, seasoned with salt, that ye may know how ye ought to answer every man" (Col. 4:6). "Comfort yourselves together, and edify one another" (1 Thess. 5:11). "Speak evil of no man" (Titus 3:2). "Exhort one another daily, while it is called To day; lest any of you be hardened through the deceitfulness of sin" (Heb. 3:13).

The blessed Jesus, who will shortly come in the clouds of heaven to judge the world, has solemnly declared that "every idle word that men shall speak, they shall give account thereof in the day of judgment. For by thy words thou shalt be justified, and by thy words thou shalt be condemned" (Matt. 12:36-37). "Not every one that saith unto me, Lord, Lord, shall enter into the kingdom of heaven; but he that doeth the will of my Father which is in heaven" (Matt. 7:21). "Why call ye me, Lord, Lord, and do not the things which I say?" (Luke 6:46). "If ye love me, keep my commandments" (John 14:15).

"Blessed Savior, be pleased to touch my lips with a live coal from Thine altar! Preserve me from a vain and trifling spirit. Solemnize my mind. Spiritualize my affections. Give me to feel the importance of eternal things. Shed abroad Thy love in my heart, and may the law of kindness dwell upon my tongue. Make me an instrument in Thy hands of good to others. While laboring to promote the cause of truth by spiritual conversation, may I feel the blessedness of Thy gospel in my own soul. Keep me from self-seeking and from slavish fear. Enable me to speak and act for Thee, and never to dread the frowns of dying worms. With increasing fervor may I love the society of Thy people, and find my happiness in sweet communion with Thee, my Savior and my God."

How sweet to bless the Lord,
And in His praises join;
With saints His goodness to record,
And hymn His power divine!

These seasons of delight,
This soul-refreshing gleam,
These rays of pure eternal light,
Demand the grateful theme.

Oh blessed Jesus, pour
Thy quickening spirit down;
That I, from this delightful hour,
Thy work of grace may crown.

May every waiting heart
His faithful witness prove;
And know its own eternal part
In Thy redeeming love.

Oh, blest assurance this,
Bright beam of heavenly day;
Sweet earnest of eternal bliss,
To cheer the pilgrim's way.

Thus will our joys increase,
Our love more ardent grow;
While all the fruits of faith and peace
Refresh our souls below.

But oh, the bliss sublime,
When joy shall be complete;
In that unclouded, glorious clime,
Where all Thy servants meet.

There shall the ransomed throng
A Savior's love record;
And shout, in everlasting song,
Salvation to the Lord!

CHAPTER 39

Christian Privilege

Under the old dispensation, many of the great privileges of the church of God were veiled under emblems and figures drawn from natural objects. The psalms of David and the writings of the prophets abound with the most beautiful images to describe the power, faithfulness, and love of Jehovah.

Under the new dispensation the veil is removed, and they are revealed in all their glory and beauty to the eye of faith. Life and immortality are brought to light by the gospel. But, as in former ages, so now, the natural man receives not the things of the Spirit of God, neither can he know them, because they are spiritually discerned—yes, they are foolishness unto him. Hence the gospel is to those who perish, foolishness; but to those who are saved, it is the power of God and the wisdom of God (1 Cor. 1:18). Happy are they who are thus taught of God, for the secret of the Lord is with those who fear Him, and He will show them His covenant.

Man is naturally blind to his real condition as a guilty, condemned sinner. Enjoying the pleasures of time, he never inquires after those of eternity. Satisfied with earth, he feels no desire for heaven, except as it presents to his mind an exemption from pain and suffering.

All men naturally prefer ease to pain. Hence heaven on this account is preferable to hell. Such is the estimate which wretched fallen man forms of heavenly bliss! Ignorant of himself and ignorant of God, he is led captive by Satan at his will, until sovereign grace redeems him out of the hand of the enemy.

The first truth which the divine Spirit discloses to the awakened conscience is our lost and undone state by nature.

This discovery is attended with the deepest self-abasement, with brokenness of heart, with anxious desires after salvation, and with a desire for salvation from present sin as well as from future punishment.

The convinced sinner, made sensible of the guilt and burden of transgression, now longs for heaven as a state of rest from sin, as well as a state of rest from suffering. But, alas, feeling his inability to think a good thought, and overwhelmed with the view of his iniquities, he anxiously inquires, "How shall man be just with God?" What must I do to be saved?

Another precious truth, hidden from the natural man, is revealed to his opening mind by the same Spirit who so graciously implanted in his heart that fear of the Lord, which is the beginning of wisdom. Jesus, as exhibited in the gospel to a dying world, is savingly manifested to the humble, trembling, believing sinner in all His glorious offices of Prophet, Priest, and King. How kind is God, how full of mercy and love! When He implants a holy fear, He imparts also a principle of saving faith.

Jesus is now beheld and apprehended as the sinner's only atonement, righteousness, and refuge; as the only way to the Father; and as the only advocate with Him. He is viewed by the eye of faith as the chief among ten thousand. He is esteemed precious, above all earthly or heavenly objects. Angels and men, as His creatures, sink into the shade, while the glories of Emmanuel, God with us, are now seen to fill heaven and earth with their resplendent brightness.

The next great secret which the Spirit reveals to those who truly fear God is the fitness of Jesus to meet all the needs of His people. Being delighted with the perfections of the Savior, the believer is filled with admiration and gratitude at the view of their suitableness to his own personal necessities.

He now loves to contemplate his gracious Redeemer in His twofold character: what He is in Himself, and what He is to His people. He knows how to appreciate and to apply, through the teaching of the

Spirit, the excellencies of Jesus to his own soul. He comes to Him daily for wisdom, righteousness, and strength. He leans wholly upon His supporting arm. He lives upon the promises of His grace and rejoices in hope of the glory of God. He delights in this way of access by faith to a mercy-seat, obtains through Jesus the blessings he needs, and thus finds Him at all times his all in all. This is happiness. This is the King's highway to heaven. This is the way in which the flock of Christ has trod in every age. "Lord, lead me forth by the footsteps of the flock. Make me a follower of it, which through faith and patience is inheriting the promises."

But this is not all. The sinner is not only made to see his lost estate by nature, the glories of the Redeemer, and the Savior's fitness to all his necessities, but another gracious truth is unfolded to him. He is enabled to know and to rejoice in his own personal interest in all the blessedness of his purchased inheritance. He can say with the church of old, "This is my beloved, and this is my friend" (Song 5:16). "This God is my God." "He is become my salvation" (Exod. 15:2). "I know whom I have believed" (2 Tim. 1:12). How sweet is this secret of the Lord! It begets humility, gratitude, zeal, and obedience. It quickens love and animates faith. It increases watchfulness and holy living. It lays the soul prostrate at the foot of the cross, while it elevates the affections to the pure regions where Christ sits at the right hand of God.

This glorious revelation is vouchsafed to those who truly fear God—not always in equal measure, but in such a degree and at such times as infinite love and wisdom deem best. All the children of God should strive after this blessed assurance of faith. It is not the presumption, but the exalted privilege, of the obedient believer. Those have low views of Christian privilege who deem it arrogant to expect the knowledge of the forgiveness of our sins.

All who believe with the heart unto righteousness, all who love the Lord Jesus Christ in sincerity, all who walk humbly with their God, may know assuredly that their sins are blotted out; for He pardons and absolves all those who truly repent and unfeignedly believe His holy gospel.

"Lord, be graciously pleased to give me a holy, filial fear; a humble, loving, obedient spirit; a deadness to the world; and a devotedness of heart to Thee; a renunciation of self, and a cordial reception of Christ, in all His saving merits and mercies. Thus, blessed Savior, let me lie passive in Thy hands, waiting Thy presence and desirous only that Thy will may be accomplished in me, until it please Thee to call me to Thy kingdom above, where all darkness and doubt shall forever flee away."

Amid all these riches of grace, another secret is unfolded: that "all things work together for good to them that love God, to them who are the called according to his purpose" (Rom. 8:28). Man is naturally anxious about tomorrow. He sees all dark before him, and imagination conjures up a thousand fears. He suffers more from imagined than from real evils. He creates a world of misery to himself by dire forebodings and anxious glances into future days. Not so when faith, love, and filial confidence in God, his heavenly Father, fill his breast. This gracious promise is then fulfilled: "Thou wilt keep him in perfect peace, whose mind is stayed on thee" (Isa. 26:3).

Calmly he leaves events with God. He studiously performs the present duties and leaves the consequences with Him, who has said: "Seek ye first the kingdom of God, and his righteousness; and all these things shall be added unto you" (Matt. 6:33).

Such is the life of faith in the Son of God. It is a life of holiness and happiness.

Many, indeed, are the afflictions of the righteous, afflictions peculiar to themselves as well as afflictions endured in common with their fellow-men; but many also are their supports and consolations. These are truly peculiar to themselves, unknown and unfelt by a suffering, unbelieving world. Even here, while sojourning through a valley of tears, they partake of the "hidden manna" (Rev. 2:17) and draw many a refreshing draught from the fountain of living waters. But their blessedness does not end here. The glorious secret, which gladdens their hearts under all their sorrows, is their future destination. They shall be "heirs of God, and joint-heirs with Christ" (Rom. 8:17). They shall sit down with Christ on His throne and reign with Him forever and ever

(Rev. 3:21). What heart can conceive the felicity of the redeemed when all terrestrial things shall have passed away!

"Lord, make me a tree of righteousness, and then I shall experience Thy heavenly beams of love! Should the rough wind of persecution, or needful trials, shake my branches, or even tear away many valued comforts, yet may I, under every bereavement, repose on Thy faithfulness and rejoice in Thy love."

As God in Christ is the fountain of all felicity, infinitely happy in Himself, and the source of true felicity to His creatures, so their blessedness is founded on His truth, secured by His oath, and sealed by His blood; for "Wherein God, willing more abundantly to shew unto the heirs of promise the immutability of his counsel, confirmed it by an oath: that by two immutable things, in which it was impossible for God to lie, we might have a strong consolation, who have fled for refuge to lay hold upon the hope set before us: Which hope we have as an anchor of the soul, both sure and stedfast, and which entereth into that within the veil; whither the forerunner is for us entered, even Jesus, made an high priest for ever after the order of Melchisedec" (Heb. 6:17-20).

Oh, what rich discoveries are these, which are experimentally and practically made known to all who fear God! Such happy souls may well join with the enraptured prophet, and say: "O LORD, I will praise thee: though thou wast angry with me, thine anger is turned away, and thou comfortedst me. Behold, God is my salvation; I will trust, and not be afraid: for the LORD JEHOVAH is my strength and my song; he also is become my salvation. Therefore with joy shall ye draw water out of the wells of salvation" (Isa. 12:1-3).

"Blessed Lord, reveal Thy truth, so full of grace and glory to my heart, in all its saving influence. Warm, yes, inflame my soul with the pure celestial fire of love. Illuminate my mind, and transform me daily more and more into Thy image until, awaking up after Thy likeness, I shall be eternally satisfied with it."

Blessed Jesus, look upon me
With a smile of heavenly love;
Draw my heart and fix it on Thee,
Never let it thence remove.

Lord, I feel a sinful nature
Tending downwards to the earth;
Save a lost and ruined creature,
Save me through the second birth.

Come, oh great eternal Spirit,
Pour Thy influence over my soul;
Let me now Thy peace inherit,
Make a wounded sinner whole.

Put Thy holy fear within me,
Make Thy gracious secrets known,
Daily may I know and love Thee,
Daily all Thy mercies own.

Jesus, plead my cause in heaven;
Be my advocate on high,
All the praise to Thee be given,
Through a vast eternity.

CHAPTER 40

Agreement Necessary to Communion

The question of Amos is of practical importance: "Can two walk together, except they be agreed?" (Amos 3:3). There can be no real communion or pleasing communion without a similarity of views and dispositions.

What can be more opposite than the carnal and the spiritual mind? A spiritually minded man delights in heavenly things. He views the world through the sacred medium of divine revelation and beholds it as the abode of sin, as a place of trial, as the valley of the shadow of death. While, therefore, he blesses his heavenly Father for every undeserved mercy and receives with gratitude the bounties of His providence, he longs for that glorious rest from sin and sorrow, which remains to the people of God. His treasure and heart are in heaven, where joy and happiness fill every ransomed soul in the beatific presence of God and the Lamb. Being born from above, he loves his heavenly Father; being united to Christ by faith, he derives all his strength from Him; being under the immediate guidance of the Holy Spirit, he is led into all truth and is made a new creature in Christ Jesus.

As he loves God, so he loves all the children of God. He delights in the company, and sedulously cultivates the friendship, of genuine Christians. He can say with David, "I am a companion of all them that fear thee" (Ps. 119:63). His delight is in the excellent of the earth, and in such as excel in virtue (Ps. 16:3). With expanded views and enlarged heart, he can love all who love the Lord Jesus Christ in sincerity, though all may not agree with him on minor points of difference. All who follow Christ in simplicity of spirit, and adorn the doctrine of God their

Savior by the purity of their hearts and the holiness of their lives, are hailed by him as brethren, traveling to the heavenly Zion.

The unconverted man is the opposite of all this. He cannot endure to bear religion discoursed upon in his presence. By a frown, a sarcasm, or a significant silence, he soon manifests his displeasure. The people of God are offensive to him. Should some unhappy characters, by their inconsistency or misconduct, dishonor the holy religion of Jesus, he ceases not to hold them up as patterns of the whole fraternity of professing Christians, thus putting the stamp of hypocrisy upon all without exception. His manner evidences the exquisitely malignant pleasure which he finds in having so plausible an opportunity of traducing the gospel, whose pure and self-denying principles his soul abhors.

To him, the world is everything. All his thoughts are exercised upon either the best mode of acquiring wealth or the most delightful way of spending it. Is he a man of fortune? Much of his time is occupied in ornamenting his grounds or in the chase. The pleasures of the field, the intricate mazes of political events, the passing news of the day, or the still more uncertain nature of the weather, form his most edifying topics of discourse, except he have a taste for literature; and then, men and books are occasionally canvassed and reviewed.

Is he a man of business? His conversation is filled with subjects connected with his calling, mixed up with all those little incidents of life which compose each passing day. And well would it be, if language awfully pernicious never stained his lips! But, in these worldly circles of business and of pleasure, the value of the soul, the dying love of Jesus, the work of grace upon the heart, all the rich and varied subjects of redemption, are never heard, unless it be to bear the lash of ridicule or the laugh of scorn. How, then, can two such opposite characters walk cordially together? It is impossible. Hence arises the danger of real Christians associating with the people of the world.

Courtesy and kindness are Christian duties to be exercised towards all; but friendship with the world is decidedly repugnant to the spirit of the gospel. In order to walk amicably together—that is, to enjoy each other's company in any tolerable degree—one party must give way to the other, at least to a certain extent.

The religious man, whose soul is supremely occupied with heavenly things, cannot help making occasional reflections on those topics which so deeply interest his heart. The carnal man, who cannot bear such conversation, must hear him patiently and even with seeming complacency, or a disagreement must ensue which would in a moment destroy all pleasing communion.

But as the men of the world are, in general, the most true to their master, they seldom fail to insinuate that such reflections are unpleasant and little better than preaching. They think it bearable, because customary, to hear them once a week from the pulpit, but quite intolerable to have such sermons forced upon them in common conversation. Consequently, they endeavor to turn the discourse to subjects more congenial with their tastes and inclinations.

Here the Christian must either give way or go away as soon as decorum will permit, since he finds that either he must be in continual dispute or else be continually making compliances to the injury of his soul.

If, then, it be evident that two cannot walk comfortably and profitably together, except they be agreed on the most important of all subjects—the salvation of the soul through faith in a crucified Redeemer—what must we think of those professors of the gospel who are constantly mixing with the world, not so much from duty, as from choice; not so much through necessity, as for pleasure? Are they never tempted to make sinful compliances that they and their party may be agreed?

Do they never sit for hours to listen to the vainest and most trifling discourse, while the dread of putting the salutary check to such idle words seals up their lips in silence? Have they never encouraged by a smile some witty jest upon religious characters or felt the blush of sinful shame glowing on their cheeks when sarcastically called a Methodist or a saint? Let conscience give the right answer.

The end of too many such unguarded professors lamentably proves that they have fallen into these snares of the devil. Rushing into temptation, without a call of duty arising from filial or conjugal relationship, they grieve the Holy Spirit, wound their own consciences, imbibe by degrees the spirit of the world, and get more and more assimilated to its taste and manners until at last they lose all relish for spiritual enjoyments and, like the apostate Julian, sit down in the seat of the scornful. "Remember Lot's wife" (Luke 17:32) is the warning voice of Jesus. "Demas hath forsaken me, having loved this present world" (2 Tim. 4:10) is the lamentation of Paul.

Some may condemn these cautionary remarks as uncharitable; but those who take Scripture for their guide, and experience for their teacher, well know the truth of these assertions. Surely, then, we may say with David: "Blessed is the man that walketh not in the counsel of the ungodly, nor standeth in the way of sinners, nor sitteth in the seat of the scornful. But his delight is in the law of the LORD; and in his law doth he meditate day and night" (Ps. 1:1-2). There are many fearful passages in the Word of God to guard Christians against the love, the deceits, and the allurements of the world.

We are, alas, too apt, even after we know better things, to be carried away by material objects. Any little trifle can divert the attention, even when the mind is engaged about heavenly things, without great watchfulness and self government; holy habits are to be attained only by frequent and fervent prayer. The world and the things of the world press upon us at all points. Our daily avocations—yes, our most lawful enjoyments—have need to be narrowly watched, lest they insensibly steal upon our affections and draw away our hearts from God.

A true Christian living in the world is like a ship sailing on the ocean. It is not the ship being in the water which will sink it, but the water getting into the ship. So, in like manner, the Christian is not ruined by living in the world, which he must necessarily do while he remains in the body, but by the world living in him. The world in the heart has ruined millions of immortal souls. How careful are mariners in guarding against leakage, lest the water, entering into the vessel, should by imperceptible degrees cause it to sink. And ought not the Christian to watch and pray, lest Satan and the world should find some unguarded inlet to his heart and thus, by entering in, bring him to destruction of both body and soul?

Let no one dare to be negligent because salvation is all of grace, since this very salvation consists in no small degree in a deliverance from pride, carelessness, and presumption, and in the implantation of holy fear, circumspection, and humility.

The Voice of wisdom says: He that despises small things, shall fall by little and little. "Watch and pray, lest ye enter into temptation" (Mark 14:38). But why give such exhortations, if no danger is to be dreaded? Every caution, every warning of Scripture, inculcates the necessity of godly fear. Thus I learn from the Word of truth and from daily experience that "ye cannot serve God and mammon" (Matt. 6:24); that there can be no fellowship between righteousness and unrighteousness, no agreement between the temple of God and idols; that a believer has no part with an infidel; and, consequently, that the children of God must not be unequally yoked with unbelievers. How, then, can two walk together except they be agreed? The blessed Savior gave Himself for us to deliver us from this present evil world. He declared to His disciples: "If ye were of the world, the world would love his own: but because ye are not of the world, but I have chosen you out of the world, therefore the world hateth you" (John 15:19).

Hence it follows, that "all that will live godly in Christ Jesus shall suffer persecution" (2 Tim. 3:12); for, said our Lord, "If the world hate you, ye know that it hated me before it hated you" (John 15:18). And so we find it, for, as "he that was born after the flesh persecuted him that was born after the Spirit, even so it is now" (Gal. 4:29). There must, therefore, of necessity, be drawn a broad line of separation between the true church of Christ and the world. This distinction must be plain and visible, not by needless singularity of dress or manner, not by sanctimonious looks or drawling tones, but by humility of mind, by kindness of spirit, by purity of conversation, by unwearied efforts to do good, even to the evil and unthankful—in a word, by a faithful exhibition of the Spirit of Christ in all the holy fruits of righteousness, goodness, and truth.

Thus true Christians must come out and be separate from the world in its principles, spirit, and practice, for the Word of God unequivocally declares that "if any man have not the Spirit of Christ, he is none of his" (Rom. 8:9).

"Oh, blessed Savior, preserve my heart from the pollutions of the world, from the influence and example of worldly men! Defend and shield me by Thy grace from sinful compliances; stop all the avenues to evil. May holy affections and heavenly desires fill my soul so that worldly desires may have no room to enter in. While I am in the world, grant that I may not be of the world. While my hands are employed about the necessary affairs of this life, may my heart be fully fixed on the next. While I use the world, preserve me from abusing it; and through the riches of Thy grace enable me to live in such a weanedness from it, and nonconformity to it, that when death shall bear me hence, I may walk with Thee in white in Thy kingdom of light and glory."

Sing, oh you saints, in sweet accord,
The wonders of your dying Lord;
While journeying homeward, sweetly sing
The praises of your heavenly King.

To you the scepter He extends;
To you a willing audience tends;
For you He died—for you He bled,
And dwelt in lodgings of the dead.

With joy His work of love survey,
As you approach the eternal day;
Behold the beauties of His face;
Admiring, own His matchless grace.

Though angry storms should seem to lower,
And over your head the deluge pour;

Agreement Necessary to Communion

Yet Jesus, by one gracious smile,
Can even the darkest hour beguile.

Soon shall your painful conflicts cease,
Soon shall you reach the realms of peace,
Where Jesus will His people own;
Where storms and tempests are unknown.

CHAPTER 41

Separation From the World

How little is the genuine nature of Christianity considered by the generality of professing Christians! The declaration of our Savior, "My kingdom is not of this world" (John 18:36), and the character of His followers, "They are not of the world, even as I am not of the world" (John 17:16), seem to be words of no import with thousands who call themselves Christians. Immersed in all the businesses and pleasures of life, they act as though no such declaration had been made or any such character been drawn by the Savior of mankind.

The commands of Scripture are most striking and clear on the duty of separation from the world. "Arise ye, and depart; for this is not your rest: because it is polluted, it shall destroy you, even with a sore destruction" (Micah 2:10). "Come out from among them, and be ye separate, saith the Lord, and touch not the unclean thing; and I will receive you, and will be a Father unto you, and ye shall be my sons and daughters, saith the Lord Almighty" (2 Cor. 6:17-18). "And be not conformed to this world: but be ye transformed by the renewing of your mind" (Rom. 12:2). "Love not the world, neither the things that are in the world. If any man love the world, the love of the Father is not in him. For all that is in the world, the lust of the flesh, and the lust of the eyes, and the pride of life, is not of the Father, but is of the world. And the world passeth away, and the lust thereof: but he that doeth the will of God abideth for ever" (1 John 2:15-17). "Know ye not that the friendship of the world is enmity with God? whosoever therefore will be a friend of the world is the enemy of God" (James 4:4).

To a soul happily delivered from this present evil world through faith in Jesus, the exhortations of Scripture are most encouraging. They breathe that holy resignation to the divine will and that cheerful contentment with the divine disposals, which, when obeyed, must cause the believer to rejoice at all times and in everything to give thanks. He is assured by the voice of infallible Wisdom that "a man's life consisteth not in the abundance of the things which he possesseth" (Luke 12:15). Hence he is warned to "take heed, and beware of covetousness" (Luke 12:15).

While carnal minds are panting after worldly riches, the believer is thus admonished by the lowly Savior: "Take no thought for your life, what ye shall eat; neither for the body, what ye shall put on" (Luke 12:22). "Consider the ravens: for they neither sow nor reap; which neither have storehouse nor barn; and God feedeth them: how much more are ye better than the fowls?" (v. 24). "Consider the lilies how they grow: they toil not, they spin not; and yet I say unto you, that Solomon in all his glory was not arrayed like one of these. If then God so clothe the grass, which is to day in the field, and to morrow is cast into the oven; how much more will he clothe you, O ye of little faith?" (vv. 27-28). "Take therefore no thought for the morrow: for the morrow shall take thought for the things of itself. Sufficient unto the day is the evil thereof" (Matt. 6:34). "Seek ye first the kingdom of God,… and all these things shall be added unto you" (v. 33).

Paul, who once possessed what the world admires—knowledge and influence—counted his possessions but loss for Christ. His knowledge, imbibed at the feet of Gamaliel, and his influence, derived from the authority of the high priest, were renounced without reserve when Jesus revealed Himself to his soul. Separated from a world which lies in wickedness, he could say: "I know both how to be abased, and I know how to abound: every where and in all things I am instructed both to be full and to be hungry, both to abound and to suffer need. I can do all things through Christ which strengtheneth me" (Phil. 4:12-13). From this sweet experience of true religion and this knowledge of the emptiness of all earthly things, he declared to Timothy: "But godliness with contentment is great gain. For we brought nothing into this world, and it is certain we can carry nothing out. And having food and raiment let us be therewith content. But they that will be rich fall into temptation and a snare, and into many foolish and hurtful lusts, which drown men in destruction and perdition. For the love of money is the root of all evil: which while some coveted after, they have erred from the faith, and pierced themselves through with many sorrows. But thou, O man of God, flee these things; and follow after righteousness, godliness, faith, love, patience, meekness" (1 Tim. 6:6-11).

The Hebrew converts he exhorted to the duty of divine contentment: "Let your conversation be without covetousness; and be content with such things as ye have: for he hath said, I will never leave thee, nor forsake thee. So that we may boldly say, "The Lord is my helper, and I will not fear what man shall do unto me" (Heb. 13:5-6).

These interesting portions from the Word of God show what are the character and spirit of true believers. They are a peculiar people, created in Christ Jesus unto good works. Their citizenship is in heaven. They are pilgrims and strangers upon earth, the temples of the Holy Spirit, the lights of the world, heirs of God and joint-heirs with Christ. On earth they bear the holy image of their Savior, and in heaven they shall shine with everlasting glory, as the sun.

The world is crucified unto them, and they unto the world. Its fascinating charms have passed away, and they themselves are no longer the delight of carnal company. Their holy walk and speech are now the subject of derision. The holy image of Jesus is beheld with aversion. They have become to their once-admiring associates as a crucified body, loathsome and disgusting.

All this discordance springs from that unalterable distinction which must ever exist between the people of God and the people of the world. This distinction is so plain that he who runs may read the living characters.

The one is born from above; the other, from beneath. The one is quickened by grace; the other is dead in trespasses and sins. The one is governed by the Spirit of God; the other is under the dominion of

Satan. The one consults the glory of God and cheerfully forsakes all for Christ; the other makes self the center round which he moves. The one, in seasons of general defection, can say with Nehemiah, "Ought ye not to walk in the fear of our God because of the reproach of the heathen?" (Neh. 5:9); the other, like Pharaoh, when called to bow to the scepter of Jehovah, exclaims, "Who is the Lord that I should obey his voice?" (Ex. 5:2).

No wonder, then, if such a disagreement renders a separation necessary—for what concord has light with darkness; what agreement has Christ with Belial? If Christians would be safe, they must separate from the world. To enforce this truth, the Bible is full of cautions, both historical and preceptive.

Before the flood, we beheld the dreadful consequences which ensued from the sons of God being captivated by the daughters of men (how strikingly the distinction is here preserved!) and taking unto themselves wives of all whom they chose, without any regard to either principle or practice. From these unnatural alliances sprung giants in wickedness as well as in stature, until the flood came and swept them all away.

The history of the Israelites teaches us, by examples the most awful, the danger of sinful connections. The following may serve as a specimen of the whole: "And the children of Israel dwelt among the Canaanites, Hittites, Amorites, Perizzites, Hivites, and Jebusites: And they took their daughters to be their wives, and gave their daughters to their sons, and served their gods. And the children of Israel did evil in the sight of the LORD, and forgat the LORD their God, and served Baalim and the groves. Therefore the anger of the LORD was hot against Israel" (Judges 3:5-8).

Let us, then, beware of compromising our principles. Let us beware of conceding to the practices of the world from a mistaken notion of conciliating prejudices or winning over the ungodly to religion. Such conduct will only excite the contempt of the world and provoke the Almighty to hide His face from us.

No, we must be singular if we would be holy; we must be consistent if we would be useful. If we are faithful, we must indeed expect reproach; if we boldly confess Christ before men, and steadily maintain that marked distinction which forms the line of separation between the church and the world, we must submit to have our names cast out as evil.

But true Christians ought never to shrink from the cross. Like Caleb, they should follow the Lord fully, when all others forsake Him; and like Joshua, they should declare, with humility and integrity of heart, in the face of a sneering world: "As for me and my house, we will serve the Lord" (Josh. 24:15).

We must let men see the foundation of our practice and the reason why we cannot do as others do. We must make them acquainted with our principles and let them know what are those secret springs of action which cause us to move in a direction so opposed to theirs.

This frank and ingenuous conduct may open the minds and touch the hearts of some who, through grace, may be led to say, "We will go with you, for we perceive that God is with you." At all events, such upright dealing will bring comfort into our own souls and preserve us from falling into those snares which Satan lays to catch the fearful and double-minded professor.

But if we are habitually afraid of being decided; if we endeavor to keep a good reputation with the world; if we want to live on the borders between the two kingdoms of light and darkness, maintaining a sort of friendly communion with the inhabitants on either side of the line; if we are ashamed of avowing our principles before men, when duty and the honor of Christ call for such an avowal; then we may be assured, on the truth of the gospel, that we have no scriptural evidence of being the children of God, for thus says our divine Savior: "Whosoever shall deny me before men, him will I also deny before my Father which is in heaven" (Matt. 10:33). "If we deny him, he also will deny us" (2 Tim. 2:12).

"Blessed Lord, keep me from the snares and fascinations of a world which lies in wickedness. May all my affections wing their way towards

Thee and be ever fixed upon Thee. Oh, be the center on which I rest and to which all my desires tend. Let my whole life be devoted to Thy service, which is perfect freedom. In all things may I seek Thy glory and, from the sweet constraining principle of faith and love, delight in every relative and personal duty, to the glory of Thy name."

What is earth and all its treasures,
Dazzling bright to mortal eyes?
When compared with heavenly glories,
Deep within the shade it lies.

Earth is but the land of shadows,
Faintly lit with glowworm light;
Where the prince of darkness reigns,
Presage of eternal night.

Oh, Thou Sun of glorious splendor,
Shine with healing in Thy wing;
Chase away these shades of darkness;
Holy light and comfort bring.

Let the heralds of salvation
Round the earth with joy proclaim,
Death and hell are spoiled and vanquished
Through the great Emmanuel's name.

Take Thy power, Almighty Savior,
Claim the nations for Thine own;
Reign, oh Lord of life and glory,
Until each heart becomes Thy throne.

CHAPTER 42

The Importance of Self-Knowledge

And did Jesus say to His disciples, "Ye know not what manner of spirit ye are of" (Luke 9:55), when, in their zeal for the honor of their Master, they wanted fire to descend upon the unbelieving Samaritans? Then, oh my soul, look well to yourself! Search deep into your principles of action, the ground of your obedience. Weigh well your motives in the balance of your sanctuary. Examine your intentions. Behold and see what manner of spirit you are of. Among the twelve disciples, I find a traitor; among the early Christians, an Ananias and Sapphira. In the judgment day, many will produce their wonderful works, to whom Jesus will say: "I never knew you" (Matt. 7:23). How important, then, is self-knowledge, the result of divine teaching and self-examination!

In the common business of life, those thrive best who examine most into their concerns. When a tradesman neglects his accounts, he will soon have a painful account to give. Negligence and bankruptcy are like substance and shadow—the latter follows closely upon the former. These remarks are still more important when transferred to our eternal concerns.

"Oh, then, before it be too late, give me grace, blessed Redeemer, to examine well what manner of spirit I am of, lest I should remain in error until that awful period, when, standing before Thy dread tribunal, every spirit shall be made manifest of what sort it is!"

With all sincerity of heart, I would inquire:

1. When I attend the ordinances of the gospel, in what spirit do I attend them? Do I come into the house of God as a poor beggar would go to the dwelling of the rich for bread to eat and clothing to put on?

Is it the bread of life and the garment of salvation which I earnestly crave at the throne of grace? Do I go as a poor debtor who has nothing to pay, as a guilty criminal on whom the sentence of death has been passed, that my debts may be canceled through the blood of Jesus and my soul delivered from the curse of the law? Do I go as one who is full of a sore disease to the great Physician for health and cure, for the gift of the Holy Spirit, to renovate my corrupted nature?

Do I go to the house of God as my exceeding joy to hear the glad tidings of salvation, to learn the way of righteousness, and to sing the praises of the Lord? Or do I go in a spirit of formality, for the sake of being thought religious, from mere custom and habit, and in a spirit devoid of devotion and love?

2. When I give to the poor, in what spirit do I give? Have I considered all my property as a trust committed to my care by the almighty Proprietor of the universe, to whom I must one day give a strict account of my stewardship? Do I view the poor as the Lord's bankers, remembering who has said: "He that hath pity upon the poor lendeth unto the LORD; and that which he hath given will he pay him again" (Prov. 19:17)? Do I esteem the pious poor—rich in faith and heirs of the kingdom which God has promised to those who love Him—as brethren whose necessities it is not only my duty, but my pleasure, consistently to relieve with the claims and necessities of my own family?

Do I relieve them for the sake of Christ, because they belong to Him, with a single eye to His glory, and as unobserved by others as circumstances will admit? Or do I relieve the poor through public institutions only that my name may be enrolled and my beneficence made known to the world, thus loving the praise of men more than the praise of God?

Are my charities confined to the body, or do I seek the spiritual good, as well as the temporal benefit of my fellow-creatures?

3. When I discourse among religious friends upon the truths of the gospel, in what spirit do I discourse upon them? Is it from a heart-felt

conviction of the sweetness, richness, and vastness of these mysteries? Is it with a view to mutual edification, to provoke one another to love and to good works, to stimulate to exertion in the cause of Christ, and to excite others to greater usefulness? Is it from a pure desire that Christ may be glorified, that His name may be honored and His righteousness exalted?

Is it from a principle of love that I converse with others on the preciousness of Jesus, the work of the Spirit, and the joys of heaven? Or do I speak of these things in a spirit of spiritual pride, to make a display of my religious knowledge, to be thought wise, and to be esteemed a saint?

4. When I perform the daily duties of my worldly calling, in what spirit do I perform them? Is it with a view to glorify God in them and to obtain an honest livelihood, through the divine blessing on my labors, that I may thereby provide for my family, and have enough to give to him that is in need?

Or is it from a covetous desire of wealth for its own sake, that I may vie in splendor with my richer neighbors, have a greater opportunity of gratifying my pride and of gaining the appellation of the opulent and of raising my family in the world?

5. When the religion of Jesus is traduced, and the gospel dispensation derided by carnal men, in what spirit do I hear these things? Do I pray that the Lord would convince them of their errors and convert them by His grace? Do I labor to do them good, if opportunity will permit, by speaking a word for Christ and exhorting them in a spirit of meekness and love?

Or, with the disciples of old, do I secretly pray for vengeance to overtake them as it overtook the enemies of Elisha, forgetting that I am a partaker of the same evil nature with themselves; and if made to differ in any measure, most humbly, yet gracefully acknowledge with the apostle: "By the grace of God I am what I am" (1 Cor. 15:10).

6. When reviled for righteousness sake, in what spirit do I treat my persecutors? Do I return good for evil, blessing for cursing, kindness for abuse? Do I bear my enemies on my heart before God in prayer and earnestly implore, like my passionate Savior when nailed to the cross, "Father, forgive them; for they know not what they do" (Luke 23:34)? Or do I resent their injuries by sourness of temper, irritation of spirit, retaliation of wrongs—returning, when possible, evil for evil?

"Almighty Savior, Thou who art the author and finisher of faith, give me a right spirit, a purity of intention, a principle of love, that all my thoughts, words, and actions may be regulated according to Thy will. With true humility of heart, may I ever study to advance the spiritual welfare of my fellow-creatures by exhortations, prayers, influence, and example. Do not allow the enemy of souls to fill me with high notions of my own excellence, but ever keep me low in my own eyes. Preserve me from spiritual pride, the bane of all true godliness. In the lowly attitude of deep contrition, may I daily come to Thy bleeding cross for renewed forgiveness and renewed strength. There may love and gratitude fill my heart, until, passing through the gates of death into the celestial city, my soul shall be forever dedicated to Thy service and glory."

Ah, who can tell the joy,
Which reigns within the breast,
Where heavenly dews of grace descend,
And Jesus is the guest.

Like some sweet summer rose,
It sheds a fragrance round
Though still, alas, the noxious thorn
Of nature may be found.

A bright celestial day
Pours light and warmth within

Yet still a cloud too often obscures
Its beams, through inbred sin.

Here is the seat of war,
Where sin and Satan rage;
The conqueror is the dying saint,
Who, fighting, quits the stage.

Blest Jesus, to my soul
Thy grace and strength impart;
'Til, clothed in perfect righteousness,
I see Thee as Thou art.

CHAPTER 43

The Spirit of Prayer

There cannot be a greater blessing imparted to us than a spirit of prayer. It is the pledge of all other blessings. When it pleases God to bestow a spirit of prayer, every other spiritual blessing is, as it were, waiting to descend upon the seeking soul. The spirit of grace and supplication is closely connected with believing contrition. "And I will pour upon the house of David, and upon the inhabitants of Jerusalem, the spirit of grace and of supplications: and they shall look upon me whom they have pierced, and they shall mourn" (Zech. 12:10).

A spirit of prayer implies faith in the promises of God and an earnest desire for the promised blessings. It includes waiting and hoping. "I waited for the LORD," says David. And what was the happy result? "He inclined unto me, and heard my cry" (Ps. 40:1). Oh, it is a blessed state of heart thus to wait upon God continually in the spirit of humble, fervent, believing prayer! Satan well knows the value of such a spirit and therefore tries hard to prevent its exercise. He labors to extinguish this sacred fire, kindled in the soul by the Holy Spirit. He endeavors to disturb the mind, to ride upon the wings of the imagination, and to fill the soul with an almost endless succession of fleeting images.

This daily interruption of the enemy constitutes no small part of the Christian warfare. The believer feels greatly distressed when his foolish heart thus wanders from its divine center. At such seasons his language is, "Oh, that I were 'near, and like my God'! But alas," I groan, being burdened. "My heart is pained within me. I am almost tempted to conclude that my experience of joy and peace is delusion."

If I am a child of God, why am I thus? And yet, I cannot but feel some encouragement from the thought, that if I were under the absolute control of natural corruption, I could not thus lament and mourn over its workings and deceits. Why do I groan, being burdened, if I feel no burden? And if I feel my burden, who has given me this spiritual sensibility? I know that in a natural state, man can neither mourn over, nor feel the weight of, spiritual evils, it being one of the marks of unregeneracy to grow in love with, rather than groan under, sin.

If I am daily anxious to possess the spirit of prayer, to be inwardly renewed in the spirit of my mind, to be more under the influence of filial love and filial fear, may I not hope that a God of grace has indeed drawn me by His loving-kindness and loved me with an everlasting love? Delightful thought! Is it too much to draw this happy conclusion? There is no merit in any creature, saint, or angel. The voice of sovereign grace is, "I will have mercy on whom I will have mercy, and I will have compassion on whom I will have compassion" (Rom. 9:15). Oh, that I may be enabled by humble faith to lie at the foot of the cross, and there to view, with growing delight, the never-ending wonders of redeeming love! Such are the feelings of every true believer.

"Lord, bestow upon me this blessed spirit of prayer. Preserve me from the incursions of the enemy, from the wanderings of my wayward heart. Take the world out of my affections. Let not its image be painted upon my imagination. But let Thine own image be deeply engraven on my soul."

As we cannot live naturally without air, neither can we live spiritually without prayer. The latter is as necessary to the soul as the former is to the body. A prayerless person is a Christless person. Living without God in the world, he must die without hope. The natural heart dislikes prayer, because it requires a frame of mind quite opposed to its corrupt views and feelings. If we feel an inward dislike to secret prayer—or if, when we pray, our hearts are habitually cold and distracted by worldly cares and sinful imaginations—we cannot have a clearer proof of our being carnally minded, which is death.

To pray aright, we must see our wretchedness, we must feel our misery, we must acknowledge our guilt, pollution, and helplessness, we must lie at the foot of the cross, plead in faith the merits of a crucified Savior, renounce our own righteousness, supplicate forgiveness through the blood of Jesus, implore the gift of the Holy Spirit, hunger and thirst after righteousness, and pour out our souls in grateful acknowledgments for redeeming grace. Now all this is contrary to the natural man. It was, therefore, no small mark of the conversion of Saul when Jesus said to Ananias: "Behold, he [Paul] prayeth" (Acts 9:11).

What an exalted privilege is prayer! How precious is the throne of grace! And yet:

> *What various hindrances we meet,*
> *In coming to a mercy-seat!*

There is even in the believer at times a painful backwardness to approach that throne on which his Father sits in the mild radiance of covenant love. Yes, even in his happiest moments, when with filial confidence he draws near the mercy-seat, the artful enemy will labor hard to impede him in his work and tempt him to give up the duty, well knowing that every relaxation in duty is a weakening of principle.

When such assaults are violent, the heart is grieved, and the believer is greatly discouraged. But if he really loves the exercise of prayer and seeks opportunities for holding communion with God, although much hindered by foolish, wandering, hated thoughts, let him not be induced to abandon the sacred work, which would only give the tempter an advantage over him.

When Satan casts his fiery darts, then must the soldier of Jesus Christ hold up the "shield of faith" (Eph. 6:16) and wield the weapon of "all prayer" (v. 18), being assured that, in spite of every opposition, victory shall be the glorious result. The divine command is: "Go forward" (Ex. 14:15). So did the Israelites when the Red Sea was before them and the Egyptians were behind them. Through the power of Jehovah, the mighty waters divided; a way was made for His ransomed to pass over, and they sang the high praises of their Redeemer, while their enemies lay dead upon the sea shore.

"So let all thine enemies perish, O Lord: but let them that love thee be as the sun when he goeth forth in his might" (Judges 5:31).

"Happy art thou, O Israel: who is like unto thee, O people saved by the Lord, the shield of thy help, and who is the sword of thy excellency! and thine enemies shall be found liars unto thee; and thou shalt tread upon their high places" (Deut. 33:29). "The eternal God is thy refuge, and underneath are the everlasting arms: and he shall thrust out the enemy from before thee; and shall say, Destroy them" (v. 27).

Yes, all the spiritual enemies of the true Israel shall sink as lead in the mighty waters in that day when Satan and his rebellious angels shall be cast into the lake of fire, never more to harass the glorified church of God, which shall shine as the sun forever and ever!

"I desire, I long, I pray to be Thine, oh blessed Jesus—a member of Thy mystical body, a sheep of Thy pasture.

"Almighty Savior, grant unto me the spirit of prayer, that, with my whole heart, I may lift up my soul unto Thee. Open my understanding to understand the Scriptures. Incline my will to choose those things which are pleasing unto Thee. Fix my affections upon Thyself, precious Redeemer. Sanctify my imagination, store my memory with spiritual treasures, sprinkle my conscience with Thy pardoning blood, cover me with Thy justifying righteousness.

"Come and dwell, oh divine Savior, in my heart by faith. Make my body the temple of the Holy Spirit; impress Thy divine image on my soul. Preserve me from the power and pollution of sin, the snares and wiles of Satan, the love and influence of the world; shed abroad Thy love in my heart; establish me in the faith of the gospel. May I ever receive Thee in all Thy glorious offices and characters as my only, my complete, salvation.

"Give me grace, oh blessed Jesus, to believe in the dignity and majesty of Thy person as the eternal Word, the everlasting Son of the Father, of equal power, glory, and eternity with the Father and the Holy Spirit. May I behold Thee with admiring love and gratitude as the virgin's Son, lying in the manger, taking upon Thyself my nature that so, being God and man in one Christ, Thou mightest satisfy eternal justice and bring in everlasting righteousness.

"Oh, may I contemplate, with mingled feelings of grief and joy, Thine agony and bloody sweat, Thy cross and passion, Thy precious death and burial—with grief when I reflect on sin, my own sin, which nailed Thee to the accursed tree; with joy when I meditate on Thy dying love, a love which angels cannot fathom, a love which fills the bright intelligences above with wonder and delight, a love which fills each humble soul on earth with gratitude and praise!

"Jesus, I—oh, that in the humble confidence of faith, I may say—I do receive Thee as my only, my beloved Savior!

"Impart into my soul this spiritual, this practical, this experimental knowledge of Thyself, who art the light of the world and the wisdom of Thy people.

"Oh, wash my guilty soul in Thy cleansing blood, Thou who art the bleeding propitiatory sacrifice, the Lamb of God.

"Now that Thou art ascended up on high and hast entered into the holiest of all, plead the cause of a poor wretched sinner who looks unto Thee as the Lord my righteousness, my great Melchisedec. Exert Thy regal power in my soul, oh King of saints, and destroy all Thine enemies and mine. Subdue every rebellious inclination of my heart which opposes itself to Thy will. Bring all my powers into subjection to Thy divine authority, and sit upon the throne of my heart as the Lord of every motion there.

"Oh, may I delight in the contemplation of those soul-reviving characters which Thou sustainest in the covenant of grace! Thou art the Redeemer, Mediator, justifier, surety, advocate, and purifier of Thy people, their friend and counselor, their shepherd and guide, their husband and guardian.

"And how beautiful are the images which the Holy Spirit employs to shadow forth Thine excellencies! Thou art 'the rose of Sharon, and the lily of the valleys' (Song 2:1), 'a plant of renown' (Ezek. 34:29). Thou art 'the true vine' (John 15:1) which supplieth each living branch with fruitfulness and verdure. Thou art the fountain in which all may wash and be clean, the rock on which Thy church is immovably fixed, the way in which Thy people journey to the heavenly Canaan, the door by which they enter into the covenant of grace, the day-star which illuminates their path and guides them safely to glory. Thou art the bread of life, the true manna whose flesh is food indeed, and whose blood is drink indeed.

"Oh, may I daily feed upon Thee by faith in my heart with thanksgiving, until I see Thee in the heavenly paradise and taste through eternal ages the sweetness of redeeming love!"

Oh, may I prize a throne of grace,
Accessible in every place;
Wherever I lift my soul in prayer,
On earth or sea, my God is there.

If in the hour of deep distress,
Its woes, my heart in sighs express;
A sweet return of love I find,
To sooth the sorrows of the mind.

Or when the grateful odors rise
Of praise—delightful sacrifice!
My soul expands with joys unknown
To every bosom, but its own.

Ah, where proceeds this sacred love,
Descending gently from above?
To Thee, Savior, and Thy blood,
I owe this precious gift of God.

Oh, may I daily love Thee more,
Of blessings, Thee, the bounteous store;
On me let every grace descend,
Oh, source of bliss, Thou sinner's friend!

CHAPTER 44

The Cautions and Warnings of Scripture

The Word of God abounds with cautions as well as encouragements, with warnings as well as invitations, with threatenings as well as promises. These are necessary and important; otherwise, they would not be as thickly scattered through the sacred volume. We find the need of cautions and warnings in proportion as we are made aquatinted with the subtlety of Satan, the deceitfulness of sin, and the treachery of our own hearts.

We learn by a thousand painful instances that "he that trusteth in his own heart is a fool" (Prov. 28:26). How short-lived are the best resolutions made in our own strength! They resemble the early dew which soon passes away, and the grass upon the house-top which withers before it grows up. What a valuable part of the Bible are the kind admonitions of a loving Savior! How should we prize the salutary counsels of Him who spoke as never man spoke, who sticks closer than a brother!

May we ever remember His gracious exhortations, for "they are spirit, and they are life" (John 6:63). "Without me ye can do nothing" (John 15:5). "Watch ye and pray, lest ye enter into temptation" (Mark 14:38). "Take heed, and beware of covetousness" (Luke 12:15). "Strive to enter in at the strait gate" (Luke 13:24). "Seek ye first the kingdom of God, and his righteousness" (Matt. 6:33). "Continue ye in my love" (John 15:9).

We are here taught by infinite wisdom that of ourselves we can do nothing that is pleasing to God or effectual towards our salvation; that our spiritual enemies are constantly plotting our destruction, spreading nets for our feet, and holding out their baits to draw us into sin; that the love of the world is a whirlpool down which millions are carried into perdition; that carnal ease and sensual indulgence form the road to hell; that to escape this dreadful end, we must strive—yes, agonize—to enter in at the strait gate which leads unto life eternal. We are exhorted to seek, as the first great object of pursuit, not the honors and wealth of the world, but righteousness, peace, and joy in the Holy Spirit. We are warned against the smallest approach towards spiritual declension; and, to avoid so great an evil, we are commanded to persevere in the good and the right way by continuing in the constant exercise of a supreme love to Jesus, who loved us and gave Himself for us. Such are the salutary counsels given to us by our divine Savior, who said to His disciples: "If ye know these things, happy are ye if ye do them" (John 13:17).

In the gospel of the blessed God, we are also cautioned against spiritual pride: "Be not highminded, but fear" (Rom. 11:20).

How prone we are to be proud, although we have nothing to be proud of! Our hearts are strongly inclined to pride, which is the very essence of the fall. Pride cast angels out of heaven and man out of Paradise. Pride fights against the mercy of God, bars the sinner's heart against the Savior, and hurries the proud rebel down the precipice of desperation into the burning gulf of hell. "Happy is the man that feareth alway" (Prov. 28:14), lest he fall into the condemnation of the devil!

"Blessed Jesus, clothe me with humility, destroy this baneful root of pride out of my heart, and make me meek and lowly, resigned to all Thy wise disposals, however painful they may be to fallen nature."

How needful at all times is this kind admonition: "Let him that thinketh he standeth take heed lest he fall" (1 Cor. 10:12). We are never in such danger of falling as when we think ourselves the most secure. Self-dependence and carnal security are those fatal props by which thousands are upheld through the delusions of Satan, until they drop into everlasting misery.

How good is this caution, also: "Let us therefore fear, lest, a promise being left us of entering into his rest, any of you should seem to come short of it" (Heb. 4:1).

Self-love blinds the eyes of the mind so that we cannot see our real state and condition. This was the case with the declining church of Laodicea. She imagined herself rich and increased with goods and as having need of nothing, when, in the eye of the all-searching Jesus, she was wretched and miserable and poor and blind and naked. Of Ephraim, it was said: "Gray hairs are here and there upon him, yet he knoweth not" (Hos. 7:9). Of Ephesus: "Thou hast left thy first love" (Rev. 2:4). Of Sardis: "Thou hast a name that thou livest, and art dead" (Rev. 3:1). So blind are we to our spiritual declensions!

All are not believers who believe themselves to be such. The divine touchstone is: "By their fruits ye shall know them" (Matt. 7:20).

When Christians are sometimes led to doubt the sincerity of their faith, it is often attributed to the temptation of Satan; but this may not always be the case. Had the church of Laodicea exercised a holy jealousy over herself, that very fear of self-deception would have indicated much self-knowledge and spiritual discernment, and might, through grace, have preserved her from degenerating into that state of lukewarmness, which evidently originated in pride and self-conceit.

Satan not infrequently harasses the true believer with desponding fears, while he buoys up the mere nominal professor with presumptuous hopes. These desponding fears, if indulged to excess, are injurious to the believer's advancement in holiness. They wound his peace and are dishonorable to a faithful, loving Savior.

Yet, if these fearful apprehensions lead him to closer self-examination and greater searchings of heart, to more fervent supplication and increased watchfulness, then Satan is foiled, and the believer, rescued from the power of the enemy through the unfailing grace of the Redeemer, is made to come off more than conqueror and to sing with joy in the ways of the Lord. When the believer in Jesus has attained to this happy state, his soul is in a right frame: humble, watchful, and holy. Being taught in the school of Christ to know himself and his Savior, he proceeds with steady step towards the heavenly Canaan, under the equalizing influence of hope and fear.

Everything which can comfort the child of God is recorded by the pen of eternal truth. As his salvation is all of grace in its origin, so is it also in its progress and consummation. "God is faithful, by whom ye were called" (1 Cor. 1:9). "He which hath begun a good work in you will perform it until the day of Jesus Christ" (Phil. 1:6). Nothing can be stronger than the following assurance of love and mercy, which is made to every penitent sinner flying for refuge to the cross of Christ: "God, willing more abundantly to shew unto the heirs of promise the immutability of his counsel, confirmed it by an oath: that by two immutable things, in which it was impossible for God to lie, we might have a strong consolation, who have fled for refuge to lay hold upon the hope set before us: which hope we have as an anchor of the soul, both sure and stedfast, and which entereth into that within the veil; whither the forerunner is for us entered, even Jesus, made an high priest for ever after the order of Melchisedec" (Heb. 6:17-20).

Yet, in the Holy Scriptures, we meet with many alarming passages which ought to awaken our solicitude and cause us to ponder the path of our feet. "The just shall live by faith: but if any man draw back, my soul shall have no pleasure in him" (Heb. 10:38). "For if we sin wilfully after that we have received the knowledge of the truth, there remaineth no more sacrifice for sins, but a certain fearful looking for of judgment and fiery indignation, which shall devour the adversaries" (Heb. 10:26-27). "It is impossible for those who were once enlightened, and have tasted of the heavenly gift, and were made partakers of the Holy Ghost, and have tasted the good word of God, and the powers of the world to come, if they shall fall away, to renew them again unto repentance; seeing they crucify to themselves the Son of God afresh, and put him to an open shame" (Heb. 6:4-6). "If after they have escaped the pollutions of the world through the knowledge of the Lord and Saviour Jesus Christ, they are again entangled therein, and overcome, the latter end is worse with them than the beginning. For it had been better for them not to have known the way of righteousness, than, after they have known it, to turn from the holy commandment delivered unto them" (2 Pet. 2:20-21).

These and other similar passages show us the importance of this proverb: "The fear of the LORD tendeth to life: and he that hath it shall abide satisfied; he shall not be visited with evil" (Prov. 19:23).

How many do we see in the course of our lives, who, after flourishing for a season, begin to fade and die! Is it not because the root of the matter was not in them, because their hearts were never savingly changed, because they were never really and truly in a state of grace?

Peter calls such characters "spots…and blemishes" (2 Pet. 2:13). Jude styles them "spots in your feasts of charity…: clouds…without water…; trees…without fruit,… to whom is reserved the blackness of darkness forever" (Jude 1:12-13)! Awful words indeed! Oh, what need there is for close examination, lest we should be found among those self-deceivers who fancy themselves to be something while they are nothing, and who, after they have made a noisy profession before men, will prove at last mere castaways! The blessed Savior has not left us at uncertainties in these important inquiries. He has given us solid marks whereby to judge of our true state and character: "If ye love me, keep my commandments" (John 14:15). "Ye are my friends, if ye do whatsoever I command you" (John 15:14). "Follow me" (Matt. 8:22).

As love is the surest evidence of faith, so obedience is the truest test of love. How vain, then, is that profession which is destitute of these graces! Universal holiness is the distinguishing mark of genuine Christianity: "Be ye holy; for I am holy" (1 Pet. 1:16) is the command of Him who is of purer eyes than to behold iniquity.

Supreme love to the Lord Jesus Christ is the governing principle of every believer. This sacred attachment to the Savior forms the grand distinction between the children of God and the children of the wicked one.

A man may make a reputable profession of religion for a season and appear like a flourishing tree and a fertilizing cloud; but if his heart be destitute of "the true grace of God" (1 Pet. 5:12), he will be found at last to resemble the character reprobated by Jude, being "without fruit" and "without water." In seasons of temptation he will wither away, not having a rooted principle of grace in his heart, and thus manifest to the church and the world, by his declension and apostasy, that he was never truly ingrafted into Christ by faith.

The force of temptation soon destroys his feeble attachment to the visible church, and he remains a solemn warning of the danger of false profession to all who call themselves Christians.

"Oh, blessed Lord, preserve me, Thy unworthy creature, from this awful state of self-delusion. Oh, give me true grace, deep repentance, and fervent love. Unite my soul to Thyself in the bonds of the everlasting covenant. Let sin be my daily aversion and holiness my everlasting delight. Prepare me for the enjoyment of Thyself here and crown all Thy mercies with the gift of Thyself, as my everlasting portion, in Thy kingdom of glory."

In seasons of doubt and gloom,
When Satan would drive to despair,
Then Christ is the life of my hope,
And hope is the life of my prayer.

My sins, like a death-bearing cloud,
Often hide the dear cross from my view;
But Jesus dispersing the mist,
Disperses the enemy too.

How kind is our merciful God!
His Word and His promise how true!
He bids me take courage and fight,
With a crucified Jesus in view.

Should Satan come in like a flood,
And fill me with grief and dismay,

The Cautions and Warnings of Scripture

The Spirit appears to my aid;
His standard drives Satan away.

By nature unable to stand,
Or vanquish temptation to sin;
Through Jesus, almighty to save,
The crown we are certain to win.

CHAPTER 45

Self-Deception

A good thought does not consist in simply thinking about good things. We may meditate upon the most excellent subjects, and even feel some delight in them, while our meditations are neither pleasing to God nor profitable to ourselves. From the habit of attending a gospel ministry and reading religious publications, we may be led into an evangelical train of thinking; and yet, both the faithful preacher and the pious author may be to us only as the summer shower falling upon the barren rock.

"Be ye doers of the word, and not hearers only, deceiving your own selves" (James 1:22) is the cautionary voice of revealed truth. There is a danger of being satisfied with the sentimentalism of religion. If a person can express himself with energy and elegance on the grand peculiarities of the gospel, and thus convey his thoughts with acceptability and usefulness, he may be in danger of substituting this knowledge and gift of utterance for humble, heart-felt religion.

As he is not a Christian who only talks about Christ, so he is not a spiritually minded man who only thinks about spiritual things. It is a great blessing to have spiritual views, but what do they avail without spiritual affections and a spiritual walk?

We are in continual danger of self-deception. What is knowledge without love? What is a ready tongue without genuine experience? David said: "I believed, therefore have I spoken" (Ps. 116:10). And Paul, when quoting this passage, adds: "We also believe, and therefore speak" (2 Cor. 4:13). Hence the apostle exhorts the Ephesian converts to speak the truth in love, that they might grow up into Christ in all things, who is the head of His mystical body the church. I would, then, with all solemnity put these searching questions to my heart: Do I esteem Jesus precious? Do I feel Him precious? Do I love Him as my only Savior? Do I trust wholly in His atonement and intercession? Do I delight in His precepts as well as in His promises? Do these views and feelings make me humble and self-denying, thankful and obedient? Is it my aim so to walk that I may please God in all things? Am I looking continually to the Holy Spirit for power to repent, believe, love, and obey? Do I daily come as a humble suppliant to the foot of the cross? Have I laid hold by faith on the promised salvation, so freely held out to me in the gospel of grace? If this be the character of my religion, then my thoughts on good things are good thoughts—they are the inspiration of the Spirit of God, from whom alone "all holy desires, all good counsels, and all just works do proceed" (the Collect for Peace, "Order for Evening Prayer," *Book of Common Prayer* [1662]). They are evidential of that spiritual-mindedness which is life and peace.

Come, oh my soul, and pour out your heart at a throne of grace. There you may ask for whatever you need, with the fullest assurance that the blessed Jesus will supply your every need out of His inexhaustible fullness.

"Blessed Savior! I ask for a more spiritual mind, a greater purity of heart, an increasing deadness to the world, a growing likeness to Thee, a more lively faith; more ardency of affection, more love for souls, more knowledge and wisdom, more meekness and forbearance—yes, more of every grace which will enable me to adorn Thy gospel and glorify Thy holy name."

How awful is the state of the self-deceiving and self-righteous professor! He builds upon a false foundation, buoys himself up with false hopes, and lulls his conscience to sleep with a false peace. He trusts to an arm of flesh, and his heart departs from the Lord. He cannot brook the thought of being altogether indebted to another, even Jesus, the eternal Son of God, for a free justification; and therefore he uses the Savior's merits only as a make-weight in the scale of his own virtues to counterbalance the weaknesses and failings incident to human nature.

> *But Christ will sooner abdicate His own,*
> *Than stoop from heaven to give the proud a throne.*

How different are the views and feelings of the convinced sinner. He sees himself ruined and undone, lying under the curse of a broken law, without strength, without righteousness, and without hope. He feels the weight of the burden of his sins. He sinks under the ponderous load and finds no help from men or angels. When he views God through the medium of a broken law, he beholds Him as an offended judge whose uplifted arm is ready to execute the awful sentence. He dreads to think upon God; a slavish fear fills his heart, and horror seizes upon his frame. He looks to the right hand, but finds no rest; and to the left, but obtains no deliverance. In some highly favored hour, some precious moment, grace, like a stream of light, darts upon his benighted soul. The clouds of despondency begin to break. The thunders of Sinai cease to roar. He hears a still small voice speaking pardon and peace through the blood of Jesus. He listens. He can scarcely believe the sound, which in an inward, yet powerful manner, reaches his trembling soul. But he is not deceived. The light gradually increases. The divine Spirit, through the written or preached Word, reveals to his now prepared mind the adorable crucified Jesus in all the glories of redeeming love. He now views the Almighty in a new, endearing aspect. He sees Him as a tender, reconciled Father in Jesus Christ, infinitely just and holy, yet forgiving iniquity, transgression, and sin. He flies to the hope set before him in the gospel and seeks refuge from the storms of wrath in the wounded side of Jesus.

> *Rock of ages! cleft for me,*
> *Let me hide myself in Thee,*

is the earnest prayer of his heart. By faith he is clothed in the Savior's righteousness, armed with strength for the spiritual combat, and sealed with the Holy Spirit of promise. Joy and peace now fill his soul; love constrains him to obedience; and childlike confidence in the promises supports him under every trial. He seeks the glory of his Redeemer, loves His cause and people, pleads nothing but His merits before the throne, and counts all things but loss for the excellency of the knowledge of Jesus Christ his Lord. He hates and resists those sins which once he loved, and renounces that world which so much enamored him. Thus, by a progressive sanctification, he goes on from strength to strength until he finally appears before God in Zion.

Such are the blessed effects of the gospel, when it comes with power, and in the Holy Spirit, and in much assurance. It invariably produces works of faith, labors of love, and patience of hope. It brings glory to God in the highest, peace on earth, and good-will towards men. It turns the lion into the lamb, the desert into the garden of the Lord. It converts the impure and savage heart into a habitation fit for the mild and holy Dove. "Old things are passed away; behold, all things are become new" (2 Cor. 5:17).

How divinely glorious, then, is the religion of Jesus! It restores the sinner to the divine favor; it renews him after the divine image; it redeems him from the depths of hell and raises him to the highest seats in glory! What tongue can speak, or what heart conceive, the richness and extent of human redemption? How cheering is the soul-enlivening truth that "all are welcome to these blessings to whom these blessings are welcome."

"Lord, make me willing in the day of Thy power. Seal this great salvation to my heart and make me Thine henceforth forever."

Come, Holy Spirit, from above,
Oh source of light and fire of love;
Come, dwell within my longing breast,
And give my troubled conscience rest.

Almighty Visitant, dispel
The dark designs and storms of hell;
Exert Thy mighty power divine;
While beams of mercy o'er me shine.

Subdue every rebel inbred foe,
Which only Thou and conscience know:
Purge out that hated leaven, sin,
How deep soever it lies within.

Take from me unbelief and pride,
That spear which pierced my Savior's side;
Destroy each lust, until Thou alone
Art seated on affection's throne.

Come, Holy Spirit, from above,
In all the energy of love;
Come, seal salvation to my heart,
And never from my soul depart.

Through all my journeyings here below,
Oh, do Thy light and truth bestow;
And when my earthly toils are o'er,
Oh, be my bliss for evermore!

CHAPTER 46

Lukewarmness

The path of the true Christian lies remote from unbelief and lukewarmness. Thousands who profess to believe the gospel are indifferent to its precepts and promises, and tens of thousands, though nominally Christian, are opposed to it through unbelief. Hence the zeal of the true believer is reviled by the infidel as fanaticism and by the lukewarm professor as unwarranted obsession.

No state of heart is more revolting to a God of love than a state of spiritual lukewarmness. Bodily sickness and earthly privations are slight evils when compared with this spiritual distemper. It is most offensive to that gracious Being who unrobed Himself of His glories, who condescended to become a man of sorrows and acquainted with grief, that we hell-deserving sinners be rescued from the burning wrath and be received into heavenly glory.

Outward prosperity, the admiration of friends, self-love, and the gradual omission of watchfulness and prayer lead us insensibly towards this dangerous precipice, down which thousands have fallen and from which nothing but sovereign grace can preserve us.

The natural inclination of the heart is from God; even when renewed in righteousness, it feels the force of this evil inclination the moment it relaxes in the exercise of faith and prayer. Believers in Jesus should therefore dread nothing so much as leaving their first love and backsliding in heart. All spiritual declensions begin in the heart and in the closet; though slow at first, yet they increase with awful rapidity as the principle of grace is weakened through the indulgence of sin.

If reason and experience tell us that the surest preservative against falling down a precipice is to keep at a distance from its edge, surely that which lies the most remote from spiritual declension must be the safest path for a Christian. Those impressions which are made merely upon the passions soon degenerate into lukewarmness when the novelty ceases or when persecution arises because of the Word. This lukewarmness is rapidly succeeded by coldness, and coldness by contempt; for "evil men and seducers shall wax worse and worse, deceiving, and being deceived" (2 Tim. 3:13).

But what is painfully true must not be withheld—even real Christians may grow lukewarm for a season through the power of temptation, the force of indwelling sin, the fear of man, or the blandishments of the world. They may fall asleep in the arbor of carnal ease or on the soft couch of worldly prosperity, and by thus grieving and quenching the Spirit, lose for a time the sensible enjoyment of divine love as well as the evidence of their adoption into the family of God. Awful state, most seriously to be dreaded! No eclipse is so dark as the hidings of the divine countenance.

For this, they shall be made to smart and mourn; for this, they shall go heavily, "as one that mourneth for his mother" (Ps. 35:14), when they are awakened by the voice of mercy and called to look upon Him whom they have pierced by their ingratitude and declension.

This sinful wandering from God does not destroy their sonship—the Word of truth declares that "the gifts and calling of God are without repentance" (Rom. 11:29)—any more than the disobedience of a child towards an earthly father makes him not a child. He is still a child, though a disobedient child. The father is displeased and withholds His regards. The wayward child is made to know this, either by correction, distance of manner, or the withholding of some favor. Hence he is brought to see, to fret, and to lament his disobedience, to long after reconciliation, and never to rest easy or become happy until the displeasure is removed and confidence and comfort are restored.

In this manner God deals with His redeemed people when they decline and disobey. He hides His face, and they are troubled. He blows upon their comforts, and they wither. He has a thousand ways of manifesting His displeasure, both in the course of His providence and in the actings of His grace.

But love is still inscribed upon all these chastening dispensations. How gracious is the voice of their heavenly Father, speaking to His wayward children through His Word! "As many as I love, I rebuke and chasten" (Rev. 3:19). "Whom the Lord loveth he chasteneth, and scourgeth every son whom he receiveth" (Heb. 12:6). "Thou shalt also consider in thine heart, that, as a man chasteneth his son, so the Lord thy God chasteneth thee" (Deut. 8:5). "I will be his father, and he shall be my son. If he commit iniquity, I will chasten him with the rod of men, and with the stripes of the children of men: But my mercy shall not depart away from him" (2 Sam. 7:14-15). "Behold, happy is the man whom God correcteth: therefore despise not thou the chastening of the Almighty" (Job 5:17). Is not this the language of a loving, tender Parent who seeks the good of His rebellious children?

All sin is productive of sorrow and naturally leads to the chambers of death. Blessed, then, are those souls whom grace has brought within the bonds of the covenant. If they wander from the fold, they shall be mercifully driven into it again through the faithfulness of the good Shepherd, who has said: "I will hedge up thy way with thorns" (Hos. 2:6); "I will never leave thee, nor forsake thee" (Heb. 13:5).

But let no one dare to presume upon the mercy of God, and sin that grace may abound. Such conduct would prove the person so acting to be destitute of faith and love. Should any deluded sinner be led by Satan so to abuse the grace of the gospel, he may be allowed to follow the wicked devices of his own depraved heart until he fall, as a vessel fitted for destruction (Rom. 9:22), into the abyss of hell.

It is the part of true wisdom to distinguish between the privileges of God's children and the abuse of those privileges. Who would condemn the noble faculty of speech, because thousands pervert it to the basest purposes? Is there any one gift of providence which is not, by some, converted into an instrument of wickedness? But let it ever be remembered that those who abuse the blessings, either of providence or grace, must bear the consequences of such impiety, whoever they be, for "God is no respecter of persons" (Acts 10:34).

It is evident, then, that if we do not enjoy peace through believing, there must be something wrong either in our views or in our hearts. Examine, oh my soul, where the evil lies, for peace is the sacred legacy which Christ left to His church when He said: "Peace I leave with you, my peace I give unto you" (John 14:27).

God in Christ is the Father of all His redeemed people. Now, a loving, obedient child delights in the society of a tender parent. He comes to his father cheerfully and without fear. He tells him his little needs and sincerely and sorrowfully confesses any fault which may have been committed against so loving a parent. But if a child dreads his parent, or feels shy, and avoids his company, even when his father is manifesting nothing but kindness towards him, must there not be something wrong in the heart of such a child? Does not the child either mistake the character of the parent, or feel a consciousness of some indulged sin, which is the latent cause of this defect in duty?

The gospel inspires confidence and love. The moment we believe in Jesus with the heart, that moment we obtain peace with God, and pass from death unto life. This peace of justification cannot be broken, because it is founded on the atonement of Christ, who is "our peace" (Eph. 2:14) and has "made peace through the blood of the cross" (Col. 1:20). The sins of believers cannot destroy this peace, which is immutable, since Jesus, foreseeing the sins of His people, atoned for them by the one sacrifice of Himself. "Being justified by faith, we have peace with God" (Rom. 5:1). The debt was paid, the satisfaction was made and fully accepted, when the Savior cried out, "It is finished" (John 19:30), and bowed His head and died!

But the peace of sanctification, that peace of God which is the sweet fruit of the Spirit, may be ruffled. Every sin disturbs this peace, like the agitating wind or the pebble cast into the glassy lake. To preserve this inward peace, we must go continually to Jesus. As the feet contract defilement by walking through a miry road, so our souls have need to be washed every hour from every hour's defilement while journeying through a sinful world.

As peace with God is not the result of our obedience, but of Christ's atonement— and, as such, cannot be broken—so the enjoyment of that peace of God which passes all understanding, and which is the work of the Spirit in our hearts, can only be maintained by constant prayer, by delighting in the study of God's Word, by watching against the workings of indwelling sin, by walking closely with God in all holy obedience, and by a daily application, through faith, to the fountain opened for sin and uncleanness.

Every approach to lukewarmness is destructive to our peace. To keep the heart under a lively sense of the love of God, we must never put our sins between our souls and the Savior. This will only obscure His grace and bring distress upon our minds. We must look at them as laid upon Christ when He hung upon the cross. Oh, that nothing, no, not a finger, may be placed between Jesus and my soul, lest it obstruct my view of His full and free redemption!

Many look at their sins, instead of their Savior, or at their sins as lying between them and their Savior, and so are discouraged by false fear from coming to Him. But this is a device of Satan. We must remember that Christ was made a curse for us when He hung upon the cross, and that He there made a full atonement for all the sins of all His believing people; for thus says the apostle: He "gave himself for us, that he might redeem us from all iniquity" (Titus 2:14), "having forgiven you all trespasses" (Col. 2:13). Oh, blessed revelation of grace and mercy! This apprehension of Christ and His all-sufficient merits will banish every doubt and fear, prevent that hateful lukewarmness which is the very bane of godliness, and cause our hearts to burn with holy love and to overflow in grateful praise.

"Oh, heavenly Father, be graciously pleased to preserve my soul from this evil of lukewarmness and from every approach to spiritual indifference and declension. Let the sacred fire of love ever burn upon the altar of my heart. Keep me humble and active, zealous and self-denying, until called to Thy courts above where all Thy servants shall serve Thee with ever-growing delight through the countless ages of eternity."

You saints, who taste the holy joys,
Which from the gospel sweetly flow;
Can you behold with unconcern
A world deep sunk in guilt and woe?

Behold the millions bound with sin,
Surrounded by the shades of night;
Behold, until pity drops the tear,
Until zeal awakens at the sight.

Arouse, you torpid saints, and bend
Your knees with humble, contrite shame,
That you so little pain have felt
For those who know not Jesus' name.

Come, join that little holy band,
Who labor to convert a world;
Join the victorious host of God,
Whose peaceful banners are unfurled.

Pour out your consecrated store;
Enrich the treasury divine;
Pour out the fervent heart-felt prayer,
Until truth through every region shine.

The cause is great—the promise sure;
The work of mercy shall be done:
Eternal love has firm decreed
The heathen to the eternal Son.

CHAPTER 47

Forgetfulness of God

How awful is this declaration of the royal psalmist: "The wicked shall be turned into hell, and all the nations that forget God" (Ps. 9:17)! Sin is a dreadful evil, under whatever guise it may appear—whether in the loose attire of wickedness, in the brazen armor of profaneness, in the fringed garment of pharisaical pride, or in the rough clothing of sanctimonious austerity. Sin is an infinite evil whose extent cannot be measured; its malignant nature may be ascertained by the poisonous fruits which it daily produces in the world and by those tremendous denunciations of wrath which are revealed against it in the Word of God.

But if we would learn what an evil and bitter thing sin really is, we must go to Mount Calvary and there contemplate the amazing price which Jesus, the eternal Son of God, paid to infinite Justice for our redemption when He Himself became the High Priest, the victim, and the altar.

"Oh, blessed Savior, give me faith to behold this great sight with a broken, believing, grateful heart. Enable me to look unto Thee and live—yes, to take shelter in Thee as in a rock of safety. While, like Moses, I stand in the cleft of the rock, may I view by faith all Thy goodness pass before me, and hear Thy gracious name proclaimed in accents of love."

The wicked and all who forget God shall be turned into hell. What a large portion of mankind does this embrace! Awfully tremendous thought! The profligate, and the comparatively amiable and moral who forget God, are here classed together.

The Scripture meaning of the term "forget" is not a total failure of the recollection respecting the being of a God, but a practical disregard of His presence and authority; it is living without God in the world, acting as if He either saw not or heeded not the conduct of His moral creatures. Those who now forget His omniscience shall before long be punished with everlasting destruction from the presence of the Lord and from the glory of His power. All His perfections, His slighted mercies, His violated laws, and His abused gospel shall be eternally glorified in their destruction. Oh, my soul, flee to the mountain, escape for your life, tarry not in all the plain, look not behind you, linger not, lest you be consumed!

How happy are they who love to meditate upon God, and to whom the Lord manifests His mercy! "A book of remembrance was written before him for them that feared the Lord, and that thought upon his name. And they shall be mine, saith the Lord of hosts, in that day when I make up my jewels" (Mal. 3:16-17). Believers are the Lord's jewels: they are precious in His sight; they are His peculiar treasure, being the purchase of His own most precious blood. They delight themselves in the Lord, in His perfections, promises, commands, and ordinances, and are filled with the abundance of peace. Oh, that I may have an increasing evidence of my interest in Jesus by thus delighting in Him and loving Him above every created good!

If forgetfulness of God be so heinous a sin, as in the very nature of things it must be, then, how important it is to have right views and feelings respecting our obligations to our almighty Creator, Preserver, and Redeemer. The divine command "Remember now thy Creator in the days of thy youth" (Eccl. 12:1) forms the basis of happiness; but the divine lamentation "My people have forgotten me days without number" (Jer. 2:32) proves us to be children of the fall.

Everything in religion depends upon the right state of the heart. If the main-spring be wrong, the whole movement of the machine must be in disorder. In Scripture, we find how great a stress is laid by Him, who looks at the heart, on the inward principle. The motive must be pure, or the work is hateful in His sight. Faith working by love is the gospel spring of action. This is beautifully set forth by Paul, in the eleventh chapter to the Hebrews, where he produces the most interesting witnesses to the power and efficacy of faith.

Though millions of wretched sinners forget God in the midst of their pleasures and pursuits, yet in every age He has had a people to show forth His praise. God never left Himself without witnesses. The apostle speaks of them as "so great a cloud of witnesses" (Heb. 12:1); and in the heavenly world, John, when wrapped in sacred vision, beheld a great multitude which no man could number, of all nations and kindreds and people and tongues, standing before the throne and before the Lamb, clothed with white robes, and with palms in their hands.

That unconverted people should habitually live in a forgetfulness of the Savior is not incredible. They have no love to Jesus, and therefore their thoughts never dwell upon Him. But that His people should so much forget Him; that they should live so little under the abiding influence of His presence; that they should be so carried away with the trifles of time, to the sinful neglect of eternity, is truly painful. Nothing can more fully testify to the power of that sin which dwells in us, or prove more forcibly the continual necessity for watchfulness and prayer, than this criminal forgetfulness of our almighty Friend and Savior.

The best preservative against the evil of forgetfulness is a heartfelt compliance with the Redeemer's command: "Seek ye first the kingdom of God, and his righteousness" (Matt. 6:33). If the glory of God be our first and chief concern; if our most anxious desire be that of the psalmist: "Whom have I in heaven but thee? and there is none upon earth that I desire beside thee" (Ps. 73:25); if Jesus is precious to us, and all else esteemed as nothing when compared with Him; then like Enoch, Noah, and Abraham, we shall walk before God with a perfect heart, upright and sincere; then like Moses, we shall endure as seeing Him who is invisible; and like David, we shall set the Lord always before us. With the apostles, we shall then do all to the glory of God, and our whole desire and aim will be that Christ may be magnified in our bodies, whether it be by life or death (Phil. 1:20).

Such is the sacred purpose of the true believer. His aim is high, yet he deeply deplores those inbred sins which prevent his constant elevation. He resembles a bird to whose foot a stone is tied. He struggles to ascend, but feels the gravitating force of nature. Yet grace enables him to rise above the level of the world and to soar higher and higher towards the heavenly regions.

Not so the generality of mankind. Most men die as they live. An awful forgetfulness marks their lives; a stupid unconcern, their deaths. If conscience should perchance be heard amid the clamor of a thousand lusts, each panting for gratification, Satan, too crafty to deny the claims of conscience, whispers the pacifying expedient in the sinner's ear: "a death bed repentance." Thus Satan lulls his fears to rest, well knowing that the heart increases in its hardness by delay and feels the less inclined to repent in proportion as it defers repentance.

"Lord, deliver me from this delusion of the artful enemy. Keep my conscience awake. Enable me to seek first Thy kingdom of grace that, at death, I may be admitted into Thy kingdom of glory through the merits of my Redeemer."

Why is my heart so wayward grown,
So prone to start aside?
Where are the joys and comforts flown,
Which once my God supplied?

Have His redeeming mercies ceased
In copious streams to flow?
Why are His judgments now increased,
To fill my heart with woe?

Alas, a cold, deceitful heart
Has grieved the holy Dove;
My sins have said—Arise, depart;
And now I mourn His love.

Forgetfulness of God

Dark and deserted is my soul;
I hear the lion roar;
Lord, make a trembling sinner whole,
Who lies at mercy's door.

In pity listen to my moan,
Return with pardoning grace;
Oh, take away this heart of stone,
And Thou shalt have the praise.

CHAPTER 48

Watchfulness

This life is a state of probation. Hence trials are necessary in order to prove us, as gold is tried in the fire. God cannot be tempted with evil, neither does He tempt any man; but we are tempted when we are drawn aside of our own lust and enticed (James 1:13-14). Satan works upon our corrupt nature, and there he finds materials ready prepared for his destructive purpose.

While we are in an unrenewed state, we are under the dominion of sin. We naturally love it and are captivated by it, for our hearts are only evil continually (Gen. 6:5).

Common prudence and worldly interest, as well as natural conscience, may prevent an unconverted man from committing many crimes which would outrage society. The fear of punishment and the dread of public infamy may operate to the prevention of those evils which would bring a man under the lash of the violated laws of his country. The certain consequence of disease and poverty attendant on some vices proves a partial check to their commission—though, alas, too weak to arrest the general torrent of licentiousness.

Thus, by the constant operation of these inferior motives and through the goodness of a restraining Providence, we are happily preserved from that inundation of iniquity which would otherwise destroy the fabric of society.

There are, it is true, many amiable characters to be found, even among those who are hostile to the spirit of the gospel, who may be considered as ornaments in the midst of surrounding depravity and pollution. Polite education and civilized society can varnish over the old Adam. But these amiable worldlings reject as fanatical those unwelcome declarations of Scripture which assert the radical corruption of our nature and the absolute necessity of being born again of the Spirit. In the midst of all this boasted morality, this vaunted amiability of temper, this studious endeavor to appear honorable in the eyes of each other, we perceive no filial fear of God, no hatred of sin, no delight in holiness, no cordial reception of the blessed Jesus as the only Savior from guilt and pollution, no self-abhorrence, no watchfulness against the sins of the heart, no deadness to the vanities and smiles of the world.

Under every garb, whether plain or splendid, the carnal mind is enmity against God. This truth cannot be too much impressed upon the mind and conscience. Hence we see the necessity for renewing grace, for, until we are united to Christ by a true faith, we cannot receive those powerful principles of love and fear which operate as perpetual excitements to holy obedience and constant checks to presumption and carnal security.

When we are thus savingly united to Jesus, we receive out of His fullness every needful grace. Being "accepted in the beloved" (Eph. 1:6), we have peace with God; we are adopted into His family; we are sealed by the Holy Spirit of promise; we enjoy sweet fellowship with the Father and the Son; and, experiencing the strengthening consolations of the Spirit, we are enabled to resist the world, the flesh, and the devil, and to perfect holiness in the fear of God. Such is the character, walk, and privilege of every true believer. "Lord, make me a branch in Jesus, the living vine. Create my soul anew, and fill me with every holy, pure, and heavenly affection."

Great, indeed, is the character of a child of God; yet, he is renewed but in part. The Canaanites are still in the land. Satan knows this well and tries most assiduously to regain possession of that heart from which grace has dislodged him. To effect his purpose, he studies tempers, natural constitutions, weaknesses, and peculiar situations in which believers are placed and thus endeavors to suit his temptations to the vulnerable parts of the Christian citadel.

How needful, then, is the duty of watchfulness! If an army, passing through an enemy's country, appoints its out-posts and sentinels to observe the motions of the inhabitants lest it should be surprised by an opposing force and be unexpectedly defeated, surely it behooves the Christian soldier to obey the command of the great Captain of his salvation: "Watch and pray, lest ye enter into temptation" (Mark 14:38).

Through the slothfulness and unwatchfulness of believers, Satan too often makes sad inroads into their peace and purity.

Mr. Winter, in one of his letters, makes this striking observation: "Watchfulness and prayer form the Christian's entrenchment. These are the lines our enemy cannot break. Be the person who uses them ever so weak, he will be sure to stand; be the person who neglects them ever so strong in himself, ever so judiciously taught, or ever so extensive in his knowledge, he is liable to fall." The farther the experienced Christian advances in his earthly pilgrimage, the more he learns how needful to his safety are watchfulness and prayer.

There are some who treat as legal this circumspection and self-distrust. But the real believer well knows that the more lively his faith is, the more alive he himself is to the motions of his spiritual enemies, lest he should be overcome by some sudden temptation.

There are three evils against which we should earnestly pray to be preserved: indecision, indifference, and insensibility. When the mind begins to be first affected with the importance of religion, many things are done which were before omitted. But no sooner is the religious feeling of the heart made known to the world by this outward change of conduct than the artillery of Satan is directed against the young professor, and too often, alas, proves successful in shaking the newly formed purpose of taking up the cross and following Christ.

The enemy of souls now plies his warlike engines with satanic violence. Worldly interest, carnal ease, false shame, the fear of man, the frowns of relations, and the raillery of sinful companions are all employed with consummate skill to undermine his good resolves. These powerful attacks, if not resisted through the energy of almighty grace, soon produce indecision in the purpose. From indecision, the step is easy to indifference; from indifference to the voice of conscience, the transition is quick to insensibility; from insensibility to the threatenings of God, how short is the road to obduracy—the very seal of perdition. Who can contemplate this awful progress of declension and not acknowledge the immense importance of watchfulness and prayer?

There cannot be a more humbling representation of the fallen state of man than in the falls of those eminent saints whose lives are recorded in the pages of Scripture. The Almighty, in His wisdom, may have permitted these falls to humble the best of men by leading them to feel that their steadfastness in holiness does not depend upon their strength, but on His grace, and that their resistance of evil is not from any natural power of their own, but entirely from the communicated influence of the Holy Spirit upon their hearts.

When Noah lived before the flood, he testified as a "preacher of righteousness" (2 Pet. 2:5) against the prevailing iniquity of the age. He walked with God in faith, fear, love, and obedience, and found grace in His sight. But when safe in the bosom of his family, a monument of mercy after the tremendous deluge, he drank wine and was drunken and lay uncovered in his tent! Can this be Noah, the holy Noah? Then let him that thinks he stands, take heed lest he fall.

Lot, whose righteous soul was vexed from day to day with the filthy conversation of the wicked, when rescued by the hand of mercy from the devoted cities of the plain and safely sheltered in the mountain, fell into the combined atrocity of drunkenness and incest. This speaks with awful voice: "Be not highminded, but fear" (Rom. 11:20).

David, the man after God's own heart, who never once defiled his soul by heathen worship, when raised to the throne of Israel and enjoying rest in his palace, was enticed by deceitful lusts into the dreadful sins of adultery and murder.

Solomon, who was honored with the name of Jedidiah (beloved of the Lord), who built a splendid temple for the worship of Jehovah, and whose wisdom attracted the Queen of Sheba to Jerusalem, when grown old, and after having witnessed the faithfulness of God in the promises made to him on ascending the throne, was turned after other gods through the allurements of his foreign wives and erected high places for the abominations of the heathen (1 Kings 11:4-8). Surely we must say, "What is man, that thou art mindful of him?" (Heb. 2:6).

Hezekiah, so mercifully raised from a bed of death, was lifted up with pride, perhaps on account of the stupendous miracle wrought on his behalf.

Peter, so zealous and confident, denied his Lord with oaths and curses.

Abraham, so eminent for faith, betrayed the evil of mistrust, showing that the fear of man brings a snare.

Jacob, under the semblance of piety and filial affection, with a lie obtained his father's blessing.

Moses, so renowned for meekness, was condemned to die in the wilderness, because he spoke unadvisedly with his lips.

Aaron, the high priest of the Lord, made a golden calf around which the people danced to their shame.

How faithful is the pen of inspiration; what indubitable marks of divinity are stamped upon the Holy Scriptures! Here, truth with impartial hand dips her pencil, now in the brighter, now in the darker colors, and thus draws her characters to the very life. Here we see man, just as he is, both by nature and grace. If characters so eminent for holiness have been stained with sin, where shall we find sinless perfection in this lower world? All need the blood of Jesus; all need the preserving grace of God; all need the constant exercise of watchfulness and prayer.

Those who take encouragement from these painful instances of corruption in the best of men in order to trifle with sin and to despise the truths of the Bible, because some holy characters recorded in it have been drawn by Satan and their own hearts into grievous crimes, evidence a total ignorance of their own hearts and a total destitution of that grace which, through the blessed truths of Scripture, leads men to holiness, to happiness, and to heaven.

While infidels tauntingly expose the sins of believers, let them behold with solemn awe the displeasure of the Almighty, as manifested in biblical characters' temporal afflictions and their heart-rending sorrows which, like piercing thorns, sprang out of their iniquities. And when believers contemplate these Scripture characters, let them seek for grace to avoid their falls and to copy their unfeigned repentance.

The all-conquering Lamb, who fought and overcame Satan by dying upon the cross for our redemption, will not allow him to exult with shouts of final victory. He raises the fallen believer through an act of inconceivable, unmerited mercy; fills him with shame and self-abhorrence; leads him to the fountain of His own most precious blood; imparts to him a fresh supply of His Holy Spirit; and thus enables him to renew the conflict with unabated vigor, in deep humility, self-distrust, and simple reliance on His almighty power, combined with constant vigilance against the motions of every inward and outward foe.

But the soul which shall dare to presume upon such mercy, and so indulge in sin, is in the utmost peril of falling into perdition; for this very spirit of daring proves a man to be a self-deceiver, an enemy of all righteousness.

A true believer may fall into sin; but he cannot sin on the principle that grace may abound or because Jesus has said, "My sheep … shall never perish" (John 10:27-28), well knowing that the character of Christ's sheep is that they hear the Shepherd's voice and follow Him.

A true believer may fall into sin, but he cannot sin habitually or with continued delight, well knowing that "whosoever is born of God doth not commit sin; for his seed remaineth in him: and he cannot sin, because he is born of God" (1 John 3:9). To do so would prove him a hypocrite, and not a child of God. The grace of the gospel gives no license to iniquity. To imagine for a moment that it grants the slightest accommodation to sin is to cast a foul reproach upon the spotless purity of that holy Being from whom all grace proceeds.

That evil men should abuse this revelation of mercy is no more marvelous than that they do every hour abuse the choicest blessings of providence. It is strange to think how incorrectly men reason, in general, about spiritual things. They can invent a thousand objections against what they do not love, which objections they would instantly repel if brought against some favorite worldly scheme.

I perceive, then, that there is great need to watch against the false reasonings of my own mind. If I feel tempted to parley with sin, to grow lukewarm in religion, or to draw back into the world, let me ask myself these solemn questions: Is my heavenly Father less kind and gracious than when I first knew the Lord? Is my Savior less lovely and precious in the eyes of saints and angels? Is the divine Spirit less holy and comforting to the tried believer? Is sin less hateful in the sight of God, and less destructive to the soul? Is Satan less watchful and subtle against the sheep of Christ? Is the world less vain and deceitful in its nature and pursuits? Is the heart less vile and treacherous in its inward workings? Is heaven less glorious and desirable to the weary pilgrim? Is hell less dreadful and tormenting to the perishing sinner?

Have any of these objects changed their nature since first the light of truth broke in upon my mind? If not, then why should I begin to change my views and feelings respecting them? Why grow lukewarm and indifferent? Oh, what need for suspicion, lest all should not be right! What need for watchfulness, self-examination, and prayer!

If these realities are still the same—if the truths of God are immutable—then why should I be less vigilant, less prayerful, less anxious about these infinitely momentous truths? Time is rapidly receding; eternity is rapidly advancing. My state must soon be irrevocably fixed in a world of happiness or misery. Then why am I so cold, so indifferent to the highest interests of my immortal soul? Is it not owing to the prevalence of inward corruption and the workings of Satan in my depraved heart?

"Blessed Jesus, look in mercy upon a wretched, lost creature. Were I to be crushed, as in a moment, and sent quick into hell, it would be righteous judgment. But Thou art gracious, Thou art full of compassion, Thou camest to seek and to save rebellious sinners. Lord, save me, help me, undertake for me. Snatch me as a brand out of the burning fire. Deliver me from the jaws of that roaring lion who is ever going about, seeking whom he may devour. Lord, give me not over to him as a prey. Allow me not to be carried captive by him at his will. Fill me with a constant dread of sin; make me ever watchful and vigilant. Bear me in Thine arms of love through all dangers of my earthly course, until, safe removed from every storm, I serve Thee in Thine everlasting kingdom."

Oh, gracious Friend of sinners,
Sanctify my guilty soul;
Speak the word, almighty Savior,
And Thy servant shall be whole.

Save me from corruption's power,
Save me from satanic wiles;
Spread Thy guardian wings around me,
Cheer me with Thy heavenly smiles.

As I wander through the desert,
Be my constant help and stay:
Shine upon my path, and lead me
To the realms of endless day.

Then, oh then, in sweetest rapture,
Free from danger, loud I'll sing,
In the grand celestial chorus,
Glory to the immortal King.

CHAPTER 49

The Danger of Riches

There is a beautiful harmony in the doctrines and precepts of Scripture, whether promulgated under the patriarchal, Mosaic, or Christian dispensation, which strikingly proves its divine origin. Every enlightened reader of the Bible will perceive a rich vein of truth running through the whole of the sacred volume. What is obscurely revealed under the patriarchal dispensation is more fully made known under the law, and exhibited in its brightest colors by the gospel.

A short review of the Scriptures, with respect to the sin of covetousness, will verify this observation.

Job, when vindicating his character, makes the following declaration: "If I have made gold my hope, or have said to the fine gold, Thou art my confidence; if I rejoiced because my wealth was great, and because mine hand had gotten much; if I beheld the sun when it shined, or the moon walking in brightness; and my heart hath been secretly enticed, or my mouth hath kissed my hand: this also were an iniquity to be punished by the judge: for I should have denied the God that is above" (Job 31:24-28). We have here the closest connection between covetousness and idolatry. The two sins are classed together as twin evils springing from one common source, the unbelief and earthliness of the heart.

This is in strict accordance with the other parts of the sacred oracle. Paul styles covetousness as idolatry (Col. 3:5) and a covetous man as an idolater (Eph. 5:5). Our Savior explains the nature of this idolatry: "How hard is it for them that trust in riches to enter into the kingdom of God!" (Mark 10:24).

To possess wealth, when imparted in the providence of God, is not sinful; for it was said of Abraham by his servant Eleazar: "And the Lord hath blessed my master greatly; and he is become great: and he hath given him flocks, and herds, and silver, and gold, and menservants, and maidservants, and camels, and asses" (Gen. 24:35). But the sin lies in trusting in these things; hence Job says: "If I have made gold my hope, or have said to the fine gold, Thou art my confidence; If I rejoice because my wealth was great, ... I should have denied the God that is above" (Job 31:24-25, 28).

David was aware of the same danger arising from the possession of wealth, and he gives this salutary caution: "If riches increase, set not your heart upon them" (Ps. 62:10), or in the words of Job: "Make them not your hope and your confidence" (cf. Job 31:24). Solomon points out the same evil: "He that trusteth in his riches shall fall" (Prov. 11:28). Moses strongly cautions the Israelites against this misuse of temporal things: "And it shall be, when the Lord thy God shall have brought thee into the land which he sware unto thy fathers, to Abraham, to Isaac, and to Jacob, to give thee great and goodly cities, which thou buildedst not, and houses full of all good things, which thou filledst not, and wells digged, which thou diggedst not, vineyards and olive trees, which thou plantedst not; when thou shalt have eaten and be full; then beware lest thou forget the Lord, which brought thee forth out of the land of Egypt" (Deut. 6:10-12).

From where does this proneness to depart from God arise, this cleaving to earthly things? It springs from the fall of Adam. It is the very fault and corruption of our nature. We are all naturally idolaters, loving the creature "more than the Creator, who is blessed for ever" (Rom. 1:25), and therefore this evil justly exposes us to eternal death. Nothing but divine grace can save us from this idolatrous attachment to earth. Who does not daily feel its influence? Oh, how much I need the sovereign grace of God to wean my affections from the world and cause me to seek my all in Him! Herein consists true happiness. Until God in Christ be my all-sufficient, my all-satisfying portion, I cannot be truly happy. A divided heart must of necessity be a wretched heart.

"Lord, unite my heart to fear Thy name. Collect my scattered powers and let them work for Thee alone. As it was with the Israelites, so may it be with me. In my departure out of a wicked world, let 'not an hoof be left behind' (Ex. 10:26). May all that I possess be wholly consecrated unto Thee."

Were we told of some highly favored individual whose every desire after wealth and pleasure might be gratified, should we not be ready to exclaim that this must be a happy man? A slight acquaintance with human character would soon dissipate this illusion. The desire of man, which is the very essence of covetousness, makes us dissatisfied with what we already possess, while an increase of possessions, by increasing our cares and troubles, tends only to diminish our portion of actual enjoyment.

The experience of Solomon, so feelingly described in the book of Ecclesiastes, speaks volumes on this subject. He made the dangerous experiment of gratifying his desires, with an eagerness which could only he equaled by his means of gratification:

> "I said in mine heart, Go to now, I will prove thee with mirth, therefore enjoy pleasure: and, behold, this also is vanity. I said of laughter, It is mad: and of mirth, What doeth it? I sought in mine heart to give myself unto wine, yet acquainting mine heart with wisdom; and to lay hold on folly, till I might see what was that good for the sons of men, which they should do under the heaven all the days of their life. I made me great works; I builded me houses; I planted me vineyards: I made me gardens and orchards, and I planted trees in them of all kind of fruits: I made me pools of water, to water therewith the wood that bringeth forth trees: I got me servants and maidens, and had servants born in my house; also I had great possessions of great and small cattle above all that were in Jerusalem before me: I gathered me also silver and gold, and the peculiar treasure of kings and of the provinces: I gat me men singers and women singers, and the delights of the sons of men, as musical instruments, and that of all sorts. So I was great, and increased more than all that were before me in Jerusalem: also

my wisdom remained with me. And whatsoever mine eyes desired I kept not from them, I withheld not my heart from any joy; for my heart rejoiced in all my labour: and this was my portion of all my labour" (Eccl. 2:1-10).

But what was the fruit of such unbounded gratification, which by thousands is esteemed the climax of human happiness? Hear the humiliating confession of Solomon, than whom no one had ever a fairer opportunity of reaping happiness, if ever it sprang out of worldly pleasure: "Then I looked on all the works that my hands had wrought, and on the labour that I had laboured to do: and, behold, all was vanity and vexation of spirit, and there was no profit under the sun" (Eccl. 2:11). And after enumerating a variety of vanities, he closes his book with these important words: "Let us hear the conclusion of the whole matter: Fear God, and keep his commandments: for this is the whole duty of man. For God shall bring every work into judgment, with every secret thing, whether it be good, or whether it be evil" (Eccl. 12:13-14).

Nothing is so restless as the spirit of a covetous man. He is continually pursuing after a phantom. Covetous men are dissatisfied and miserable, "for they have sown the wind, and they shall reap the whirlwind: it hath no stalk; the bud shall yield no meal: if so be it yield, the strangers shall swallow it up" (Hos. 8:7). "Surely every man walketh in a vain shew: surely they are disquieted in vain: he heapeth up riches, and knoweth not who shall gather them" (Ps. 39:6). Solomon felt this when he said: "Yea, I hated all my labour which I had taken under the sun: because I should leave it unto the man that shall be after me. And who knoweth whether he shall be a wise man or a fool?... This is also vanity" (Eccl. 2:18-19).

How contentedly happy is the child of God! He views every event as directed by infinite wisdom and reviews every gift as the expression of infinite love. He knows that God is well acquainted with the nature of His own gifts, and he is therefore satisfied with the portion which infinite love bestows, as well as with the dispensation by which infinite wisdom takes away. With childlike acquiescence in the divine disposals, he learns in whatever state he is, therewith to be content. He does not labor to be rich. He finds by experience that riches cannot confer happiness or health or honor. He sees many rich men miserable, and many poor men happy. He blesses God for his daily bread, eats his food with gladness and singleness of heart, and praises God for His hourly mercies flowing to him through that precious medium of communication between heaven and earth, the Lord Jesus Christ.

He has, however, covetous desires. He covets earnestly the best gifts. He longs and labors to possess these eternal blessings, which never cloy, but increase the joy and happiness of the soul by their increased possession. He prays with fervent desire for the graces of faith and love, for humility and purity, for the filling of the Spirit, for the presence of the Savior, for the love of the Father, for a heart filled with all the fullness of God.

This is the happy man, whose desires are accomplished. He delights in the Lord, and the God of all grace gives him the desires of his heart. The character of his life is contentment with moderation in earthly things, combined with ardent desires after the increase of spiritual blessings. He is diligent in business as a duty, fervent in spirit as a blessedness, active in serving the Lord as his highest honor.

Oh, for this contentment, this thirsting after God, this devotedness to His service and glory! He who trusts in riches is like one who endeavors to repose upon the foam of a tempestuous sea. No sooner does he throw himself upon it than it separates, and he sinks as lead in the waters; while he who trusts in the Lord resembles the man who, securely stationed upon a rock, sees the billows spend their fury at his feet. He views the wild uproar and smiles at the storm.

In this fallen world, where sin has planted sorrows in awful profusion, is it not amazing that creatures, liable to continual change, are not solicitous to find a shelter from the tempest? They are anxious, indeed, to obtain rest, but they seek for it where it never can be found—in earthly things.

Men are apt to imagine that if they can only amass a fortune and reach the hill of prosperity, they shall escape those troubles which overwhelm the many who dwell in the valley below. But are not mountains the most exposed to storms? Are they not the most bleak and barren parts of the earth, while the sheltered valleys stand so thick with corn, that, in the poetic language of David, they laugh and sing (Ps. 65:13)?

History furnishes abundant proofs that elevated stations expose men to perpetual dangers and cause the soul to be barren in those fruits of peace, contentment, and piety, which enrich the heart of the lowly, retired believer. Why, then, should I envy the great, or labor to be rich? Even if I should happily escape the common snares of wealth, yet death will soon transfer it into other hands, and then what will all my riches profit, if at that solemn period I should be destitute of faith and love?

"Lord, make me anxious for the true riches. May I daily lay up my treasure in heaven. May my heart be there. Let no idol be seated on the throne of my affections. May Thou reign the sovereign Lord within. Oh, may all my powers be subject unto Thee. May I own no sway but Thine. All will then be well. Whether prosperous or afflicted, all things shall work together for my good."

The Scriptures point out in the strongest manner the danger of riches. Many monuments of wrath are there presented to our view. Achan, Gehazi, Judas, and Ananias and Sapphira, being dead, yet speak with warning voice. The love of money proved their downfall.

We all naturally love ease. We have a natural love of rest. Toil and pain are alike irksome to the savage and the sage. Those earthly possessions which promise the greatest portion of enjoyment are the most coveted by mankind in general. In civilized countries it may be said, in the expressive language of Solomon: "Money answereth all things" (Eccl. 10:19). It is able to procure for us those various conveniences which tend to smooth the path of life. It provides us with food and clothing; with innumerable elegancies and superfluities; with opportunities of extending our researches after knowledge, of visiting distant countries, and of treasuring up the labors of the dead. Money can command almost everything, but what is most essential to our happiness: peace of conscience, joy in God, and victory over sin and death.

Here, then, arises the danger of riches. They furnish us with every requisite to earthly pleasure. They give us a commanding influence over our poorer neighbors and an importance in the circle in which we move. Hence we secretly pant after their increase. They engross the affections, they fill the mind, they captivate the will, they usurp the place of God in the soul.

When riches flow into the coffer, trouble is never apprehended; but when they cease to flow, the darkened clouds seem rapidly to threaten the destruction of our earthly joys. The smile then forsakes the worldling's countenance, gloom settles upon his once laughing face, despair seizes on his heart, and death not infrequently closes the fatal scene.

Such a state of mind as this infallibly proves the love of money to be the predominating passion in the soul. And such a state of mind is incompatible with salvation. Our blessed Lord has declared, in words too plain to be misunderstood: "It is easier for a camel to go through the eye of a needle, than for a rich man [trusting in his riches] to enter into the kingdom of God" (Matt. 19:24). Paul in like manner bears his testimony against this sin of our nature: "Charge them that are rich in this world, that they be not highminded, nor trust in uncertain riches, but in the living God, who giveth us richly all things to enjoy" (1 Tim. 6:17). He cautions believers most solemnly against the evil of covetousness by declaring that "the love of money is the root of all evil: which while some coveted after, they have erred from the faith, and pierced themselves through with many sorrows" (1 Tim. 6:10).

If true believers, we ought again and again to impress upon our hearts this sacred truth: that real happiness consists in having God for our portion; in being satisfied, yes, thankful for the allotments of His providence; in feeling ourselves to be pilgrims and strangers upon earth, hastening along the stream of time to that blessed world, where every trial will be forgotten—or, if remembered, will only, by its recollection, enhance our everlasting joy.

This state of mind, this holy frame of heart, is the work of the Spirit, the fruit of faith. "And all thy children shall be taught of the LORD; and great shall be the peace of thy children" (Isa. 54:13). "Thou wilt keep him in perfect peace, whose mind is stayed on thee: because he trusteth in thee" (Isa. 26:3). "Be careful for nothing; but in every thing by prayer and supplication with thanksgiving let your requests be made known unto God. And the peace of God, which passeth all understanding, shall keep your hearts and minds through Christ Jesus" (Phil. 4:6-7). "Our light affliction, which is but for a moment, worketh for us a far more exceeding and eternal weight of glory; while we look not at the things which are seen, but at the things which are not seen: for the things which are seen are temporal; but the things which are not seen are eternal" (2 Cor. 4:17-18).

"Oh, blessed Savior, wean my foolish heart from the world. Save me from the love of money, which is spiritual idolatry. Raise my affections to high and heavenly things. May Thou be in time and through eternity my all in all."

Why, oh my soul, should earthly joys
Detain you prisoner here below?
The richest gems are trifling toys,
Compared with those believers know.

How glorious their immortal crowns,
More dazzling bright than mid-day sun.
Jesus their happy souls adorns
With wreaths, which He Himself has won.

How vain are all the scenes of earth,
Beneath their now exalted view!
They feel the honors of their birth,
The friends of God, and angels too.

Oh, blissful state of holy joy!
Awake, my soul, and upward soar;
Your rebel passions now destroy,
Let earth engross your heart no more.

Yet, Lord, I look alone to Thee,
Exert Thy sovereign, saving power;
Oh, set my captive spirit free;
Be this redemption's joyful hour!

CHAPTER 50

The Thorns in the Parable

In the instructive parable of the sower, our divine Redeemer, who spoke as never man spoke, has discovered to us the nature of those thorns which choke and render unfruitful the good seed of the Word of God. "And that which fell among thorns are they, which, when they have heard, go forth, and are choked with cares and riches and pleasures of this life, and bring no fruit to perfection" (Luke 8:14).

Worldly cares are thorns. If we are anxious and troubled about many things—anxious about the events of tomorrow and forecasting evils which have no existence but in our own minds—we are sowing tares and thorns, which must of necessity destroy all the vigor and fruitfulness of the gospel seed.

The work of faith is to perform present duty and then leave the issue with God, who works all things after the counsel of His own will. We have no power over the varied events of life. Circumstances arise which cannot be foreseen, nor prevented if foreseen. Prudence may lay her plans, but He who rules on high can thwart them all. "There are many devices in a man's heart; nevertheless the counsel of the Lord, that shall stand" (Prov. 19:21). It is, then, the part of Christian wisdom to obey the beautiful precept of Solomon: "Trust in the Lord with all thine heart; and lean not unto thine own understanding. In all thy ways acknowledge him, and he shall direct thy paths" (Prov. 3:5-6).

In such a world as this, which is made up of vicissitude and agitations, how highly privileged is the man who can say with David: "The Lord is my rock, and my fortress, and my deliverer; my God, my strength, in whom I will trust; my buckler, and the horn of my salvation, and my high tower" (Ps. 18:2). How calm is that soul whose cares are laid upon God! This is the Christian's privilege: "Casting all your care upon him; for he careth for you" (1 Pet. 5:7). "Cast thy burden upon the Lord, and he shall sustain thee" (Ps. 55:22). Oh, my soul, remember who it is that invites you to this rest. It is Jesus, the friend of sinners. How affectionate is His invitation: "Come unto me, all ye that labor and are heavy laden, and I will give you rest" (Matt. 11:28).

Cares are vexatious to a worldly mind. Afflictions are viewed as so many suspensions of worldly happiness. Poverty is dreaded as the greatest worldly evil, and even religion itself is treated as an enemy, because it demands the separation of the heart from worldly lusts and pleasures. And yet, it is owing to the absence of true religion that the varied dispensations of providence become crosses. We meet them in an unsubdued frame of spirit. We murmur and rebel against the correcting hand of our heavenly Father, and thus render that burden heavy and that yoke grievous which would otherwise be easy and light. While in this unhappy state of mind, we hear the gospel with perpetual distraction. The cares of life, like prickling thorns, cover the ground of our heart and prevent the good seed from springing up and bearing fruit to the glory of God.

"Oh, blessed Spirit, awaken my soul to a due solicitude about my everlasting state. Let me not be sowing tares while Thy ministers are sowing wheat. Let not my foolish heart by worldly cares choke the precious seed of holy truth. Make me watchful and vigilant. Break up the fallow ground of my heart by deep and abiding convictions, that I may no longer sow among thorns, but yield abundant fruit to the praise of the glory of Thy grace."

Riches are thorns. What can riches, so coveted after by the world, do for wretched man, simply considered in themselves? They cannot produce happiness. How many families, overladen with wealth, are made unhappy by the very wealth which they possess! They cannot insure usefulness. How many people do we continually see, who, with the most extensive means of usefulness, are little better than cumberers of the ground! They cannot promote health. How many are rendered the victims of disease by the facility which wealth affords for gratifying their carnal appetites and luxurious inclinations! They cannot prolong life. How many are cut off in the midst of their splendor, when they were fondly promising to themselves a long succession of joyous years!

If riches cannot procure temporal blessings—if they cannot, by their mere possession, even to their greatest extent, make us happy in ourselves, or useful to others; if they cannot promote health, or prolong life—how much less can they procure spiritual or eternal blessings: the pardon of sin, peace with God, purity of heart, and perpetuity of bliss in heaven!

And yet, wealth is the grand desire of the world. To obtain riches, men are willing to risk the loss of soul and all the glories of heaven. The nominally Christian world is bowing down to the golden image which Satan has set up, while all kinds of music are employed to celebrate its praise. Even real professors of godliness have need to watch continually against the seductive influence of the god of this world. He can paint upon the imagination the shadowy glories of the world, and then whisper to the soul: "All these things will I give thee, if thou wilt fall down and worship me" (Matt. 4:9).

But truth lifts up her warning voice to guard her children against the snares of this father of lies: "But they that will be rich fall into temptation and a snare, and into many foolish and hurtful lusts, which drown men in destruction and perdition. For the love of money is the root of all evil: which while some coveted after, they have erred from the faith, and pierced themselves through with many sorrows" (1 Tim. 6:9-10).

Our blessed Lord, whose love is infinite, has given us a double caution: "Take heed, and beware of covetousness: for a man's life consisteth not in the abundance of the things which he possesseth" (Luke 12:15). And Paul, writing under the influence of the Spirit of Christ, exhorts us to "let your conversation be without covetousness; and be content with such things as ye have: for he hath said, I will never leave thee, nor forsake thee" (Heb. 13:5).

Riches, when loved and coveted after, become our idols. And even when they do not captivate the affections, they will soon choke the precious seed of divine truth, if not carefully guarded against. Hence our Lord calls it "the deceitfulness of riches" (Mark 4:19). They draw away the heart insensibly from God, and then they become a curse, and not a blessing. Many who, while in the valley of humiliation, adorned the gospel and labored with unwearied diligence to promote its extension, have become lukewarm when wealth has filled their coffers.

These characters present an awful instance of the danger of worldly prosperity and should make every professor of the gospel tremble, lest, when riches increase, his heart should be lifted up and he forget the Lord his God. Worldly prosperity is almost always followed by declension. How many Christian families, once the ornaments of the church, have, in their posterity, lost all semblance of piety through the growing prosperity which attended their secular concerns!

"Oh, blessed Lord, give me grace to covet earnestly the best gifts, even the unsearchable riches of Christ; to labor after the attainment of those riches whose value can never be fully known in this lower world, but after which all, without exception, are graciously invited to seek, that they may obtain everlasting life. Blessed Jesus, pearl of great price, may Thou be my treasure."

> *Give what Thou wilt; without Thee, I am poor;*
> *And with Thee, rich; take what Thou wilt away.*

Worldly pleasures are thorns. Man has a natural thirst after happiness; but, being blinded through the fall, and having all his appetites vitiated, he is continually seeking that from the world which can only be found in God.

Fallen man, like Cain of old, is a fugitive. He is ever flying from the presence of his Creator, who is the source and center of true felicity. He is daily committing two evils, forsaking the fountain of living waters and hewing out to himself broken cisterns which can hold no water (Jer. 2:13).

Hence he is miserable while in quest of happiness. He drinks of the intoxicating wine of carnal gratification; revels for a time in sensual pleasure; and if he awakens to sober recollection, feels a thousand stings, which too often drive him to despair and death.

Consistent professors of godliness readily allow the sinfulness of gross sensual indulgences and of such worldly amusements as lead directly to the violation of chaste feeling, or into the vortex of fashionable dissipation.

There are, however, pleasures of a sober and innocent kind, which, from their friendly aspect, are unsuspectedly admitted into the heart, and, like the "little foxes,… spoil the vines" (Song 2:15). Few seem to consider that even lawful pleasures, when too eagerly pursued, become sources of pain by secretly alienating the heart from God.

Hence serious Christians have need to guard against giving too much of their mind and time to those pursuits which may insensibly draw them off from private devotion and the daily duties of social life. The acquirements of music and drawing, as well as the prosecution of literary and philosophical studies, are lawful and agreeable when pursued in subservience to that great end of life so plainly enforced by the apostle: "Whether therefore ye eat, or drink, or whatsoever ye do, do all to the glory of God" (1 Cor. 10:31). Religion does not forbid the improvement of our intellectual faculties; it only guards against their abuse.

Lawful things are not always beneficial; and, if abused or used to excess, they become injurious. Society is pleasant; yet it becomes a snare if it leads us from our secret chamber by its incessant attractions and thus makes us strangers to God and our own hearts.

We are everywhere surrounded with danger. Each pleasure has its poison, and each sweet its snare. And yet, how fleeting! Worldly delights resemble the rose, which droops almost as soon as gathered. Our blessed Lord warns us against those pleasures which too frequently choke the Word, as thorns do the growing plant. The enemy knows this well; and, therefore, when young people, especially, begin to feel their consciences awakened under the faithful preaching of the gospel, he stirs up their carnal friends to carry them into the various gayeties of life, that the incipient workings of divine grace may be destroyed in the very germ.

Oh, then, let us be upon our guard, not only against distracting cares and deceitful riches, but also against delusive pleasures, which, by their smiling face and winning form, would steal away our hearts and rob us of eternal glory! Worldly pleasures, like Solomon's many wives, entice the soul to idolatrous attachments and departure from God. There are, however, pleasures pure and peaceful, holy and heavenly, which never cloy or injure the believer. Communion with God in Christ—the enjoyment of the divine favor, through faith in the blood of Jesus; the varied exercises in reading, meditation, and prayer; the society of experienced Christians; visiting the sick; instructing the young; relieving the poor and needy; pouring the balm of consolation into the troubled breast; directing the wanderer to Jesus; restoring the backslider; reproving the profane; promoting peace; and supporting by active and financial exertions those noble institutions which bless our happy land—form so many streams of pleasure which at once refresh and fructify the soul.

If to these are added the duties of our secular calling, the endearments of domestic life, the well-timed relaxations of music, painting, and gardening, with the higher gratifications of mental study—where, we may ask, is the lack of enjoyment to the real Christian? He needs not the vanity of the ball-room, the irritations of the card table, the pollutions of the theater, the snares of the race-track, the frivolity of the circus, nor the debaucheries of the club.

If poor, he seeks not for the noisy mirth of the ale-house, which ends in rags and misery; he is happy in the bosom of his family, with his Bible and his God. Oh, that my thirst may daily increase for the holy enjoyment of pure and undefiled religion!

How insipid are the boasted pleasures of the world, when compared with these soul-reviving delights, which a God of mercy has provided for the enjoyment of Christian pilgrims!

"Blessed Jesus, fill my soul with Thy presence, and then I shall never lack a stream of pure delight while journeying through this barren wilderness to the heavenly Canaan. Let no cares disturb my peace, no riches deaden my affections, no pleasures enchain my heart. Like the wise husbandman, in mercy eradicate every noxious thorn and prepare me by Thy Spirit to receive and cherish the good Word of Thy grace, that I may bring forth fruit a hundred-fold to the glory of Thy holy name."

Touched by a sense of love divine,
Thy goodness, Lord, I feel;
What joy to call the Savior mine!
Of endless joys the seal!

Though round my path a thousand snares
Are laid by Satan's art;
Though often assailed by earth-born cares,
Those traitors of the heart.

Yet still, dear Lord, beneath Thy smiles,
A heaven of joy appears;
While faith the weary way beguiles,
And hope the prospect cheers.

If, through affliction's darksome vale,
I downward bend my way,
Oh, may Thy comforts never fail
To shed their cheering ray.

Or, should I mount the dangerous steep,
Where earthly honors shine,
Upheld by Thee, nor height nor deep,
Shall part my love from Thine.

Whatever I be, or rich or poor,
I'll trust Thy saving name;
To all the seed Thy Word is sure,
To all who love the Lamb.

Oh, let me taste Thy goodness more,
Each moment as it flies;
Until, landed safe on Canaan's shore,
Where glory never dies.

I see my Savior face to face,
Without a veil between;
And sing loud praises to His grace,
Who saved my soul from sin!

CHAPTER 51

The Parable of the Rich Man and Lazarus

The parables of our Savior are full of wisdom and beauty. They are intended to convey some great truth to which the various appendages are in general to be considered rather as natural accompaniments than as each requiring a forced or fanciful interpretation. We should, therefore, endeavor to ascertain what was the primary object which our Lord had in view when He delivered these exquisitely beautiful lessons of divine truth, that we may derive that instruction which is inculcated by them.

The parables of the net, containing good and bad fish; of the ten virgins, five of whom were wise, and five foolish; of the marriage feast, where one guest was found without a wedding garment; of the tares which sprang up among the wheat; of the vine with fruitful and barren branches—all are designed to show that, in the visible church, the righteous and the wicked will live together until the general separation at the day of judgment.

The parables of the seed springing up imperceptibly, of the grain of mustard seed, growing from the smallest seed to a great tree, and of the leaven, secretly working until the whole lump is leavened, beautifully point out the progress of the gospel throughout the earth.

The parables of the lost sheep, of the lost piece of money, and of the prodigal son reveal to us, in the most affecting manner, the great love of God in coming to seek and to save that which was lost, the readiness with which He receives returning sinners, and the joy which angels feel at the salvation of men.

The parables of the great supper and of the husbandman in the vineyard most strikingly show how men in general, and the Jews in particular, to whom our Lord then addressed Himself, despise the offers of divine mercy and persecute the faithful servants of God, who speak to them in His name.

The parables of the treasure in the field and of the pearl of great price call upon us, from the common feeling of worldly prudence, like the wise merchantman, to part with a smaller possession for one of superior value—to give up the trifles of time for the glories of eternity.

The parables of the ten pounds, of the talents, and of the sheep and goats, speak directly to the heart and are calculated to produce the deepest concern respecting that strict account which we must render of every talent committed to our trust.

The parable of the barren fig-tree exemplifies the divine patience through the intercession of Jesus. The parable of the Good Samaritan beautifully enforces the extensive duty of loving our neighbor as ourselves. The parable of the unmerciful servant is a faithful picture of divine compassion and of man's hard-heartedness and ingratitude.

The parable of the unjust judge, by way of contrast, conveys consolation to the suffering church under all her protracted trials. If this judge, so unjust, avenged the poor widow because she wearied him, shall not a God of justice much more avenge His own elect, though He bear long with them?

The parable of the Pharisee and the publican gives us a striking view of spiritual pride and spiritual humility. The parable of the laborers in the vineyard is full of comfort to the Gentile world, which shall be called by the gospel, even though it be at the eleventh hour, into the church of God.

The parable of the two sons very pertinently shows the vast difference between saying and doing. The parable of the two debtors, spoken to Simon the Pharisee, and which, from its simplicity, drew from him the confession that he would love the most to whom the most was forgiven, proves how pardoning mercy melts the heart into love.

The parable of the sower, by its beauty and perfect adaptation to the human heart, is calculated to enlighten every mind in quest of truth, respecting those hindrances which prevent our profitable hearing of the Word of God. The parable of the servant waiting for his lord shows us in what posture every believer should be: not sleeping, not rioting, but diligently waiting to meet his Lord at His coming. The parable of the rich fool, addressed to the man who so unseasonably interrupted our Savior in His discourse, manifests the folly of heaping up treasure to ourselves instead of laboring to be rich towards God.

So, in like manner, the parable of the rich man and Lazarus (Luke 16) contains much valuable instruction on a subject which men in general treat with awful indifference—the realities of a future world. This very impressive parable teaches us:

1. That riches and poverty are no sign either of God's favor or of His displeasure. His enemies often abound in temporal mercies, His friends in temporal affliction. His enemies grow harder under the beams of prosperity, his friends are softened and melted in the furnace of adversity. Hence the latter pant more ardently after heaven; the former cleave more closely to the earth.

2. That death is making steady advances towards all, both rich and poor. The rich man's wealth could not bribe death, nor avert his blow. The poor man's poverty did not cause him to be overlooked as too insignificant for the notice of this general destroyer.

3. That our state in the next world has no connection with our outward condition in this world. Here, the rich man fared sumptuously every day; there, he was destitute of a drop of water to cool his tongue. Here, Lazarus was hungry and wretched; there, he was blessed and happy in Abraham's bosom.

4. That there is no mitigation of pain in hell. Not one drop of water could be allowed by inexorable justice to alleviate his sufferings or allay the intensity of the flame.

5. That the torments of hell are eternal. A great gulf is fixed which forever prevents escape from hell or relief from heaven. Oh, wretched state of unutterable woe!

6. That the soul in hell is in a state of consciousness. The rich man looked back and remembered his former life and connections. He had five brethren. He dreaded their coming into the same place of torment—knowing, probably, that his example had helped forward their impiety. He anticipated only five additional tormentors.

7. That the appearance of a spirit would not convert a soul. Conversion is the work of God. He has appointed means for this blessed end: "If they hear not Moses and the prophets, neither will they be persuaded, though one rose from the dead" (Luke 16:31).

> "Lord, make me wise in time,
> that I may be happy in eternity!"

This parable speaks at once to the understanding, the conscience, and the heart. Yet, it is painful to think how little the human mind is affected by the most solemn truths of revelation. People who profess to believe in the divine inspiration of the Holy Scriptures, and who would on no account be deemed infidels, can and do act, from day to day, as if the future eternal world were unreal and all the promises and threatenings of the Bible without a meaning. If their earthly prospects are likely to be blasted by some improvident connection, and they are timely forewarned of the coming danger, how anxious are they to avail themselves of such friendly intimation, placing the most implicit reliance upon the veracity of their informant and acting promptly and decidedly upon it.

But the reverse is the case as it respects their spiritual concerns. They are forewarned and admonished in vain. They hope things will end better than religious people imagine, and thus madly venture upon the awful issue, rather than act as in temporal matters they would have acted. With all their boasted faith, they are unbelievers in practice. They acknowledge the veracity of Scripture but refuse to obey its dictates. They have loved idols, and after them they will go (Jer. 2:25).

The state of Christendom, it is to be feared, too much resembles this picture. There is a verbal veneration for the Word of God, combined with a secret aversion to its holy requirements. But what is faith without works? No better than a tree destitute of its fruit. The faith of God's elect is according to godliness. The Word of truth must be not only believed, but practiced; not only acknowledged, but felt. Its solemn, its consoling, its purifying doctrines must have a transforming influence on the heart. Then, and only then, will the believer be made clean, being sanctified by the truth as it is in Jesus. This change constitutes the characteristic difference between the nominal professor of Christianity and the real believer. They are known by their fruits.

It is truly surprising that the human heart is so little impressed with the nearness of eternity. This insensibility only proves the powerful prevalence of unbelief. A very slight accident or disease, if it affects a vital part of our frame, soon dissolves the natural union between soul and body.

We are constantly walking upon the very borders of the invisible world, where all is unchangeable and eternal; yet we live as if time would never end; or, at least, as if its termination were very distant from us. This can arise only from the earthliness of our hearts, from the astonishing power which visible objects have over us, and from the small influence which unseen, future, eternal realities have upon our hopes and fears. But this small influence springs solely from unbelief. We know that we must die; and yet we live as if we did not believe it. We know that life is uncertain; and yet we lay our plans for years to come, as if nothing were so certain as our continuance here. We profess to believe that God will render unto every man according to his works; and yet we act as if our works would never be noticed in the day of general retribution. We acknowledge that out of Christ there is no salvation, that without holiness no man shall see the Lord; and yet we neglect the Savior and treat the work of grace upon the heart as fanatical and delusive.

"Lord, what is man! What a compound of contrarieties and inconsistencies! Oh, give me a heart devoted to Thy glory, broken off from sin, and weaned from the world."

Dear Jesus, to Thy cross I bring

This treacherous heart of mine;
Oh save me from the serpent's sting,
And make me wholly Thine.

From unbelief and inward guile
Oh, keep my conscience clear;
Midst every deep satanic wile,
Preserve my heart sincere.

Whatever I am, or wish to do,
Whatever my thoughts devise,
Is all exposed to Thy view,
Though hid from mortal eyes.

Whenever my devious footsteps stray,
May I remember Thee;
And know, through all the dangerous way,
That "Thou, God, seest me."

CHAPTER 52

The Three Enemies

Why are so many souls deceived and plunged into destruction? Because they will not think. Lack of thought is one of the fruitful sources of human misery. "My people doth not consider" (Isa. 1:3). A thoughtless mind is one of the characteristics of that broad road which leads to destruction, while anxious inquiry, a solicitous concern, a serious consideration about eternal things, is the first step through grace into that narrow way which leads unto life eternal. "Give me, blessed Savior, a thoughtful, serious, reflecting mind; a deep sight into myself; a watchful eye over my spiritual enemies; an unshaken confidence in Thee."

From the Word of God, and my own experience, I find that there are three powerful enemies which are incessantly laboring to destroy my soul.

The first is *the world*. Being rescued from its snares through the mighty power of God, it still seeks to effect my ruin: 1. By its smiles, hoping thereby to win me back again and allure my poor, vain heart by its soft, seductive influence. This is a most dangerous temptation, and few withstand its force. 2. By its frowns, thinking thereby to terrify my soul and cause me to renounce the faith of Jesus, rather than suffer affliction with the people of God for a season. "Lord, strengthen my faith, and arm me for the combat." 3. By placing before my eyes its riches, honors, and pleasures to captivate my affections and wean me from the unseen glories of a future world. Fatal temptation! "Demas hath forsaken me," said Paul, "having loved this present world" (2 Tim. 4:10). To withdraw the affections from the things of time, to sit loosely even to lawful enjoyments, and to wait with anxious desire for the signal of departure to a better world is what unassisted nature can never perform; yet, genuine religion consists in this happy state of mind. "Lord, help me. Without Thee, I can do nothing; but, oh, glorious triumph, 'I can do all things through Christ which strengtheneth me'" (Phil. 4:13).

The second enemy, who labors to oppose my progress to the realms of bliss, is *the flesh*—dangerous enemy indeed, because never separated from me. Wherever I go, I carry this enemy in my bosom. "Lord, save me from this sinful man, myself!" The flesh harasses my soul: 1. By exciting evil affections and lusts and stimulating to wicked and unlawful actions. 2. By resisting the good motions of the Spirit, stifling its convictions, and craving a little more indulgence on the lap of sinful pleasure. 3. By laboring to blind my understanding by false reasoning, and thereby aiding the tempter in his work of destruction. Thus inbred sin is always at work. I am safe only while vigilant and constant at a throne of grace.

The third enemy, by whose subtlety and malice man became a child of misery, is *the devil*. This great adversary of the human race, as well as of the world and the flesh, has many devices and stratagems to deceive and to destroy. May I never forget my helplessness and danger, but ever look to Him who fought this warrior in my nature and overcame him by His own most precious death upon the cross.

The devil harasses my soul: 1. By injecting evil thoughts, those firebrands of hell, which fill the mind with anguish and almost drive the trembling sinner to despair. The feeble-minded and the low-spirited are exposed to this artillery of Satan, from which even the strongest and most joyous believer is not wholly exempted. When the enemy comes in like a flood, oh blessed Spirit, lift up a standard against him. When the overflowings of ungodliness make me afraid, then arise, oh mighty Conqueror of death and hell; so shall Thine enemies be scattered; then shall those who hate Thee flee before Thee! 2. The devil tempts me to ruin by presenting the bait of sin under false names and alluring colors. How many are destroyed by this temptation! The object of Satan is to represent the religion of Jesus as gloomy, unsocial, and forbidding, and the pleasures of the world as smiling, sociable, and enchanting. "Lord, make me watchful. 'In vain the net is spread in the sight of any bird'

(Prov. 1:17). Enable me to examine every thing by the light of truth, to prove all things, and to hold fast that which is good." 3. He seeks my destruction by stirring up the wicked to persecute my soul, and by spreading stumbling-blocks to impede my progress towards the heavenly Canaan. These are but a small part of his devices, of which the believer is not ignorant. We are in an enemy's country. This is the field of battle. Here we must fight; but, if we endure faithful unto the end, we shall triumphantly join in the Conqueror's song.

My prayer must daily be that I may never be allowed to indulge a thought which I would not dare to express, or do an action in secret which I should blush to have known. I do not expect, while in this state of mortality, to be free from every sinful thought, or effectually to prevent their entrance into the mind. This is the perfection of heaven. Yet I must labor after this blessedness by faith and prayer, or I am only a hypocrite and self-deceiver.

The ready access which Satan has to the imaginative powers of the soul, and the quickness with which he can dart his poisonous suggestions into the heart, are most astonishing. No season is too sacred to prevent his bold intrusion. The house of God and the table of the Lord do not afford a sanctuary from this enemy. Judas stands on record as an awful witness to this truth.

The Christian's private retirement is often greatly disturbed by this restless invader, who tempted the holy Jesus in the desert. He raises visionary schemes of profit or pleasure to amuse the fancy or engage the passions. No art or stratagem is left untried to tempt the harassed soul to forego its duties or meditate on anything rather than Christ and holiness and heaven.

Oh, how precious at such a season are prayer and the Word of God! The sword of the Spirit and all-prayer are the weapons which Satan cannot long withstand, when wielded by the arm of faith. "Resist the devil, and he will flee from you" (James 4:7) is written for the encouragement of tempted pilgrims.

But who can prevent the injections of Satan? I might as soon attempt to check the whirlwind in its course or stop the flowing tide.

Yet I may and must resist them by faith and prayer, or I shall perish by them. All-sufficient help is offered. Jesus has said: "My grace is sufficient for thee: for my strength is made perfect in weakness" (2 Cor. 12:9). The promise is: "God…shall bruise Satan under your feet shortly" (Rom. 16:20). I must daily seek this promised aid by humble, persevering prayer. Then, as surely as the promise stands recorded in the Bible, so surely shall I come off more than conqueror through the blood of the Lamb.

This is not, however, the work of an hour. The believer's warfare ends only with his life. He puts off his earthly tabernacle and his earthly troubles together. Oh, my soul, take encouragement from that consoling question which was put to doubting Sarah: "Is any thing too hard for the Lord?" (Gen. 18:14).

"Almighty Savior, when sin is working within me, and my soul is bowed down with sorrow; when Satan buffets me with his horrid assaults, and all seems darkness and despair; when unbelief would tempt me to give up all for lost—then may I hear Thee speak in cheering accents to my soul, 'Is any thing too hard for the Lord?' (Gen. 18:14).

"Oh, let me never forget this animating question, which puts to flight a host of unbelieving fears. May I daily live upon Thy grace and rest on nothing, blessed Lord, but Thee."

When I contemplate myself, what do I behold? A polluted nature; a deceitful heart; a body every moment tending to decay; a beclouded understanding; a depraved will; affections in disorder; a memory retaining things forbidden; a creature, in short, born in sin; a child of wrath; an heir of hell. Awful as this portrait is, and humbling to the pride of carnal man, yet it gives but a faint representation of the original.

And can such a hateful creature enter into heaven? Impossible! I must be born again. But can the Lord renew so vile a being and cause the graces of His Spirit to abound in such a heart as mine?

Hear, oh, my soul, the words of your Savior which he spoke to Sarah, as the *angel of the covenant*: "Is any thing too hard for the Lord?"

"Lord, I believe—help my unbelief. I believe Thou canst in a moment raise me from a death in sin to a life of righteousness; and shall I doubt Thy willingness? Thou didst come to call sinners to repentance, to seek and to save that which was lost. Thousands in every age who have felt the power of Thy regenerating grace can witness to this delightful truth, that nothing is too hard for Thee.

"Oh, heavenly Father, bestow on me, the vilest, the most unworthy of Thy creatures, a look, a smile of love, for His dear sake in whom my soul delights, even Jesus, the sinner's friend.

"Thou art almighty; nothing is too hard for Thee. Let not unbelief, for one moment, stop the current of Thy grace; but cause Thy saving mercy to flow onward in my soul, until unbelief and pride, and every sin, shall be forever lost beneath the powerful stream. Then shall I be able to tell some fearful, doubting saint what Thou hast done for my soul, and to the latest moment of my life proclaim, with heartfelt joy, that nothing is too hard for Thee."

I will plead Thy promise, Lord,
I will trust Thy faithful Word;
Since this precious truth I see,
"As thy days, so shall thy strength be."

Often I feel an evil heart,
Prone to wander and depart;
But Thy Word still speaks to me,
"As thy days, so shall thy strength be."

Satan, with his crafty wile,
Seeks to fill my heart with guile;
Yet the promise says to me,
"As thy days, so shall thy strength be."

In whatever strait I come,
While I journey to my home,
This shall be my stay and plea:
"As thy days, so shall thy strength be."

CHAPTER 53

Indwelling Sin

Nothing grieves the believer in Jesus so much as the sin which dwells in him. He can feelingly adopt the language of the apostle, "O wretched man that I am!" (Rom. 7:24), and with him acknowledge, "We that are in this tabernacle do groan, being burdened" (2 Cor. 5:4). Yet, let not the worldling imagine that the believer has no inward enjoyment. This very grief on account of sin is accompanied with holy peace and joy through faith in the atonement of Jesus.

How great is the change which grace makes in the soul! Sin, which once was sweet, now becomes bitter. Sin, which once wore the mask of beauty, now appears in all its native deformity. The mind, enlightened from above, beholds sin in the mirror of truth as hardening and deceiving, unprofitable, shameful, and deadly. Its evil effects are seen in the destruction of original innocence, the desolating judgments of heaven, and the miseries which cover the earth.

Its evil effects are felt in the corruption of our nature, the stings of conscience, and the abounding iniquities of mankind. But, above all other views, we behold the infinite evil of sin in the agonies and death of Jesus, the Son of God.

Oh, that I may have grace to bewail, at the foot of the cross, the exceeding sinfulness of sin. There I would confess both my guilt and pollution; and there, looking with an eye of faith to the bleeding sacrifice, I would wait in humble hope, until Jesus would speak those soul-transporting words: "Be of good cheer; thy sins be forgiven thee" (Matt. 9:2).

Sinless perfection is the bliss of heaven. There, believers who die in the Lord become "the spirits of just men made perfect" (Heb. 12:23). While they sojourn here below, they are called to wrestle and fight both with inbred sin and outward temptations. Hence we find in that faithful Word, which is the light and counselor of the church of God, continual calls to vigilance and activity and reiterated cautions against negligence and sloth. There are four evils against which the most advanced believer has daily, yes hourly, to contend.

The first is *unbelief*. This is a powerful enemy to our peace. It was unbelief which gave Satan the first advantage over the once-happy pair in Paradise. They doubted, they disbelieved, they fell. Unbelief is the parent of numberless evils, which, although of different complexions, yet, like the human race, may be traced to the same source.

Doubt, distrust, evil-surmisings, murmurings, complainings, slavish fears, despondencies, creature dependencies, contempt of divine threatenings, slighting of divine promises, rejection of Jesus, neglect of the gospel, ridiculing the work of the Spirit, atheism, deism, Socinianism, carnal security, lukewarmness, backsliding in heart or life, false profession, hypocrisy—all these, and a thousand other evils, spring from unbelief. "Lord, deliver me, I humbly and earnestly beseech Thee, from these soul-destroying, hell-deserving sins."

The second inbred evil is *pride*. Pride is a subtle enemy. It spoils all that we think and speak and do, until the Spirit of Christ destroys its power in the soul. Pride is the last sin which dies, expiring only with the life of the believer. Through his whole pilgrimage, he has to contend against spiritual pride in all its specious and multiplied forms.

In heaven, pride cannot exist. There, all is humility and peace. Self-love, self-seeking, self-will, self-confidence, self-righteousness—all spring from pride. Pride, like unbelief, is a root of bitterness from where grow in dreadful luxuriance vain-glory, love of human applause, seeking of honor, independence, rebellion, revenge, anger, contempt of others, resentment of real or supposed injuries, ambition, presumption, etc. There is no end to this extensive evil which infects the hearts of sinners and fills the earth with misery and blood.

"Blessed Jesus, Thou humbled Thyself even unto death to make an atonement for my pride. Oh, make me humble and lowly in heart. Clothe me with humility, that, with all lowliness of mind, I may walk before Thee to Thy honor and glory."

The third enemy is *sensuality*. This dreadful evil is the parent of crimes, which the apostle declares ought not so much as to be named among the holy followers of Christ. How awful, then, is the thought that the nominally Christian world is, at this very moment, stained with crimes of so polluting a nature as to oppose a barrier, in many instances, to the conversion both of the heathens and the Jews! Our Lord has told us that offenses will come; but He has also denounced: "Woe unto him, through whom they come" (Luke 17:1).

Self-indulgence, sloth, luxury, gluttony, and drunkenness unite with carnal gratifications and impure desires in binding chains around the captive sinner until death consigns him to the dungeon of hell. "Oh, Thou holy and ever-blessed Spirit, purify and purge my heart from this dreadful enemy, the flesh, which wars against the soul. Wash me in the precious blood of Jesus. Pardon all my sins of impurity and fill me with holy affections and pure desires."

The most solemn threatenings are denounced in Scripture against these inbred sins: "He that believeth not shall be damned" (Mark 16:16). "Every one that is proud in heart is an abomination to the Lord" (Prov. 16:5). "If ye live after the flesh, ye shall die" (Rom. 8:13).

But there is another enemy which lodges within the human heart—*covetousness*, or the *love of the world*. This sin ever opposes the exercise of love to Christ and heavenly things in the soul of the believer. The world assumes an undue importance, owing to our coming into continual contact with its fleeting possessions, while eternal realities are the objects of faith and hope. Hence, even the advanced believer finds frequent occasions to use the lamentation of David: "My soul cleaveth unto the dust: quicken thou me according to thy word" (Ps. 119:25). The conviction of this evil should lead us to more earnest prayer for that spiritual-mindedness which is life and peace.

Worldly prosperity too frequently produces lukewarmness and declension from the ways of God. But if we possessed more of that faith which is the substance of things hoped for and the evidence of things not seen, more of that telescopic eye which looks within the veil and views, as near, the distant glories of Emmanuel's kingdom, we should be less attached to earth—yes, altogether weaned from it—and be enabled to say with the apostle: "God forbid that I should glory, save in the cross of our Lord Jesus Christ, by whom the world is crucified unto me, and I unto the world" (Gal. 6:14).

This proves the necessity of regeneration, since the love of the world is the natural affection of the unrenewed heart. Nothing can eradicate this idolatrous attachment to earthly things but the love of Christ shed abroad in the heart by the Holy Spirit. The more we see of the preciousness, glory, and excellency of Jesus, the more we discover of the emptiness, vanity, and insufficiency of all earthly good, and the more will our souls be withdrawn from present things and fixed upon things above, where Christ sits at the right hand of God.

The evils flowing from this sinful love of the world are many and great. Idolatry (for whatever supremely engages the heart, be it a diadem or a feather, is our idol), avarice, greed, the love of money, of earthly possessions, of splendid equipages, and of all those things which "the nations of the world seek after" (Luke 12:30); fraud, deceit, over-reaching, theft, envy at the prosperity of others; repining at our own condition, if lower than our neighbor's; an unwillingness to part with all for Christ; a shrinking from the cross; a dread of suffering for righteousness' sake—these, and many other evils, flowing from covetousness, prove the soul to be in a state of enmity against God, for "whosoever…will be a friend of the world is the enemy of God" (James 4:4).

From these four dreadful sources of evil—unbelief, pride, sensuality, and covetousness—spring all the miseries which inundate the earth and fill hell itself with horrors.

These sins are so interwoven with our fallen nature that, until we are created anew in Christ Jesus, they form, as it were, part of ourselves. How needful, then, is self-examination! How important to consider our ways! We may leave the world with respect to its vain amusements and yet never have the heart disengaged from it. Withdrawment from the world does not necessarily produce a crucifixion to it. It is one thing to leave the sinful customs and company of the world, and another to sit loosely to its fading pleasures and possessions. We may be worldly in a lonely desert, and spiritual in the midst of a crowd. The world may reign in the cell of the monk, and be renounced in the counting-house of the pious merchant.

The exhortation of Paul is at all times most appropriate and seasonable: "But this I say, brethren, the time is short: it remaineth, that both they that have wives be as though they had none; and they that weep, as though they wept not; and they that rejoice, as though they rejoiced not; and they that buy, as though they possessed not; and they that use this world, as not abusing it: for the fashion of this world passeth away" (1 Cor. 7:29-31).

"Blessed Lord, implant in my heart that lively faith, that deep humility, that heavenly purity, that spiritual-mindedness, which will evidence my union to Thee and prepare me for Thy beatific vision in the world to come."

When I survey my treacherous heart,
So base, so vile in every part;
How wondrous, Lord, that sovereign grace
Should make this heart Thy dwelling-place!

It is true, I hate each rebel sin,
And long for purity within;
Yet, ah, what evils still remain,
The purest act of love to stain.

Were this my only hope and plea,
What I have said, or done for Thee,
Dread loads of guilt would sink me down,
Beneath the terrors of Thy frown.

Indwelling Sin

But Jesus is my living way,
My only trust, my hope, my stay;
From Him, I all my strength receive,
And daily on His fullness live.

When death shall loose the silver cord,
Obedient to Thy mandate, Lord,
My soul shall joy and peace possess,
If Jesus be my righteousness.

CHAPTER 54

Trials

When I look into the world and see around me many pursuing happiness in unpossessed yet desired objects that elude the grasp of thousands, who think they have just to make one effort more to seize the flattering shadow and be happy, I ask, Why all this restlessness, this feverish thirst for that which cannot satisfy an immortal soul? Is it not that man, blinded by his passions, fondly hopes to find happiness in a world from where it long since took its flight when Adam ate of the forbidden tree?

"Thorns…and thistles shall it bring forth to thee" (Gen. 3:18) was the language of Jehovah to His fallen creatures when He cursed the ground for man's sake; and if the divine inspiration of the Bible rested upon the truth of this one declaration, every age and every heart must feelingly witness to its holy origin.

Vain man would attempt to be happy while remaining at a distance from his God. He plucks the flower, and it withers in his hand. His fond expectations of earthly bliss, like wave succeeding wave, roll along in quick succession without bringing him any nearer to the desired haven of rest and happiness.

This world is not a resting-place to the wicked, nor the resting-place of the righteous. "There is no peace, saith my God, to the wicked" (Isa. 57:21). His desires are restless, his passions are restless, his spirit is restless. He needs what he has not, and does not truly enjoy what he has. He is of the earth, earthy. His aims, pursuits, and pleasures, all spring out of and settle upon the world. Thus he reaps those thorns and thistles which spring up in such abundant crops wherever he erects his dwelling. Disappointed and chagrined that happiness is ever eluding his grasp, he grows peevish in his spirit, or a complainant against his kind, yet insulted, Creator. No wonder that misery marks his steps, even though, like those of Asher, they be dipped in oil (Deut. 33:24).

Worldly riches cannot give quietness when God gives trouble. Oh, my soul, learn true wisdom from what you see around you. Every situation is planted with thorns in this wilderness of sin. Vain, then, is the expectation of man to find a place of pure, uninterrupted rest below the skies. And yet, what crowds are daily in search of such a place of rest in the midst of a polluted and tempestuous world! Some think it lies in the region of wealth, others in that of pleasure, others in that of honor. Some fancy it is found in the busy throng, and some in the stillness of retirement. But all who seek it in the world shall never find it.

Thou, blessed Jesus, art the true and only resting-place for guilty sinners. Believing in Thee, they enter into rest. Thy people, it is true, must bear Thy cross, but they enjoy Thy consolations also; they feel a peace and calm within, which all the panting candidates for worldly happiness can never obtain. They have peace with God, peace in their own consciences; and they study, as much as lies in them, to live peaceably with all men.

Thus they are enabled to bear with composure the varied trials of life, looking with assured hope to that rest which remains to the people of God, when this stormy world shall have passed away and its votaries be doomed to that doleful place where they have no rest day nor night, but where the smoke of their torment ascends up forever and ever!

"Oh, divine Savior, be my portion, the lot of my inheritance! Then shall I rejoice in the midst of sorrows and be calm in the midst of storms. Oh, speak peace to my troubled soul, and then all shall be still. Blessed Redeemer, all who come to Thee find rest unto their souls; and I would now come. Receive me in mercy. Cause me to know Thee as my Savior and to rejoice daily in the joyful sound of mercy extended to the chief of sinners."

When a sinner is first brought to the knowledge of the truth and experiences the joys of faith and the sweets of pardoning love, he fancies that the bare mention of his own comforts will be sufficient to make all around him anxious to possess them too. A little experience, however, shows him that the hard heart of man is not so easily to be moved.

Instead of converting those about him, he raises up a host of foes, even in the bosom of his own family and among his kinsfolk and acquaintances. He becomes the object either of their pity or their scorn and meets with cold neglect, or many sharp rebukes, where once he enjoyed a hearty welcome. His name is cast out as evil; his motives are maligned; his actions deemed precise and singular; his conversation whining cant; yes, his whole life condemned as unbecoming a true man or even a person endued with common sense. The consistent believer in Jesus must, therefore, expect trials and opposition from an ungodly world. "As then he that was born after the flesh persecuted him that was born after the Spirit, even so it is now" (Gal. 4:29).

The blessed Savior has given His people clear and repeated intimations to that effect. "Blessed are ye, when men shall hate you, and when they shall separate you from their company, and shall reproach you, and cast out your name as evil, for the Son of man's sake. Rejoice ye in that day, and leap for joy: for, behold, your reward is great in heaven" (Luke 6:22-23).

The Christian's trials arise from various sources. They spring from *his general character*. If the believer be divested of all unnecessary singularity in dress or deportment, yet his attachment to the Redeemer, evidencing itself by a firm adherence to the precepts of the gospel and a rooted aversion to all sin, will, of itself, create dislike and beget such a secret enmity in the hearts of the ungodly as cannot fail of showing its malignity by outward contempt or ridicule.

There was nothing of singularity in the character of the blessed Jesus, except His unspotted holiness; His unbounded benevolence; His perfect conformity to the divine law; His heavenly wisdom; His deadness to the world; His boldness in reproving sin; His entire resignation to His Holy Father's will; His divine power in healing diseases, feeding the hungry, casting out devils, and stilling the raging elements; and yet, with all this display of majesty and glory, of tenderness and compassion, how hated, how despised, how persecuted, was the Savior of mankind! If they thus treated the Master of the house, they will also despise those of His household. If, said our Lord, they hated Me, they will also hate you (John 15:18).

Have you, oh my soul, reason to believe that you are born from above—that a divine change has passed upon you? Where are the fruits of faith? Where is the opposition of the world? Examine well, for it is declared: "Woe unto you, when all men shall speak well of you" (Luke 6:26). Is the image of Jesus stamped upon you? Are you bold in confessing Christ before men, faithful in discountenancing every thing that is contrary to His blessed Word? Do you acknowledge Him to be the Lord your righteousness, your only atonement, advocate, and friend? Lord, grant that I may, through grace, be able to say: "Thou knowest all things; thou knowest that I love thee" (John 21:17).

I need not court opposition—only let me live a life of faith in the Son of God, and opposition will be excited as naturally as fire introduced into water occasions a contest between the two elements, for "all that will live godly in Christ Jesus shall suffer persecution" (2 Tim. 3:12).

The believer's trials frequently arise from *his peculiar situation*. This, added to the former, namely, his general character as a true Christian, whereby he tacitly condemns the conduct of a wicked world, brings still greater odium upon him and puts all his graces to the severest test.

A pious wife, child, or servant is often severely tried in the furnace by being brought into immediate contact with an ungodly husband, parent, or master. The natural enmity of the heart, aided by natural authority, receives additional strength and fails not to vent its utmost malice against the unoffending lambs of Christ's flock. Like the savage wolf of the forest, such characters seem to take delight in devouring the weak and defenseless and satiating themselves with the miseries of others.

Many hearts are made to bleed by the unkindness of these adversaries to the truth, whose only charge against the objects of their cruelty is that they dare not comply with their sinful commands in direct violation of the law of God.

But Jesus is the good Shepherd. He watches over the people of His flock with tender care in the dark and cloudy day. In the midst of all their outward troubles, He gives them inward peace. While trusting in His unchanging love, they experience a joy of which the utmost rage of persecution cannot deprive them.

If such be the blessedness of the lambs of Thy flock, oh gracious Savior, give me a holy courage in Thy cause, a holy confidence in Thy mercy, a holy consolation from Thine exceeding great and precious promises. Let me never dread the sneers nor the frowns of the ungodly. Preserve me from sinful compliances with the customs, and from sinful conformity to the spirit, of the world. Make me valiant for the truth, ever daring to be singular in the cultivation of Christian tempers and scrupulous in the choice of Christian companions, whom Thou hast called the salt of the earth and the light of the world and to whom it is Thy good pleasure to give the kingdom.

The believer's trials sometimes spring from *the immediate hand of God*. The wife is deprived by death of her earthly support, a tender husband; the husband, of an affectionate wife. The parent sees the hope of his declining age sink into the grave; the child is left an orphan in a wicked and ensnaring world. The tenderest ties are snapped asunder by the unrelenting hand of death. Diseases of various kinds are commissioned to invade our frames. One faculty after another is taken away, or greatly impaired. Earthly comforts droop and die. Riches fly away, poverty advances, and nothing but clouds and storms appear in sight.

In such a situation, the poor, trembling believer is sorely assaulted by the tempter to doubt of his interest in Christ, of the love of God to his soul, of the truth of the promises, of the power of his Redeemer, of His willingness to save. In short, he is tempted to unbelief and hard thoughts of God.

At such bereaving seasons, injudicious friends are apt to suspect his character and, like those of Job, to charge him with hypocrisy. The ungodly rejoice over him, saying, "There, there, so would we have it. You see what is the end of his prayers and religion. If he be a child of God, let Him deliver him, if He will have him."

But the triumphing of the wicked is short. The very storm which purifies the humble believer often strikes the scorner dead. Death, like a tiger, darts upon him in a moment when he is least aware of his approach. "He that being often reproved hardeneth his neck, shall suddenly be destroyed, and that without remedy" (Prov. 29:1), while the child of God calmly waits the hour of his dismissal and even longs to depart, that he may be with Christ.

Oh, the depth of the goodness and severity of God! By these trials, the Lord brings the faith and love of His people into lively exercise and thus demonstrates the efficacy of true religion.

The graces of the Spirit generally thrive most in a rugged soil and in tempestuous seasons. Like the Israelites in Egypt, they increase in the midst of oppression, persecution, and suffering; for, as gold shines brightest in the furnace, so the Lord's people glorify Him most in the fires (Isa. 24:15).

The believer's trials arise also from *his inward corruptions*. This is more painful to him than all the rest, because the sufferings he endures from indwelling sin are the bitter fruits of that evil nature which is so offensive to God, his Savior.

He can bear with calm composure the taunts of men; he can patiently submit to be accounted a fool for Christ's sake; yes, he can suffer joyfully the spoiling of his goods and even the loss of life itself; but he cannot endure the inward workings of corruption. He cannot submit to the power of indwelling sin. He cannot tamely allow his mind to be assaulted by his spiritual enemies. He cannot bear the thought of losing that joy and peace through believing, which is the very foretaste of heavenly felicity. Oh, the anguish of his mind when corruption rages! How fervently does he pray for deliverance! How precious is the blood of Jesus at such seasons! He flies to the strong for strength. He takes refuge in the wounds of Jesus and is safe.

This trial, like every other, is overruled for good. A holy watchfulness, an increased dread of sin, a jealous, godly fear, a spirit of prayer, a more simple dependence on Christ, a more hearty loathing of self, a more ardent breathing after holiness and heaven, are excited in the soul. Thus, through grace, Satan is defeated, and the tempted believer comes out of the furnace as gold tried in the fire, leaving nothing but the dross behind.

"Happy art thou, O Israel: who is like unto thee, O people saved by the Lord, the shield of thy help, and who is the sword of thy excellency! and thine enemies shall be found liars unto thee" (Deut. 33:29). "The eternal God is thy refuge, and underneath are the everlasting arms" (v. 27).

Oh, 'tis sweet to trust in Jesus,
To rely upon His Word;
Cares and sorrows fly before us,
When we trust a pardoning God.

Here we meet with heavy crosses;
Many burdens we must bear;
But the Lord can make our losses
Lighter than the ambient air.

Then, my soul, why so distressed?
Why cast down with anxious fear?
Jesus helps the weak oppressed,
He the drooping soul can cheer.

Gird your loins, let hope support you;
Speed with cheerful haste your way;
He who called you to the journey,
Will conduct to endless day.

CHAPTER 55

Affliction

All the ways of God are good; yes, all the paths of the Lord are mercy and truth, unto such as love Him and keep His commandments (cf. Ps. 25). Should any one ask, "Why, then, does the Lord afflict His people?" We answer, "Because He loves them." "As many as I love, I rebuke and chasten" (Rev. 3:19). This will appear from a few reflections on the nature, design, and end of affliction.

Its nature is indeed unpleasant to the children of men: Paul declares it to be not "joyous, but grievous" (Heb. 12:11). The cup of affliction is composed of bitter ingredients at which our nature revolts. But should we commend the physician, who prescribed only luscious medicines for a distempered stomach? His skill would rather appear in administering a bitter, yet salutary, draught. And so it is with our heavenly Physician. He knows our inward malady, and He has medicine to heal our sickness. Affliction is one of His medicinal dealings which is more or less bitter, according to the spiritual malady of His people. But our heavenly Father, who does not willingly afflict or grieve the children of men, never infuses more wormwood and gall than is needful to correct our vitiated souls.

Hence we plainly see what is the design of affliction. It is to do us good. The tender-hearted physician for the body aims at nothing but his patient's recovery. He calls every day; he watches every term of the complaint. And is our heavenly Physician less attentive to His dear afflicted children? Ah, no! He calls not merely once a day. He is always near them. His eye is always upon them. His ears are always open to their prayers. When He sees a favorable change in their spiritual state,

He administers the cordials of His promises to strengthen and restore them to that peace and comfort and joy which, before the afflictive dispensation, they were not in a proper frame of spirit to receive.

Thus we see the gracious end of affliction. Before the trial came, they were perhaps growing lukewarm or insensibly gliding into a sinful compliance with the customs of the world, or they were settling upon the lees and feeling quite at ease in Zion. Surrounded with earthly comforts, they were forsaking the Fountain of living water and idolizing some created good in the bosom of domestic life. But now, they return unto the Lord and find their happiness in their God.

Our heavenly Father, in perfect accordance with His covenant of life and peace, sends the needful trial: "If his children forsake my law, and walk not in my judgments; If they break my statutes, and keep not my commandments; then will I visit their transgression with the rod, and their iniquity with stripes" (Ps. 89:30, 32). Thus for a season, if need be, we are in heaviness through manifold temptations.

The Lord deals graciously with His people. Though He puts them into the furnace, yet He will not allow it to be heated one degree more than is needful to consume the dross and purify their souls. He presides over it Himself. His wisdom and love regulate its strength. Thus, in the midst of all their trials, He never leaves them nor forsakes them.

In this way, the Holy Spirit carries on the great work of sanctification in their souls, manifesting their sonship by these fatherly corrections and fitting them for that pure region where nothing can enter that defiles or makes a lie.

And is it thus with God's dear children? Then, oh my soul, receive the cup of affliction with humble resignation and adoring love. Kiss the hand that smites. Bless the rod which chastises.

While the bramble is allowed to grow wild, the vine is pruned; while God says of the wicked, "Let them alone," He scourges every son whom He receives (cf. Heb. 12:6). And truly His "loving correction" shall make you great.

How consoling, then, to the true believer, is this sweet assurance of the royal psalmist! "All the paths of the LORD are mercy and truth unto such as keep his covenant and his testimonies" (Ps. 25:10). David was a tried saint. He had often been made to pass through the furnace of affliction and always found himself the better for his trials. In the 119th Psalm he says: "It is good for me that I have been afflicted; that I might learn thy statutes" (Ps. 119:71). "Before I was afflicted I went astray: but now have I kept thy word" (v. 67). And then he adds: "Thou art good, and doest good; teach me thy statutes" (v. 68), thus acknowledging the goodness of his heavenly Father in not leaving him to follow the devices and desires of his own deceitful heart.

It is delightful to consider that the sufferings which believers are now called to endure are the only sufferings which they shall ever experience. In heaven there is neither sighing nor sorrow. None of its inhabitants say, "I am sick"; for the former things are passed away. What an animating thought! It should make the children of God exclaim with the apostle: "I am filled with comfort, I am exceeding joyful in all our tribulation" (2 Cor. 7:4).

If we read the Word of God with due attention, we shall find that the most eminent saints have been the most tried. The faith of Abraham, the patience of Job, the meekness of Moses, the purity of Joseph, the devotion of Daniel, would not have been so conspicuous had not these peculiar graces been brought into exercise by trials remarkably adapted to each.

God is sovereign, wise, and good. He can overrule the sorest temptations of Satan to the establishing of His people. "Who is he that will harm you, if ye be followers of that which is good?" (1 Pet. 3:13) is a question full of comfort to the tempted believer. Suffering he may endure, but real injury he shall not sustain, since eternal truth has declared that "all things work together for good to them that love God, to them who are the called according to his purpose" (Rom. 8:28). "Wherefore let them that suffer according to the will of God commit the keeping of their souls to him in well doing, as unto a faithful Creator" (1 Pet. 4:19).

The happiness of man consists not in an exemption from trials, but in having his will swallowed up in the will of God. For this we are taught to pray: "Thy will be done in earth, as it is in heaven" (Matt. 6:10). Just in proportion as we approximate to the unreserved obedience of the heavenly host, we shall be happy. Our trials are sent for this very purpose: to mold our will into the divine will and consequently to make us holy and happy.

From these few reflections, it is evident that the advantages which believers derive from sanctified afflictions are many and great. In affliction, we often detect the sin which most easily besets us. This is the most difficult sin to find out, though the most in operation, on account of its blinding and deceiving nature. We have therefore cause to bless God for showing to us the accursed thing and wherefore He contends with us.

In affliction, we obtain clear views of the insufficiency of all earthly things. A dark shadow is thrown over the smiling scenes of busy life. We discover the little value of those possessions, the attainment of which once appeared so desirable.

In affliction, we learn to estimate, above all treasures, an assured interest in Jesus Christ. The blessedness of the believer is then felt and acknowledged. His peace of mind and hope of glory—the fruits of saving faith—are esteemed more precious than rubies.

In affliction, the promises of God's holy Word are sweeter than honey and the honeycomb. They are sacred cordials administered by infinite love to revive and strengthen the drooping saint.

Thus, while the prosperous worldling in the midst of his abundance despises the "hidden manna" (Rev. 2:17) the contrite believer in his heaviest trial can extract sweetness from the wormwood and the gall. A Savior's love, experienced in the soul, renders all palatable, however distasteful to our nature.

If man had never sinned, suffering would have been unknown; but, having lost the divine image, infinite Wisdom is pleased to appoint sundry trials as means in His hands for restoring us to that filial spirit which we lost through the fall. Sanctified affliction can bend the stubborn will and bring us to the frame and temper of little children.

Hence we find in Scripture much to this effect: "And ye have forgotten the exhortation which speaketh unto you as unto children, My son, despise not thou the chastening of the Lord, nor faint when thou art rebuked of him: for whom the Lord loveth he chasteneth, and scourgeth every son whom he receiveth. If ye endure chastening, God dealeth with you as with sons; for what son is he whom the father chasteneth not? But if ye be without chastisement, whereof all are partakers, then are ye bastards, and not sons. Furthermore we have had fathers of our flesh which corrected us, and we gave them reverence: shall we not much rather be in subjection unto the Father of spirits, and live? For they verily for a few days chastened us after their own pleasure; but he for our profit, that we might be partakers of his holiness. Now no chastening for the present seemeth to be joyous, but grievous: nevertheless afterward it yieldeth the peaceable fruit of righteousness unto them which are exercised thereby" (Heb. 12:5-11).

Under affliction, the believer is like a city set on a hill. His faith and patience, his meekness and resignation, cannot be hidden. They manifest the reality of his religion and prove to an unbelieving world the blessedness of serving God. His mind is kept in perfect peace. His heart is full of holy joy. He lies as clay in the hands of the potter; and with his suffering Savior he can say, "Father,... not my will, but thine, be done" (Luke 22:42). If doubts and fears are permitted to overshadow his soul, they only resemble the dark clouds which pass athwart a summer's sky. The manifestation of a Savior's love soon dispels the gloom.

The afflicted believer is stirred up to closer communion with God. He girds his loins. He trims his lamp. He waits for the coming of his Lord in the daily exercise of faith and prayer. When his trials are heavy, his prayers are more fervent and frequent; for the same wind which extinguishes a less fire causes the greater to burn with increased intenseness. What says our divine Master? "Because iniquity shall abound, the love of many shall wax cold. But he that shall endure unto the end, the same shall be saved" (Matt. 24:12-13).

In seasons of deep distress, Satan is sometimes very busy in suggesting hard thoughts of God, exciting doubts, and creating murmurings.

Many battles are then fought, and the faith and love of the believer are tried to the uttermost. But He who is in him is greater than he who is in the world. Jesus, who vanquished Satan in our nature, by His Spirit destroys the power of the adversary in the hearts of His people. Thus, He enables them to rise superior to all their trials, through His grace which is sufficient for them.

In tribulation, the child of God experiences many sweet tokens of his heavenly Father's care. His sick chamber is the abode of grace, mercy, and peace. The bright beams of hope dispel the gloom which gathers round the grave, and raises his enraptured soul far above a sorrowing world. At such a season of unspeakable delight, his heart is loosened from every earthly tie; and in the language of the exulting apostle, he can say: "O death, where is thy sting? O grave, where is thy victory?" (1 Cor. 15:55).

Thus, affliction has a two-fold effect. Like the wintry blast, it kills the noxious weeds of lust, pride, and covetousness; while, like the genial warmth of summer, it cherishes all the kindly graces of the Spirit, humility, purity, and love.

Many people are apt to imagine that if they are not deeply afflicted in some way or other, they cannot be the children of God. We see instances, however, of excellent characters passing through life with comparatively few trials, and yet maintaining a peculiar spirituality of mind. There is certainly no necessary connection between affliction and resignation or prosperity and gratitude.

When adversity meets a man destitute of grace, it stirs up within him a rebellious spirit against the moral government of God; or, at least, it calls forth his natural corruption into more active operation.

When prosperity pours its profusion upon an unconverted person, it tends to foster all the evils of pride, insolence, and independence so that the man almost forgets that he is mortal, a being accountable to his Maker. It is grace alone which makes all the real difference between one man and another. "By the grace of God," said Paul, "I am what I am" (1 Cor. 15:10). And to the Corinthians he adduced this argument as a ground for humility: "Who maketh thee to differ from another? and what hast thou that thou didst not receive? now if thou didst receive it, why dost thou glory, as if thou hadst not received it?" (1 Cor. 4:7).

We may therefore conclude that when affliction renders a man humble and resigned to the will of God, when it tends to wean him from the world and produces a change in his whole spirit and conduct, it is because the God of all grace is employing it as a means whereby to lead him to deep consideration and, through the accompanying power of the Spirit, to true repentance, faith, and holiness.

So, when in prosperity the heart expands with benevolence; when a man is cheerfully employed in diffusing a portion of that comfort around him which he himself enjoys; when he is laboring to glorify his Redeemer by aiding those institutions which have for their object the dissemination of divine truth; when he is led to consider himself as a steward of the manifold gifts of God; and when all this is accompanied with true humility, unostentatiousness, and self-denial—then we may safely conclude that God has blessed his basket and his store; that all his fruitfulness is the effect of grace alone and is not the natural consequence of mere worldly abundance.

How precious, then, is the grace of God! Natural evils are converted into spiritual blessings when thus sanctified by divine grace; and, without this grace, natural blessings such as health, plenty, friends, and influence, become snares and excitements to sin and rebellion."Oh, then, let me ever pray for grace to use both affliction and prosperity aright. Lord, impart unto me this inestimable treasure. When Thou givest grace, Thou givest Thyself: 'Thyself, of all Thy gifts, is the crown.'"

Be still, my soul, and know the Lord,
In meek submission wait His will;
His presence can true peace afford,
His power can shield from every ill.

Your path is strewed with piercing thorns;
Each step is gained by arduous fight

Yet wait, until hope's bright morning dawns,
Until darkness changes into light.

Soon shall the painful conflict cease;
Soon shall the raging storm be o'er;
Soon shall you reach the realm of peace,
Where suffering shall be known no more.

There shall your joy forever flow
In one unbroken stream of bliss;
There shall you God the Savior know,
And feel Him yours as you are His.

CHAPTER 56

The Character of Martha and Mary

With what beautiful simplicity is the interview between Jesus and the sisters of Lazarus related by Luke in the tenth chapter of his gospel. How gentle and yet how forcible is the reproof which our Lord gave to Martha. How gracious the testimony which He bore to the piety of Mary. Mary sat at Jesus' feet and heard His words. Happy and favored station! She sat at the feet of Him who is infinite wisdom and heard, with teachableness and delight, those gracious truths which proceeded from His lips. The Lord inclined her heart, as He did Lydia's, to attend unto the things which He spoke unto her. His words fell like good seed into a soil prepared by sovereign grace and brought forth the blessed fruits of righteousness.

Martha was cumbered with much serving and careful about many things. Her mind was ruffled at the apparent inattention of Mary, who had left her to serve alone. But Jesus, instead of reproving, bestows His commendation on Mary's conduct, since He came to their house not for the purpose of feasting Himself with their earthly dainties, but to feast them with the delicious truths of gospel grace.

This family picture is often exhibited in the Christian world. We are naturally more inclined to the bustle of religious occupations than to the retired devotional exercises of meditation and prayer. Martha's hospitality was in itself commendable, and sprang from love to her Savior; but the hurried state of her mind, and the neglect of a precious season for spiritual improvement, were highly reprehensible. She forgot her own spiritual needs and the great object of Christ's visit. She was cumbered with much serving. Her spirit got ruffled. An improper feeling carried her away beyond the bounds of affection and decorum. She even interrupted our Lord in His discourse with Mary and wished Him to dismiss her with a suitable reproof for neglecting her household concerns. "Lord, dost thou not care that my sister hath left me to serve alone? bid her therefore that she help me" (Luke 10:40). The reproof, however, unexpectedly fell upon herself. "Martha, Martha, thou art careful and troubled about many things: but one thing is needful: and Mary hath chosen that good part, which shall not be taken away from her" (v. 41-42). This faithful admonition was no doubt sanctified to her, for "Jesus loved Martha, and her sister, and Lazarus" (John 11:5).

We cannot contemplate this family scene without being struck with the value of a meek and quiet spirit, which is in the sight of God of great price. A mind active and ardent, alive to neglect and susceptible of irritation, is generally admired by the world, as indicative of a noble spirit; while a retired, noiseless, yet humble and obedient frame of heart is ridiculed or despised as low and unmanly.

But the Lord sees not as man sees. Man looks at the outward appearance, but God looks at the heart. "That which is highly esteemed among men is abomination in the sight of God" (Luke 16:15).

Like Mary, I, too, am privileged to sit at Jesus' feet; for when I read the Holy Scriptures, I read the Word of Jesus. When I hear the gospel faithfully preached, I hear the gospel of Jesus. With what reverence, then, should I listen to the words of eternal truth; with what delight should I receive the glad tidings of salvation, proclaimed by Him who came down from heaven to seek and to save that which was lost and who has graciously declared that all who look unto Him, who come unto Him, who receive Him and believe in His name, shall not perish, but have everlasting life.

"Lord, give me faith and hope and love, that all my affections may be fixed upon Thee and my whole life devoted to Thy glory. But alas, how often do I resemble Martha! Daily do I need her salutary reproof."

The various occupations and businesses of life, the multiplied cares and anxieties about earthly things—no, even the very labors required in actively conducting religious institutions—have a tendency, without great watchfulness and prayer, to weary the spirits, to clog the wheels of the mind in its ascent heavenward, and to render us unfit for that tranquil, spiritual posture of soul in which Mary was found when she sat at her Savior's feet.

To be actively employed is good for the Christian, while a too great seclusion unfits the mind for general usefulness. There is, however, a happy combination of activity and retirement which at once strengthens the mind and preserves its spirituality from decay.

The characters presented to our view in the Holy Scriptures are drawn by the unerring pencil of truth. There we see man as he really is, both in his best and worst estate. The excellencies of the saints are recorded with remarkable conciseness, while their defects and falls are dwelt upon with awful particularity. The reason seems to be apparent—to humble the natural pride of man and to demonstrate that he who glories must glory in the Lord.

The Bible tells us the unwelcome truth that "man at his best state is altogether vanity" (Ps. 39:5); that "there is not a just man upon earth, that doeth good, and sinneth not" (Eccl. 7:20). It is absurd, then, to expect perfection, but not unreasonable to expect consistency.

While I labor to promote the spread of the gospel through the benighted regions of the earth, I must beware lest I neglect to cultivate, by close communion with Jesus, the work of grace in my own soul. When, like Martha, I find my mind cumbered with much serving—when I begin to feel an increasing distraction of thought and a growing unfitness for spiritual meditation—then let me betake myself with redoubled frequency to Mary's happy station.

At the feet of Jesus, I am permitted to ask for every blessing. In secret fervor of spirit, I may there implore that all-sufficient grace which is so freely promised to all who sincerely seek the heavenly treasure.

"Lord, enable me to cultivate diligence with devotion, to employ my humble powers in Thy service, both in the active range of Christian benevolence and in the passive exercise of self-denying resignation. Mold my will to Thine; let holy love be the ever-moving spring of all my actions, that whatever I do in word or deed, I may do all with a view to Thy glory and to the spiritual good of a perishing world."

Descend, blest Spirit, in my heart,
And give me Mary's better part;
An interest in the Savior's love,
A foretaste of the joys above.

Dispel the darkness of the mind:
In Thee alone sweet peace I find;
Whose kindly office it is to bless,
Through Christ the Lord, my righteousness.

Oh, may I walk with holy fear,
While journeying as a pilgrim here;
Feel my weak soul by Thee sustained;
And in the path of life maintained.

Descend, blest Spirit, from above,
Thou God of peace, of joy, and love,
Seal Thy salvation to my heart,
And never from my soul depart.

CHAPTER 57

The Character of the Bereans

The character and conduct of the Berean Jews, as recorded in the seventeenth chapter of Acts, is very instructive. As pride and prejudice shut out the light of truth, so humility and openness prepare the way for its admission. These Bereans were more noble than those of Thessalonica. They were people of a more ingenuous spirit. They did not resort to the base refuge of ridicule and persecution. They possessed a more elevated mind. Knowing the importance of the apostles' doctrine, if true, they judged it not only expedient, but, due to the greatness of the message, essential to receive the Word. They admitted them into their synagogue and with all readiness of mind, with a cheerful disposition of heart, listened to their preaching.

Having thus permitted the light to shine upon them, they did not, like the Thessalonians, immediately expel it by driving the holy messengers of mercy out of their city; but they proceeded to search the Scriptures. They brought the doctrine of the apostles to the test of God's holy Word. This they did, not superficially, but carefully: they "searched the scriptures." They dug deep into the sacred mine. This they did, not occasionally, but constantly—they "searched the scriptures daily" with unwearied assiduity, like those who were in earnest to discover the pure gold of divine truth. This they did, not critically, but sincerely—not to cavil with the apostles' doctrine by finding out objections against it, but to see "whether those things were so," whether they were so revealed in the Scriptures as the apostles declared them to be (Acts 17:11).

The effect of this ready reception of the Word, of this daily searching of the Scriptures, was that they believed. The Holy Spirit graciously guided their inquiring minds into all truth so that they heartily embraced the Word of salvation. "If any man will do his will, he shall know of the doctrine, whether it be of God, or whether I speak of myself" (John 7:17). This blessing was not confined to a few. It is said: "Many of them believed"; also, "of honorable women which were Greeks, and of men, not a few" believed (Acts 17:12). What a bright example, and what an encouragement is here held out to us!

Many of the Jews of Thessalonica, no doubt, acted like these Bereans, for we read in the fourth verse: "A great multitude believed." And in that city, the apostles planted a church which shone exceedingly bright in faith and love.

The carnal mind in every place is enmity against God. Even in Berea, the unbelieving Jews who came from Thessalonica stirred up the people so that it was found needful to send Paul away. What a striking picture the Word of God gives us of the human heart! We see man under all circumstances an enemy of God. Whether he live in ruder or more polished times, the heart, until renewed by grace, is the seat of sin. Whether he be enveloped in ignorance or enlightened by science, he naturally hates the pure and holy light of evangelical truth. The sensual shuns its purifying tendency, the self-righteous its humbling tendency. All, without exception, love darkness rather than light, because their deeds are evil (John 3:19).

Yet, God has never left Himself without witness. In every age He has had a seed to serve Him who are accounted to the Lord for a generation. Neither has He ever left His people without sufficient evidence whereby to prove the truth of His own revealed will respecting them. Among the many facts which may be adduced to prove the divine inspiration of the Bible, the two following may perhaps deserve some notice.

First, as it respects the Old Testament. It is well known that the Jews were never either a philosophical or a literary people. There are no works among their ancient uninspired authors which can lay any claim to genius. Yet the books of their prophets surpass all the celebrated writers of antiquity. What heathen poet, however laureled by admiring ages, can exceed the sublimity of their conceptions, the grandeur of their descriptions, and the exquisite taste and beauty of their imagery when describing the glorious majesty and unsullied purity of the one, only true God, the works of His hands, the ways of His providence, and the wonders of His love?

How skillfully do they dissect the human heart and delineate to the very life the character of man in his lapsed and restored condition! How pure are the precepts, how precious the promises, how dreadful the threatenings, how solemn the warnings, with which their writings abound!

When contrasted with the fables of the heathen poets, with their deification of the worst passions of mankind, with the impure character which they give to their gods (though embellished by all the flowers of rhetoric and sweetened by the enchanting flow of numbers), it must surely convince every unprejudiced mind that such writings as the Jewish prophets have left for the benefit of mankind cannot be the product of unassisted fallen reason, but the gracious revelation of the divine Spirit, under whose influence these holy men both spoke and wrote.

Secondly, as it respects the New Testament. The writers of the New Testament, with the exception of Luke and Paul, were men of no education; and yet their writings are the only standard of truth respecting the character and work of the Savior of the world. These unlettered men elevated the standard of morals to the highest pitch and revealed those heavenly principles which alone are able to restore man to the lost image of his Maker. So did not the most renowned and wisest philosophers of antiquity. The authors who immediately followed the said writers, called the primitive fathers, fell into many fancies, and even errors, on certain points, as if it had been permitted in order to draw the line of distinction between divine inspiration and the ordinary illumination of the human mind more clear and defined.

But the two great evidences for the truth of Christianity are miracles and prophecy. At the time when the Lord Jesus declared Himself to be the Messiah and proclaimed the glad tidings of salvation to a lost world, miracles were needful in order to prove the truth of His mission, to manifest the divine approbation to His doctrines, and to fulfill the prophetic character of the Messiah, as recorded in the thirty-fifth chapter of Isaiah.

Miracles were also necessary after His ascension to evidence the truth of those doctrines propagated everywhere by His apostles, which declared Jesus to be the Son of God, the true Messiah, the Savior of the world. When these doctrines were thus fully attested by the power of God accompanying the preaching of the cross, miracles ceased in the church, as being no longer needed.

Yet a still more important evidence was reserved for future ages, no less declarative of the divine approbation to the Christian religion than miracles; that evidence is prophecy. The gradual fulfillment of those prophecies which were foretold by Christ and His apostles may be considered as a standing miracle, since it is utterly beyond the power of man to insure the accomplishment of any predicted event independently of the will and purpose of God. Any man may predict, but the accomplishment must prove the truth of the prediction.

Christ, as God in our nature, foretold what would come to pass through His own prescience. The prophets and apostles, as His servants, spoke under the immediate influence of His Spirit dwelling in them (1 Pet. 1:10, 11). Thus the prophecies which have been fulfilled, and which are now fulfilling, and which still remain to be fulfilled to the end of time, form a chain of evidence to the divine origin of Christianity which Satan and his emissaries can never destroy.

These two external evidences of miracles and prophecy, taken together with the whole character of the blessed Jesus, answering in every minute particular to the ancient prophecies of the Old Testament, and also connecting with the internal evidence of the gospel arising from its agreement with the nature of God and its adaptation to the needs of fallen man ought—yes, and will—satisfy every honest inquirer after truth that Christianity is of God.

Such an one, through grace, will be led to acknowledge with heartfelt gratitude, like the Bereans of old, that Jesus Christ is God manifest in the flesh, the only Savior and hope of perishing sinners. The joyful exclamation of such an enlightened soul will be: "We have found him, of whom Moses in the law, and the prophets, did write" (John 1:45). And should any skeptic reply, "Can there any good thing come out of Nazareth?" the simple answer will be, "Come and see" (v. 46).

In every age, a generation of men has sprung up, the Serpent's brood, who have labored to bring the Word of eternal truth into discredit by false statements and sophistries of every kind. "Thy word is very pure: therefore thy servant loveth it" (Ps. 119:140) was the language of David in his day.

It may appear strange, in this age of light and information, that the New Testament should be arraigned by modern infidels as the most immoral book that is extant. Surely this must be the dying gasp of infidelity, for what can be more feeble than such an attack? They may as well assert that the sun, when shining without a cloud in its meridian splendor, is the darkest part of the visible creation. The sun is indeed as darkness to those who are blind, and so are the things of God to those who are unenlightened by the Spirit of truth.

How strange! A Roman emperor placed a statue of Jesus among his idol deities on account of the excellence of His moral precepts, while modern infidels, reaping the benefits of His morality in the inestimable blessings of established governments, dare—in defiance of common sense, common honesty, and common experience—to denounce the holy gospel of Jesus as the chief of immoralities!

It is truly awful to behold how far men may travel in the road of sin and rebellion against the almighty Governor of the universe! Is there in the whole world a morality so elevated, so pure, so influential, as the morality of the gospel? We need only compare the lives of those who reject the Christian revelation with the lives of those who truly believe it and live under its purifying influence in order to ascertain where true morality is to be found.

It lies in the pages of the Bible and is exhibited in the spirit and conduct of its sincere believers. The history of the church in all ages attests this delightful truth, that "the gospel of Christ…is the power of God unto salvation to every one that believeth" (Rom. 1:16). Men of the most savage natures have become mild; the most impure have become chaste; the most ungovernable have become obedient. In short, the whole moral change from darkness to light, from sin to holiness, from Satan unto God, has been effected solely by the Spirit of God, through the instrumentality of the gospel of Christ.

"Oh, blessed Suit of righteousness, Thou who art the light of the world, let Thy bright beams shine upon it, that the deep shades of error, superstition, and sin may flee before Thy powerful rays, until all the earth shall be filled with Thy glory.

"Shine, blessed Jesus, upon Thy church. Let all Thy people become burning and shining lights in the world, shining by a reflection of Thy glory. Illuminate my dark mind. Take away the thick film from my mental vision. Remove the veil from my heart, and let me behold Thy glory with unveiled face. Yes, let me daily contemplate Thy glorious character, offices, and perfections until I am changed into Thy holy image and made fit for the enjoyment of Thy heavenly kingdom."

How rich, how varied are the themes,
The sacred page contains,
Like oceans deep, or lucid streams
That fertilize the plains.

Here, humble souls are sweetly taught
Salvation through His blood;
By whom alone mankind are brought
To happiness and God.

Here, lofty philosophic minds,
Deep versed in learned lore,

Are lost amid those vast designs
The cherubim adore.

The sacred mysteries of grace
Confound their reasoning pride;
They see no beauty in His face,
Who bowed His head and died.

But firm as on a solid rock,
The saint on Christ relies;
He smiles in death's dissolving shock,
And mounts into the skies!

CHAPTER 58

The Living Water

How beautifully instructive is our Savior's conversation with the woman of Samaria, given while sitting, wearied with His journey, on Jacob's well! What an example to His followers does the benevolent Redeemer exhibit of condescension to ignorance and of affectionate improvement of trivial occurrences to the spiritual good of all around us! The human mind, until taught of God, is equally blind, whether clothed in the imposing vestment of a Jewish doctor or in the simple attire of a Samaritan female. Nicodemus was as ignorant respecting the nature of the new birth as this poor woman was of the living water.

Human learning, though called theological, can never make us savingly acquainted with the first principles of the gospel of Christ. Many an unlettered peasant may be a scribe well instructed in the mysteries of the kingdom, while the learned doctor, filling the professor's chair, may be a very babe in the things of Christ. This view is humiliating to the pride of man and should teach us to call no man master upon earth, but in child-like simplicity to sit at the feet of Jesus and drink of that living water which alone can purify and refresh our souls.

How delightful is the thought that Jesus, the Savior and friend of sinners, is the giver of this spiritual blessing! "If thou knewest the gift of God, and who it is that saith to thee, Give me to drink; thou wouldest have asked of him, and he would have given thee living water" (John 4:10). How consoling the truth that this living water shall be in all His believing people as a well of water, not drying up as earthly springs too frequently do when most needed, but daily rising higher and higher until it issues into everlasting life.

"Jesus answered and said unto her, Whosoever drinketh of this water [the well of Jacob] shall thirst again: but whosoever drinketh of the water that I shall give him shall never thirst; but the water that I shall give him shall be in him a well of water springing up into everlasting life" (John 4:13-14).

The joys of earth are only top springs. Many are delighted with these bubbling waters in seasons of outward prosperity. But in adverse times, when comfort is most needed, they become wells without water. Where, then, must the poor worldling go to quench his thirst? He must go to Jesus. "If any man thirst, let him come unto me, and drink" (John 7:37). "Whosoever will, let him take the water of life freely" (Rev. 22:17).

The Holy Spirit is this living water whose sacred streams can satisfy the most thirsty soul with joys which strengthen and purify the heart. He who drinks of this fountain shall thirst no more as once he did. His thirst shall now be after righteousness, after the enjoyment of God Himself. Blessed thirst! Oh, that I could feel this thirst increasing every hour and every hour betake myself to this spring!

But what says the Savior? It shall be in you a "well of water springing up into everlasting life" (John 4:14). Happy experience, when sensibly enjoyed! Have I this precious internal spring? Have I the Spirit of Christ? This forms the grand indisputable evidence of being a child of God, an heir of glory. Were the whole world my own, I could find no real happiness separate from Jesus Christ. There are indeed many counterfeits which bear the image and superscription of happiness, but all shall finally be detected and leave their possessors miserably poor.

"Man that is born of a woman is of few days and full of trouble" (Job 14:1). Such is the portrait which Job draws of human life. But man was created happy, and would have remained so, had not Satan beguiled him into sin. Yet being "full of trouble," he naturally desires rest. Hence all men are in quest of happiness, and every one expects to find it. Many fancy that they have obtained it, and wrap themselves up in this fond conceit, until death hurls them headlong down the precipice into the burning gulf below!

While we view the many millions of mankind in search of some imaginary good, and greatly thirsting after it, how gracious, how condescending, is the invitation of mercy to the only fountain of true felicity: "Ho, every one that thirsteth, come ye to the waters, and he that hath no money; come ye, buy, and eat; yea, come, buy wine and milk without money and without price" (Isa. 55:1). A world thirsting after happiness, but mistaking its true nature and source, is here most lovingly, most freely, invited to accept of the inestimable blessing. "Wherefore do ye spend money for that which is not bread? and your labour for that which satisfieth not?" (v. 2) is the powerful appeal to the hearts and consciences of sinners.

Much labor and expense are bestowed towards obtaining some supposed good; but being altogether of an earthly nature, it cannot nourish the soul or satisfy its enlarged desires. Hence follows this gracious declaration: "Hearken diligently unto me, and eat ye that which is good, and let your soul delight itself in fatness. Incline your ear, and come unto me: hear, and your soul shall live; and I will make an everlasting covenant with you, even the sure mercies of David" (v. 2-3).

Oh, what rich display of grace is here. Well may the Almighty say: "My thoughts are not your thoughts, neither are your ways my ways" (v. 8). But it does not stop here. The voice of mercy still cries: "Seek ye the LORD while he may be found, call ye upon him while he is near" (v. 6), evidently implying that a time is coming when He will not be found; an hour is approaching when He will not hear. He is now waiting to be gracious and may be found in Christ upon a mercy-seat to bless every returning penitent. But if the day of grace be once ended—if death find the sinner still impenitent and unbelieving—the Lord will be found indeed, but found seated on a throne of judgment; and the wretched criminal will be driven far from His presence, never more to hear the sweet call of slighted mercy.

In this beautiful invitation to a world of sinners, grace reigns through righteousness, for it is added: "Let the wicked forsake his way, and the unrighteous man his thoughts: and let him return unto the LORD, and he will have mercy upon him; and to our God, for he will abundantly pardon" (v. 7). A sweet assurance of joy and peace is given to every sinner who thus, through grace, turns unto the Lord with a true penitent heart and living faith: "Ye shall go out with joy, and be led forth with peace: the mountains and the hills shall break forth before you into singing, and all the trees of the field shall clap their hands" (v. 12).

Here is nothing but joy and rejoicing! Oh, what a precious salvation! The ransomed soul shall be filled with joy and peace through believing. "There is joy in the presence of the angels of God over one sinner that repenteth" (Luke 15:10). The ministers of Christ ardently long after and rejoice in the conversion of sinners. "My heart's desire and prayer to God for Israel is, that they might be saved" (Rom. 10:1). "God is my record, how greatly I long after you all in the bowels of Jesus Christ" (Phil. 1:8). "I have no greater joy than to hear that my children walk in truth" (3 John 1:4). Such were the feelings of Paul and John.

The whole church rejoices to behold the wandering sheep brought safe into the fold and heartily welcomes the chief of sinners when he becomes the loving disciple of the church's beloved Lord. "But they had heard only, That he which persecuted us in times past now preacheth the faith which once he destroyed. And they glorified God in me" (Gal. 1:23-24). So wrote Paul to the church in Galatia, respecting his reception by the apostles at Jerusalem.

The Almighty Himself thus addresses His beloved people, redeemed through the blood of Jesus: "The LORD thy God in the midst of thee is mighty; he will save, he will rejoice over thee with joy; he will rest in his love, he will joy over thee with singing" (Zeph. 3:17). Thus the Lord will bless the righteous, and with favor will He compass him as with a shield. The certainty of all this blessedness is declared: "So shall my word be that goeth forth out of my mouth: it shall not return unto me void, but it shall accomplish that which I please, and it shall prosper in the thing whereto I sent it" (Isa. 55:11).

The glory of God is also secured: "Instead of the thorn shall come up the fir tree, and instead of the brier shall come up the myrtle tree: and it shall be to the LORD for a name, for an everlasting sign that shall not be cut off" (Isa. 55:13). This glorious change from sin to holiness, which is figuratively expressed by the thorns and briars, the cypress and the myrtle, shall be for a sign, an everlasting sign of the divine origin of the gospel of Christ, and for a perpetual memorial of the converting grace of God.

Oh, my soul, after what object are you thirsting? After what are your desires tending? Look around you, and see if any created good can satisfy those desires. Be assured that nothing can make you truly happy but an interest in the blood of Jesus, nothing but a union to Him by faith, nothing but a sweet experience of His pardoning mercy and sanctifying grace, nothing but an entire and unreserved dedication of yourself to Him who gave Himself for you. Oh, then, cast yourself now at the feet of a loving Savior! He will not spurn you from Him, though you deserve to be cast into the nethermost hell.

"Oh, may I daily thirst for these blessings! I would now draw near to the Fountain of living water. May I freely take of Thee, oh Spirit of consolation. By Thy sacred influence may I feel my soul refreshed and strengthened while journeying to the land of which sovereign Grace has said, 'To thee will I give it' (Gen. 13:15).

"Blessed Jesus, I am not worthy to approach Thee. But here is my encouragement: that those only are invited who have no 'money,' no merit of their own; and I have none. Thy righteousness is my only boast and plea. Thou camest not to call the righteous, but sinners, to repentance. How gracious, then, is this gospel call to a world of perishing sinners! 'Ho, every one that thirsteth, come ye to the waters' (Isa. 55:1). Oh, that all may hear and embrace the offered mercy.

"Hasten the glorious period when all shall come with singing unto Thee, when the church shall lengthen her cords and strengthen her stakes—yes, when the whole earth shall be filled with Thy glory. Come, Lord Jesus, come quickly. Amen."

Thou fountain of eternal life,
Whose streams forever flow,
Spring up within my waiting heart,
And all Thy bliss bestow.

The Living Water

Refresh my soul with living streams,
Until holy fruits abound;
A chosen tree of righteousness,
On Zion's sacred ground.

Come, Holy Spirit, Thy grace impart;
Put forth Thy quickening power;
Vain is the hope of bliss below,
The pageant of an hour.

Like tender flowers, we open the bud,
And greet the morning ray;
But before it is noon we droop and fade,
The creatures of a day.

Yet on this little day of life
What mighty things depend;
Eternal torments, or the joy,
That knows nor bound nor end.

Then haste, blest Spirit, to my breast,
Renew my guilty soul;
Speak peace, Thou blessed Comforter,
And make the wounded whole.

CHAPTER 59

The Burning Bush

Much valuable instruction and consolation may be derived from the consideration of the vision with which Moses was favored in the desert of Midian. "And the angel of the LORD appeared unto him in a flame of fire out of the midst of a bush: and he looked, and, behold, the bush burned with fire, and the bush was not consumed" (Ex. 3:2). Like Moses, I would now turn aside and contemplate "this great sight" (v. 3), at once so instructive and consoling.

This bush, which in the original signifies a thorny bush, is a fit emblem of the church of God. Considered in itself, it is weak and worthless, a bramble bush, the lowest among the shrubs. "Ye see your calling, brethren," writes the apostle to the church at Corinth, "how that not many wise men after the flesh, not many mighty, not many noble, are called: But God hath chosen the foolish things of the world to confound the wise; and God hath chosen the weak things of the world to confound the things which are mighty; and base things of the world, and things which are despised, hath God chosen, yea, and things which are not, to bring to nought things that are: that no flesh should glory in his presence" (1 Cor. 1:26-29).

"The bush burned with fire" (Ex. 3:2) justly represents the state of the church in this evil world. The malice of Satan, the persecutions of the ungodly, the corruptions of the heart, and the trials and afflictions which come immediately from God for the purification of His people may well be compared to fire.

The bush, though on fire, "was not consumed" (Ex. 3:2). This is a wonderful sight indeed. Here the grace and power of Jesus are eminently displayed. The church has always been in a furnace, and yet never consumed—yes, rather purified and brightened in proportion to the intensity of the flame. The cause of the church's preservation is revealed to us. The Lord was in the bush. "God is in the midst of her; she shall not be moved" (Ps. 46:5). "The gates of hell shall not prevail against it" (Matt. 16:18). "Fear thou not; for I am with thee: be not dismayed; for I am thy God" (Isa. 41:10). "No weapon that is formed against thee shall prosper" (Isa. 54:17). "Let not your heart be troubled, neither let it be afraid" (John 14:27).

This remarkable vision should teach us humility. The church is not compared to a stately cedar, but to a bramble-bush. We must have low thoughts of ourselves. Man is naturally proud. This inbred evil, even after conversion, rebels against the motions of the Spirit. Hence arises spiritual pride.

When the Lord graciously imparts His gifts for the edification of the church, how prone we are to take the praise of these endowments to ourselves. This made the lowly minded apostle expostulate with the Corinthian converts: "Who maketh thee to differ from another? and what hast thou that thou didst not receive? now if thou didst receive it, why dost thou glory, as if thou hadst not received it?" (1 Cor. 4:7). "Knowledge puffeth up, but charity edifieth" (1 Cor. 8:1).

Moses equally cautioned the ancient people of God against this subtle poison. "The Lord did not set his love upon you, nor choose you, because ye were more in number than any people; for ye were the fewest of all people: But because the Lord loved you, and because he would keep the oath which he had sworn unto your fathers" (Deut. 7:7-8). "Not for thy righteousness, or for the uprightness of thine heart, dost thou go to possess their land: but for the wickedness of these nations the Lord thy God doth drive them out from before thee, and that he may perform the word which the Lord sware unto thy fathers, Abraham, Isaac, and Jacob. Understand therefore, that the Lord thy God giveth thee not this good land to possess it for thy righteousness; for thou art a stiffnecked people" (Deut. 9:5-6). How slow are we to learn this humbling, yet precious, truth—that salvation is all of grace, rich grace, abounding to the chief of sinners.

The beauty and glory of the church are derived from Christ. He is the glory, as well as the glorifier, of His people Israel. Filled with His Spirit, and bearing His image, the church "looketh forth as the morning, fair as the moon, clear as the sun, and terrible as an army with banners" (Song 6:10). Jesus beautifies the meek with salvation. "I will greatly rejoice in the Lord, my soul shall be joyful in my God; for he hath clothed me with the garments of salvation, he hath covered me with the robe of righteousness, as a bridegroom decketh himself with ornaments, and as a bride adorneth herself with her jewels" (Isa. 61:10). "By the grace of God I am what I am" (1 Cor. 15:10). "In the Lord shall all the seed of Israel be justified, and shall glory" (Isa. 45:25).

From this vision we are taught to expect trials while journeying through this desert world. Sometimes the storm rages violently and the flame burns with awful intenseness, yet nothing of the church shall be consumed but its dross. Thus the malice of Satan and the world is overruled for good. Persecution tends only to refine the saints of God. It quickens their graces and puts new life into their prayers. They run to the stronghold and are safe under the fostering care of an almighty Savior. At such trying seasons, the chaff and the withered branches are consumed. Mere nominal professors cannot endure those persecutions, which are designed in God's providence to separate the precious from the vile. "It must needs be that offences come" (Matt. 18:7), "that they which are approved may be made manifest" (1 Cor. 11:19).

The consideration of "this great sight " (Ex. 3:3) should teach us confidence in the faithfulness and power of Jesus. He is in the bush. He never leaves nor forsakes His people. "When thou passest through the waters, I will be with thee; and through the rivers, they shall not overflow thee: when thou walkest through the fire, thou shalt not be burned; neither shall the flame kindle upon thee" (Isa. 43:2) is the gracious sustaining promise.

This vision of a bush burning, yet unconsumed, affords a striking view of the perpetuity of the church of Christ. Nothing shall be allowed to destroy this treasure of Jehovah. It may be reduced, and often has been reduced to the lowest ebb, but in the most degenerate times God never left himself without a church, however small, to show forth His praise. From Abel down to the present hour, there has ever been "a remnant according to the election of grace" (Rom. 11:5). When the whole earth was filled with violence, and all flesh had corrupted its way before God, "Noah found grace in the eyes of the Lord....Noah was a just man and perfect in his generations, and Noah walked with God" (Gen. 6:8-9). The desolating flood at length descended, and everything wherein was the breath of life perished, except the little church of God, which was preserved in the ark on the bosom of the tempestuous waters!

After the deluge, iniquity began to spread with awful rapidity. Idolatry reared its rebellious tower in the plain of Shinar, and the knowledge of the true God became gradually shrouded in ignorance and superstition until the Almighty called Abraham by His grace and caused genuine piety to flourish once more in himself and in his family.

When planted in the land of Canaan, the Israelites soon forsook the God of their fathers. In the midst of abounding idolatry, the Lord raised up a prophet in whom seemed to center all the religion of the land. In the grief of his heart he said, "It is enough; now, O Lord, take away my life; for I am not better than my fathers" (1 Kings 19:4). "I, even I, only am left; and they seek my life, to take it away" (v. 10). But what was the answer of the Lord to Elijah? "I have left me seven thousand in Israel, all the knees which have not bowed unto Baal" (v. 18).

When our blessed Lord came in the flesh, darkness covered the earth and gross darkness the people (Isa. 60:2); yet even then there were a chosen few who in faith "waited for redemption in Israel" (cf. Luke 2:38).

During the dark period of 1260 years, foretold in the Revelation, wherein the dragon, the beast, and the false prophet would wage continual war with the church of Christ, the Lord appointed two witnesses (a constant succession of faithful men) who should testify to the power and grace of Jesus, even though they prophesy in sackcloth. In this period we now live and can only attest to the truth of this remarkable prophecy.

All this is in virtue of the everlasting covenant. How extensive the promise of the Father to His eternal Son! "He shall have dominion also from sea to sea, and from the river unto the ends of the earth" (Ps. 72:8). "His name shall endure for ever: his name shall be continued as long as the sun: and men shall be blessed in him: all nations shall call him blessed" (v. 17).

From this manifestation of the Almighty to Moses, we are led to adore the sovereignty of God. He ordinarily chooses not the great ones of the earth, but the poor and the despised. Some, indeed, but not many, noble are called. Worldly riches and elevated stations have a tendency to beget self-sufficiency and vain-confidence. "Poor in spirit, rich in faith, and heirs of the kingdom" is the genuine character of the church of Christ. Divine grace, however, can as easily bring the proudest monarch, as the lowest beggar, in the lowly attitude of contrition to the foot of the cross.

Happy will be that period when the kings of the earth and its nobles shall esteem it their highest glory to become the subjects of the Prince of Peace and their chief joy to promote the extension of His kingdom of righteousness throughout the world.

We are hereby led to admire also the wisdom and power of God. He can promote the enlargement of His church by those very means which its enemies employ to destroy it. The children of Israel grew and multiplied, in spite of Pharaoh's efforts to prevent it.

The gospel spread with wonderful rapidity, notwithstanding all the threatenings of the Jews and Romans to check its progress. Those persecutions which scattered the disciples abroad tended only to widen their field of labor; for they went everywhere, preaching the Word. The sacred fire, thus dispersed by the rude hand of violence, multiplied itself in proportion to its dispersion. Hence it became proverbial that the blood of the martyrs is the seed of the church. "So mightily grew the word of God and prevailed" (Acts 19:20). Even its enemies wondered whereunto all this would grow.

While the kings of the earth set themselves and the rulers took counsel together against the Lord and against His Christ, the almighty Sovereign of the universe proclaimed: "Yet have I set my king upon my holy hill of Zion" (Ps. 2:6). Jesus by His resurrection was declared to be the Son of God with power, and "of the increase of his government and peace there shall be no end.... The zeal of the LORD of hosts will perform this" (Isa. 9:7)....

Oh, my soul, rejoice in this great salvation! Lord, grant unto Thine unworthy servant a portion of this felicity. Make me even now a living member of Thy mystical body, poor in spirit and pure in heart, patiently enduring every trial, daily exercising faith in Thy truth and mercy, adoring Thy sovereignty, admiring Thy power, and rejoicing in the perpetuity of the grace which lives in all Thy faithful people and preserves them unto Thy eternal kingdom and glory.

Let my whole heart praise Thee, Thou God of my salvation. Let my whole life be consecrated unto Thee. The work, oh Lord, is Thine. Thou alone canst new-create the soul. Perform this act of grace, this miracle of mercy, for Thine own glory and to Thine everlasting praise. Amen and amen.

Oh, come, you servants of the Lord,
Whose will is your delight;
His boundless love and grace record,
While heart and tongue unite.

Strike up your harps, and sweetly sing
Of Jesus' lovely name;
To Him your grateful tribute bring,
His endless praise proclaim.

Declare what wonders He has done,
Make all His glories known;
Adore the Father's equal Son;
The Priest upon the throne.

Sing of His rich and sovereign grace,
Transcendent and divine;
Sing how He died to save our race
From misery and sin.

He died for us—He made our peace;
He pleads our cause on high;
Oh, may our praises never cease,
Hosannahs never die!

May each revolving year inflame
Our zeal, delight, and love;
Until round the throne we chant His name
In purer strains above.

Oh, come, you servants of the Lord,
His endless praise proclaim;
In gladsome notes His love record,
For, "Worthy is the Lamb."

CHAPTER 60

Adoption

How rich, how varied are the blessings of redemption! Like the gracious Giver, they are infinite and eternal, reaching from everlasting to everlasting. Fully to know the gifts of grace, we must know the fullness of Him from whom they flow. Surely gratitude ought to swell our hearts when we contemplate the Author of our mercies and the abject worms on whom those mercies are bestowed.

Happy is that heart which can appreciate the love of Jesus and to which the Savior is increasingly precious. Thus to feel is heaven begun, and it forms one of the brightest evidences of adoption into the family of God.

According to the natural order of things, we are first made the children of God, and then we receive the spirit of children. This is in perfect accordance with Scripture: "Ye are all the children of God by faith in Christ Jesus" (Gal. 3:26), and "because ye are sons, God hath sent forth the Spirit of his Son into your hearts, crying, Abba, Father" (Gal. 4:6). For "God sent forth his Son, made of a woman, made under the law, To redeem them that were under the law, that we might receive the adoption of sons" (Gal. 4:4-5). Hence, "he that believeth on the Son of God hath the witness in himself" (1 John 5:10), the indwelling Spirit testifying to his spirit, or conscience, that he is a child of God; for thus says John: "Hereby we know that he abideth in us, by the Spirit which he hath given us" (1 John 3:24). Therefore, filial affections towards God as our covenant Father, produced in the soul by the Holy Spirit, constitute the Spirit of adoption and prove us to be His redeemed children.

This delightful feeling of sonship, with all its attendant blessedness, creates a peace and joy such as a loving child experiences in the society and under the smiles of an affectionate parent. But we must never forget that this state of heart is not the mere effect of contemplating the change which may have passed upon us. When we look into ourselves, we find continual need for the deepest humiliation, even when we can praise God for His distinguishing mercy towards us.

Our peace and joy are the fruits of faith in the blood of Christ, wrought in us through the mighty power of God. We can have peace and joy only through believing. But as we become the children of God by faith, so true peace in the conscience and joy in the heart can be maintained and increased only through an abiding reliance on the blood and righteousness of Jesus.

From this foundation arises a sacred edifice of heavenly graces. "Know ye not," says the apostle, "know ye not that your body is the temple of the Holy Ghost which is in you, which ye have of God, and ye are not your own? For ye are bought with a price: therefore glorify God in your body, and in your spirit, which are God's" (1 Cor. 6:19-20). All the delightful experiences of true believers are inseparably connected with the witness of the Spirit. For though, for perspicuity's sake, we may endeavor to speak of them as so many steps ascending to the highest privileges of the gospel, yet they are so blended together that to separate them would be like separating the superstructure of a building from its foundation or disjointing the members of a beautifully formed body.

Every grace of the Spirit has its counterfeit in the hypocrite. Oh, what need we have to pray for wisdom to "try the spirits" (1 John 4:1). All joy is not the fruit of the Spirit. The joy of the hypocrite is but for a moment (Job 20:5). All peace is not the peace of God. "When they shall say, Peace and safety; then sudden destruction cometh upon them" (1 Thess. 5:3).

The enemy of souls can sow his tares, which at a distance may appear like true wheat, while, on closer inspection, they are found to be destitute of the precious grain. The renewed mind, on the contrary, unfolds its native excellencies the more minutely it is viewed, just as the insect and the flower spread before us their exquisite forms and beauties in proportion to the power of the lens.

Thus the more we become acquainted with a real child of God, the more of the divine image we shall discover. Humility, love, and purity will equally spread before us their beauties and prove that the workmanship is of God.

What remains of fallen nature will indeed be uncouth and forbidding, but what is of God will be attractive and delightful. Oh, that my heart may be molded into this lovely image! There is in the blessed Jesus every thing to kindle our love to the highest flame. Lord, inflame my whole heart with constant, fervent love to Thee.

Some professors of religion consider every affection short of ecstasy as worth nothing. Hence many, it is to be feared, substitute mere animal excitement for joy in the Holy Spirit and thus deceive themselves.

A person may bring forth the fruits of the Spirit, have much of the meekness and gentleness of Christ, and yet not be able, from some mental cause, to exercise that filial confidence towards God in which the Spirit of adoption in a great measure consists, although none can possess the Spirit without bringing forth the fruits of righteousness.

Others, from some peculiar temperament of body, may be prevented from feeling high transports of joy, while, at the same time, they can taste the sweets of inward serenity and composedness of mind. Others again, from a deep view of their own corruption, cannot or dare not recognize in themselves a holy conformity to God, though they hate sin and truly love the Savior.

Now, shall we say that such characters have not the Spirit's witness because they cannot feel this ecstasy of delight? Must the work of the Spirit be overlooked in the absence of rapturous feeling? Shall we make those sad whom the Lord has not made sad? Oh, how needful it is for the enjoyment of true comfort to place our experience on the right foundation!

Now, if joy, which is the Christian's delightful privilege, be the effect of the Spirit's witness, rather than the witness itself, then the humble follower of Jesus, who has the testimony of his conscience that he has chosen God for his portion and cleaves wholly to his Savior for righteousness and strength, ought not to despond because he cannot rise to those heights of joy which some favored believers are permitted to attain. He may, however, and he ought, to take courage from this inward witness of the Spirit to his conscience to aspire after so happy a state of mind which conduces so much to the glory of God and to the spiritual growth of his own soul, for "the joy of the Lord is your strength" (Neh. 8:10).

May we not then conclude that, when joy overflows the heart through a lively sense of redeeming grace, it forms a sunshine in the soul; and that when this joy is accompanied with love and confidence and reverence and trust in God, we have the Spirit of adoption in its most genuine exercise? We also perceive that joyful emotions arising from some powerful impression or animal excitement may be transient, as is evident from the stony ground hearer who anon received the Word with joy but in time of temptation fell away.

It is to guard against such a delusion as this that we should endeavor to form a solid and scriptural basis on which to repose our hopes and consolations. Joy may be unhallowed, but submissive obedience to the will of God cannot be. How important, and yet how determinate, is the declaration of Paul "as many as are led by the Spirit of God, they are the sons of God" (Rom. 8:14). Am I led by the Spirit of God? Oh, how much of happiness is contained in the right answer to this question! The Spirit leads the sinner to the foot of the cross. Have I ever reached that place of mercy? The Spirit leads the sinner from the love of sin to the love of holiness. Do I abhor whatever is contrary to the mind of my Redeemer and seek my happiness in the performance of His will?

The Spirit leads the soul from the vanities of the world to the enjoyment of momentous gospel blessings. Have I been graciously withdrawn in heart and affection from an evil world and led into the purifying delights of fellowship with the Father and with His Son, Jesus Christ?

How blessed is the Spirit of adoption, that childlike Spirit which enables us to come to our heavenly Father, neither doubting His power nor distrusting His grace. When we consider our weakness and His strength, our needs and His fullness, we may well feel happy while possessing in all its vigor this Spirit of adoption.

Sickness may invade our frame; poverty may diminish our substance; friends may prove unfaithful; yes, even Satan may harass our minds; and sin, dwelling within us, may lust and rebel; yet with God, the great God, as our reconciled Father in Christ Jesus, we shall rise superior to every grief and loss and feel and maintain a peace which the world can neither give nor take away.

While in this happy frame of mind, the Spirit bears witness with our spirit that we are the children of God. But if we are children, then we are heirs—oh, amazing thought, surpassing human intellect to conceive—heirs of God, and joint-heirs with Christ (Rom. 8:17)! Heirs of that Being, whom Abraham styles "the possessor of heaven and earth" (Gen. 14:22), and joint-heirs with that Savior, who declared: "All power is given unto me in heaven and in earth" (Matt. 28:18). Surely, then, with delightful propriety might the apostle say: "All things are yours;… and ye are Christ's; and Christ is God's" (1 Cor. 3:21, 23).

Are the children of God, while thus exalted in privileges, exempt from affliction? Ah, no! While here below, they must tread the path of suffering, the path by which the blessed Jesus went to glory, for it is added: "if so be that we suffer with him, that we may be also glorified together" (Rom. 8:17).

"Oh, Thou adorable Savior, may I never shrink from bearing Thy cross when called to endure it; if I suffer with Thee, I shall also reign with Thee. But who is sufficient for these things? Of myself, I am perfect weakness, but in Thee there is fullness of strength; and through faith in Thee, I shall assuredly overcome.

"Oh, that I may daily possess this sacred evidence of my adoption into Thy family, an evidence which will stand the test of trial and temptation, which will keep me humble in prosperity, patient in affliction, peaceful in death, and joyful through eternity. Impart this blessing for Thine own mercies' sake, my only helper and deliverer."

You happy souls, the Savior praise,
Whose grace has made you sons of God;
To Him devote your fleeting days,
Who bought you with His precious blood.

With childlike confidence repose
Each care on His paternal breast,
Whose love no end nor measure knows;
The center of eternal rest.

How sweet to dwell beneath His shade,
Removed far from toil and care;
Where none can make the soul dismayed
That seeks and finds its refuge there.

Unite my heart, dear Lord, to Thee,
To Thee be every moment given;
On earth may I Thy goodness see,
Thy glory in the highest heaven.

CHAPTER 61

Faith

The heart of man is like a weight, whose natural bias is downward. Nothing but a power outside of itself can cause it to ascend heavenward. The attraction of gravitation is not more powerful in its effects on the various parts of the universe than is the debasing force of natural corruption in the heart of fallen man.

There is, however, a counteracting principle, an attracting influence which can draw the soul from earth to heaven and unite it to the blessed God. This principle is faith. Without faith it is impossible to please God, because until we truly believe in Jesus, we are in a state of guilt and condemnation.

True faith is not a mere passive impression or an inoperative notion. It is a holy principle wrought in the soul by the Spirit of God, producing gracious habits, holy affections, filial reverence, and obedience. Faith is seated in the heart, influencing and purifying the whole inner man.

Faith unites the soul to Christ, as the branch to the vine. It draws virtue from Him, whereby the believer is rendered fruitful in every good work. The sweet fruits of the Spirit appear and abound in rich luxuriance on these favored branches, to the glory of God.

Faith places the soul upon Christ, as the only foundation on which it is built up a holy temple unto the Lord, unhurt by all the winds and storms which beat upon it. Faith feeds upon Christ continually, as the true bread which came down from heaven, of which whoever eats shall live forever. Faith works by love to God, His people, and His Word. It evidences its vitality by its fruits. Faith purifies the heart from sin, waging war against all internal and external evil. Faith overcomes the world, both when it smiles and when it frowns. Faith views the glorious land of promise as its own and triumphs over all intervening difficulties and dangers which bestrew its path to Zion.

Faith makes the believer confident, yet watchful; bold, yet cautious; aspiring, yet humble. He is confident, since the promises of God are kindly given him to rest upon; watchful, since he feels the deceitfulness of his rebellious heart; bold, since the honor of the Savior demands his confession; cautious, lest he should be only gratifying a vain-glorious spirit; aspiring after that honor which comes from God only; yet humble, since he remembers his own vileness and utter unworthiness of the least of the divine mercies.

If it be asked, How can faith effect such wonders? The reply is, Because faith is the gift of God, and the power of God. The believer, abiding in Christ and deriving continual supplies of grace and strength out of His fullness, becomes mighty through this power which works in him mightily. He is strengthened with might by His Spirit in the inner man to fight the good fight of faith and to lay hold on eternal life. Weak and helpless in himself, he is strong in the grace that is in Christ Jesus his Lord and finally obtains the palm of victory through the blood of the Lamb. Thus, faith in Christ at once gives peace to the conscience and leads it to all true holiness, for when peace is imparted to the conscience, purity is produced in the heart.

Such is the faith of God's elect, a faith which is according to godliness. That system of religion must be awfully defective which would dare to lower the standard of holiness under the false—I would say impious—notion of thereby exalting the grace of God. Because Christ is a Savior, shall we make Him the minister of sin? Because God is merciful, must He therefore be unjust? He who is glorious in holiness cannot save sinners in their sins or admit them into His kingdom while sin has the dominion over them; it is impossible. The whole of divine revelation—yes, the very plan of the gospel—is designed to preserve unsullied the infinite perfections of Jehovah, while the vilest of sinners are saved from hell and made, through grace, to reflect the divine image in all the beauties of holiness, righteousness, and truth.

None are saved by Christ but those who are saved from their sins. If any man be in Christ, he is a new creature.

The apostle Paul, writing to the Galatians, says: "If there had been a law given which could have given life, verily righteousness should have been by the law" (Gal. 3:21).

This declaration is most important. If God could have given a law less spiritual in its requirements and less awful in its sanctions, if He could have given a law lowered in its standard and yet compatible with His infinite holiness and man's truest happiness, then life might have been attained by such a law.

But as this, in the very nature of things, is impossible; as God cannot, from the absolute perfection of His nature, command less than infinite holiness approves or less than infinite justice demands; as His law is immutably holy, though man has rebelled against it and lost all power to obey it; it remains an unchangeable truth that life cannot come by a law which condemns the very thought of sin and lays the whole human race under merited condemnation.

On this account, the Scripture has concluded all under sin, that the promise by faith of Jesus Christ might be given to those who believe. This divine truth strikes at the root of those errors which would make the gospel a mitigated law or mix man's works and the Savior's merits in the great act of justification or, denying the necessity of an atonement, make man's repentance and obedience sufficient to insure the approbation of heaven. The law is given to us, not for the purpose of obtaining eternal life by our obedience to its requirements, since "by the deeds of the law there shall no flesh be justified" (Rom. 3:20), but as a rule of life by which we are to walk under the influence and guidance of the Holy Spirit.

The gospel is revealed for the all-gracious purpose of redeeming us from all iniquity and purifying our hearts from sin through faith in the atonement of Jesus the Son of God. Here spring all our hopes of forgiveness, all our peace of conscience, all our joy in the Holy Spirit. From this source of mercy we derive all our power to love and serve God in the filial spirit of adoption.

Thus it is evident that where infinite justice finds its satisfaction, there, and there only, can my guilty soul find its salvation. The Lamb of God, bleeding upon the cross as the divinely appointed sacrifice for the sins of a fallen world, is the sinner's only refuge from the storm of eternal vengeance. To this blessed atonement I would look, and from it I would draw all my hopes of pardon, peace, and purity.

"Oh, for more faith and love! Lord, without Thee I can do nothing. I feel my helplessness and my inward depravity. Lead me to the Rock which is higher than I. Wash me in the fountain opened for sin and for uncleanness. Sprinkle clean water upon me, and I shall be clean. Put Thy Spirit within me. Cause the south wind to blow, that my soul may be filled with precious fruits, that the spices may flow out, that my Beloved may come and eat His pleasant fruits and abide with me forever!"

Oh, what a happy life is a life of faith in the Son of God! To have the humble, yet scriptural, assurance that my sins are forgiven, and to know from the Word of truth and to be persuaded that all things shall work together for my good, are the divine alchemy which turns all to gold.

Sickness, adversity, persecution, and the buffetings of Satan are all overruled for good when the soul is accepted and pardoned through faith in the blood of Jesus. Nothing can separate such a soul from the love of God while abiding in Christ by faith.

How safe, how happy, how rich, is the true believer in Jesus. He is safe under the protecting wing of the Almighty, happy in the enjoyment of the divine favor, rich with all the treasures of grace and glory. He is Christ's, and Christ is God's.

And yet, how is such a state despised by the world! Those who live in the enjoyment of it are deemed enthusiasts, or perhaps insane. Numbers who would be thought religious treat such a state of feeling with coldness or receive it with caution. They seem to dread everything that is fervent or transporting in religion, as if the affections had no share with the understanding in the great transactions between Christ and the soul.

Oh, that I could feel my heart more alive to God, more active in His service! A lukewarm spirit is hateful to a God of love. I am convinced that faith is the gift of God, not only because I read it in my Bible, but because I feel my utter inability, by any natural power of my own, to produce it in myself. I am taught to pray for this blessing in the name of Jesus. But true prayer is equally the gift of God.

Thus I perceive that I am indebted to sovereign grace alone for the whole work of salvation from first to last, from the first incipient desire after God to the full fruition of Him in glory. Then what must I do? Must I sit still and do nothing? Ah, no! This would, indeed, be enthusiasm. Satan and my own indolent heart would have me act in this manner. But such reasoning would condemn, and not excuse, me in the day of judgment. God has given me an understanding which, though darkened through the fall, is still capable, under the advantages of Christian instruction, of knowing that the Creator ought to be loved and feared and served above all other beings.

He has given me a conscience which, though awfully defiled, yet, under such instruction, is capable of making me feel that I do not love and fear and serve this almighty Creator above all other things, and therefore, that I am a guilty creature and deserving of His eternal wrath.

God has cast my lot in a land where Jesus is preached, where sinners are invited to come unto Him for all those blessings which they have lost through the fall and of which they stand in need. My responsibility is, therefore, increased by this offered mercy.

What, then, must I do? Surely it is my duty, as a rational and responsible creature, to listen to the call of my heavenly Father. It is my duty to come to the cross of Christ, just as I am—blind, ignorant, helpless, guilty, and polluted—that I may obtain, through the riches of His grace, light and strength and righteousness and sanctification.

If I do not come, the fault is altogether my own; it is because I will not. The guilt lies in the bad state of my heart. If I do come, it is through the secret, yet powerful, operation of divine grace, seeing God is the first mover of the heart to Himself. Infinite Wisdom knows how to reconcile these seeming differences, and what the believer knows not now, he shall know hereafter.

Hence it is evident that all the specious pleas and excuses which sinners make for not coming to Jesus will before long be found to originate in their love of sin and in the corrupt state of their will. Hell will be filled with self-reproaches and with eternal self-condemnations. Let not Satan, then, oh my soul, and a perverse rebellious will, keep you from the Savior. Press to Him through the crowd. Do not be afraid of meeting with a repulse. His heart is full of tenderness and love.

Bartimeus could not heal his blindness, nor the leper his leprosy, nor the poor woman her issue of blood. They all felt their respective maladies. They believed that Jesus could restore them. They applied to Him and were healed. Go and do you likewise. Cry also to the Savior, touch the hem of His garment, and He, who is all power, and grace, and love, will impart this saving faith and enable you to draw virtue from Him, saying: "I will: be thou clean" (Luke 5:13). Only believe. "All things are possible to him that believeth" (Mark 5:6; 9:23).

"'Lord, I believe; help thou mine unbelief' (Mark 9:24). Lord, increase my faith. Enable me to come to Thee now in humble confidence and love, that I may receive out of Thy fullness grace for grace. Lord, shine upon Thy work. Make me a monument of Thy mercy, that I may live to Thy glory and sing Thy everlasting praise."

Oppressed with grief, overwhelmed with fear,
Where can I find a refuge near?
Dear Savior, unto Thee I flee,
Oh, hide me in Gethsemane!

My sins assume an awful form;
Around I view the rising storm;
I fly, my only Lord, to Thee,
Oh, hide me in Gethsemane!

In that sweet garden, Thou didst bear
Of guilt and pain my awful share;
Thy bleeding form methinks I see
Extended in Gethsemane.

Oh, fill my heart with fervent love;
To Thee, let each affection move;
From sin preserve me ever free,
While sheltered in Gethsemane.

CHAPTER 62

Hope

Paul, when writing to the Corinthians, declared, "Some have not the knowledge of God: I speak this to your shame" (1 Cor. 15:34). And may not the same reproof be directed to multitudes of professing Christians of our day? The ignorance of many is lamentably great. Light is in the dwellings of the righteous, and the spiritual Goshen is illuminated by the beams of heavenly truth; but what an awful extent of territory still remains enveloped in Egyptian darkness, under the tyranny of Satan and in bondage to sin! With Isaiah we must lament, while casting our eyes over the world, that darkness covers the earth, and gross darkness the people (Isa. 60:2).

With what fervency, then, should true believers supplicate for the promised out-pouring of the Holy Spirit, who alone can enlighten the understanding and guide the wretched slave to Jesus Christ for spiritual redemption! Too many, it is to be feared, seek their knowledge from human sources, rather than from the fountain of divine wisdom. The writings of good men may be lawfully used as little rills flowing from the sacred fountain of inspiration, but woe be to that church or people who substitute them for the blessed spring itself. It is a never-failing mark of a fallen church when human traditions or human systems are raised above, made equal with, or set in opposition to the revealed Word of God.

The Bible is the grand depository of every truth that is necessary to be known, believed, and practiced in order to have eternal salvation. But even the Holy Bible itself is but a dead letter, without a spiritual discernment of its doctrines and a spiritual relish for its precepts. "But the natural man receiveth not the things of the Spirit of God: for they are foolishness unto him: neither can he know them, because they are spiritually discerned" (1 Cor. 2:14). But, says the apostle, "God hath revealed them unto us by his Spirit: for the Spirit searcheth all things, yea, the deep things of God" (1 Cor. 2:10).

How affectionately did Paul pray for the Ephesian converts, that God would give unto them "the spirit of wisdom and revelation in the knowledge of him: The eyes of your understanding being enlightened; that ye may know what is the hope of his calling, and what the riches of the glory of his inheritance in the saints" (Eph. 1:17-18). Many professing Christians would be at a loss to give a reason of the hope that is in them. They tell us, indeed, that God is merciful, that they trust to Jesus Christ, that they do the best they can and want to injure no one and therefore hope that all will end well at the last, though they do not pretend to so much religion as some people who are perhaps no better than others, notwithstanding their preciseness and apparent sanctity of character.

This is a creed which satisfies the consciences of thousands, while their affections are glued to the world and the love of Christ is a stranger to their hearts. Such people have no sublime views of the Christian hope. A mist of ignorance rests upon it, which obscures its glory and damps its joy.

"Lord, give me, through the teaching of Thy Spirit, a sweet realizing view of this blessed hope which bears up Thy people under all their trials and enables them to glorify Thee, even in the fires."

The hope of the believer in Jesus flows from the free, sovereign love of almighty God; therefore it is called "a good hope through grace" (2 Thess. 2:16)—"good" because it issues from the fountain of goodness, and "through grace" because it originates solely in unmerited mercy. This hope rests upon an immovable foundation, even on the divinity and atonement of Jesus Christ, who is called by the Spirit of Truth "our hope" (1 Tim. 1:1) because all our hope of salvation is treasured up in Him and flows from Him. All who possess this hope have Christ dwelling in their hearts by faith; therefore, says the apostle, "Christ in you, the hope of glory" (Col. 1:27). The Spirit of Christ is the pledge and seal of future glory and abides in the hearts of all the faithful in Christ Jesus.

But how are we to know when we truly possess this hope of glory? John informs us: "Every man that has this hope in him purifieth himself, even as he is pure" (1 John 3:3). It is therefore a holy principle, sanctifying and cleansing the soul. He who has the hope of dwelling with Christ in glory, cannot delight in the service of Satan, or in the pleasures of sin. They are an offence unto him. To live in sin, while professing to enjoy the hope of glory, forms an indisputable mark of hypocrisy or self-delusion.

Oh, with what jealous care should real Christians watch against those destructive tenets which, under the cloak of evangelical doctrines, would break down the barrier of gospel holiness and let in the wild boar of the woods, or trample under feet the sacred ground of Zion! "He that saith, I know him, and keepeth not his commandments, is a liar, and the truth is not in him" (1 John 2:4).

The believer, who is taught from above, well knows that sin separates between him and his God and prevents the communication of His gracious beamings on the soul. He, therefore, hates and loathes this infinite evil. He longs for more of his Savior's presence and love, and mourns over every corruption of his nature and every contracted defilement of which his heart is made conscious. Knowing what numberless deviations from the holy law of God his Savior's eye beholds continually in his daily walk and conversation, he lifts up the prayer of David with self-abasement: "Cleanse thou me from secret faults" (Ps. 19:12). He pants after that blessed period when sin shall no longer rebel against the Spirit dwelling within him, and therefore the "hope of glory" (Col. 1:27) is to him a glorious hope and makes him long to be dissolved, that he may be with Christ.

The Christian's hope is a living hope. It gives the believer vigor in running the race that is set before him. It animates him in his arduous warfare. It enables him to endure, with patience and fortitude, the rugged path through which he has to travel Zionward.

The Christian's hope is full of immortality. It traverses the valley of the shadow of death and opens to his view the boundless prospect of eternal glory. It gathers, by delightful anticipation, many a precious cluster of the grapes of Eshcol and thus gives a foretaste of the joys of heaven.

The Christian's hope "maketh not ashamed; because the love of God is shed abroad in our hearts by the Holy Ghost which is given unto us" (Rom. 5:5). It forms a divine evidence of his union to Christ. He can now say with Paul: "I am not ashamed of the gospel of Christ: for it is the power of God unto salvation to every one that believeth" (Rom. 1:16). He is not ashamed to confess Christ before men as his only hope of glory. He can declare with humble confidence and heartfelt sincerity: "I know whom I have believed, and am persuaded that he is able to keep that which I have committed unto him against that day" (2 Tim. 1:12).

The Christian's hope is a helmet of salvation (1 Thess. 5:8) which covers his head in the day of battle, when the fiery darts of Satan are leveled against him. It is "an anchor of the soul" (Heb. 6:19), both sure and steadfast, which preserves the tempest-tossed soul from being driven into the ocean of doubts and despondencies or dashed against the rocks of presumption or despair. Surely, then, it is a "blessed hope" (Titus 2:13). All who possess it are blessed. This made the apostle pray so sweetly for the Roman converts: "Now the God of hope fill you with all joy and peace in believing, that ye may abound in hope, through the power of the Holy Ghost" (Rom. 15:13).

Diligence and privilege are inseparably united by the wisdom of God. Hence Paul thus exhorts the Hebrews: "God is not unrighteous to forget your work and labour of love, which ye have shewed toward his name, in that ye have ministered to the saints, and do minister. And we desire that every one of you do shew the same diligence to the full assurance of hope unto the end: That ye be not slothful, but followers of them who through faith and patience inherit the promises" (Heb. 6:10-12). Examine well, oh my soul, what is the hope of your calling. You have been and are continually called by the outward preaching of the Word; but here is the turning point: have you been drawn to Christ by the inward, effectual call of the Holy Spirit?

To ascertain this important fact, inquire what is the nature of your hope. Is it a good hope, a blessed hope, a hope full of immortality? Have you cast the anchor of hope within the veil? Have you put on the helmet of salvation? Do you find your hope to be a lively hope, animating and invigorating your endeavors after the attainment of everlasting life? Does the hope which you possess purify all your affections? Is Jesus really dwelling in you as the hope of glory? Are you resting on Him as the only foundation of hope? And, in the full assurance of this Christian hope, do you enjoy that peace which passes understanding, that joy which is unspeakable and full of glory? If this be your experience, then rejoice and be exceeding glad—for happy, unspeakably happy, will be your lot through the countless ages of eternity.

But, oh, have you not reason to mourn over the little progress which you have made in the divine life, since the bright beams of grace first dawned upon you? "Thou knowest, blessed Lord, that I want to love Thee more than I have ever yet done; yes, I want those unerring marks of real love, which never fail to prove it to be genuine. I want to feel a greater delight in prayer, to pour out my heart before Thee with more childlike simplicity, to tell Thee more freely all my needs, to mourn more deeply over all my corruptions, to trust more unreservedly to the blood of Jesus, to dread all approaches to sin and earnestly to covet the best gifts of faith, hope, and charity, humility of mind, holiness of heart, deadness to the world, and an entire subjection of the soul to Thee. Thou canst in a moment impart these blessings. Thousands have been partakers of them without diminishing Thy fullness. Open the doors of my heart, enlarge it by Thy grace, and let it be filled with Thy grace and heavenly benediction.

"Thou wilt be inquired of by Thy people, not that Thou needest to be informed, but that they may feel their need of Thee. Oh, that I may approach Thee at all times sprinkled with the atoning blood, until the angel of death shall bear me to the mansions of glory, where hope shall be swallowed up in the enjoyment of Thy everlasting love."

Unite, you saints, in cheerful praise,
To heaven your joyful voices raise;
Unite in melody divine,
Until all in heartfelt chorus join.

Let sacred hope your breasts inspire;
While love, that pure celestial fire,
Burns with an undiminished blaze,
Amid the symphonies of praise.

Praise Him, who gave His only Son,
For crimes which rebel worms have done;
Praise Him, who died upon the tree,
Who bled and groaned on Calvary.

Praise Him, who long in patient love,
Our stubborn hearts has sought to move;
Praise Father, Son, and Holy Ghost,
You ransomed souls, you heavenly host!

Oh, may our praises never cease,
While journeying towards the realms of peace;
Where saints in lovelier accents raise
A never-ending song of praise!

CHAPTER 63

Love

True Christian love is of an enlarged, unselfish nature. It loves all who love the Lord Jesus Christ in sincerity.

Party spirit is confined within the limits of a sect. But Christian love outsteps the narrow boundary and can recognize a brother in each humble believer who practically exemplifies the holy doctrines of the gospel. When we love our own party exclusively, or people only of our own peculiar train of thinking, we love ourselves in them. We see our own image and admire it. But when we love those who differ from us in nonessentials, because we discover in them the humility, meekness, purity, patience, and benevolence of the Redeemer, then our love is truly Christian. It is Christ in them whom we love. How little of this enlarged affection on pure Christian principles do we discover in the professing world! We hear much about it, but see little of it. It is highly extolled, but little cultivated. The heart of man is naturally selfish and contracted, bigoted, and full of jealousies. It suspects a foe where charity hails a friend.

Nothing is more evident than this truth, that Christian charity increases our happiness with its own increase. A narrow, contracted spirit, under the influence of prejudice, and blinded by fond partialities, can never enjoy the refined pleasures of Christian communion. Such a spirit chills and freezes the soul; it checks exertion, except when its party is concerned, and looks badly on those, however excellent, who "do not follow us." Distinctions seem necessary in this state of imperfection; but real Christians know well how to distinguish between the expansive charity of the gospel and that undefined latitudinarianism which would level all distinctions.

There is a perfect consistency in preferring our own peculiar communion, to which we are attached from judgment and conscience, and in loving those of other communions who bear the image of the blessed Jesus.

"Lord, preserve me from all selfish and uncharitable feelings. Be the center of my affections, and may their only boundary be Thyself, oh unbounded ocean of eternal love! Enable me to give the right hand of fellowship to all who truly love Thee, and to rejoice in being in any measure instrumental in hastening on that glorious period when Judah shall not vex Ephraim, nor Ephraim envy Judah, but when all shall love as brethren."

God is love. Love, therefore, brings heaven into the soul and diffuses happiness wherever its influence is felt. Where love reigns, there is peace and joy, gentleness and goodness. How clearly does this consideration prove to us the divine origin of the gospel of Christ, which breathes nothing but peace. Earth would indeed be blessed, if pure Christian love dwelt in every breast and regulated every thought.

The period so glowingly depicted by Isaiah is fast approaching, when they shall not hurt nor destroy in all God's holy mountain (Isa. 11:9). But what is described as the cause of this blessedness? "The earth shall be full of the knowledge of the Lord, as the waters cover the sea" (Isa. 11:9). What a stimulus should this be to strenuous exertion and fervent prayers! Every true believer should esteem it his privilege and duty, according to his ability, to aid in building the spiritual temple and in ushering in the latter day of glory.

Daniel has foretold that "many shall run to and fro, and knowledge shall be increased" (Dan. 12:4), while the diligent laborers are thus encouraged by Zechariah: "I will strengthen them in the Lord; and they shall walk up and down in his name, says the Lord" (Zech. 10:12). Happy are those servants who shall be found so doing; may an increasing company of faithful missionaries ever abound in their labors of love, until all shall know the Lord, from the least unto the greatest;

until judgment shall run down as water, and righteousness as a mighty stream (Amos 5:24).

Heaven is the place where love is enjoyed without alloy. In that blessed region of delight, no pride, no envy, no discord, dwells. In the angelic world, God is supremely loved and feared and obeyed. Each blessed spirit loves its fellow, and all are knit together in one family bond of love. Happy state! "Lord, mold my soul to theirs, or rather to Thine own most lovely image. Let me drink deep into Thy Spirit and be daily preparing for those mansions where all is harmony and peace and purity and joy."

From the Word of truth we are clearly taught that notions however correct, forms however excellent, creeds however orthodox, ordinances however scriptural, labors however abundant, and sacrifices however costly will avail nothing in the sight of God if genuine love be lacking in the heart.

Love is the very essence of true religion. It is the main spring which puts all in motion.

Precious faith unites the sinner to the Savior, while love, the fruit of faith, produced in the soul through the power of the Holy Spirit, gives vitality to the new creature and enables him to act for God alone. It is evident, then, that without love, all religious profession is hypocrisy. Our real character is not estimated by Him who looks at what we know, or what we say, nor even what we do; but from the inward ruling principle of the mind.

We may speak with the tongues of men and of angels, we may understand all mysteries and all knowledge, we may give all our goods to feed the poor and our bodies to be burned, and yet be accounted by a heart-searching God as no better than sounding brass or a tinkling cymbal (1 Cor. 13:1). We may attend the house of God with scrupulous exactness, and yet have no heart in the work. We may admire the preacher, without loving the Word, and extol a form of devotion, while destitute of pious feeling. Oh, what need there is for inward searching of heart! True religion is less common than many imagine. "Strait is the gate, and narrow is the way, which leadeth unto life, and few there be that find it" (Matt. 7:14).

Formality and hypocrisy are two powerful and successful agents of Satan. The enemy of souls is not very anxious whether men travel to hell by the road of profaneness or false profession. The latter, being more creditable, is generally the most frequented. Gross vice startles the conscience, while the garment of decency thrown over the general conduct quiets the mind and makes the deluded sinner more easy in his sins.

"Blessed Lord, save me from the delusions of Satan and the deceitfulness of my own heart. Let me know myself. Guard me against self-deception, self-love, and vainglory. Make me humble, simple, and sincere. Fill me with love, and fit me for Thy service and glory."

Love is the distinctive characteristic of all God's people. The soul which is savingly enlightened by the Spirit of truth must, as a natural consequence, love God. There is a knowledge which may be acquired by reading, hearing, and reflection. Religion may be learned as a science. Its doctrines may be arranged with all the accuracy of systematic precision, and its precepts be admired as lessons of the purest morality. But such knowledge, springing only from the exercise of the intellectual faculties, leaves the soul in its natural state of pride, earthliness, and self-sufficiency. Such knowledge puffs up, while charity edifies (1 Cor. 8:1).

Every awakened soul needs to feel the love of God as its actuating principle and the glory of God as its constant aim. Oh, that I may experience these blessings more and more! Nothing can eradicate the love of the world from the heart, but this ardent and supreme love to God as the highest good, implanted in the soul through the power of the Holy Spirit. God is love. When, therefore, He draws forth the arrows of conviction and lodges them in the sinner's conscience, He graciously dips them in the blood of Jesus, that He may heal as well as wound. Thus, the blessed Spirit, by first convincing of sin and then revealing the Savior, gives the broken-hearted penitent a crown of beauty instead of ashes, the oil of gladness instead of mourning, and a garment of praise instead of a spirit of despair.

How gracious are the operations of mercy! No sin, however great, can exclude that soul from heaven whom the Lord makes a monument of His sovereign grace. As soon might the black vapors of the night which skirt the horizon prevent the rising of the sun. "By grace are ye saved" (Eph. 2:8). "By the grace of God I am what I am" (1 Cor. 15:10) is the language of Paul, who styles himself the chief of sinners, and whose delight is to magnify the exceeding riches of redeeming love.

God is love. Hence all holiness proceeds from Him. He must first draw the heart to Himself by the powerful attractions of His own eternal love, or it will forever remain hard as adamant and vile as hell. "I have loved thee with an everlasting love: therefore with loving-kindness have I drawn thee" (Jer. 31:3) are the sweet accents of mercy to a family of backsliding children.

The Spirit of God can alone fill the heart with love. The apostle gives love the first place among the fruits of the Spirit, for if this heavenly grace be lacking in us, all the rest of our benevolent or amiable qualities will profit us nothing.

How important, then, is self-examination on a subject which involves our present and eternal happiness! If I am a child of God, I shall love Him supremely. It is impossible to be in the family of God and not love God, for every one that loves is born of God and knows God. "He that loveth not knoweth not God; for God is love" (1 John 4:8). Oh, my soul, think what you owe to your great Creator! I am indebted to God for my being, my daily preservation, my hourly comforts. From Him I receive every blessing: health, friends, and domestic enjoyments. To Him I owe myself and all my powers—yes, all that I am and have. He not only made me; but, oh wonderful love, He took my nature upon Him and died, the just for the unjust, that through His atoning blood I might be saved from sin and the wrath to come.

If I am a child of God, I shall love all His children. If I am in the family of God, I shall love all the members of His family. This John declares as evidential of a state of salvation: "We know that we have passed from death unto life, because we love the brethren" (1 John 3:14). "Every one that loveth him that begat loveth him also that is begotten of him" (1 John 5:1). Thus Christian love passes over the threshold of home, sect, and nation and embraces all who love the Savior, whether inhabiting the torrid or the frigid climates.

If I am a child of God, I shall love the commandments of God. His law will be my rule of life, while Christ crucified is the sole foundation of my hope. I shall have more delight in His Word than in all manner of riches, for these can only gratify my carnal nature, while that can satisfy my immortal soul.

If I am a child of God, I shall be anxious to live to His glory, to employ my talents in His service, and to promote His cause among men. I shall not be ashamed to confess myself His servant. If reproached, I shall rejoice in being counted worthy to suffer shame for His name, and shall be willing to be accounted even the offscouring of all things for Jesus' sake (1 Cor. 4:13).

If I am a child of God, I shall bear the image of God. In God's family there is a family likeness. All the children resemble their heavenly parent. They have the mind of Christ and are renewed in knowledge after the image of Him who created them. "If any man be in Christ, he is a new creature" (2 Cor. 5:17); but "if any man have not the Spirit of Christ, he is none of his" (Rom. 8:9). I may possess an extensive knowledge of divine truth and a facility of utterance which, when combined with strong natural warmth of feeling, may cause me to make an imposing appearance. But what will knowledge avail if destitute of humility—or glowing eloquence, if devoid of love?

Let me, then, seek most earnestly the sweet graces of the Spirit: love, humility, and purity. These will make me like the blessed Jesus, whose whole character bore these sacred features and whose gentle command is: "Learn of me; for I am meek and lowly in heart: and ye shall find rest unto your souls" (Matt. 11:29).

"Blessed Jesus, be pleased to sanctify the desires of my heart. This is Thy will, even my sanctification. Let it be my will also. Oh, put forth Thy healing hand and touch my leprous soul; yes, speak the word only, and Thy servant shall be healed. Let me never for one moment doubt Thy willingness to save, though I be the very chief of sinners. Thy grace is infinite; if it were not infinite, I might indeed despair; but being infinite, how can I despond? Oh, what a word is infinite! There is no depth of guilt in which infinite mercy cannot reach me, and no height of glory to which infinite love cannot raise me."

Rejoice, then, oh my soul, and be filled with thanksgiving. Jesus is your all-sufficient Savior. Believe in Him, trust in Him, come to Him, and love Him, and then shall you be saved with a present and everlasting salvation.

How blest are they who love the Lord,
Who lean upon His Word;
They feel a joy, a peace within,
Which earth cannot afford.

By faith they see the heavenly world,
And taste the Savior's grace;
The bliss concealed from carnal eyes
They view "with open face."

They know their interest in His love,
Who bought them with His blood;
And with assured faith can say,
My Savior, and my God.

You blessed flock—you chosen few,
Let grateful praise ascend;
And, as you pass the vale of life,
Extol the sinner's Friend.

CHAPTER 64

Joy

Christian joy is not a tumultuous passion or feverish affection, but a calm and composed frame, a holy serenity of soul, a gladsome rest in the faithfulness and grace of Jesus. It sheds a luster over the countenance, beams forth at the eye, and often causes it to be suffused in tears. It creates an indescribable delight in the heart.

Paul was in this heavenly frame when he said: "I am filled with comfort, I am exceeding joyful in all our tribulation" (2 Cor. 7:4). This holy joy does not depend on outward circumstances, for the apostle could say: "As sorrowful, yet always rejoicing" (2 Cor. 6:10). No one possesses this inward joy but the real believer. "A stranger doth not intermeddle with his joy" (Prov. 14:10). It is the fruit of the Spirit, and flows from a living faith in the divinity and atonement of Jesus.

So inseparable from Christian joy are right views of the blessed Savior, that John commences his first epistle, as he did his gospel, by refuting those two heresies, which, like poisonous weeds, were then springing up. The one was propagated by the Gnostics or Docetae, who denied the real humanity of Jesus; the other by the Ebionites, who denied the essential divinity of the Redeemer. How conclusive are the declarations of John: "That which was from the beginning, which we have heard, which we have seen with our eyes, which we have looked upon, and our hands have handled, of the Word of life" (1 John 1:1). What language can more fully describe the real humanity of the Son of God?

"For the life was manifested, and we have seen it, and bear witness, and shew unto you that eternal life, which was with the Father, and was manifested unto us" (v. 2). What a striking attestation to the divinity of Christ! "That which we have seen and heard declare we unto you, that ye also may have fellowship with us: and truly our fellowship is with the Father, and with his Son Jesus Christ" (v. 3). "And these things write we unto you, that your joy may be full" (1 John 1:4).

Thus the apostle clearly and unequivocally states that Christian communion can only be maintained in its blessedness, and Christian joy possessed in its fullness, by a cordial reception of Jesus Christ as "God…manifest in the flesh" (1 Tim. 3:16).

It were well if all who profess to believe in Jesus would examine the ground of their faith and the source of their joy by this highly important passage in the Word of God. Holy joy is a portion of heaven brought down into the soul, and it enables the believer to soar above the troubles which assail him. Like the Alpine traveler, he looks down upon the storm which agitates the valley beneath. Even when compelled to exclaim, "Without were fightings, within were fears" (2 Cor. 7:5), he can "rejoice evermore" (1 Thess. 5:16).

Habakkuk was truly happy when, raised above all the changing scenes of life, he thus sang to the harp of prophecy: "Although the fig tree shall not blossom, neither shall fruit be in the vines; the labour of the olive shall fail, and the fields shall yield no meat; the flock shall be cut off from the fold, and there shall be no herd in the stalls: yet I will rejoice in the Lord, I will joy in the God of my salvation. The Lord God is my strength, and he will make my feet like hinds' feet, and he will make me to walk upon mine high places" (Hab. 3:17-19).

The apostles sang in the prison. The martyrs praised God in the fires. They rejoiced in hope of the glory of God and were made more than conquerors through Him who loved them and gave Himself for them. This holy joy, this peaceful state of heart, is, nevertheless, susceptible to be disturbed and ruffled.

Through the remaining corruption of his nature, the believer is often sorely harassed and distressed. The enemy plies him very closely with his temptations. Thus he finds hourly need for watchfulness and prayer, as well as for deep humiliation and self-abhorrence. If ensnared through the subtlety of Satan or by sudden surprises of temptations, the enemy exults, and his heart is grieved. Yet, what must he do? Through grace, he betakes himself to the blood of sprinkling. He goes mourning to his heavenly Father, acknowledging his sin; he pleads the merit of his Savior; he implores the continued aid and protection of the Holy Spirit; he lies low in self-abasement at the foot of the cross and there receives this gracious word applied powerfully to his soul: "Be of good cheer; thy sins be forgiven thee" (Matt. 9:2). Light beams once more in his heart; joy once more fills his soul. He hates himself and loves his Savior, watches more narrowly over the inward motions of his spirit, distrusts himself, and relies more confidently on the grace of his covenant God.

Thus the enemy of souls is baffled; his growth in humility is promoted; and God, through His restoring grace, is glorified.

Chastening, says the apostle, is not joyous, but grievous (Heb. 12:11). Hence outward troubles may dampen the believer's joy while he looks off from the Savior to the boisterous wind and waves which rage around him. Peter did so and began to sink. Faith, however, clings fast to the Savior and exults in the storm.

Paul was compelled at times to say: "I have great heaviness and continual sorrow in my heart" (Rom. 9:2). But where arose this grief? It sprang from the deep concern which he felt for his perishing brethren according to the flesh. Thus many favored souls who are happy in the love of God, and who rejoice in Jesus with a joy unspeakable and full of glory, can sympathize with David and say: "Rivers of waters run down mine eyes, because they keep not thy law" (Ps. 119:136). Their personal joy may be in lively exercise, while their hearts are greatly grieved for a world which lies in wickedness. Is not this the characteristic feeling of the children of God?

Christian charity is a compound of active benevolence and tender compassion, flowing from a supreme love to Jesus Christ. The true believer is, therefore, the genuine philanthropist. He not only feels for the miseries of others, but labors to remove them by prayer and suitable exertion. His heart can melt at another's woe and gladden at another's welfare. Hence he rejoices over one sinner that repents. He feels his own joy increased by each increase to the church of God. He rejoices not in iniquity, but rejoices in the truth. As sin pains him, both when felt in himself and seen in others, so holiness delights him, when, like Barnabas, he beholds its growing influence in those around him. The joy of the Lord is his strength. When faith is in lively exercise, and joy is springing up in his soul, he can brave every danger and boldly encounter every enemy which may oppose his way to glory.

Such is the happy experience of the believer in Jesus. It is his privilege to rejoice. A God of sovereign love wills the happiness of His people. As nothing but sin can separate the soul from God or cause Him to hide His face from us, so nothing but sin ought really to dampen our joy. Woe be to him who can feel joyous in his sins!

The gospel is good news, glad tidings of great joy. Those worldly people greatly mistake its nature, tendency, and design, who suppose it to be a mere system of restraints, an enemy to innocent enjoyment. Its ways are ways of pleasantness, and all its paths are peace. The gospel bids us to be happy. All that it condemns is an abuse of divine mercies and that alienation of heart which leads us to seek from the broken cisterns of the world that happiness which can only be derived from the eternal fountain of uncreated excellence.

The gospel, while it faithfully reveals to us our ruined state as sinners and our utter unworthiness of the least of God's mercies, graciously opens to our view the way to unspeakable felicity, through the incarnation and death of the eternal Son of God. Those who reject the gospel and choose the forbidden pleasures of sin find the fruit of their choice to be bitterness and death, while those who cheerfully renounce the world and yield themselves unto God through Jesus Christ have a spring of holy joy opened in their souls, which shall flow onward until it issues in everlasting life. Oh, my soul, is this your experience? Do you feel this inward joy in a crucified Jesus? Are you leaning on the bosom of your Savior, resting on covenant faithfulness and unchanging love?

"Enable me, blessed Lord, with joy to draw water out of the wells of salvation and to come daily unto Thee, the fountain of consolation, who has said: 'Drink, yea, drink abundantly, O beloved' (Song 5:1). When I feel my inward depravity, oh give me grace to see, with the eye of faith, the glorious remedy which Thou hast provided. May I lay hold on Jesus Christ, and never let Him go, until He bless me. Shine into my heart with the bright beam of Thy heavenly grace. Shed abroad Thy love in my soul. Give me the witness of the Holy Spirit. Grant that I may taste Thy goodness here, in the sweet refreshing streams of gospel joy, until, borne with gladsome wing to the fountain-head in glory, my soul shall be lost in wonder, love, and praise."

---

*How sweet the sacred joy that dwells
In souls renewed by power divine;
Where Jesus all His goodness tells;
Oh, may this joy be ever mine!*

*Descend and bless Thy servant, Lord,
Thy loving Spirit now impart;
Speak the all-enlivening Word,
And seal salvation to my heart.*

*From earth, and all its fleeting toys,
Be all my fond desires withdrawn;
Oh, fill my soul with heavenly joys,
Of endless bliss the glorious dawn.*

*Then shall my raptured spirit sing,
In strains of pure celestial love;
When, borne on some kind seraph's wing,
I soar to brighter worlds above.*

CHAPTER 65

Peace

There is something peculiarly calming to the soul in these beautiful words: "Thou wilt keep him in perfect peace, whose mind is stayed on thee: because he trusteth in thee" (Isa. 26:3). This is a world of sin and trouble. Here, thorns and thistles grow around us, painful emblems of the human heart and of the sad change which passed on Adam at the fall.

Though painful the change, yet, with a pleasing mournful recollection, our minds delight to contemplate the first parents of our race enjoying communion with their God and happy communion with each other in the bowers of Eden. All was then serene and peaceful. No indulged sin poisoned their joys or caused the divine countenance to be turned away from them. They had no feeling but love and gratitude, no desire but to serve and please their almighty Creator. This happy state was, alas, of short duration. They listened to the voice of the tempter and fell from holiness, from happiness, and from God.

He, who lately held sweet converse with His creatures, now banished them from Paradise, denied them all access to the Tree of Life, that pledge of immortality, and, in righteous judgment, pronounced the curse upon them. They now became dying creatures, doomed through their willful disobedience to present and eternal misery. The ground was cursed for their sake. Refusing its spontaneous fruitfulness, it required their toil and labor, while the prickly thorn and thistle sprang up as silent monitors to remind them of their sins.

May we not ask with anxious solicitude, How can such fallen, wretched creatures be kept in peace, "in perfect peace" (Isa. 26:3)?

What warrant have we to trust in God or stay our minds upon Him as our righteousness and strength? This important question has been answered by God Himself. He graciously promised a Savior, even at the time when justice pronounced death on the transgressors. Thus mercy rejoiced against judgment and shed a ray of heavenly light over the benighted souls of our fallen parents.

In the fullness of time, Jesus, the promised seed of the woman, was born. The ransom-price was paid by His precious blood-shedding upon the cross, and the gates of heaven were opened to all believers. The gospel was preached and pardon proclaimed to every humble, penitent, believing soul. All who lived before the advent of Christ, looking to the promise and resting in the covenant of grace, were accepted in the Beloved; and those who have lived since His advent in the flesh can say: "Whom having not seen, we love; and in whom, though now we see him not, yet believing, we rejoice with joy unspeakable and full of glory" (1 Pet. 1:8). To all such, the prophet proclaims peace: "Thou wilt keep him in perfect peace, whose mind is stayed on thee" (Isa. 26:3).

Here, then, we learn the nature of true religion. It is staying the mind upon God. As unbelieving sinners, we cannot do this; as believing penitents, we may. Yes, it is the privilege of every contrite soul thus to repose upon the mercies of God in Christ Jesus.

Oh, blessed truth! Though by nature far from God, we are brought near by the blood of Christ; though lying under the curse of a broken law, we are delivered from condemnation through the death of Jesus; though helpless, restless, and wretched in ourselves, we are privileged, through faith, to stay our minds upon God as our strength, our rest, and our peace. Oh, what a work of grace, mercy, and love! "Bless the Lord, O my soul: and all that is within me, bless his holy name" (Ps. 103:1).

We also learn where true stability is to be found. It is in God. Everything here in this world is fickle and changing. But that God who gives peace unto His people changeth not, nor knoweth the shadow of a turn (James 1:17). The soul, therefore, which is stayed on Him finds rest and peace. If I rest my hopes upon an earthly friend, death removes the prop, and I fall and mourn and weep. If I place my confidence on riches, they fly away as an eagle towards heaven and leave me to regret the folly of my covetous desires. If I build upon the breath of fame, it dies away or changes into scorn or slander. If I repose upon the rosy couch of earthly comforts, however lawful and endearing, these lovely flowers will quickly fade and leave me nothing but the thorns. Jesus is the only source of comfort, the only spring of joy. From Him proceed all the peace and purity which gladden and beautify the church of God.

Oh, my soul, never look for peace from the creature; never expect it from yourself. He who made peace for you by the blood of His cross can alone impart peace to your trembling conscience. Jesus is the Prince of Peace. While rejecting His salvation, peace can never be enjoyed. "There is no peace, saith my God, to the wicked" (Isa. 57:21). Solemn truth, no less engraven on the sinner's heart than recorded in the book of God. How can peace dwell in a bosom on which the heavy curse of the Almighty continually abides?

The world may appear smiling and happy, but its appearances are deceitful. True peace descends from above. It is the fruit of faith. The Holy Spirit alone can produce this blessedness in the soul; and, therefore, none can possess it but the faithful in Christ Jesus. The world can yield no solid peace to its most zealous votaries. Whatever I possess, without the presence of my heavenly Father, is unsatisfying and unstable. Oh, my soul, seek a higher bliss than any which earth can give!

"Blessed Spirit of peace and love, place me on the Rock of Ages; let me never, never stray from Thee. Be the guide of my steps and the guardian of my days. Give me Thy peace always by all means, and make me a living temple consecrated wholly unto Thee."

How great the peace, how blest the joy,
Each true believer only feels!
Satan can never the bliss destroy,
Which faith in Jesus sweetly yields.

Peace

Amid the ruffling scenes of life,
Amid the storms which rage below,
A calm retreat, removed from strife,
Does Jesus on His saints bestow.

He kindly spreads His loving arms,
As parent wings protect their brood;
He shields from danger and alarms;
He fills His saints with every good.

Oh, could I call this blessing mine;
How rich, how vast the sacred store!
Blest Savior, grant one gracious smile,
And earth shall hold my heart no more.

One gracious smile of heavenly love
Would melt my heart and lay me low;
One blissful smile, which saints above,
Which happy angels ever know.

CHAPTER 66

Humility

Pride and vanity cannot thrive at the foot of the cross. It is only when we remove from this holy ground that they shoot out their pestiferous branches in awful luxuriance. True humility loves the sacred mount of Calvary, on which the lowly Savior bowed His head and died! There, repentance sheds the contrite tear. There, faith views with joy the great atonement. There, love glows with fervent desires to the Friend of sinners.

Man is naturally a proud, selfish creature. Morality may teach him the badness of such a character, but it can never produce in him any principle of renovation. He tries indeed to appear humble and unselfish, but the monster Pride is easily seen through the thin veil of false humility, which is thrown over its frightful visage; while Self, like another Proteus, assumes a thousand forms to escape detection.

It is only when the divine Spirit puts forth His new-creating power, through the instrumentality of the everlasting gospel, that the proud, selfish sinner becomes the lowly follower of the Lamb. He then learns to bear with cheerfulness the burden of a suffering brother, while, with all lowliness of mind, he esteems others better than himself.

Humility is, then, the work of grace. Without it, there can be no salvation; for God resists the proud and sends the rich empty away. If angels in glory hide their faces with their wings when standing before the Lord of hosts, if glorified saints cast their crowns before the throne of their Redeemer, if the humblest believer is the greatest in the gospel kingdom, what a heaven-born grace is humility! How beautiful is the exhortation of Peter: "Be clothed with humility" (1 Pet. 5:5)!

Oh, that my soul may be arrayed in this lovely grace, the brightest ornament of the Christian character! We talk of humility. "But oh, bleeding Lamb, what is the humility of a sinful creature, when compared with Thine? Thou, who humbled Thyself to behold the things that are in heaven and earth, did stoop in infinite condescension to leave the throne of Thy glory, to lay aside the robes of Thy majesty, to be made in the likeness of men, to become the son of a poor virgin, to be made of no reputation, to take upon Thyself the form of a servant; and having thus humbled Thyself, to become obedient unto death, even the death of the cross!

"And why didst Thou thus humble Thyself with a humility surpassing all conception? It was that Thy humility might atone for my pride and, by this Thine infinite abasement, exalt a proud, rebellious, hell-deserving creature to a participation of Thy felicity and to a place near Thy throne!"

Enter into yourself, oh my soul, and earnestly entreat the quickening Spirit of your Lord to search and try you. Can you dare be proud while viewing the deep humiliation of the Son of God? Where would you have been, if Jesus had not died? And where will you be, if, through pride, you reject this great salvation? Are you willing to be nothing in your own estimation—yes, less than nothing in the sight of infinite Perfection? Can you renounce your own fancied righteousness as filthy rags? Do you throw yourself with absolute entireness upon the infinite mercies of a crucified Savior? Can you delight in the praise and prosperity of others, even when, through their superior luster, you are cast into the shade? Do you feel no envious risings when others are made much of in your presence, and yourself studiously overlooked? Are there no workings of mortified pride within, when the conversation of others is anxiously listened to, and yours is altogether disregarded?

Is the glory of God the only object of your wishes and the good of souls your only desire? Are you willing to be esteemed a fool for Christ's sake, and glad to lose the present good-will of your friends so that you may win Christ and be found in Him? If it be your heartfelt prayer to be delivered from pride and, like your lowly Savior, to be clothed with humility, then your graces are the graces of the Spirit, your conversion is sound, your state is safe, and your eternal habitation shall be with the once abased, but now exalted, Jesus.

Cultivate, oh my soul, this lovely grace of humility. Bless God sincerely for every occasion which tends to mortify your pride and crucify your vain-glory. Do not be angry with those who slight you, who treat you with contempt and scorn. Rather receive it as a "needs be," as a corrosive to eat out your overweening love of self, as one of those things which form a touchstone to try your inward state and which, through the power of the Spirit, shall be overruled for the advancement of your spiritual good.

Be thankful for reproof, whether conveyed with the smoothness of Christian meekness or the keenness of satirical asperity. Remember that God's people are a tried people, that all who will live godly in Christ Jesus shall suffer persecution, that they who are not of the world must expect the world's hatred. Let no contempt or suffering be allowed to abate your fervor or slacken your speed, since the trial of your faith is much more precious than of gold that perishes, though it be tried with fire, and shall before long be found unto praise and honor and glory at the appearing of Jesus Christ.

What rich promises are made in the gospel to humble souls! Jesus pronounced His first blessing on the poor in spirit. The Lord gives grace unto the humble. He fills the hungry with good things. He condescends to dwell in the lowly heart. He beautifies the meek with salvation. The Scriptures abound with beautiful descriptions of the privileges and blessings which are the portion of every humble believer in Jesus. All who are truly convinced of sin by the powerful application of the law to their consciences, all who are led to see their awful state by nature and to feel their need of Jesus as their only Savior, all who are enabled by the Spirit of truth to apprehend Christ by faith in all His offices and covenant relations, are clothed with humility.

Weaned from self-righteous dependencies, they trust in Christ alone for pardon and acceptance, and find rest unto their souls. Receiving a new taste and a spiritual appetite, they live upon Christ by faith and derive daily strength and comfort from Him. The love of Christ constrains them to obedience, and the language of their heart is: "Whom have I in heaven but thee? and there is none upon earth that I desire beside thee" (Ps. 73:25).

To these humble souls the promises belong. They are the very members of Christ's mystical body, and it is their Father's good pleasure to give them the kingdom. The world frowns upon them, but God shines into their hearts. The carnal mind hates them, but Jesus loves them with an everlasting love. The devil sets himself in battle array against them, but the Holy Spirit lifts up a standard against him and compasses them about as with a shield. Though weak in themselves, they are strong in the Lord; though unable of themselves to overcome the least temptation, they become, through Christ, even more than conquerors.

"Oh, Spirit of holiness, without whom nothing is strong, nothing is holy, open my blind eyes to see the wonders of Thy grace. Quicken my dead soul to feel its sacred influence. Make me truly humble in heart, emptied of every self-exalting thought, which would oppose the freeness of Thy love. Mold my whole soul into the lowliness and meekness of Jesus. Preserve me from the subtle influence of pride and vainglory. Keep me ever low in my own eyes. Root out every sinful, selfish principle, and give me a single eye which aims at nothing but Thy glory. Shed abroad Thy love in my heart; then will my understanding, will, and affections be light in the Lord, and each unite their powers in loving and obeying Thee."

Oh, dear, anointed Jesus,
All my hopes are fixed on Thee;
In Thy tender, sweet compassion,
Cast a smile of love on me.

Come in all Thy full salvation,
Deign within my heart to dwell;
Then, with all Thy ransomed people,
Of unbounded love I'll tell.

Fill my soul with heavenly graces,
Gently falling from above;
Meekness, patience, pure affection,
Sweet humility and love.

Come, oh blest anointed Savior,
To Thine earthly temple come;
Until the hour of death remove me
To my everlasting home.

CHAPTER 67

Meekness

The apostle Peter exhorts us to put on "the ornament of a meek and quiet spirit, which is in the sight of God of great price" (1 Pet. 3:4). May I ever prize what infinite Excellence esteems so precious! And yet, alas, how soon do we disfigure this holy ornament, when any little thing crosses our temper! This is highly sinful. We should not so readily cast away a diamond, because of some trifling opposition to our will. Oh, may I learn wisdom in the school of Christ and seek for more grace from that Savior, who has so kindly said: "Ask, and it shall be given you; seek, and ye shall find" (Matt. 7:7).

The greatest part of our unhappiness in life arises not so much from cross providences as from cross tempers. The former only happen occasionally, to try our faith; while in some families the latter occur daily, to try our patience. Now, in proportion as we become truly Christians, in that proportion we shall resist and overcome these wasps which nestle in our bosom. He who torments others torments himself, while he who labors to promote the happiness of his fellow creatures very greatly augments his own.

We see, then, how beautiful is the religion of Jesus, which is all love and peace and goodness. Wherever its influence is felt, there a little heaven is enjoyed. Where it is unknown, there darkness and discord reign. The world, proud and turbulent, despises this heavenly ornament, this workmanship of the Holy Spirit. May I have grace to esteem it above all those splendid ornaments which dazzle and attract the admiration of mankind. "Learn of me; for I am meek and lowly in heart," was the condescending exhortation; "and ye shall find rest unto your souls" (Matt. 11:29) was the gracious promise of the heavenly Savior. Rich blessings are, indeed, promised to the meek. "The meek…shall inherit the earth" (Matt. 5:5). "The meek…shall delight themselves in the abundance of peace" (Ps. 37:11). "The meek will he guide in judgment: and the meek will he teach his way" (Ps. 25:9). "The LORD…will beautify the meek with salvation" (Ps. 149:4).

To possess this sweet ornament of a meek and quiet spirit, I must be clothed with humility, for humility and meekness are inseparable. No mere nominal professor of Christianity ever possessed this celestial ornament. The world endeavors to counterfeit this lovely spirit by what is termed politeness, a kind of spurious meekness and humility. When slights or insults arise, this worldly gem soon discovers its worthless composition, while the gospel jewel brightens by attrition.

Meekness, humility, love, and purity form the Christian character. These graces, growing out of a true faith in Jesus, evidence a vital union to Him, from whom every blessing is derived.

As deformed people give no just idea of the beautiful symmetry of the human frame, so there are some professors of the gospel who have their minds so twisted by prejudice, and their wills made so crooked by obstinacy, that they exhibit a mere distortion of Christianity. Such people sometimes hold high doctrines and talk much about election and final perseverance. They regard the humble, circumspect believer as living below his privileges, and condemn his holy walk as legal and beneath the liberty of the gospel. Sin, they say, cannot hurt them, for they are not under the law, but under grace. They scruple not to charge their neighbors with hypocrisy, while they never, for one moment, suspect themselves.

What an awful perversion is this of the beautiful religion of Jesus! How deformed, how unlike the new creature in Christ Jesus! In these unhappy people, we behold no ornament of a meek and quiet spirit, no garment of humility. They love to live in the storm, either of controversy or contradiction. Every word is misconstrued, every action is ascribed to some improper motive. Pride and uncharitableness mark their character. Others cannot please them; because their bosoms are the seat of conflicting passions, they cannot please themselves. Devoid of the mind which was in Christ, they resemble the ground which the Lord has cursed, yielding thorns and briars.

But how lovely does the image of the Savior appear when reflected by the spirit and conduct of the true believer. It resembles the sun shining with unbroken luster on the peaceful lake, while the wicked are like the troubled sea, which cannot rest, whose waters cast up mire and dirt.

These angry, contentious, loud-sounding, presumptuous professors are spots and wens in the visible church, stumbling-blocks to weaker brethren, and scandals to the world.

"Lord, preserve me from this awful state. Let me ever hold the truth in righteousness. Oh, that I may ever dread that presumptuous spirit which would seize on the sacred fruits of the Tree of Life, without one gospel warrant so to do; which would dare, with sacrilegious hand, to divide the precept from the promise, and, under the impious idea of exalting free grace, sin, that grace may abound. Lord, give me a holy fear of falling into sin, a jealousy over my own deceitful heart, a cleaving unto Thee, a delight in keeping Thy commandments. Enable me to walk circumspectly and warily along the slippery path of life, to watch and pray always, to guard against the first approaches to temptation and every incitement from my spiritual adversary to transgress Thy law. Put on me the lovely ornament of a meek and quiet spirit. Let all anger, bitterness, and evil-speaking be put away from me, with all malice. Let love reign in my heart and purity adorn my soul. Oh, blessed Jesus, cover me with Thy spotless robe of righteousness and make me all glorious within, through the renewing influence of Thy grace. Let me never forget whose I am and whom I serve. Cause me to bear Thy cross with holy rejoicing until, in Thy kingdom of glory, the cross shall be exchanged for the crown, and sorrow be swallowed up in everlasting joy."

Father of mercies, God of love,
To Thee my wishes all aspire;

Descend, blest Spirit, from above,
And guard and feed the sacred fire.

Preserve me from those thousand snares,
Which Satan weaves around my path.
On Thee I cast my hourly cares;
On Thee I look in humble faith.

Behold me at the bleeding cross;
Wash out, dear Lord, each guilty stain;
Oh, may I count the world but loss—
Thy love, my great, my richest gain.

In mercy help a feeble worm,
Whose strength is all derived from Thee;
Thou canst appease the wildest storm;
And Thou canst set the captive free.

In cheerful hope my soul relies,
Blest Savior, on Thy dying love,
Until I reach the blissful skies,
And strike the golden harp above.

CHAPTER 68

Purity

"Blessed are the pure in heart: for they shall see God" (Matt. 5:8). What a wonderful change must pass upon a soul born in sin before it can become pure. Wherever this change takes place, we must exclaim: "What hath God wrought!" (Num. 23:23). It is the work of Omnipotence thus to new-create the soul and to transform the sinner into a pure and holy being. But great and radical as this work is, there still remains the seed of corruption, which would be continually budding in the heart and bringing forth fruit unto death, were it not for the constant operation of divine grace, checking the growth of inbred sin.

Though unlike Adam when in a state of innocence, and unlike the spirits of just men made perfect in heaven—yet, if we are true believers in Jesus, we are quite different from what we once were, and are different from the carnal world around us. "Old things are passed away; behold, all things are become new" (2 Cor. 5:17).

We have, it is true, much to root out and destroy, so long as the law in the members wars against the law of the mind; yet, while journeying to the land of promise, we are favored with many delightful foretastes and many cheering views of the celestial Canaan to animate us to persevere.

Gospel holiness is therefore a progressive work. Like the process of vegetation, there is first the blade, then the ear, and then the full corn in the ear. From the first workings of grace to its full consummation in glory, there is a gradual advancement towards perfection. We read of little children, of young men, and of fathers in Christ, and are commanded to grow in grace and in the knowledge of our Lord and Savior Jesus Christ.

But as we are equally exhorted to crucify the flesh and to mortify our members which are on the earth, we learn that the old man is not yet dead, but dying; he is in a state of crucifixion, dying daily. Those who are best acquainted with their own hearts, and with human nature in general, being taught by the Spirit of God according to the revealed truth of his holy Word, know from painful experience that sin is still in them. They hate it and fight against it; and in this hatred of sin, and warring against it, consists, in no small degree, that purity of heart which our Lord pronounces blessed.

We cannot truly hate sin as being an offence to God, and resist it with the whole bent of our will, until we are born from above. We must love God as an infinitely holy and gracious being before sin can be so hated as to be uniformly and strenuously opposed.

Therefore, though we cannot say, "I am pure from sin," under a consciousness of so much remaining corruption; yet, if conscience bears its inward testimony to our irreconcilable hatred of sin, if we groan under its burden and resist its workings, we ought to take encouragement and go on seeking strength from above, being assured that He who has begun the good work will perform it until the day of Jesus Christ.

No unconverted man, by any mere natural power of his own, ever yet hated and opposed sin as an evil directed against the majesty, holiness, and goodness of God. As soon might water run up a steep ascent, contrary to experience and the laws of nature. If, then, I would bear the image of Christ in glory, I must bear His image now in holiness, through the power of the Holy Spirit.

Oh, how happy is that soul which is renewed in righteousness! Jesus dwelling in the heart by faith is heaven begun. A holy light then irradiates the mind, a sweet glow of sacred love warms the affections, and all the powers of the soul are made willing to glorify Him who is the chief among ten thousand, the altogether lovely! Oh, that I could feel my heart always alive to God! Man was originally made to glorify

God. If, then, I do not live to His glory, I am not answering the great end of my being.

Here lies my guilt: my heart, through the fall, is naturally averse from every thing that has God for its object. I am prone to sin, prone to earth, prone to depart from God. Hence my condemnation is just, and hell would be my deserved portion through a countless eternity. But how can I express the inconceivable love of God in giving His only begotten Son for such a rebel, such an apostate creature! Oh, that I could feel my whole soul burning in one constant flame of holy love for such amazing grace!

How beautiful is true religion! It commends itself to every man's conscience, notwithstanding the natural enmity of the heart against it. There is something so amiable in Christian graces, so winning in the simple movements of Christian love, that even the bitterest enemies of the gospel are compelled in their reflecting moments to acknowledge its intrinsic excellence. We have abundant evidence of this from the page of history, when Christians lived and acted under the high principles of their holy religion. The reason why so little good is done by professing Christians may be owing to their own defect of character, to the lack of that purity of heart from where all outward holiness proceeds.

When we read the Acts of the Apostles and the epistles which they wrote to the several churches, we cannot but be struck with the spirituality of mind, the purity of heart, the simplicity of spirit, the contempt of the world, the patience under suffering, the love of the brethren, the dependence on the Savior, which appeared so conspicuous in the primitive believers and which caused them to shine as lights in the world. All who beheld them were constrained to confess that they were not as other men. They saw the change and persecuted them for it. But now, the shades of difference between many professors of Christianity and the men of the world are so faint that it often becomes difficult to discover the line of separation.

Inward purity and outward sanctity are the only true marks of God's children, however rarely these marks are to be found. Jesus gave Himself for us that He might redeem us from all iniquity and purify unto Himself a peculiar people zealous of good works. Without holiness, no man shall see the Lord; but every one who is pure in heart shall see God and become an heir of God. Amazing inheritance! What mind can conceive the vastness of this eternal blessedness—an heir of God through Christ!

The man that is pure in heart shall inherit that glorious God as his portion, in whom he lives and moves and has his being and by whose almighty power all things consist. He shall inherit Him who fills heaven and earth with His presence, who is the fountain of felicity and at whose right hand are pleasures for evermore. Oh, my soul, you can never thirst enough after this exalted privilege! What are earthly kingdoms, crowns, and scepters when compared with such a portion? Rejoice evermore while this promise stands recorded in the page of truth.

"Lord, perform Thy whole work of mercy in my heart. Let me never rest satisfied with any present attainment, but continually forgetting those things which are behind and reaching forth unto those things which are before, may I daily press towards the mark for the prize of the high calling of God in Christ Jesus (Phil. 3:13-14), until I see Thee as Thou art and love Thee as I ought in Thine everlasting kingdom and glory."

Make me simple and sincere,
Keep, oh Lord, my conscience clear;
Lead me in the living way;
Bring me to eternal day.

Oh, preserve my soul from sin,
Slay each rebel lust within;
Take away the heart of stone,
Make me Thine—and Thine alone.

Jesus, Thou art all my trust;
When consigned to native dust,

Purity

Take, oh take my soul to Thee,
And where Thou art—let me be.

Let me rise on wings sublime,
Far beyond the scenes of time;
Rise, to meet my God and King;
Rise, Thy endless praise to sing.

CHAPTER 69

Godly Fear

Fear is a most powerful passion in the human breast. Its natural effect is painful; hence we instinctively fly from everything which excites its agitating influence. Our minds are easily wrought upon by sensible objects or imaginary evils, while those which are remote or unapprehended give us little concern.

If we receive the alarm of some approaching danger, how readily do we magnify the dreaded calamity beyond its real extent. Some people, indeed, are so bold and daring that they seem to rise above the influence of every fear and to face danger, and even death in all its forms, with a coolness and intrepidity which are truly astonishing. Yet, in general, this natural passion operates in almost every case of serious apprehension but one, which of all others should awaken its sensibility.

We can fear almost anything more than the wrath of God, and any event more than approaching death and judgment. Strange infatuation and obduracy! An unregenerate man will sit unmoved and unawed under the most awful displays of divine vengeance as exhibited in the preached Word, while a slight shock of an earthquake, or the falling of a steeple, would cause him to start from his seat and fly with fearful steps to some place of safety. Unbelief lies at the bottom of our indifference to eternal things and is the true cause of that stupid unconcern, that fearless state of heart, which we manifest towards the infinitely important realities of a future world. There are, indeed, checks of natural conscience, but these are transient and seldom felt, except when our misconduct has sensibly affected our worldly prospects, our health, our reputation, or something of an earthly nature.

The immediate apprehension of death and judgment may appall the sinner and awaken all his solicitudes. Like Felix, the proud worldling sometimes feels an involuntary tremor, an inward misgiving of heart; but, like him, he labors to overcome the painful sensation by removing, if possible, the cause of his uneasiness: "Go thy way for this time; when I have a convenient season, I will call for thee" (Acts 24:25). Thus he goes on until death strikes the blow and hurries him into the abyss of endless horrors.

"Lord, deliver me from this most awful state. How distressing that my foolish heart should be so little affected by those rich displays of divine grace and those tremendous exhibitions of divine wrath which are revealed in the Word of God. Blessed Lord, give me a stronger faith, that I may continually realize to my mind those great things which Thou hast done, and dost still promise to do, for Thy believing people; and give me a more solemn fear of those awful threatenings which Thou hast denounced against thine enemies."

There is a fear of which excellent things are spoken and to which many precious promises are made. This holy fruit of the Spirit is peculiar to the children of God. It is one of the blessings of the new covenant. It is the beginning of wisdom. It tends to life (Prov 19:23). "In the fear of the LORD is strong confidence" (Prov. 14:26). "Happy is the man that feareth alway" (Prov. 28:14), who is "in the fear of the LORD all the day long" (Prov. 23:17). "The LORD taketh pleasure in them that fear him" (Ps. 147:11). He has promised to look with peculiar favor to him who trembles at His Word.

This heavenly grace is quite different from that slavish fear which tends to bondage. The fear which grace implants in the heart harmonizes with love and joy. The first Christians, on whom the Spirit was poured in such rich effusion, walked in the fear of the Lord and in the comfort of the Holy Spirit. To such renewed souls the apostolic command is: "Sanctify the LORD of hosts himself; and let him be your fear, and let him be your dread" (Isa. 8:13). The admonition of the Savior is most impressive: "I will forewarn you whom ye shall fear: Fear him, which after he hath killed hath power to cast into hell; yea, I say unto you, Fear him" (Luke 12:5). The Scriptures abound with exhortations to this duty. The most solemn appeals are there made to the heart and conscience, while promises of the most delightful nature are given to those who walk humbly with their God.

It is characteristic of the wicked that "there is no fear of God before his eyes" (Ps. 36:1). If, then, I would form a part of the assembly of the saints, I must daily seek by fervent prayer a reverential fear of God. "Let us have grace [says the apostle] whereby we may serve God acceptably with reverence and godly fear: For our God is a consuming fire" (Heb. 12:28-29).

John saw a multitude of the heavenly host "having the harps of God. And they sing the song of Moses the servant of God, and the song of the Lamb, saying, Great and marvellous are thy works, Lord God Almighty; just and true are thy ways, thou King of saints. Who shall not fear thee, O Lord, and glorify thy name? for thou only art holy: for all nations shall come and worship before thee" (Rev. 15:2-4).

I must cultivate a cautionary fear. "Let us…fear," says Paul, "lest, a promise being left us of entering into his rest, any of you should seem to come short of it" (Heb. 4:1). "Let him that thinketh he standeth take heed lest he fall" (1 Cor. 10:12). "Be not high-minded, but fear" (Rom. 11:20).

I must possess a filial fear which, combined with love and obedience, forms that spirit of adoption which is the sweetest evidence of admission into the family of God. For, perfect love, while it casts out that servile fear which has torment, cherishes a holy fear of grieving the Spirit, wounding the Savior, and displeasing the Father of mercies.

"Oh, blessed Lord, give me this holy preservative against falling into sin, that, fearing Thee from a principle of filial, reverential love, I may go on steadily in the narrow way of faith and holiness until I reach with joy and gladness the holy hill of Zion."

How happy is the humble soul,
Who lives in holy fear;

Godly Fear

While troubles in succession roll,
He feels the Savior near.

While others climb the dangerous steep,
And build their Babels high;
He loves that lowly path to keep,
Which leads him to the sky.

Content with all his God bestows,
He needs not wealth nor power;
Perpetual blessing round him flows,
Increasing every hour.

Rich with the riches of His grace
Who saved him by His blood;
He views by faith the Savior's face,
And knows that God is good.

Through life's uneven path upheld,
Preserved from every ill;
He views at length the heavenly field,
And reaches Zion's hill.

Oh, may I thus be sweetly blest,
With humble souls below;
Then enter the eternal rest,
Where endless pleasures flow.

CHAPTER 70

The Believer's Aim and Hope

How beautiful and glorious is the plan of human redemption! Angels may well desire to look into it. At the birth of our Emmanuel, they declared its gracious design, even that of bringing "glory to God in the highest, and on earth peace, good will toward men" (Luke 2:14). The apostle felt the happy effect of this salvation in his own soul when he could say: "For me to live is Christ, and to die is gain" (Phil. 1:21).

Jesus is the eternal spring of light, life, and glory. He made all things, and by Him all things are held together. Dead souls are quickened to a life of faith and holiness by His almighty power; and through Him they are preserved, in the midst of a wicked world, unto His everlasting kingdom. Oh, my soul, is Jesus the source of your spiritual life? Am I looking to Him and living upon Him daily by faith? Have I learned that by nature I am dead in trespasses and sins; that of myself I am unable to do anything that is pleasing unto God; that I may have a form of godliness, and a name to live, while destitute of saving grace? This religious complexion of my character may arise from education, the force of example, or a self-righteous principle. But this is not spiritual life. With every exterior of devotion, I may be spiritually dead. Can I in such a state say with the apostle: "For me to live is Christ" (Phil. 1:21)? Surely not. If I am truly quickened by the Spirit of Christ, Christ will be the acknowledged source of my life. As I derive all my powers from Him, so will those powers be devoted to His glory. I shall love Him with a supreme affection.

"Blessed Jesus, graciously communicate Thy saving strength to my soul. Raise me from a death in sin to a life of righteousness. Enlighten my dark mind. Warm my cold affections. Melt my hard heart. Subdue my stubborn will and make me a new creature, that I may walk before Thee in newness of life."

Jesus is the great example to His people. "He that saith he abideth in him ought himself also so to walk, even as he walked" (1 John 2:6). He left us an example, that we should follow his steps (1 Pet. 2:21). "As ye have therefore received Christ Jesus the Lord, so walk ye in him" (Col. 2:6). "Let this mind be in you, which was also in Christ Jesus" (Phil. 2:5). "If ye love me, keep my commandments" (John 14:15). "Follow me" (Luke 9:23).

Oh, that I may have grace to set the Lord always before me and to contemplate the meek and lowly Savior with increasing admiration, until my soul is transformed into His likeness. While treading in His steps and copying His example, I shall enjoy the light of His countenance and the consolation of His Spirit, for the precious promise is: "If a man love me, he will keep my words: and my Father will love him, and we will come unto him, and make our abode with him" (John 14:23).

The great end and aim of the believer's life is to promote the glory of Jesus. Paul declared to the Philippians that the one object of all his labors and sufferings was that Christ might be magnified in his body, whether it be by life or death. And then he adds: "For to me to live is Christ, and to die is gain" (Phil. 1:21). Those who love the Lord Jesus Christ in sincerity will be anxious to glorify Him with their bodies and their spirits, which are His. All their desire will be to Him and to the glory of His name. Is this my happy experience? Am I seeking to promote the interest of the Redeemer's kingdom? Do I esteem every enjoyment joyless which is not sweetened by His love, and every effort useless which is not connected with His glory? If Jesus is the author of my spiritual life, light, and fruitfulness; if He is the great example, ever present to my mind; if the promotion of His glory is the one aim of my united powers; then may I say with the apostle: "For me to live is Christ." What object so noble, what end so glorious, as thus to live simply and entirely to Him who is Lord of lords and King of kings! While thus living, I may join with Paul in his happy experience and say: "I am crucified with Christ: nevertheless I live; yet not I, but Christ liveth in me: and the life which I now live in the flesh I live by the faith of the Son of God, who loved me, and gave himself for me" (Gal. 2:20).

While thus living, I may scripturally take the full comfort of his joyful expectation and exclaim: "For to me…to die is gain" (Phil. 1:21). "When Christ, who is our life, shall appear, then shall ye also appear with him in glory" (Col. 3:4), for he has said: "Because I live, ye shall live also" (John 14:19); "Where I am, there ye may be also" (John 14:3); "Father, I will that they also, whom thou hast given me, be with me where I am; that they may behold my glory" (John 17:24). Glorious hope! Blessed expectation!

To every humble believer, death will be everlasting gain. It is only a quick transition from earth to heaven. To be absent from the body is to be present with the Lord. No wonder, then, that the apostle longed to be dissolved, that he might be with Christ. How happy is the death of every true believer in Jesus! That dreadful sting, which gives death all its terror, was extracted by the Savior when, expiring on the cross, He exclaimed, "It is finished" (John 19:30). He "bare our sins in his own body on the tree" (1 Pet. 2:24). "Through death he might destroy him that had the power of death, that is, the devil" (Heb. 2:14).

No dire foreboding, no agonizing fears of approaching dissolution, rend the heart of the humble believer or accelerate the wasting disease. Hope bears up the heir of glory amid all his sufferings. Faith pierces the veil which hides the heavenly world from mortal eyes, while love burns brighter as it reaches the source from where it came.

Oh, my soul, are you prepared to die? Have you fled for refuge to lay hold on the hope set before you in the gospel? Are you washed from your sins through the blood of the Lamb? Have you experienced a new and divine change? Have you passed from darkness unto light and from Satan unto God? "Oh, blessed Savior, perform in me all the good pleasure of Thy goodness, and the work of faith with power."

Death is gain to the believer because it will increase his knowledge beyond all that he can now conceive. Here we see as through a glass, darkly. We behold spiritual objects as in a mirror, through the medium of natural things; but in heaven, we shall behold the adorable Savior, not as now veiled under figures and emblems, but face to face. We shall see Him as He is, and be made like Him in the beauty of holiness. Oh, what a vision will that be! Who can describe the glorified person of our Emmanuel? Who can paint the resplendent Sun of Righteousness, whose beams gladden and illuminate all the realms above?

The apostles were favored with a glimpse of His glory on Mount Tabor, when the Savior shone as the sun and when His clothing was white as the light. John was permitted to enjoy a rich display of the Redeemer's glory when he was an exile in the isle of Patmos. But how faintly does human language set forth the glories of that Being from whose presence the heaven and earth shall flee away and who inhabits eternity! If all created glories are thrown into the shade when Jesus is revealed to the soul while the believer dwells in a house of clay, how will they be lost amid those radiant perfections which shall hereafter be revealed when the believer, admitted into the Savior's presence, shall behold all heaven unveiled to his sight! Well might the apostle count all things but loss for the excellency of the knowledge of Christ Jesus his Lord.

Oh, blessed Spirit of wisdom and truth, give me an increasing knowledge of Jesus and the glories of His kingdom. Impart unto me a spiritual, experimental knowledge of that love of Christ, which passes knowledge, that I may be filled with all the fullness of God.

Death will be gain to the believer, because it will increase his holiness. Here on earth, we have to contend with an evil nature, although subdued by almighty grace and changed in a considerable degree through the power of the Holy Spirit. Yet the Canaanites are still in the land. The remainders of corruption require continual watchfulness and circumspection, lest they increase and regain their former possession of the heart. Sin still dwelling in the believer causes that warfare, which must never cease until this body of death is laid in the grave, never more to harass the disembodied spirit encircled with heavenly glory.

Oh, that I may daily hunger and thirst after righteousness! I want to be holy, as God is holy, to have my will swallowed up in His. I feel sin daily working within me, but oh, may I hate and abhor it! May I ever feel it to be my grief, my burden, and my cross, and rejoice at every victory obtained over it through the blood of the Lamb.

How unspeakably blessed must heaven be, where sin can gain no admittance, where every object shall administer the purest felicity, and where Jesus Himself will be the eternal source of joy!

Death must, then, indeed be gain to the believer; for it shall put him in complete possession of everlasting happiness.

Here on earth we groan, being burdened. Here we live in an enemy's country through which we must pass, contending every inch of our way to Zion. Here we live as in a great hospital between the dying and the dead. Here we are surrounded with all kinds of natural and moral evils flowing from that poisoned source, the fall of man. Here we must drink the bitter waters of Marah, made still more bitter by our love of ease, our lack of resignation to the will of God, our selfishness of spirit, our rebelliousness of heart to His disposals.

The believer, it is true, experiences daily mercies which compass him about, for the Lord will not forsake His inheritance in the waste howling wilderness. His supplies, like the ancient manna, are continually falling around his tent. He has light in his dwelling and can, therefore, rejoice in the Lord and joy in the God of his salvation. He glories in tribulation for Christ's sake and, like the martyr of old, can kiss the fagot which, as another chariot of fire, is appointed to convey his soul to heaven. But still his happiness is greatly interrupted through the vestiges of indwelling sin, the wickedness of mankind, and the malice of Satan. He, therefore, looks forward with joyful expectation to that glorious period when his happy spirit will take its station near the throne of his beloved Savior, and he rejoices in hope of the glory of God.

How passing strange that dying, sinful worms of the earth should ridicule and despise such a hope and end as this! "Oh, almighty Spirit, descend into my soul! Banish every thing which is contrary to Thy holy nature and obstructive to my spiritual progress towards the realms of bliss. Fill me with light and love, with joy and peace. Take me under Thy guardian care. Guide me by Thy unerring hand through all the dangerous mazes of this mortal state, until I am brought to the full fruition of Thy glorious Godhead through the all-sufficient merits of my Lord and Savior Jesus Christ."

How happy is the dying saint,
Whose sins are all forgiven;
With joy he passes Jordan's flood,
Upheld by hopes of heaven.

The Savior, whom he truly loved,
Now cheers him by His grace;
A glory gilds his dying bed,
And beams upon his face.

Ecstatic joy and heavenly bliss
Swell his enraptured heart;
He views the promised land of rest,
And pants for his depart.

Terror and dread are both unknown;
Sweet peace and hope appear,
To guide the blessed traveler home,
And all his footsteps cheer.

Angels of light attendant wait
His spirit to convey
Beyond this drear abode of night,
To realms of endless day.

Oh, may I live the life of faith,
Abound in holy love,
Until death shall bear my joyful soul
To Zion's courts above.

CHAPTER 71

True Happiness

There is one important truth which cannot be too deeply engraven on the heart—that *to be holy is to be happy*. This truth, being once admitted, accounts for the misery of thousands who are in search of happiness. They mistake its real nature and the way which leads to it. They thirst, indeed, for the refreshing stream, but find it not, because their minds being unholy, they cannot discern—nor even relish, if they could discern—the true felicity of man.

Where, then, is this sacred treasure to be found? What shall we answer to the thousands who inquire: "Who will shew us any good?" (Ps. 4:6). The blessed gospel reveals the important secret. While worldly minds are toiling through the valley of life to reach the envied spot, the imaginary paradise of affluence, where happiness is supposed to dwell, the humble Christian, living day by day on Christ by faith, enjoys the real blessing in every situation and condition of life.

Riches cannot confer happiness. Grace can, and does. Herein is the goodness of God strikingly manifested, that true happiness is not the result of human wisdom, power, or grandeur. The poor may enjoy it, while the most wealthy are destitute of it. The illiterate may discern its excellence, while the wisest philosophers may be blind to its beauty.

We see this continually verified. The rich rejecting the true riches; the wise of this world despising the true wisdom; the men who are struggling after happiness, refusing that gospel which alone can make them happy.

And why is this? Because man is naturally blind to the things of God, and his own true interest, until enlightened by the Spirit of God.

Truly, man by nature is dead in trespasses and sins. He is alive indeed to evil and active in the pursuit of earthly good, but towards God he is dead. His heart has no impulsive feeling of love and gratitude. His will has no holy bias in childlike simplicity and obedience to his great Creator. He is averse from God. The carnal mind has not only no desires towards God but is rooted in enmity against Him.

This is the true state of man by nature. He is up in arms against his Maker. Hence he is an object of deserved condemnation. His natural conscience testifies indeed against him. But he breaks through all restraints and sins with awful determination.

The Almighty could, by a single volition of His will, consign the rebel to eternal death. But oh, how sweetly do grace and mercy shine! Yes, how wonderfully does mercy rejoice against judgment! Jesus descends, satisfies the demands of the law, removes the curse, and opens the kingdom to all believers. To believe this mystery of love, to receive Christ into the heart by faith, to live under the abiding influence of this heavenly truth, is to attain the grand secret of happiness. All else is but vanity and vexation of spirit, for "there is no peace, saith my God, to the wicked" (Isa. 57:21). It is evident, then, that true happiness consists in being at peace with God through Jesus Christ, and consists in the habitual enjoyment of that peace in the conscience through the power of the Holy Spirit.

This delightful state of reconciliation with God is connected with inward purity as the blessed fruit of the Savior's death, for holiness is an essential part of Christ's salvation. Thus peace and purity, felt and enjoyed, form that happiness which creates a heaven in the soul and prepares the soul for the enjoyment of heaven.

In proportion to the clearness of our views of gospel grace, and the strength of our faith in the atonement of Jesus, will be our victory over sin and the abundance of our peace and joy. All believers are not equally happy, because all are not equally strong in faith or equally advanced in inward holiness. When, therefore, we are dejected and fearful; when we find an uncomfortable restlessness within, corroding and damping our spiritual enjoyment; or when we feel a dread of the judgment to come; we should look well to ourselves, lest there be some root of bitterness, some secret sin indulged in the heart, which, as it grieves the Holy Spirit, never fails to intercept the smiles of our heavenly Father, to becloud our evidences, and to mar our joy.

Happiness is inseparable from holiness, and cannot exist without it. Some constitutions are prone to melancholy, and if any pious people have such a natural predisposition to sadness, the world immediately ascribes it to religion. But surely this is most unjust, and shows how readily we throw the blame on what we do not love.

How perverted is man in his feelings and affections! He smiles when he should sigh; he laughs when he should mourn; he appears gay and sprightly when he should be of a sorrowful spirit. But oh, the blessed change which takes place when the gospel comes to the heart, not in word only, but in power, in the Holy Spirit, and in much assurance! He sighs and mourns over his guilt and misery, but his sorrow is turned into joy. Jesus, who is anointed to preach glad tidings unto the meek, to bind up the broken-hearted, and to comfort all that mourn, gives him beauty for ashes, the oil of joy for mourning, and the garment of praise for the spirit of heaviness. He can now rejoice in the Lord with joy unspeakable and full of glory; a heavenly light shines into his soul, and he delights himself in the abundance of peace.

Oh, happy, blissful state! Who would not long to be a genuine disciple of the blessed Jesus, who has assured His obedient people that He will manifest Himself unto them as He does not unto the world; that He will come and make His abode with them? What heart can be unhappy in which Jesus deigns to dwell, to which He manifests His grace and love?

Such favored souls are the temples of the Holy Spirit, the habitation of God through the Spirit. They are led by the Spirit into all truth; they are preserved from the corruption which is in the world through lust; and they bring forth the fruits of righteousness. They ripen daily for the paradise above, where they shall eat of the Tree of Life and walk in white with Him whom they love above every created being.

Oh, my soul, receive with joy the reconciliation! Nothing can make you happy, but a simple laying hold of Christ by faith.

Oh, what a blessing is the simplicity of faith! "Lord, enable me to look to Thee as revealed in the gospel and to rely with unshaken confidence on Thy atonement and intercession."

If I believe with the heart unto righteousness, I shall be saved—saved from guilt and condemnation, saved from the power and pollution of sin. If thus saved, I must be happy—happy in the love of God and happy in the sweet assurance of being with my Savior forever and ever.

"Lord, I believe—help my unbelief. I would credit Thy Word. It is unerring truth. Now let its sacred power be felt in my heart. From this moment seal Thy pardon to my soul, by the indubitable impression of heavenly love."

Who can describe the holy joy,
The calm that reigns within;
When Jesus speaks the pardoning word,
And breaks the power of sin!

Sweet peace, composing all the mind,
Bids angry passions cease;
Graces descending from above,
Like flowing waves increase.

Dear Savior, let Thy healing beams
In softest radiance shine;
Let humble fear and love abound,
To prove the work divine.

Then will my grateful heart each day
Its Ebenezer raise,
Until angels teach me, near Thy throne,
Eternal songs of praise.

CHAPTER 72

True Religion

True religion neither courts the observation nor seeks the applause of men. It grows and thrives most in retirement. Its effects, indeed, are widely felt, and its blessings extensively diffused, but its salutary streams are fed by communion with God by holy meditation, fervent prayer, and much converse with the Holy Scriptures. It aims at the glory of God. Jesus Christ is its sum and substance, and to promote the happiness of the whole human race is its delightful occupation.

True religion is the very opposite to hypocrisy and formality. It is made up of truth and sincerity, and its love is without pretense. It hates every false glare, all ostentatious parade, all desire to be seen; and it labors to approve itself to Him who looks at the heart and examines the motives of men.

True religion is founded on the truth of God's holy Word. There, man is declared to be not only guilty, but unable to save himself, and wholly indebted to the sovereign grace of God for life and salvation. To know God in His Word, to love Him in the heart, and to honor Him in the life is the daily work of every real believer. Hence, to love the Lord Jesus Christ in sincerity is the essence of true religion.

Many fatally deceive themselves respecting the nature of genuine Christianity.

True religion does not consist in having a name to live, but in having a reputation for godliness. "Thou hast a name that thou livest, and art dead" (Rev. 3:1).

It does not consist in outward forms, however excellent. "Having a form of godliness, but denying the power thereof: from such turn away" (2 Tim. 3:5). "The kingdom of God is not meat and drink; but righteousness, and peace, and joy in the Holy Ghost" (Rom. 14:17).

It does not consist in attending divine ordinances. "This people honoureth me with their lips, but their heart is far from me" (Mark 7:6). "And they come unto thee as the people cometh, and they sit before thee as my people, and they hear thy words, but they will not do them: for with their mouth they shew much love, but their heart goeth after their covetousness" (Ezek. 33:31).

It does not consist in outward profession. "They profess that they know God; but in works they deny him" (Titus 1:16).

It does not consist in the mere performance of moral duties. "Except your righteousness shall exceed the righteousness of the scribes and Pharisees, ye shall in no case enter into the kingdom of heaven" (Matt. 5:20).

It does not consist in head knowledge, great gifts, liberality to the poor, or even martyrdom itself. "Though I speak with the tongues of men and of angels,… though I have the gift of prophecy, and understand all mysteries, and all knowledge;… though I have all faith, so that I could remove mountains;… though I bestow all my goods to feed the poor, and though I give my body to be burned, and have not charity, it profiteth me nothing" (1 Cor. 13:1-3).

The religion of the Bible is pure, spiritual, experimental, and practical. It is the devotion of the heart, for God is a spirit and requires those who worship Him to worship Him in spirit and in truth (John 4:24).

It is then evident that the whole of evangelical religion may be summed up in four short words: "Faith … worketh by love" (Gal. 5:6). Without love, faith is dead, like a tree destitute of sap. Without faith, love can have no existence, for the sap cannot exist if the root be wanting. Good works are the blessed fruits of faith and prove the existence and soundness both of faith and love.

God, in grace, as in nature, is the creator of the root, the sap, and the fruit. He gives life and fertility. Without Him, we are nothing and can do nothing. Hence, believers are called "trees of righteousness, the planting of the Lord, that he might be glorified" (Isa. 61:3), they are also branches in Jesus Christ, the true vine, who has said, "I am the vine, ye are the branches: He that abideth in me, and I in him, the same bringeth forth much fruit: for without me ye can do nothing" (John 15:5).

True religion is exemplified in the conscientious discharge of all the social and relative duties. It fills the domestic circle with peace and every community where it reigns with unity and concord.

The Christian's life is a life of desire and enjoyment. His desires are ever on the wing towards Jesus, and at times he enjoys the smiles of his Savior, which gladden his heart and quicken his desires after a perpetual increase of this blessedness.

He pants continually after true happiness in the exercise of true religion; and every taste of this sweet refreshing fountain, while it alleviates his thirst after earthly pleasures, only serves to increase his desires after more spiritual communion with his God and Savior. Thus he proceeds, until his most enlarged desire is satisfied in that blessed region where all the saints are led to living fountains of water, proceeding from the living God.

How little is the Christian's life known by the world in general! How little is it valued even by those who profess to esteem it! How true the apostolic declaration: "All seek their own, not the things which are Jesus Christ's" (Phil. 2:21). The warrior, pursuing fame even to the pinnacle of glory, braving all the horrors of the blood-stained field; the man of letters, deeply entrenched in ponderous folios, seeking by research to immortalize his name; the busy merchant, stretching out his arms, and holding in his wide embrace a world of traffic to enlarge his fortune and enrich his family; ten thousand times ten thousand human beings of every rank and station all feel, while unrenewed, a secret wish that Scripture truth may not be true. Else why dispute the plain, yet awful declarations of the Word of God? Why argue, contradict, and gainsay—yes, deny—the solemn revelation of His will, whose Word is truth, whose nature is unchangeable, whose counsel shall stand, and who will do all His pleasure?

How inveterate is the natural enmity of the human heart to true religion! Hence every call from earth to heaven is neglected and despised.

The heart, deeply rooted in the earth, derives its nourishment from thence, and finds no relish in enjoyments or pursuits which stretch beyond the boundaries of time or bid the worldly mind forsake the groveling pleasures of this passing scene.

The religion of Jesus is unalterable in its very nature. It is founded on the perfections of Jehovah and on the necessities of man. Its promises and precepts, its prospects and privileges, are the same now as they ever were. Then why is the face of the Christian world so changed? It is owing to the prevalence of that evil heart of unbelief against which Paul so feelingly cautions the Hebrew converts, and which occasions our present luke-warmness, slothfulness, and departure from God.

There are four evils which mark the decayed state of Christians in general: their love of the world, their love of ease, their fear of man, and their distrust of providence. The primitive believers were just the reverse of all this. They despised the world and its flattering allurements, they took up the cross and denied themselves, they boldly confessed Christ and suffered for His sake, they trusted God for all things and so took joyfully the spoiling of their goods. And what was the blessed fruit? They abounded in consolation, they grew in grace, they shone as lights in the world, they felt joy and peace in believing.

But now we see professing Christians—even many of whom we charitably hope well—languid in their graces, timid in their confession, fearful of consequences, and fearful of offending. Sad symptoms, these, of spiritual decay! Hence the spirit of the gospel is not exhibited. Its character is not exemplified, and Christ is not glorified.

No marvel that the work of evangelizing the world has proceeded so slowly, since the power of true religion is so little felt by the bulk of professing Christians. An awful charge of guilt thus rests upon the visible church of Christ. But as the church is composed of individual members, so each must take his share of criminal supineness and neglect. And you, oh my soul, must stand condemned before that gracious Savior, whose love demands the exercise of all those powers which He Himself bestowed upon you. Oh, that the Lord may quicken His people and revive His work in the midst of the days!

Jesus said: "If any man will come after me, let him deny himself, and take up his cross daily, and follow me" (Luke 9:23). This cross is heavy to bear when earthly affections, or pride, or unbelief, work in the heart. But when the heart is filled with love to the Savior, then the greatest cross is light, and even pleasant, to endure. Thus the apostles counted it all joy, when they fell into diverse temptations (James 1:2). They rejoiced that they were counted worthy to suffer shame for the name of Jesus. Multitudes of loving believers gloried in tribulation and sealed the truth with their blood. If Christianity can effect such wonders in the hearts of sinners, how powerful, and yet how beautiful, is true religion!

As God will be for a crown of glory and for a diadem of beauty unto the remnant of His people, so His people shall be a crown of glory in the hand of the Lord, and a royal diadem in the hand of their God. But while we admire the work of grace, it is to be deeply deplored that the world has made such sad inroads into the territories of the visible church.

The love of ease, of splendor, of worldly distinction, of family comforts, has greatly destroyed that spirit of martyrdom which should practically operate in every believer in Jesus.

Every Christian should be a martyr in spirit. He should be ready to leave all and sacrifice all for Christ. That excellent reformer Oecolampadius, writing to a friend, said: "The greatest happiness of this life is to venture for the sake of Christ." Many will venture their all in some profitable speculation, which promises a large increase of worldly property. But happy indeed is that man who can venture all for Christ in faith and love. He may lose all that the world calls great and good—but he shall receive, through the merits of the Redeemer, a crown of glory which fades not away.

It is easy to rejoice at the bestowment of temporal favors, and sometimes of spiritual mercies—but are we as ready to render thanks unto the Lord for pains and trials, for losses and crosses, endured for righteousness' sake, or in the wise dispensations of a good and unerring Providence?

Now the apostolic command is: "In every thing give thanks" (1 Thess. 5:18). But oh, how little of this primitive spirit is there among us! Who can bear with joy the loss of all things for Christ's sake? Who can glory in tribulation?

"Blessed Lord, pour out Thy Holy Spirit upon Thy drooping church, that it may 'flourish like grain and blossom like grapevines.' Oh, that I may sit loosely to the world and its passing enjoyments, and be ready to arise and follow Thee wheresoever Thou callest me, either to labor or endure. Make me sincerely thankful for hourly mercies; and with these mercies, be pleased to bestow a heart weaned from creature comforts and supremely devoted unto Thee. Increase in me true religion that so, amid the manifold and sundry changes of the world, my heart may surely there be fixed, where alone true joys are to be found. Give me that spiritual perception and that spiritual relish for heavenly truths, which are the experience and portion of Thy children here and which form the delightful foretaste of their eternal blessedness in the world to come."

Oh, Thou in whom all comfort lies,
The source of all my inward joys;
To Thee I look, to Thee I call,
My only hope, my life, my all.

With Thee, oh God, is holy peace;
Thy flowing mercies never ccase;
They fill the spacious courts above
With odors sweet of grace and love.

Blest Savior, with delight I dwell
On themes no mortal tongue can tell;
The glory of Thy cross exceeds
All human, all angelic deeds.

Oh, may the love which brought Thee down
Continue still Thy work to crown;
Until every nation shall confess
Thy grace, Thy blood, and righteousness.

CHAPTER 73

Election

It is very dangerous to indulge a spirit of curiosity respecting the deep things of God. There are mysteries in the kingdom of grace, and in the kingdom of nature, which surpass the highest powers of created intelligence to comprehend. But, as in the natural world, enough is made level to our capacity, to render us comfortable and happy with respect to food, clothing, and other temporal conveniences; so likewise in things pertaining to the spiritual world, sufficient is revealed to make us wise unto salvation, through faith in Jesus Christ.

That desire of being wise above what is written, which is the effect of a proud, unhallowed curiosity, is strongly reprehended in the Holy Scriptures. Our blessed Lord frequently repressed this spirit of curious inquiry which is so natural to us. When one asked Him, "Lord, are there few that be saved?" (Luke 13:23), His practical answer was: "Strive to enter in at the strait gate" (v. 24). It was as if He had said: "Trouble not yourself about the secret counsels of heaven; take heed to yourself; or you shall likewise perish."

At another time, when His disciples asked Him, saying, "Lord, wilt thou at this time restore again the kingdom to Israel?" (Acts 1:6), He replied, "It is not for you to know the times or the seasons, which the Father hath put in his own power" (v. 7). When Jesus had been foretelling Peter by what death he should glorify God, Peter, seeing John, the disciple whom Jesus loved, felt a curiosity to know what would become of him also, and said: "Lord, and what shall this man do?" (John 21:21). Jesus said unto him: "If I will that he tarry till I come, what is that to thee? follow thou me" (v. 22). Thus we see how pointedly our

Lord checked that prying into secret things, which, if indulged, would take us from the plain path of childlike obedience and draw us into labyrinths, where our minds would soon be "in wandering mazes lost."

But although we cannot fathom, we are nevertheless to believe from the heart the mysterious truths of God. Should any of these truths seem to contradict each other, it arises altogether from the finite nature of our own minds. Instead, therefore, of laboring to reconcile the apparently opposing statements of eternal truth by systems of human invention, it is the part of humility to receive each, in the simplicity of faith, as God has been pleased to reveal them to us in his holy Word. By adopting this mode, we shall not be shackled by human opinion nor be afraid of inconsistency while we state the simple truth as it is in Jesus.

How rich, how full, and how extensive are the blessings which Paul declared to the Thessalonian church. They reach from everlasting to everlasting and are calculated to animate all true believers to works of faith, labors of love, and patience of hope, since He who has promised is faithful and will never forsake the work of His own hands.

"But we are bound to give thanks alway to God for you, brethren beloved of the Lord, because God hath from the beginning chosen you to salvation through sanctification of the Spirit and belief of the truth: Whereunto he called you by our gospel, to the obtaining of the glory of our Lord Jesus Christ" (2 Thess. 2:13-14).

Some may ask, How could the apostle know that the Thessalonians were the chosen of God? Had he ever been favored with a view of the Book of Life? Had he ever seen their names written in heaven? Had he ever explored the secret decrees and counsels of the Almighty? No. This eminent servant of Christ searched another Book, even the volume of grace, the revealed Word of God. There he discovered the clear marks and evidences of God's redeemed people. And being himself under the immediate inspiration of the Holy Spirit, he was enabled to draw just conclusions respecting the state and character of those who embraced the gospel.

In the first chapter of this epistle to the Thessalonians, the apostle displays in glowing colors the faith, love, patience, zeal, and hope of this infant church in their readiness to receive the Word, their professed subjection to the gospel, their cheerful waiting for Christ, and their joy under manifold afflictions. Hence he drew the conclusion that they were the chosen of God, "knowing, brethren beloved, your election of God" (1 Thess. 1:4). Whether these words mean God's choice of them or their choice of God, it comes to the same thing, for if we love Him, it is because He first loved us (1 John 4:19).

All, then, who truly believe in Jesus, and who are renewed in the spirit of their minds through the power of the Holy Spirit, evidence their election of God. "We are bound to give thanks alway to God for you, brethren beloved of the Lord, because God hath from the beginning chosen you to salvation through sanctification of the Spirit and belief of the truth" (2 Thess. 2:13).

But another work of grace is mentioned by the apostle—they were effectually called by the gospel. Thousands are called by the faithful preaching of the gospel every Sabbath day to flee from the wrath to come and to lay hold on the hope set before them in a crucified Savior. Yet how few obey the call and come unto Jesus, weary and heavy-laden with the burden of their sins.

How few are effectually called! The great mass of baptized Christians hear the words of life, but regard them not. They love the world and cling to it. They love sin and will not part with it. They love darkness rather than light, because their deeds are evil (John 3:19). And if it be asked, Why do they thus act? the answer is given by Paul himself, writing under the guidance of the Holy Spirit: "But if our gospel be hid, it is hid to them that are lost: In whom the god of this world hath blinded the minds of them which believe not, lest the light of the glorious gospel of Christ, who is the image of God, should shine unto them" (2 Cor. 4:3-4).

We may therefore conclude that all who believingly obey the call of mercy and draw near unto God through Jesus Christ evidence their election of God, according to the plain, grammatical meaning of the apostle's declaration.

The other blessing mentioned by Paul, and which crowns the whole, is the eternal glorification of all who are thus effectually called and evidence their election in Christ by faith and holiness: "Whereunto he called you by our gospel, to the obtaining of the glory of our Lord Jesus Christ" (2 Thess. 2:14). Our divine Master has declared: "He that endureth to the end shall be saved" (Matt. 10:22). Peter assured the Christian strangers who were scattered abroad that they were "kept by the power of God through faith unto salvation" (1 Pet. 1:5).

Hence it follows that all who are effectually called by the gospel shall finally obtain the glory of our Lord Jesus Christ, being preserved through faith unto God's everlasting kingdom. Thus grace reigns through righteousness unto eternal life by Jesus Christ our Lord.

The gospel is designed to stain the pride of human glory and to lay man in the dust of humiliation. "For by grace are ye saved through faith; and that not of yourselves: it is the gift of God: Not of works, lest any man should boast. For we are his workmanship, created in Christ Jesus unto good works, which God hath before ordained that we should walk in them" (Eph. 2:8-10). Such is the humbling, yet delightful, language of the inspired apostle.

The carnal heart rises against these abasing, purifying doctrines of the cross, which strip the sinner of all self-righteous dependence and strike at the root of all fleshly indulgences. The proud sinner must become a fool in his own estimation and feel himself to be nothing before he can receive with gratitude these stupendous blessings offered for his acceptance in the gospel.

Divine grace alone can effect this mighty change. But what cannot the power of omnipotence accomplish? "Yea, before the day was I am he; and there is none that can deliver out of my hand: I will work, and who shall let it?" (Isa. 43:13) is the voice of the Sovereign, "who worketh all things after the counsel of his own will" (Eph. 1:11), and who has said: "My counsel shall stand, and I will do all my pleasure" (Isa. 46:10).

Man, if left to himself, would never seek after God. His language is: "I have loved strangers, and after them will I go" (Jer. 2:25). But when God says, "*Live,*" the soul shall as assuredly live, as when at the creation He said: "Let there be light: and there was light" (Gen. 1:3). The chaotic mass was formed to order and beauty when the Spirit of God moved upon the face of the deep, and so shall the disordered soul be transformed after the divine image when almighty grace puts forth its new creating power. "This people have I formed for myself; they shall shew forth my praise" (Isa. 43:21).

When the leper said, "If thou wilt, thou canst make me clean" (Mark 1:40), Jesus replied: "I will; be thou clean. And…immediately the leprosy departed from him" (v. 41-42). In Jesus, we behold "the mighty God" (Gen. 49:24), "God…manifest in the flesh" (1 Tim. 3.16), exerting His benevolent power in healing diseases, in stilling the raging elements, in casting out devils, in multiplying provisions, in raising the dead, in revealing men's thoughts, in forgiving sin.

And now that He is in glory and reigns as sovereign Lord, no darkness of the understanding, no hardness of the heart, no rebellion of the will, no alienation of the affection, no outward opposition or inward repugnance to the truth, can prevent the conversion and final salvation of that soul whom God loves with an everlasting love and draws with loving-kindness to the cross of Christ.

"Herein is love, not that we loved God, but that he loved us, and sent his Son to be the propitiation for our sins" (1 John 4:10). This is the wonderful announcement of the messengers of peace.

As believers in Jesus are declared to be chosen in him before the foundation of the world, that they should be holy and without blame before him in love (Eph. 1:4), so the change which passes upon the soul when brought by the Spirit to the love and practice of holiness, as evidential of its election in Christ, is described in Scripture by the boldest figures.

"And you hath he quickened, who were dead in trespasses and sins" (Eph. 2:1). "We know that we have passed from death unto life, because we love the brethren" (1 John 3:14). "For ye were sometimes darkness, but now are ye light in the Lord" (Eph. 5:8). "Giving thanks unto the Father,... who hath delivered us from the power of darkness, and hath translated us into the kingdom of his dear Son" (Col. 1:12-13), "that ye should shew forth the praises of him who hath called you out of darkness into his marvellous light" (1 Pet. 2:9). "Except a man be born of water and of the Spirit, he cannot enter into the kingdom of God" (John 3:5). "If any man be in Christ, he is a new creature: old things are passed away; behold, all things are become new" (2 Cor. 5:17).

This blessed conversion from sin to holiness is thus declared by the apostle to the Romans: "Ye were the servants of sin, but ye have obeyed from the heart that form of doctrine which was delivered you" (Rom. 6:17). To the Thessalonians: "Ye turned to God from idols to serve the living and true God" (1 Thess. 1:9). To the Corinthians: "Know ye not that the unrighteous shall not inherit the kingdom of God?... And such were some of you: but ye are washed, but ye are sanctified, but ye are justified in the name of the Lord Jesus, and by the Spirit of our God" (1 Cor. 6:9, 11).

The way and means of the church's salvation were also foreordained. Jesus is declared to be the Lamb slain from the foundation of the world. Faith is the divinely appointed instrument by which the sinner is enabled to lay hold on Christ. The Holy Spirit is promised to all who ask for this unspeakable gift. "Ho, every one that thirsteth, come ye to the waters" (Isa. 55:1) is the gracious call.

The gospel is designed to be a universal blessing, for the command is: "Go ye into all the world, and preach the gospel to every creature" (Mark 16:15). The invitation is general; the command to preach the gospel is unlimited. None are excluded but such as, through unbelief, exclude themselves; for God has "no pleasure in the death of the wicked; but that the wicked turn from his way and live" (Ezek. 33:11); He is "not willing that any should perish, but that all should come to repentance" (2 Pet. 3:9); He "will have all men to be saved, and to come unto the knowledge of the truth" (1 Tim. 2:4).

Such are the views which God's infinite wisdom and love have given us in the pages of inspired truth. Eternal misery is there declared to be the fruit of man's willful apostasy and rebellion, and eternal happiness to be the free gift of sovereign grace through Jesus Christ. Thrice happy, then, are they who experience the saving grace of God, who hear in faith, who obey the call of mercy, and who follow the Lord fully and perseveringly in filial obedience.

These are the objects of the Savior's love and care, theirs are the promises, and to them belong the glories which shall shortly be revealed. Oh, happy people, saved by the Lord!

"Blessed Savior, draw my heart sweetly and powerfully to Thyself. Oh, make me Thy temple! May Thy Word reach my heart and Thy love constrain my soul to love and obedience. Like Matthew, may I cheerfully obey Thy call, leave all, and follow Thee. Subdue every rebellious inclination, and let nothing dwell within me that is contrary to Thy will. Root out of my heart all evil affections, and fill me with the fruits of righteousness. May my happy position ever be at the foot of the cross. There wean my heart from earthly things and bind me to Thyself by cords of everlasting love. Oh, let me never, never wander from Thee, but preserve me to Thy kingdom and glory for Thine infinite mercies' sake."

Dear Shepherd of the chosen flock,
I love to hear Thy voice;
When full of kind, redeeming love,
Thou bidst my heart rejoice.

Oh, let me never leave the road,
That leads to Thine abode!
Oh, suffer not my feet to stray
From Thee, the living God!

It is Thy delightful work to save,
Thy pleasure and Thy joy;
Then let Thy praise each fleeting hour
My grateful thoughts employ.

A stranger, Lord, I will not know,
Through Thy preserving grace;
But follow Thee with cheerful steps
To heaven, Thy dwelling-place.

CHAPTER 74

Spiritual Vision

It is a pleasant thing for the eye to behold the sun and all the varied objects which are illuminated by its rays. If the natural eye be such a precious gift of providence, the eye of faith must be an invaluable gift of grace. Through the weakness of the natural eye, distant objects are dimly seen; but, by the eye of faith, we can pierce the veil which bounds our sight and view the unseen glories of the heavenly world.

"Lord, impart unto Thy servant this spiritual vision, that I may daily contemplate the wonders of eternity and the blest abodes of heavenly purity and joy."

When I look with an eye of faith towards heaven, what do I there behold? The glorious habitation of Him who fills all space with His presence, who dwells in the light which no man can approach unto. I there behold the throne of grace and mercy, in the midst of which appears a Lamb slain, even Jesus, the friend of sinners, the advocate of guilty man.

I there behold myriads of glorified spirits hymning the praises of Him who was, and is, and is to come. They appear as flames of fire, burning with zeal and love. Their outstretched wings express their readiness to fulfill the mandate of their God.

I there behold rivers of pleasures, mansions of bliss—yes, more than tongue can speak or heart conceive. There dwells the great, the glorious God-Man, Emmanuel, God with us. Around Him are assembled all His faithful ministers and people, clothed in white, with palms of victory in their hands, singing to their golden harps the praises of redeeming love. To be ever near this gracious Savior, to behold His glory, to experience the fullness of His love, to enjoy His smiles, to be filled with His Spirit, is the heaven, the felicity, the glory of the saints in light.

When from these high abodes I cast my eyes upon this earth on which I tread, how wretched does it appear. The believer may at that very moment be treading upon a scorpion, but he feels not its painful sting; some acute disorder may be striking through every nerve, but his exalted views of heavenly glory benumb the pain and blunt the edge of suffering. Through the power of his realizing faith, he is even more than conqueror. He can glory in tribulation and triumph in death. The world may frown, but it troubles him not. It may smile, but he regards it not. His whole soul is full of heaven, of Christ, and of eternal glory.

"Oh, Thou ever-blessed Spirit of grace and truth, impart this precious faith, this realizing view of Jesus, this sweet foretaste of everlasting bliss. Give me to know and feel my interest in His atoning blood. Make me more active for Christ, more devoted to His cause, more attached to His people, more alive to His honor, more simple in my dependence, more sincere in my professions, more simple in all my aims to glorify my God and Savior."

When I look into the grave, what do I there behold? The dire effects of sin, the vanity of all created things, the end of pomp and pride. But when, with the eye of faith, I look beyond this cold and dreary mansion of the dead, what awful scenes present themselves before me! There I behold the rich man who, when on earth, fared sumptuously every day, lifting up his eyes in torment, without one cooling drop to quench his flaming tongue. And why does he thus suffer? Because he trusted in his riches and forgot his God.

The grave is the concluding scene of splendor and magnificence. There, the now-pampered body must become the food of worms! There, the body now arrayed in purple and fine linen must be covered with corruption!

Methinks this humiliating end of human greatness would convince the fondest worldling of the vanity of earthly things. And surely it would impress the mind, and deeply too, if men would but consider.

Vain, thoughtless man! Ah, when will he be wise? The opening grave creates a slight alarm when some beloved object is laid within its cold embrace. But soon the transient tear is wiped away, and every serious thought, like writing on the sand, is rapidly effaced by the world's returning tide of business or of pleasure.

Lord, grant that it may not be so with me. Teach me so to number my days, that I may apply my heart unto wisdom. Preserve me from the folly of building the fabric of my hopes upon so mutable a foundation as human life. Oh, may I never boast of tomorrow, but labor to improve today. Oh, may I seek Thee now while Thou mayest be found, and call upon Thee while Thou art near; for now is the accepted time, now is the day of salvation. May I learn wisdom from the folly of others and pray that they also may become wise unto salvation. Remembering that the end of all things is at hand, may I be sober and watch unto prayer. May I live in a constant preparation for a dying hour and find the last retiring moment the happiest of my life, being brightened by faith in Jesus and by an assured hope of glory.

When I look around me in the world, what do I there behold? A scene of complicated misery; an Aceldama; a field of blood; a huge hospital filled with all manner of diseases; an asylum full of maniacs, fancying themselves immortal in the region of mortality and happy in a valley of tears.

I behold a multitude of faithful prophets, now blowing the brazen trumpet of the law, and now the silver trumpet of the gospel, each laboring to alarm or to allure this miserable, this dying, crowd. Some few, through grace, are arrested in their mad career; their eyes begin to open, the scales drop off, they stand confused and amazed, they look around in terror and cry out: "What must we do to be saved?" (Acts 16:30). Through grace, they behold the Savior; through grace, they repent and believe; through grace, they love and obey the gospel. They now lament the dreadful situation of their poor companions and become themselves the objects of derision.

"Lord, what is man! How astonishing Thy forbearance, how surpassing thought Thy boundless grace and mercy!

"Enable me to see the madness and folly of living at a distance from Thee. Lead me from the ways and customs of the world. Fix my heart more steadfastly upon heavenly joys; upon Christ, the fountain of bliss; upon Christ, the hope of glory; upon Christ, Thy well-beloved; upon Christ, the adoration of angels, the joy and portion of the church on earth, the bliss and glory of the general assembly and church of the first-born in heaven.

In those blest regions of delight,
Where Jesus is unveiled to sight,
No mortal tongue can e'er express
The ransomed sinner's blessedness.

His joys are all alike unknown,
As seated on Emmanuel's throne,
He drinks the living streams of bliss,
And views all heaven's joys as His.

Amazing grace! Stupendous love!
Oh, may each warm affection move;
Until all my soul is knit to Thee,
In time and through eternity!

Thou of all joy the center art;
Oh, never from my soul depart;
Blest Jesus, let Thy saving love,
Like dew, drop gently from above.

Blow on Thy garden, fairest One;
Oh, be my bliss, and Thou alone;
Let sweetest spices ever flow
To beautify Thy church below.

CHAPTER 75

Heaven

Come, oh my soul, and meditate on the joys and glories of the heavenly world! Lift up your eyes unto the hills from where comes your help (Ps. 121:1), those everlasting hills, where all the precious flock of Christ will eternally feed and where the great Shepherd of the sheep immediately dwells. Nothing tends more to ennoble the mind and refine the faculties of the soul than frequent and pious contemplations on the grace of Jesus, on the love of the Father, on the communion of the Holy Spirit, on the felicities reserved in heaven for all who love the Lord Jesus Christ in sincerity. When the mind is once filled with these stupendous, yet endearing, subjects, how contemptible and trifling do all earthly things appear!

The Word of God reveals much that is captivating to the soul respecting the abodes of glory; yet language cannot describe, nor the mind conceive, the blessed reality. What heaven really is we must die to know. All the glories of kingdoms, all the beauties of gardens, all the splendors of palaces—yes, all the riches of creation—form but a faint sketch of the sublime original.

Earth can afford only a shadowy representation of heavenly glory. The Holy Spirit reveals far sweeter views to our minds than those which are drawn from sublunary scenes.

Heaven is a state of rest. "There the wicked cease from troubling; and there the weary be at rest" (Job 3:17). How delightful is rest to the weary traveler, to the sons and daughters of affliction, to those whose bodies are "chastened ... with pain" (Job 33:19) or whose souls are "filled with the scorning of those that are at ease, and with the contempt of the proud" (Ps. 123:4).

How cheering is the prospect of rest to the persecuted followers of Jesus, who find no abiding city here, being driven from place to place by the rude hand of arbitrary power. How happy was the exchange for Lazarus when carried by angels from a leprous body, wasted with hunger, to Abraham's bosom, to the mansion of the blessed, the paradise of God.

Heaven is the abode of peace. Pleasing thought indeed, to those who are constrained to dwell with Mesech and have their habitation among the tents of Kedar, who are compelled to say with David, "My soul hath long dwelt with him that hateth peace" (Ps. 120:6), wounding the feelings and destroying the happiness of all around them. But in heaven all is harmony and love. There, every heart vibrates in unison and swells with pure affection.

The sons of peace shall dwell with their heavenly Father who is the God of peace; with Jesus their Redeemer, who is the Prince of Peace; with the Holy Spirit, whose fruit is peace. The Triune God will cause their peace to flow like a river fed by a perennial spring, whose waters fail not, ever issuing, clear as crystal, from the throne of God and of the Lamb.

Heaven is a state of perfect holiness. How ardently does the true believer in Jesus pant after perfect holiness. Here, indeed, he cannot attain unto it. Every moment bespeaks his infirmity. Too often, alas, his deep corruption, inwardly felt and deplored, makes him cry out in bitter anguish of spirit: "O wretched man that I am! who shall deliver me?" (Rom. 7:24). In heaven, he shall be forever delivered from the workings of inbred sin. In heaven, he shall be perfected in holiness. He loves, therefore, to anticipate the bliss of heaven, which consists in seeing God in all His unutterable glories, in being made like Him in the perfection of beauty, in being forever with Him in the enjoyment of His love.

In heaven, he will be pure as God is pure, holy as God is holy—not, indeed, in degree, but in nature. All the loveliness of the Savior will be reflected from the heavenly bride, when, adorned with every grace and clothed in the righteousness of her beloved Lord, she shall shake herself from the dust at the morning of the resurrection and arise and shine in the full splendor of eternal glory.

Oh, how glorious will that period be when all the elect of God shall be gathered in; when not a grain of the precious seed shall be lost; when every, even the feeblest, lamb shall be housed from the storm.

Heaven is a state of unmixed happiness. No tears bedew the cheeks, no sorrow rends the hearts of its blissful inhabitants. In those celestial regions there is no pain, neither painful separation of kindred souls. All is blooming health and immortal vigor. There, death shall strike its dart no more, for death is swallowed up in victory (1 Cor. 15:54).

Sin, which now embitters every blessing, cannot shed its baneful influence over the glorified spirits surrounding the throne of God. Satan can find no admittance into those realms of bliss. The world, and all which it contains, shall have passed away. Every enemy shall be destroyed, and Christ shall reign forever and ever.

Heaven is a state of never-ending bliss. This stamps a value which all the gilded happiness of this world cannot boast. "The perpetuity of bliss, is bliss." Here, in this present world, all is transitory and unsatisfactory. The utmost point of earthly enjoyment is vanity and vexation of spirit. He who grasps the most grasps only a delusive shadow. Nothing beneath the eternal source of blessedness, God in Christ, can give abiding peace or joy. How endearing, then, are the words of the Savior: "These things I have spoken unto you, that in me ye might have peace" (John 16:33). "These things have I spoken unto you, that my joy might remain in you, and that your joy might be full" (John 15:11).

Heaven is the assemblage of all that is lovely and excellent. There dwell the cherubim and seraphim; the angels and archangels; principalities, thrones, dominions, and powers. There will all the friends of Jesus, who have lived in successive ages of the world, meet in blissful harmony and adoring praise. There all the holy intelligences will have one mind, one voice, one will, one spirit. All will be filled with the love of God. All will be holy, and all will be inexpressibly happy.

The divine image, which is the real excellence and beauty of the moral creation of God upon earth, will be seen in all its glory when the bride, the Lamb's wife, the church triumphant, shall be presented to the heavenly Bridegroom, without spot or wrinkle or any such thing.

Oh, my soul, rest not day nor night, until the Lord makes you fit for the inheritance of the saints in light. To taste something of the blessedness of heaven, I need not travel in imagination over mighty kingdoms or picture to my mind the varied beauties of art and nature; I must descend into my own heart and there, in "secret silence of the mind," contemplate by faith the infinite loveliness of the Savior, until a flame of holy love warms every affection, and a beam of holy joy gladdens every power of my soul. Such glimpses of uncreated glories, such tastes of redeeming grace, such views of Jesus and His great salvation, purifying the heart and raising the transported spirit above this poor, polluted world, may well be called a heaven begun below.

If it be heaven to behold God without a veil, to bear His image, and to dwell in His presence, then the preparation for heaven and the foretaste of it must consist in beholding God now by the eye of faith, as revealed in His holy Word, in being now transformed by the renewing of the mind, and in holding daily converse with Him by a diligent perusal of the Scriptures and by prayer. This is the life of faith. All profession of religion, without this, is mere delusion. Such barren profession may be full of words, while destitute of works; full of notions, while devoid of holy affections; full of zeal for doctrines, while empty of all saving graces.

But oh, how calm and tranquil is the humble Christian, who enjoys an assured hope of glory! He resembles a person standing on some mighty eminence. Above him shines the sun, without an intervening cloud, while far beneath his elevated station roars the dreadful thunder.

The great mass of mankind is compared in Scripture to the sea. This emblem is most accurate. The sea is always varying in its form—ever restless, ever fluctuating. Its waves, at one time, rage with tremendous fury; at another, they undulate in gentle motion or subside into a peaceful calm. Thus the heart of man is compared to that element which, with the most appropriate significance, denotes deceitfulness, instability, and change. In the blessed world of glory, which John saw when wrapped in vision in the isle of Patmos, "there was no more sea" (Rev. 21:1). No turbulent elements, no ungovernable passions, no wild uproar to disturb its everlasting rest, no bar to communion or sweet communion among the heavenly hosts.

The true Christian is a citizen of the New Jerusalem. He daily walks with God by faith. His heart is separated from a vain and noisy world through which he is indeed hastening, but to which he does not belong. He needs not to busy himself about its passing vanities or to contend about its fleeting honors. He shuns the angry disputes of fiery politicians and the crowds of maddening multitudes. He feels the force of the prophet's exhortation, "Let the potsherd strive with the potsherds of the earth" (Isa. 45:9), and seeks to lead a quiet and peaceable life in all godliness and honesty, well knowing that this is good and acceptable in the sight of God his Savior.

He has a nobler conquest to obtain than that which occupies the worldling's mind. He labors to obtain the conquest over himself, since "he that is slow to anger is better than the mighty; and he that ruleth his spirit than he that taketh a city" (Prov. 16:32). He has to contend against those very evils which are fostered by the world and which lead the heart directly from God.

He honors and obeys the laws; he cheerfully submits to the powers that be, not only because of punishment, but also for conscience' sake. He regards his neighbor's welfare as his own, and studies to be quiet and do his own business. He wishes to "owe no man any thing, but to love one another" (Rom. 13:8). Love he considers to be a debt which he should always be laboring to discharge, although he knows it can never fully be paid.

Such is the believer in Jesus. Such is the heir of glory. He is a son of peace and is hastening to the mansions of peace. As his life is, so is his death. "Mark the perfect man, and behold the upright: for the end of that man is peace" (Ps. 37:37).

There is a world of rich delight,
Where warm affections glow;
Where reigns the everlasting light,
Where crystal waters flow.

Those happy saints securely dwell
From Satan's deadly power;
Their bliss no mortal tongue can tell,
"Unfolding every hour."

They dwell with Jesus, and behold
The beauties of His face;
Secure in the celestial fold,
And crowned by sovereign grace.

From earth, and all it's empty joys,
Blest Jesus, set me free;
How vain the worldling's painted toys,
Compared with heaven and Thee!

Thou art my hope, my way, my bliss,
My glory, and my crown;
Descend, oh blessed Prince of Peace,
And make my heart Thy throne.

CHAPTER 76

The Blessedness of the Saints

The book of Revelation not only contains the most important prophecies respecting the church of Christ to the end of time, but it also unfolds to us the happy and glorified state of true believers in the heavenly world. The apostle John saw a door opened in heaven, and scenes of the most solemn, grand, and delightful nature were presented to his view. "Oh, blessed Savior! Thou who art the light and glory of the heavenly world, take away the scales of unbelief and ignorance from my eyes and enable me to look through the veil and contemplate with delight those joys which are prepared for Thy people, that my affections may be fixed upon things above, where Thou sittest at the right hand of God."

From the book of Revelation I find what graces of the Spirit accompany the believer to the celestial Canaan. Love, joy, peace, gratitude, humility, adoring awe, and an ineffable delight in the triumphs and glories of Jesus form part of that felicity which the redeemed experience in the presence of God and the Lamb.

The seed is sown and the bud is formed here, but the flower expands and the sacred fruits ripen under the eternal beams of the Sun of Righteousness. The more my soul is filled with these graces, the more shall I be assimilated to the spirits of just men made perfect in heaven.

Pride can find no entrance into heaven. There, the saints are all humility. Boasting is forever excluded. They are filled with that charity which boasts not itself, is not puffed up. They sing unceasing praises to Him who washed them from their sins in His own blood. Casting their crowns before the throne in token of their own unworthiness, they cry: "Worthy is the Lamb" (Rev. 5:12). Every motion to pride is the effect of the fall. The whole scheme of redemption is calculated to humble the sinner, while it exalts the glory of Jehovah Jesus and promotes the sanctification of every believing soul.

From the interesting vision vouchsafed to the apostle as recorded in the seventh chapter, I learn that the blessings of salvation are not confined to any particular age or nation; for multitudes out of all nations and kindreds and people and tongues stood before the throne and before the Lamb, clothed with white robes and having palms in their hands.

Jesus, therefore, may justly be called "the Lamb of God, which taketh away the sin of the world" (John 1:29), once typified by the lamb, sacrificed every morning and evening on the Jewish altar, and symbolically represented by a lamb slain (Rev. 13:8) in the apocalyptic vision.

I here behold the amazing honor which Jesus puts upon His people. The apostle saw three circles round about the throne; and, wonderful to contemplate, those blessed angels who never sinned composed the outer circle! No envy or jealousy lurks in their holy bosoms. It is only on this polluted earth that such unhallowed fires are found to burn. Oh, that every unholy flame may be quenched in my soul!

"Blessed Jesus, impress Thy sacred precepts on my heart. Weave them into the very texture of my soul. Thou hast said by Thine apostle: "Be clothed with humility" (1 Pet. 5:5). Oh, make me humble, and, under an abiding consciousness of my own unworthiness, may I ever esteem Thee above all created beings and my fellow sinners better than myself."

The Christian's life is affectingly described by the Elder, who spoke to John. The words are few, but comprehensive. "These are they which came out of great tribulation" (Rev. 7:14). Yes, those who will live godly in Christ Jesus must suffer persecution. It is through much tribulation that we enter the kingdom. This tribulation is both inward and outward.

Outward trials may vary in different periods of the world. In our days, we are privileged to worship the God of our salvation under the protection of a mild and paternal government, not making us afraid.

There have been ages, and those not a few, when believers, of whom the world was not worthy, were compelled to seek an asylum in mountains, and dens, and caves of the earth, being destitute, afflicted, tormented (Heb. 11:38). The danger, with respect to Christians, now is, lest outward prosperity and the absence of persecution should produce inward languor and spiritual decay.

The graces of the Spirit generally thrive best in tempestuous seasons, when the saints are driven, as it were, to their place of refuge by the brandishing sword of tyranny or superstition. But God is all-sufficient, who can impart grace equal to the day either of ease or of trouble.

In every age, the believer will experience inward trials arising from his own heart and the busy temptations of Satan. He will find himself surrounded with snares and dangers, whether he be in outward prosperity or in adversity. Hence he will always stand in need of watchfulness and prayer. Like David, however, he may encourage himself in the Lord his God (1 Sam. 30:6), since all things shall work together for good while, in the exercise of faith and love, he labors in patience to possess his soul.

From this sublime vision I learn that salvation is all of grace. The blood of Jesus freely and gratuitously poured out upon the cross is the sole procuring cause of eternal salvation. The soul of the heavenly saint, once guilty and polluted, was pardoned and purified through faith in the atonement of Jesus. On this account, and on this only, does he stand before the throne of God. All human righteousness is forever excluded. He that glories must glory in the Lord. None will ever be admitted into the presence of God but those whose robes are washed and made white in the blood of the Lamb.

None will ever be admitted to sing the praises of self. All the redeemed unite in one grand everlasting chorus: "Worthy is the Lamb that was slain to receive power, and riches, and wisdom, and strength, and honour, and glory, and blessing" (Rev. 5:12). "Blessing, and honour, and glory, and power, be unto him that sitteth upon the throne, and unto the Lamb for ever and ever" (Rev. 5:13). The employment of redeemed saints is also described in this glorious vision. They shall serve God day and night in His temple (Rev. 7:15). Idleness is not happiness. The rest of heaven is not inaction, for "absence of occupation is not rest." Activity characterizes the heavenly world. Here, we are soon wearied, even in the sweetest seasons of devotion. The spirit is often willing when the flesh is weak. But in heaven, the believer shall serve God without weariness and distraction. Here on earth, we often groan, being burdened, and at the close of a blessed Sabbath have to mourn over a dead and lukewarm heart. But in heaven, the soul shall be filled with ecstasy and delight while serving the eternal Jehovah day and night in His temple.

Oh, the happy state of that glorious world, where sin and its baneful influence shall molest the ransomed soul no more!

How awfully do those people deceive themselves, who hope for happiness in heaven while averse to holy meditation and praise! The disposition of the saints in light must now be wrought in every believing soul. The exercise of heavenly graces forms the beauty and happiness of the saints on earth, as well as their qualification for the enjoyment of the heavenly felicity.

What tongue can describe the blessedness contained in these few words, "He that sitteth on the throne shall dwell among them" (Rev. 7:15)? When Jesus manifests Himself to His people but for a short period, He makes their delighted spirits like "the chariots of Amminadab." They are borne aloft upon the wings of fervent love—yes, like Elijah, they are carried to heaven in a chariot of fire. But for Jesus to dwell among them, and that forever and ever—oh, what heart can conceive the unutterable bliss! Here, indwelling sin often grieves the Holy Visitant and quenches the sacred flame, but in heaven it is not so. "Lord, fit and prepare me for this glorious state, crucify every wrong desire, and make me a humble follower of the Lamb."

In heaven, the believer will be removed out of the reach of evil. Those happy souls who have washed their robes and made them white in the blood of the Lamb "shall hunger no more, neither thirst any more; neither shall the sun light on them, nor any heat" (Rev. 7:16).

"God himself shall be with them, and be their God. And God shall wipe away all tears from their eyes; and there shall be no more death, neither sorrow, nor crying, neither shall there be any more pain: for the former things are passed away" (Rev. 21:3-4).

The ransomed host who stand upon Mount Zion as conquerors through the blood of the Lamb shall be admitted to the enjoyment of the highest good. They shall eat of the Tree of Life, which is in the midst of the paradise of God. They shall eat of the hidden manna; and receive a white stone, in which is written a new name, which no man knows, only he who receives it (Rev. 2:17). They shall be clothed with white clothing, and their names shall not be blotted out of the Book of Life (Rev. 3:5). "The Lamb which is in the midst of the throne shall feed them, and shall lead them unto living fountains of waters" (Rev. 7:17). They "shall inherit all things" (Rev. 21:7) and reign with Christ forever and ever (Rev. 11:15).

Such is the blessedness of the saints. To this blessedness, the Spirit and the Bride say: "Come. And let him that is athirst come. And whosoever will, let him take the water of life freely" (Rev. 22:17).

"Almighty Redeemer, make me willing to receive with joy and gratitude these rich blessings of Thy grace, so dearly purchased and so freely offered. Impart Thy whole self to my longing soul, and enable me to give my whole self to Thee. Oh, grant that I may possess Thee as my present and eternal portion. With inextinguishable desire may I seek Thy face and favor. Never let me rest in outward forms nor in any of Thine appointed means of grace; but, ever bearing the blessed end in view, may I labor to apprehend that for which also I am apprehended by Thy grace, until I attain at length the prize of the high calling of God, even eternal life, through the exceeding riches of Thy love and mercy. Thou hast said, 'Surely I come quickly' (Rev. 22:20); amen. Even so come, Lord Jesus."

Though billows of sorrow should roll,
And surround me on every side;

Yet Thou canst the tempest control,
My Savior, my refuge, and guide.

Thy smile maketh the soul to expand,
And graces celestial to grow;
With rapture I gaze on the land,
Where pleasures incessantly flow.

It is there my dear Savior resides,
In fullness of glory and grace,
And there the pure river that glides
Through regions of joy and of peace.

The life-yielding tree there shall spread
Its branches luxuriantly round;
The saints robed in white shall be fed
With fruits from Emmanuel's ground.

How deep is the mystery of grace,
The theme of bright seraphs above;
To see the sweet beams of His face,
To dwell in the essence of love!

My Father! Thy nature is love;
In Jesus, Thine image I view;
Oh, may I behold Him above,
And praise Him eternally, too.

May this my delight ever be,
On earth His rich grace to record;
And when from these temples set free,
With joy ascend up to the Lord.

CHAPTER 77

Christian Obedience

Obedience to the divine command is essential to the character of a child of God. "A son honoureth his father…: if then I be a father, where is mine honour?… saith the Lord of hosts" (Mal. 1:6). "If ye love me, keep my commandments" (John 14:15). "He that hath my commandments, and keepeth them, he it is that loveth me" (John 14:21). How far removed from the truth as it is in Jesus are those who do not consider it legal to enforce obedience to the moral law! The life of Christ was an undeviating display of perfect holiness and sinless obedience to the will of His Father. From the manger to the cross, He has left us an example that we should follow His steps. The obedience of Christ was without reserve: "I seek not mine own will, but the will of the Father which hath sent me" (John 5:30). "My meat is to do the will of him that sent me, and to finish his work" (John 4:34). "O my Father, if this cup may not pass away from me, except I drink it, thy will be done" (Matt. 26:42). Oh, that we may have grace to drink deeply into the spirit of our divine Emmanuel, and under every suffering dispensation to say: "The will of the Lord be done."

What blessedness is treasured up in this single petition: "Thy will be done in earth, as it is in heaven" (Matt. 6:10). If we could live under the daily influence of believing prayer, we would indeed be happy. Our wills being molded into the will of God, we would acquiesce in all the divine dispensations. With Eli, we would say: "It is the Lord: let him do what seemeth him good" (1 Sam. 3:18). With Aaron, we would hold our peace. With Job, under the deprivation of earthly comforts, we would exclaim: "The Lord gave, and the Lord hath taken away;

blessed be the name of the Lord" (Job 1:21). With David, our language would be: "I was dumb, I opened not my mouth; because thou didst it" (Ps. 39:9). With Habakkuk, we would sing: "Although the fig tree shall not blossom, neither shall fruit be in the vines; the labour of the olive shall fail, and the fields shall yield no meat; the flock shall be cut off from the fold, and there shall be no herd in the stalls: Yet I will rejoice in the Lord, I will joy in the God of my salvation. The Lord God is my strength, and he will make my feet like hinds' feet, and he will make me to walk upon mine high places" (Hab. 3:17-19). Thus, with holy Paul, we would learn, in whatever state we are in, therewith to be content. Oh, how happy we would be if we never felt in our hearts one desire or affection contrary to the will of our heavenly Father! It is the lack of perfect conformity to the commands of God which occasions so much darkness and distress, so much sin and suffering in the world. The more we resemble Jesus in His life and spirit and the more we are made willing to do and to suffer the holy will of God, the more of joy and peace will dwell in our souls. If the will of God were done on earth as it is in heaven, what showers of blessings would descend upon it! Then would be realized the glowing descriptions of the latter-day glory, when the kingdoms of this world shall become the kingdoms of our Lord and of His Christ, and He shall reign forever and ever.

As pilgrims journeying through a darksome wilderness, our heavenly Father has provided for us a lamp to lighten our path and to cheer us on our way. David prized this blessing: "Thy word is a lamp unto my feet, and a light unto my path" (Ps. 119:105). Oh, how greatly should we value it, now that it contains the full revelation of the will of God to man! Let us daily study and pray over the book of God; then the Word of Christ will dwell in us richly in all wisdom and spiritual understanding and make us fit, through the Spirit, for the inheritance of the saints in light.

Are any asking, What does the Lord require of us? Hear, and your souls shall live.

1. "God…commandeth all men every where to repent" (Acts 17:30). "This is his commandment, That we should believe on the name of

his son Jesus Christ" (1 John 3:23). Have we done the will of God by turning away from all our iniquities and receiving Christ as our only Savior? Repentance and faith are the gifts of grace: "Him hath God exalted with his right hand to be a Prince and a Saviour, for to give repentance to Israel, and forgiveness of sins" (Acts 5:31). He is the "author and finisher of our faith" (Heb. 12:2). Under the conviction of our own helplessness, and His fullness of power and love, have we prayed to Him for strength to repent and believe with the heart unto righteousness? What evidence do we possess of having obtained help from the Lord? Is our stubborn will subdued? Are our earthly desires mortified? Have we renounced our own righteousness and thrown ourselves upon Christ for every blessing, as the fruit of His perfect atonement and obedience to the law for man? Are we willing to be nothing, that Christ may be all in all?

2. "This is my commandment, That ye love one another, as I have loved you" (John 15:12). Sweet and delightful precept! To a renewed mind, the commandments of Jesus are not grievous: His service is perfect freedom; His yoke is easy, and His burden is light. Holiness would be our happiness, were it not for that carnal mind which is enmity against God. Love reigns wherever Christ dwells. God is love, and he that dwells in love dwells in God, and God in him. Oh, what a happy world would this be, if love governed every heart and directed every action. Are our hearts alive to the welfare of our fellow-creatures? Passing over the boundaries of kindred, sect, and nation, can we feel a Christian affection for all, of every climate and of every color, who bear the Savior's image, who are the objects of His love and the subjects of His kingdom? Does our charity manifest its indwelling by acts of kindness, liberality, and sympathy; by spiritual communion and intercessory prayer? Is the love of Christ to us the pattern of our love to others? "Lord, shed abroad Thy love in our hearts, that we may prove our discipleship by dwelling in the element of holy love."

3. "I say unto you, Love your enemies, bless them that curse you, do good to them that hate you, and pray for them which despitefully use

you, and persecute you" (Matt. 5:44). Difficult and self-denying duty! Oh, how counter does this precept run to the stream of natural corruption! And yet, divine grace can enable us to practice this command of love also. It is true, we cannot, nor are we required to, love our enemies, if they be enemies for the gospel's sake, as we would love our dear Christian friends; yet, we must feel towards them a love of compassion for their souls; we must pray for their conversion, and requite them good for evil. We must resemble Him who makes His sun to rise on the evil and on the good, and sends rain on the just and on the unjust.

4. "This is the will of God, even your sanctification" (1 Thess. 4:3). The great design of Christ's coming into the world was to save sinners—to save them from their sins, from this present evil world, and from the wrath to come. Having made atonement for us by His death upon the cross, and ascended up, far above all principality and power, He now sheds forth the Holy Spirit to purify unto Himself a peculiar people, zealous for good works. He has promised and encouraged us to pray for the Spirit of truth, the Comforter. Are we daily seeking after this blessing by fervent, believing prayer? What evidence have we that our prayer has been answered? Have our minds been guided into all truth? Are we led by the Spirit out of ourselves to the cross of Christ? Do we walk in the Spirit, under the daily power of His sanctifying grace? Do we seek the extermination of every bosom-sin and labor to crucify the flesh with its affections and lusts?

5. "In every thing give thanks: for this is the will of God in Christ Jesus concerning you" (1 Thess. 5:18). Gracious command! Truly God wills the happiness of His people when He wills that they shall have a thankful heart. Who is so happy as the rejoicing believer, saved through the blood of Jesus? How varied soever be his crosses and trials, he can bless God for them all, because on each he can read, in legible characters: "Whom the Lord loveth he chasteneth" (Heb. 12:6). As the affliction abounds, the consolation does also abound; for when all around him is storm and tempest, he can sing: "God is our refuge and strength, a very

present help in trouble" (Ps. 46:1). Thus he rejoices in the Lord always and in everything gives thanks.

Have we thus done the will of God, endeavoring, through the Spirit, to maintain a praising frame? Filled with gratitude for the blessing of redemption, do we delight in speaking good of His name and telling of His salvation from day to day? Oh, what happiness we lose by not cultivating a thankful spirit! Were we deeply sensible of what we deserved as sinners, we would be overwhelmed at the sight of our mercies, so freely and abundantly poured out upon us through Jesus Christ. May the Lord make us duly thankful; then, we shall devote all our powers to His service and glory, who has redeemed us at so rich a price.

"Come, oh Spirit of holiness, come into our hearts, and make Thy abode within us. Come, precious pledge of all spiritual and eternal blessings, and be within us, as the witness of our adoption into the family of God, as the seal of our salvation. Make us willing to welcome Thine approach and to receive Thee with joy and gladness. Mold our souls into the image of Jesus; conform our wills to the will of God. Fill us with the light of truth and the fire of love. Oh, give us a foretaste of celestial happiness by the inward manifestations of Thy favor. Teach us to know ourselves. Guide us into the way of peace. Preserve us from the wiles of Satan, the deceitfulness of sin, the corruption of the flesh, the allurements of the world. Arm us for the spiritual combat. Strengthen us by Thy power, and make us more than conquerors through Him who has loved us and given Himself for us. Sustain us as we pass through the valley of the shadow of death, and bring us, with songs of triumph, into the heavenly Zion. To free, sovereign, boundless love, be all the praise."

Gracious is our heavenly King,
Let us each His praises sing,
Ever loving, ever kind,
Seek—for all who seek shall find.

Let us seek Him in His Son,
Who by grace our hearts has won;
Seek Him, through the Spirit's power,
Wait the soft refreshing shower.

Lord, to us Thyself impart,
Cheer and bless each longing heart;
Keep us all from evil free,
Make us live for heaven and Thee.

May we all Thy love possess,
Traveling through this wilderness,
Until we reach Thy dwelling place,
And behold Thee face to face.

CHAPTER 78

The Day of Judgment

He who said, "Behold, I come quickly; and my reward is with me, to give every man according as his work shall be" (Rev. 22:12), will soon appear seated on His great white throne as the glorified God-man, the judge of the living and the dead. How all-absorbing should the consideration of this period be! And yet, alas, how little does it interest the minds of thoughtless millions! Occupied with ten thousand vanities, men seldom think upon—much less prepare for—death and judgment. The ever-varying concerns of life fill up each fleeting hour, until, reaching the verge of their earthly existence, they are hurried, in all their unpreparedness, into the presence of their God. Oh, that they were wise, that they understood this, that they would consider their latter end.

The day of judgment will be a day of final separation. Now, the wheat and the tares grow together; but then, we shall discern between the righteous and the wicked, between him that serves God and him that serves Him not. Many who were first in the estimation of men will be found last in the sight of God, while many who were last in the esteem of the world will be exalted in the presence of saints and angels. The once flaming professor of godliness will be cast into outer darkness, when his secret thoughts shall be revealed to an assembled world. Self-love, spiritual pride, vainglory, and a thousand unhallowed springs of action will then be disclosed to his utter confusion and prove the worthlessness of his boasted righteousness.

What self-reproaches, what gnawings of conscience—that worm which never dies—will tear the hearts of those who were once enlightened and tasted of the heavenly gift, yet apostatized from the faith through the fear of man or love of the world, thus manifesting that their hearts were never right with God. What dismay and anguish will be seen in the countenances of others who, when on earth, despised the riches of divine mercy or trifled away their day of grace. The man of business, whose time was engrossed in amassing wealth as his chief good; the voluptuary, who devoted all his powers to sinful pleasures; the man of ambition, who sacrificed his conscience to the idol of worldly greatness; the man of science, (falsely so called) who disdained to bend his reason to divine revelation—each will be found to be a fool and a madman, while the holy, self-denying believer in Jesus, whose life was counted madness and his end to be without honor, will appear most glorious when his lot is among the saints. "Remember me, O Lord, with the favour that thou bearest unto thy people: O visit me with thy salvation; that I may see the good of thy chosen, that I may rejoice in the gladness of thy nation, that I may glory with thine inheritance" (Ps. 106:4-5).

Would we be found among the redeemed in the day of judgment, we must be willing to drink of their cup. Jesus was a man of sorrows and acquainted with grief, and His people have ever been an afflicted people. The offence of the cross has not ceased, for, as "he that was born after the flesh persecuted him that was born after the Spirit, even so it is now" (Gal. 4:29). "All that will live godly in Christ Jesus shall suffer persecution" (2 Tim. 3:12). The poison of the old serpent is as active and deadly in its nature as ever. It is only through the restraining power of God when its destructive effects are checked. "If the world hate you," said our blessed Lord, "ye know that it hated me before it hated you" (John 15:18). "The servant is not greater than his lord. If they have persecuted me, they will also persecute you" (John 15:20). Oh, then, you servants of Jesus, do not be afraid of those who kill the body, and, after that, have no more that they can do. Your souls are safely guarded by your almighty Savior; because He lives, you shall live also.

This world is designed to be a place of trial. The enemies of Jesus may, for a season, be permitted to harass His church. But He who is in the midst of her is omnipotent. The very storm which threatens her destruction shall be overruled to promote her stability and purity. The triumphing of the wicked is short. Oh, what fearfulness will seize upon the enemies of Zion when her King shall be revealed from heaven in flaming fire to take vengeance on those who know not God and that obey not the gospel of our Lord Jesus Christ, and when He shall come to be glorified in His saints and to be admired in all those who believe. Then will the pilgrim's sigh be exchanged for the song of heaven.

"The trumpet shall sound, and the dead shall be raised" (1 Cor. 15:52). But oh, how awful the thought; some shall awake to "shame and everlasting contempt" (Dan. 12:2). This doom Jesus pronounced when on earth: "Whosoever shall be ashamed of me and of my words, of him shall the Son of man be ashamed, when he shall come in his own glory, and in his Father's, and of the holy angels" (Luke 9:26). Ashamed of Jesus! Yes, thousands of 'decent Christians,' who, while they dread to commit acts of gross immorality, lest a stain should be affixed to their character, are not afraid to deny Christ before men. They are ashamed to appear in the rank of His faithful followers; they shrink from the imputation of being righteous over-much. They are willing to conform to the duties and decencies of religion, as far as the world approves, and to common custom sanctions; but beyond this, they dare not go. They love the praise of men more than the praise of God.

Oh, all you Christians of this highly favored age, who refuse to deny yourselves, to take up the cross, and to follow Christ through evil report and good report, how overwhelming will be your condemnation! When standing before His judgment-seat, methinks the glorified Savior will say, "Behold, you cowardly professors, that noble army of martyrs, now standing at My right hand, who lived in the days when *pagan Rome* bathed its sword in the blood of My saints. In the view of racks and tortures, of savage beasts, of flames and crosses, they confessed Me, their God and Savior. When the awful crisis came—deny or die—they freely yielded up their lives to death for My sake and the gospel's. See also this glorious company of the faithful who lived in the days when *papal Rome* issued its bloody mandates against My chosen flock. These also chose to die, rather than bear the mark of the beast and worship his image. But you, double-minded professors, denied Me in the midst of outward peace and personal security, when My gospel was faithfully preached, and My followers were protected by the laws of your country. What, then, deterred you from confessing Me before men? Was it something more dreadful than racks and flames? Hear, oh heavens, and be astonished! These wretched souls denied Me, only lest they should encounter the shyness of friends, the cold looks and unkind speeches of carnal relatives, the raillery of unbelievers, the sacrifice of some temporal gain, or the crucifixion of some beloved lust. They preferred sin and the world to My favor and heaven; therefore, they shall have their part in the lake which burns with fire and brimstone."

Such will be the doom of all faint-hearted and false-hearted professors of the gospel, who shrink from suffering, who dread to sustain the consecrated cross. The Word of God, which cannot be broken, expressly declares that "the fearful, and unbelieving, ... and all liars, shall have their part in the lake which burneth with fire and brimstone: which is the second death" (Rev. 21:8).

The day of judgment, so full of horrors to the wicked, will be a day of blessedness to the righteous. The voice of the archangel and the trumpet of God will announce the joyful hour of deliverance. Their sleeping dust shall be changed in a moment, in the twinkling of an eye. They shall be made like unto Christ's glorious body and dwell forever with the Lord. Oh, blissful state, when sin shall no longer defile nor sorrow distress, when Satan shall never again be permitted to tempt or terrify the sheep of Christ.

The day of the Lord will come as a thief in the night. When men are saying peace and safety, then sudden destruction comes upon them, and they shall not escape (1 Thess. 5:3). As it was in the days of Noah, so shall the coming of the Son of man be. How important, then, is a spirit of watchfulness and prayer! Blessed are they, who, with their loins girded, and their lamps burning, are waiting for the coming of their Lord; yes, looking for and hastening unto the coming of the day of God. But let us remember the foolish virgins. Have we oil in our vessels with our lamps? Without the indwelling Spirit, an outward profession will avail us nothing. Oh, how awful was the cry when the approach of the Bridegroom was announced: "Our lamps are gone out" (Matt. 25:8). They slept in carnal security and awoke to endless horrors. Then would they have entered the heavenly mansion, but "the door was shut" (v. 10) and, being once closed, was closed forever.

Nothing will stand the test of death and judgment but the religion of the heart, a real union to Christ by faith. Every earthly thing, when weighed in the balance of eternity, is less than nothing, and is vanity. Yet, strange to tell, the smallest trifle can drive futurity from our minds until we are taught the value of the soul at the cross of Christ. Have we experienced the converting grace of God? How wonderful is the power of the Spirit in the regeneration of a sinner! He turns the wilderness into a fruitful field and makes all things new. Do we loathe our once beloved sins and love the once neglected Savior? Are our affections tending heavenward, which before were buried in the earth?

How happy is the believer in Jesus! He is filled with joy and peace. Knowing in whom he has believed, he can repose with calm reliance on the faithfulness of his Redeemer. While journeying through the wilderness, he feeds upon the heavenly manna and is refreshed by living water from the smitten Rock. The pillar of fire and the cloud guide and protect him. Underneath and around him are the everlasting arms. He realizes the sweetness of the promise "The beloved of the LORD shall dwell in safety by him; and the Lord shall cover him all the day long" (Deut. 33:12). And as he approaches the banks of Jordan—the cold stream of death which rolls between him and his promised rest—he hears a voice from heaven proclaiming: "Blessed are the dead which die in the Lord from henceforth: Yea, saith the Spirit, that they may rest from their labours; and their works do follow them" (Rev. 14:13). Full of faith and hope, he falls asleep in Jesus and enters into the joy of his Lord. "Mark the perfect man, and behold the upright: for the end of that man is peace" (Ps. 37:37).

www.ingramcontent.com/pod-product-compliance
Lightning Source LLC
Chambersburg PA
CBHW030259080526
44584CB00012B/367